The Miracle Houseplants

THE
Miracle
Houseplants

THE GESNERIAD FAMILY

New, Enlarged Edition
African Violets and Other Easy-to-Bloom Plants
in the Gesneriad Family

Virginie F. and George A. Elbert

CROWN PUBLISHERS, INC., New York

Manufactured in the United States of America

Design: Deborah Daly

Library of Congress Cataloging in Publication Data
Elbert, Virginie.
 The miracle houseplants.
 1. Gesneriaceae. 2. House plants. I. Elbert,
George, 1911-   II. Title.
SB413.G37E4 1984   635.9′3381   83-15355
ISBN 0-517-55136-5
ISBN 0-517-55137-3 (pbk.)

First Updated Edition

10   9   8   7   6   5   4   3   2   1

DEDICATION

TO
FRANCES BATCHELLER
WHOSE
HELPFULNESS AND KNOWLEDGE
MADE THIS BOOK POSSIBLE

Contents

ACKNOWLEDGMENTS xi

PREFACE TO THE NEW, ENLARGED EDITION xiii

THE GESNERIAD FAMILY 1

CULTURE 13

PROPAGATION 27

PLANT LIST 43

NAME CHANGES IN THE GESNERIADS 44

Naming Intergeneric Hybrids 45

Plant Societies 46

TERMINOLOGY 47

CULTURAL LIST OF GESNERIADS 47

Achimenes 47
  Species and Cultivars 50
    Achimenes Species 50
    Achimenes Cultivars 52
Aeschynanthus 55
Agalmyla 60
Alloplectus, Cobananthus,
  Corytoplectus 61
Alsobia 62
Bellonia 64
Besleria 66
Boea 66
Capanea 68
Chirita 68

Chrysothemis 72
Codonanthe 74
Columnea 77
  Culture 78
  Species 79
  Cultivars 84
  The Cornell Hybrids 85
  Cultivars—General List 86
Diastema 90
Didymocarpus 92
Drymonia 93
Episcia 96
  Culture 98
  Other Species 100

*Episcia Look-Alikes and
Cultivars* 101
  The Look-Alikes 102
  Episcia Cultivars 103
Gesneria 107
Gloxinia 111
Hypocyrta 116
Koellikeria 117
Kohleria 119
  Kohleria Hybrids 120
Lietzia 122
Lysionotus 122
Monophyllaea 123
Monopyle 123
Nautilocalyx 123
Nematanthus 126
  The Saylor Hybrids 129
Niphaea 131
Paliavana 132
Paradrymonia 132
Pearcea 133
Petrocosmea 134
Phinaea 135
Rechsteineria 137
Rhabdothamnus 139
Rhynchoglossum 139
Rhytidophylum 139
Saintpaulia 139
  Mini-history 141
  The Species 142
  The Hybrids 147
  Honor Roll of African Violets
   148
  Culture 152
Sarmienta 153
Sinningia 155
  Sinningia Speciosa 157
  Sinningia Speciosa Cultivars
   158

Florist Gloxinia Cultivars
  162
List of Florist Gloxinias 163
Species Sinningias 166
*Cultivars Derived from
  Crosses Between S. Pusilla-
  S. Concinna and
  "Original" Sinningias
  Culture* 179
*Hybrids Between Sinningia
  and Former Rechsteinerias
  and Others* 183
Bee Dee Hybrids 185
Culture 187
Smithiantha 188
  Smithiantha Hybrids 189
Solenophera 190
Streptocarpus 190
  *Species of Subgenus
   Streptocarpus* 193
  *Species of Subgenus
   Streptocarpella* 197
  Streptocarpus Hybrids 200
  *Culture of Subgenus
   Streptocarpus* 206
Titanotrichum 208
Some Alpine Gesneriads 210
Asteranthersa 210
Briggsia 210
Conandron 210
Corallodiscus 211
Haberlea 211
Jankaea 211
Loxostigma 212
Mitraria 212
Opithandra 213
Oreocharis 213
Platystemma 214
Ramonda 214

GESNERIAD UPDATE 215
GLOSSARY OF WORDS USED IN THIS BOOK 251
PLANT SOURCES 257
HOUSEPLANT SUPPLIES 263
INDEX 267

The plants shown in the color section (following page 114) are listed in the order of their appearance:

Streptocarpus × *Cyanandrus*
Streptocarpus 'Tina'
Streptocarpus 'Netta Nymph'
Agalmyla parasitica
Sarmienta scandens
Chrysothemis villosa
Gloxinia perennis
Nautilocalyx lynchii
Titanotrichum oldhami
Aeschynanthus obconicus
Diastema vexans
Episcia 'Cygnet'
Episcia lilacina
Episcia 'Jinny Elbert'
Columnea teuscheri
Kohleria eriantha
Gesneria cuneifolia cv. Talpeyi
Columnea 'Moonglow.' A Lyon cross
Phinaea multiflora
Nematanthus perianthomegus
Nematanthus 'Green Magic.' A Saylor cross
Sinningia 'Cindy'
Sinningia pusilla
Saintpaulia 'Lisa'
Sinningia 'Rex.' A Lyon cross
Bellonia aspera
Florist Gloxinia. A Buell cross
Smithiantha
Gloxinia 'Chic.' A Lyon cross

ACKNOWLEDGMENTS

We are deeply indebted to the following:

Mr. Paul Arnold of Binghamton, N.Y., Registrar of AGGS, who made valuable records available in time for our manuscript.

Mrs. Joseph D. (Frances) Batcheller, of Durham, N.H., for constant help and guidance.

Laura, Judy, and Ray Becker of Lauray of Salisbury for photographing facilities.

Dr. A. G. Brown of John Innes Institute for valuable information about *Streptocarpus.*

Albert and Diantha Buell for photographing facilities.

Mrs. Henry P. (Grace) Foote, Editor of *African Violet Magazine* for photographs and information.

Miss Elizabeth C. Hall, the greatest of botanical librarians, for her constant assistance.

Mr. Michael Kartuz for photographing facilities and much helpful assistance.

Mr. Lyndon Lyon for much helpful advice, information, and photographing facilities.

Dr. Harold E. Moore of Cornell University for making the facilities of the Bailey Hortorium available.

Mr. William Saylor for much information on *Nematanthus.*

Dr. Laurence E. Skog of the Smithsonian Institution for generous assistance.

Dr. Margaret Stone, Curator of the L. H. Bailey Hortorium, for her guidance and assistance.

Last in the alphabet but first in importance for this book we are both deeply grateful for the help of our editor Mr. Philip Winsor, whose constant concern has been to aid us in producing a creditable work and a handsome book.

PREFACE TO THE NEW, ENLARGED EDITION

During the eight years since the first edition of this work was published, a taxonomic cyclone hit the gesneriads as many new species were introduced from the wild and botanists attempted to rearrange many genera and species. We had been cheered by the warm welcome accorded to the book and further reassured when it continued to retain its appeal for gesneriad enthusiasts during the intervening years.

A revision of the work now seemed overdue. Even though none as yet has merited wide popularity, we had to note the introduction of a number of new species. Of the numerous proposals establishing new genera and the transfer of many older species to different genera, some have been widely accepted by leading botanists as sufficiently justified. Others are still in limbo, not totally rejected yet viewed with suspicion as lacking a sound basis. Nevertheless, they cannot be ignored. There are many new cultivars and as many old ones that are no longer being grown extensively. Above all, we felt that a new edition would help clear up some of the inevitable confusion of amateur growers regarding the names of their plants and the availability of many species and cultivars from nursery sources.

It is fun to grow gesneriads. It is no fun at all to wrestle with all the shifts in the taxonomy of the family and to fit them in the older text without giving our publisher economic megrims. It was far easier to deal with new developments, for which we have been provided additional space with a new chapter, our Gesneriad Update. Altogether, though scars and bandages may show here and there, we feel that we have covered our subject sufficiently well to retain the loyalty of our knowledgeable readers.

You will not find every single species that has been discovered, but certainly most of those that have promise as houseplants. We foresee that many more will be discovered and described in due time, especially from the relatively uncharted gesneriad world of the orient. Of these, too, only a few will be successful in attracting the attention of hobbyists for long. Even in so large and wonderful a family as the *Gesneriaceae,* the winners are always few in number. We would wish it different of course. But at least this fact increases the likelihood that our new edition, like the first, will survive intact for a stretch of years and contribute to the spread of interest in gesneriads.

Working through the complexities of name changes, Mrs. Frances Batcheller has, as usual, been of immeasurable assistance. Others who have been most forthcoming are Dr. Margaret Stone and Mrs. Helen Beaufort-Murphy for their valuable lists in *The Gloxinian,* and Miss Judy Becker for advice on Columneas.

We offer our warmest thanks to Mrs. Renee White. *The Gloxinian* has always been a fine publication but never more so than since she assumed the editorship. She has been at all times generous with assistance and we owe a number of our lists to the pages of *The Gloxinian.*

Our editor for the new edition, Brandt Aymar, has shepherded a number of our other books through the final stages and deserves all our thanks for his patience with this one.

We have incorrectly given credit for many of the illustrations to the L. H. Bailey Hortorium of Cornell University. All of these were owned and supplied to us by Dr. Stone. We apologize to her and are deeply grateful for her generosity in making the photographs available for publication.

The Gesneriad Family

THE SUPERIORITY OF THE GESNERIADS

In the indoor plant revolution which has only just begun, the family of the African violet and the florist gloxinia has emerged as the leader in the race for popularity. This is due not to chance but to the interaction between new life-styles, new techniques, and plants which have demonstrated an extraordinary degree of adaptability to the needs of our times. Recent years have witnessed the introduction of great numbers of plants grown indoors essentially for their foliage. And this enrichment of the repertory has introduced a new era in the history of horticulture.

How wonderful it is that everybody can now, with relative ease, grow so many of these beautiful plants indoors—plants that formerly were rarities, seen only in botanical gardens or the greenhouses of the very rich! What a difference it makes in the lives of people in our cities and cramped suburbs! But great as is this achievement, we are also becoming aware of a still more exciting possibility. If we enjoy our ability to make gardens of greenery in our homes, how much more thrilling it would be to have the added beauty of flowering plants. The idea would have been laughed at a mere fifty years ago. Yet we can predict with reasonable certainty that flowering plants will become a normal feature of the home within a relatively short span of time. And these will not be summer gardens, like those outdoors which last only half the year. Our future flower gardens will be continuous, unaffected by changes of seasons, and everblooming. That is a kind of miracle—one that is as extraordinary in its way as anything in science itself and with an impact on the home environment perhaps as great as television. If you think this is farfetched, consider the changes in leisure activities, in time allocation, in attitudes toward nature, in home decoration, which will take place when everyone has flower gardens indoors—which is inevitable.

Though there are many contributing factors which have supplied the means to launch this horticultural revolution, one family, the *Gesneriaceae,* has provided the type of plants without which it would be impossible. Experience with these plants has contradicted the most cherished traditions of pseudoscience. Because of them we now know that it is possible to have bloom daily throughout the year—in other words, that plants do not "bloom themselves to death." We have found out that they can be subjected to continuous twenty-four-hour illumination without necessarily causing harm and that some plants will bloom well with this treatment. For the first time we have tuberous plants which do not go into dormancy. So, we have found out that dormancy is not necessarily automatic. It has been discovered that the tissue of some gesneriads can produce plants from single cells and that the rate of mutation can, thereby, be greatly increased. We have a number of examples of plants which bloom at light levels that were formerly considered impossibly low. The myth that plants need ventilation—change of air—was blasted long ago by Dr. Ward and the Wardian Case. But gesneriads proved to us that we can also have normal flowering in hermetically sealed vessels. Each one of these attributes of the gesneriads is shared by some member of another family, but we do not believe there is at present known to be any other which matches it in the variety of traits that directly contribute to our ability to grow them well indoors. The fact that this family also encompasses an extraordinary variety of ways to propagate the plants means that commerical production—essential to popularity—is greatly facilitated.

These are some of the reasons why we feel justified in calling this the Miracle Family and attempting to direct the attention of more indoor growers to its great potential. Of course, there is nothing new about gesneriads. The African violet *(Saintpaulia)* is the most popular blooming houseplant, and gloxinias have enjoyed prominence for over a century. But there are, in addition, a growing number of species which have some of the qualities of these great plants and which with further breeding will be on their way to mass popularity.

In the United States there are millions of indoor gardeners. Most of them stick to the foliage plants as outdoor gardeners take the easy way, growing nothing but zinnias, marigolds, and petunias year after year. But sooner or later everyone will discover the added pleasure of having blooming houseplants. The opening of flowers in our homes is a first experience which takes on the character of an event. And, in our contacts with indoor growers, we have observed the excitement with which it is greeted, as if a new world had opened up along with the expanding bud. If people do not attempt to meet this challenge, it is due to the same inertia which always finds an excuse for doing the same things over and over again. Those who have made the switch to flowering plants usually find that they cannot account for their unwillingness to do so long ago.

But growing blooming plants does not mean deserting the fine foliage ones. In the first place a garden entirely devoted to bloom indoors lacks contrast. And, secondly, there are certain sculptural large tropical exotics which are essential in home decoration. But growing gesneriads offers the best of both worlds, for there is no other family except the begonias which offers such a variety of foliage. Gesneriads have rather simple uncomplicated leaves but the textures and colors are extraordinary. Smithianthas, sinningias, *Nematanthus*, episcias, and many other genera make splendid foliage plants and are worth growing for that alone. You never have to suffer through months of ugly stiff greenery, as you do with orchids, to enjoy a short period of magnificent bloom.

The very qualities which have confounded scientists, which we mentioned above, make gesneriads particularly adaptable to culture in our homes. Many of them like the same conditions in which we live and require no sacrifice of comfort to grow well. Following a few simple rules of modern horticultural technology, they are easy to grow. Those that are happy in a terrarium environment can be left for months without any attention at all. And, if some perform best with artificial lighting, that is a plus, for the fluorescent light garden is the greatest decoration you can have in a home. A well-built and maintained garden puts the finest furniture to shame and provides a sense of color and luxuriance that brightens a whole room.

In writing a book entirely devoted to the gesneriads, we hope that we will help win over thousands of indoor gardeners to these wonderful plants. Indoor plants are said to be the fastest-growing industry in America and, in our opinion, gesneriads and other blooming houseplants will lead the parade for the next stage in the expansion of this national hobby. Get aboard now and learn about them and grow them. It will enrich enormously your leisure time at home.

WHY WE CAN GROW BLOOMING PLANTS INDOORS

Although it is a matter of fifteen or twenty years at the most since we have received a flood of new tropical foliage plants that can be grown indoors most people simply take them for granted and are not aware that our homes had to change before these plants could survive in them. Actually it is not just the home which has become a different environment. The same has happened to the environment in all buildings, industrial, commercial, and institutional.

The essential change has been in the mastery of temperature control indoors, both in summer and winter. In summer improved insulation keeps out excessive heat and air conditioners maintain even temperatures. In winter the far more important and difficult task of maintaining unbroken warmth throughout the season has been accomplished. That is due to improved heating equipment and distribution. In other words most Americans can maintain a minimum temperature of between 60° and 65° all the year round. Air conditioning in summer keeps temperatures at a maximum of 80°. Although the equipment is not in universal use, its absence is not as serious for plants as a temperature drop in winter. Most apartment buildings are equipped with air conditioning, and the homes that are not are mostly out in the country, where better ventilation prevails and the temperatures rarely if ever soar as high as they can in the city.

In addition to these basics, we also can control humidity with automatic humidifiers. Not everybody has them but they are not very expensive and are at hand if we feel we need them.

Before we had good temperature control, very few plants did really well indoors without considerable attention. And these were all plants which, if the furnace conked out and the indoor temperature dropped to the high forties, would not keel over and die immediately. That was a very considerable limitation and meant that the list of houseplants was confined to such tough foliage plants as aspidistras, certain ferns and palms, a few begonias, and a fairly large repertory of bulb plants. Begonias bloomed seasonally but were beautiful at all times. The bulb plants were a drag except when in flower which was usually in spring.

The essential temperature range of 60° to 80° or above means that we must grow tropical plants indoors. They offer an inexhaustible variety of foliage plants of every shape and size. There are certainly several hundred now being cultivated for the trade. The majority are either cast-iron plants which need next to no attention or plants that need some care but no expertise. This is due to the simple fact that our normal home conditions suit them. In England, where the popular temperature range is at least 10° cooler on average, most of the new plants we are growing would collapse immediately.

When we come to flowering plants, the situation is no longer so simple. Invariably more light is required to bloom a plant than to maintain its foliage. This brings in another element in plant growth. For the foliage plants, selected as shade loving and tolerant of low light conditions, we have window light which can be supplemented by spot- or flood-lighting for several hours a day. Incandescent light won't make these plants bloom but adds just enough illumination to keep them going. As incandescent lighting is a normal feature of homes and institutions, this presents no great problem.

Window light is strong enough to bloom some plants if sunlight is available for periods of sufficient length. Unfortunately it is an unreliable source because of periods of cloudiness distributed throughout the year and especially prevalent in winter. This means that flowering at all may be a matter of luck. If a plant is in bud and a week of gray weather intervenes, the chances are good that flowering will be inhibited. As a practical matter it is only in summer that bloom can be counted upon at all. The wonderful windowsill blooming we hear about is actually very spotty and people make a big thing of it because it is by no means easy.

So we see that, although our indoor environment has been greatly improved in regard to temperature and this factor alone permits us to grow more flowering plants on the windowsill than ever before, the light is still not sufficiently reliable to keep plants in continuous bloom or to achieve any real success during the winter months. Previously this was not felt to be a handicap for the simple reason that nobody considered such blooming possible anyway. Now, with so many flowering houseplants available, there is only one solution—the fluorescent light garden.

Efficiency and low cost have made light gardening available to everybody. And fluorescent lamps permit us to bloom plants all the year round. Although there are more powerful and more economical light sources which have been produced in the last few years, none of these is as yet designed to be used in the home. But fluorescent light is altogether adequate and, where there has been failure with some groups of plants, it has been due rather to improper cultural adjustments than to the light itself. However, this is not a problem in regard to gesneriads, which is another major reason why they are paramount in the blooming houseplant category. No major gesneriad in cultivation requires more light than can be provided by an ordinary fluorescent fixture. Low light needs and adaptability to the rest of our home environments are the reasons why we can grow and bloom them indoors.

INTRODUCTION FOR GESNERIAD HOBBYISTS

Much has changed in the gesneriad world since Dr. Harold E. Moore of Cornell University wrote *African Violets, Gloxinias and Their Relatives* in 1957. Not only has the repertory increased considerably, but the whole technology of houseplant growing has changed. Several years have passed since the last book was published which dealt in a popular way with the subject, and a new one is long overdue.

A first plan, to produce a combination of popular information and a fairly complete survey of the gesneriads for the amateur expert, soon was dropped as we realized the magnitude of the task even if we only considered, as did Dr. Moore, all the plants in collections in the United States. A work for specialists would also be very restricted in its readership, and a publisher would be hard to find. In the end we decided to use our own judgment as to the plants to be included and to write in a style sufficiently popular to be understood by those not familiar with esoteric botanical terms. After all, the main purpose is not to catalog, but to promote the wider cultivation of these beautiful plants.

Due to the extremely fluid situation in the gesneriad family—the constant trial of new introductions, the new hybrids, the taxonomic changes now taking place, and the fact that many potentially important plants are being grown by very few commerical nurseries and therefore are unavailable to the public—there has been plenty of room for error and oversight. We are certain that they will be found in this work and that they are inevitable. Many have considered tackling a book on this subject, but they have been wise in restraining themselves for we have found it is the most difficult of our several books.

If anyone is tempted to be hypercritical, let him consider the magnitude of the job. It would have been possible, and far easier than what we have done, for us to consult purely botanical sources for these plants and then paraphrase them. To find out about the appearance of these many plants and their cultural idiosyncracies has been a task of organization as well as research. Fortunately we have grown many of them and to a certain extent could proceed by analogy. The pages of *The Gloxinian* in particular, and *Gesneriad-Saintpaulia News* (GSN), have been helpful, especially in regard to descriptions, but many plants have not been discussed with any thoroughness in their pages. Mrs. Frances Batcheller's descriptions have been the most useful and have filled in many blank spots. Without them a very large part of the family which is cultivated here would be without specific record in print.

Thus, except for these few references, we have been thrown back very much on our own resources. And if we had realized ahead of time to what degree this would be the case, we might not have ventured into this maze at all.

We believe that our book will be helpful to beginners and experienced growers alike and will spread the message regarding gesneriads to innumerable growers who have never attempted them. It is to this latter group that we hope to appeal most strongly, for a group of plants which remains the challenge of the few also remains of little more than botanical interest. Therefore, we beg your forbearance and hope that this work will prove entertaining as well as useful to all lovers of good houseplants.

WHAT ARE THE GESNERIADS?

As we have no intention of providing precise botanical descriptions of the plants, it may be of interest to give some definition of the family itself for those who want to know its place in the order of nature.

The Family, *Gesneriaceae*, belongs to Division 7 of the Plant Kingdom—the *Spermatophyta* or seed plants. It also belongs to Subdivision 2, the *Angiospermae*, or flowering plants. Subdivision 1 consists of woody plants whose ovules (female organs) are *not* enclosed in an ovary, are freely exposed, and are directly pollinated. The *Angiospermae*, on the other hand, have ovules enclosed in a structure called the ovary. Consequently pollen grains cannot attain direct access to the ovules, but must come into contact with a special organ, the stigma, on which they germinate, grow a pollen tube which penetrates the ovary wall, and thus carry the sexual cells to the ovules.

In the subdivision *Angiospermae*, the *Gesneriaceae* belong to Order No. 34, the *Personatae*, closely related to the previous Order 33, the *Tubiflorae*. Both of these orders have superior ovaries. That is to say that the whole ovary and its stigma stand above the calyx, the base of the stamens, and of the petals or flower tube if present. Note, as an exception, that in *Sinningia* of the *Gesneriaceae*, the ovary is half inferior, or partly imbedded in the calyx tube.

The above two orders are also very much alike in other ways. However, the *Tubiflorae* usually have two carpels (sections of the ovary) with only two ovules per carpel (each ovule is an incipient seed). These carpels split into four one-seeded portions at maturity. You can easily observe this in the ripe morning glory pod, with its four sections and large seeds or nutlets.

The *Personatae*, on the other hand, with a similar structure of carpels and ovary, produce in each, as a rule, a large number of ovules, and the fruit is a capsule or berry with many seeds. The big, spiny seedpods of *Datura stramonium*, a common weed, split into four sections, each one filled with a great number of seeds. You will be able to observe that, no matter how small the pod of a gesneriad, it always contains a large number of proportionately small seeds.

Within the *Personatae*, the Family *Gesneriaceae* is not easy to separate from closely related ones, and there are gray areas around the fringes which have always puzzled botanists. There is, for instance, a very close similarity, in appearance and other details, to the *Scrophulariaceae (Verbascum, Digitalis, Antirrhinum)*, the *Orobanchaceae* (squawroot, Indian pipes, etc.), and the *Bignoniaceae*.

It is separated from the orobanches because its members are nonparasitic. In the early days of botany, many gesneriads were placed in this family. The *Scrophulariaceae* come under the rule of two-celled ovaries, while the *Gesneriaceae* are exceptional and are *one celled.* The *Bignoniaceae* have compound leaves and winged seeds. Gesneriad leaves are simple, and the seeds are not winged.

The following summation contains more information on the flowers, and so on.

1. The *Gesneriaceae* are a family of plants with a geographical distribution around the world, including the tropical and north and south temperate zones. There are some 125 genera and over 2,000 species, which make it a medium-size family. The majority of species originates in the tropics, but some are found at considerable altitudes and are semihardy, while a few are hardy—similar to the perennial plants of our northern gardens. Many of the tropical plants are evergreen. About 300 species are in cultivation, and there are now many more cultivars (hybrids and selected plants). Many are still to be found only in scientific collections.

2. The flowers have the petals joined at the base so that they are reduced to being the lobes of a tube. The resultant tube, sometimes very short, as in African violet, has five, occasionally four, lobes. The form is zygomorphic: that is to say, it can be divided symmetrically along only one plane. The flower is generally two lipped, consisting of two smaller superior and three larger inferior lobes.

There are at present two exceptions to this rule resulting from peloria, a recessive mutation. In the flowers of the florist gloxinia, the flower is not two lipped and the five, or more, lobes are equal in size, producing a circular flower. The same applies to *Sinningia cardinalis* 'Kalmbacher.'

Inside the cup of a florist gloxinia. The petals are joined. Notice the single stigma whose tip varies in shape in different species. The stamens are joined in an oval.

The ovary at the base of the stigma in the florist gloxinia. The glands show up as black shapes at the base. The corolla has fallen off, and what remains are the lobes of the calyx.

3. The calyx is five parted, sometimes large and leafy in form. The calyx lies between the flowering stalk and the corolla of the flower.

4. The ovary is superior and one celled, containing a large number of ovules which develop into seeds. There are two to four stamens (the male organs), which are usually fused in pairs or may be all joined together in a ring or square. This is a prominent feature of many gesneriad flowers and has the appearance of a tangled cluster, whereas in most flowers, where the stamens are visible, you will notice that they are separated. On some anthers the pollen dries on the surface and is free. In others, for instance *Saintpaulia*, it is enclosed in an anther sac.

5. The flowers are generally borne in pairs on a peduncle (a flower stalk with multiple buds) or on pedicels (a flower stalk with single bud) from the axils or node of the leaves.

6. The leaves are simple. This means that they do not consist of several leaflets. Also you will see that gesneriad leaves are not deeply notched, like many begonias for instance, but are variations of oval or spatulate shapes.

7. The family includes terrestrial and epiphytic (growing on trees) herbs and also shrubs and small trees.

Fruit of a species of *Columnea*.

8. The seeds are numerous and small. The seedpod is not usually compartmentalized.

9. Gesneriads have a variety of forms of root, namely: fibrous, tuberous, and scaly rhizomatous.

10. Certain gesneriads bear propagules in the axils of their leaves which are similar to the underground scaly rhizomes.

11. The family shows great variety in means of propagation: normal seed, often spontaneously produced; rhizomes; tuberous offsets. Pieces of leaf and stem root readily. Some leaves are capable of producing new plants from single cells.

12. In a number of gesneriad species only one half of the cotyledon (both halves of the seed) continues to grow after germination. Unequal opposite leaves are common in the family—one being much larger than the other. In some species of *Streptocarpus*, the one cotyledon becomes a leaf which constitutes the whole plant above ground. Thus each leaf is a separate plant and the flower stalks rise from its base.

Old World Subfamily **Cyrtandroideae**

Cyrtandreae
Hexatheca
Rhynchotechum
Protocyrtandra
Sepikaea
Cyrtandra

Trichosporeae
Micraeschynanthus
Oxychlamys
Euthamnus
Aeschynanthus
Agalmyla
Lysionotus
Loxostigma
Dichrotrichum

Klugieae
Rhynchoglossum
Monophyllaea
Moultonia
Epithema

Loxonieae
Stauranthera
Loxonia
Whytockia
Cyrtandromoea

Didymocarpeae
Conandron
Tengia
Bournea
Orcocharis
Dasydesmus
Tremacron
Briggsia
Corallodiscus
Beccarinda
Jerdonia
Cathayanthe
Isometrum
Ancylostemon
Platsytemma
Didissandra
Boeica
Leptoboea
Championia
Anna
Raphiocarpus
Opithandra
Petrocosmea
Orchadocarpa
Hemiboea
Chirita

Petrocodon
Didymocarpus
Primulina
Trisepalum
Tetraphyllum
Phylloboea
Loxocarpus
Paraboea
Codonoboea
Ornithoboea
Rhabdothamnopsi
Boea
Dichiloboea
Chlamydoboea
Saintpaulia
Acanthenema
Trachystigma
Linneaopsis
Streptocarpus
Ramonda
Jankaea
Haberlea

Unclassified
Titanotrichum

New World Subfamily **Gesnerioideae**

Beslerieae
Besleria
Cremosperma
Pterobesleria

Columneae
Episcia
Drymonia
Chrysothemis
Alloplectus
Columnea
Nematanthus
Codonanthe
Hypocyrta
Nautilocalyx

Bellonieae
Bellonia
Niphaea
Phinaea
Monopyle
Anodiscus

Gloxinieae
Achimenes
Koellikeria
Smithiantha
Heppiella
Seemannia
Gloxinia

Kohlerieae
Diastema
Kohleria
Pearcea
Vanhouttea
Capanea
Paliavana

Sinningieae
Sinningia
Lietzia
Rechsteineria

Solenophoreae
Solenophora

Gesnerieae
Gesneria
Rhytidophyllum

Coronanthereae
Depanthus
Negria
Coronanthera
Rhabdothamnus

Mitrarieae
Sarmienta
Asteranthera
Fieldia
Mitraria

Unclassified
Anetanthus
Napeanthus

ABOUT KONRAD GESNER

Konrad (not Conrad) Gesner, after whom the *Gesneriaceae* were named, lived long before the first plants of this family were described and had absolutely nothing to do with them. He was, indeed, an important savant of the sixteenth century, and his studies were of the natural world. But, if we were to do justice to merit as far as the history of the family is concerned we would have to honor such students of old as Clarke, de Candolle, Engler, von Martius, Hanstein, Lindley, Regel, Nees, and Wendland among others. In more recent times Burtt, Hilliard, Clayberg, Moore, Lee, Morley, Teuscher, Skog, Saylor, Lawrence, Broertjes, Talpey, and many others have contributed to our knowledge of the plants or to their improvement.

However, for those who are curious, here is a quick synopsis of the life of Konrad Gesner.

He was born on March 26, 1516, in Zurich, Switzerland, the oldest of eleven children. His father was a furrier and tanner. His early years coincided with the first stages of the Reformation. When he had completed grade school, Ulrich Zwingli, a leading theologian, provided a scholarship permitting him to study medicine and theology at the University of Strasbourg and later at Bourg-en-Bresse.

Driven from France by the persecutions, Gesner returned to Zurich, where the town council supplied the means to continue his education at the University of Basel. There he wrote a Greek-Latin lexicon for a local publisher and was then called to the University of Lausanne as professor of Greek—at the age of twenty. After three years and a short session of study at the University of Montpellier, he received his degree in medicine in Basel when twenty-four.

He had already begun a work entitled *Bibliotheca universalis,* in twenty large folios, which was a catalogue of works by Greek, Hebrew, and Latin authors.

From then on he was constantly busy with various natural studies. For instance he made investigations of the mineral content and medicinal efficacy of European spas. Travels in the Mediterranean countries and North Africa resulted in his *Historia animalum,* published between 1551 and 1558, and *Icones animalum,* the major works on the subject until that time and considered the basis of modern zoology. Another work, *Theatrum insectorum,* was not published until 1634. In between these major efforts, he managed to put together a compendium of plants used in medicine and *Mithridates de differentiis linguis,* a description of 130 known languages. Another major work, the *Historia stirpium*—history of plants—was never finished. He died on December 13, 1565, at the age of forty-nine.

Gesner was undoubtedly a major influence on the development of a number of sciences, and his books were reprinted many times, their influence continuing for two hundred years. In 1693 the French botanist Charles Plumier suggested the use of his name for the family of plants we know today as the *Gesneriaceae.*

Culture

FLUORESCENT LIGHT GARDENING WITH GESNERIADS

It is no accident that the development of African violet popularity and the introduction of the fluorescent lamp coincided. The plant is circular and not easy to grow to perfection with the light coming through a window from one direction. With a couple of fluorescent tubes over their heads, they grew evenly in all directions. And when hobbyists discovered that plants which ceased to flower during long periods of bad weather in winter would continue to bloom right through a period which had always been considered no time for that sort of thing, indoor light gardening was born.

There had never been a plant like the African violet before. It had been known for a long time in England and on the Continent, but home temperatures were not favorable, and it was, at best, a summer bloomer even in greenhouses. In 1938 when fluorescent lamps were first marketed, American homes were warmer and the plants did far better here than in England. Once the results of the first trials became known, the boom was on.

In spite of the expansion of light gardening, many people still grow African violets in their windows, and nurserymen, who cannot ship during the winter months, confine their fluorescent light growing to the leaf cuttings under the benches. But this plant was not to remain alone. Trials of other gesneriads revealed their adaptability to artificial light culture. It must be remembered that the early light output of the tubes was lower than at present. The gesneriads could bloom under that light, and other plants could not. It seemed hardly believable that a large flowering plant like the florist gloxinia could be as vigorous in a light garden in a home as in a greenhouse. Until this discovery, flowering plants of this kind were considered only as gifts for temporary display. Other tropicals grew only in greenhouses and were a luxury of the relatively rich.

Suddenly horticulture became democratic to a greater degree than ever before. Those rare and beautiful plants which people saw in botanical gardens could be grown in their own homes with little cost and effort. Obviously that also started a bigger market for houseplants and meant that commercial and scientific plant explorers started to send more and more plants from the tropics to northern horticultural institutions and amateurs for testing. All down the line the gesneriads repeatedly demonstrated their superiority under light gardening conditions. And so we now have a growing body of material to grow and enjoy and the expectation that there is much more still to come.

We have no intention of fully discussing fluorescent light gardening here. Readers can refer to *The Indoor Light Gardening Book* (Crown) and our other books, all of which have some details. Here we will assume that you are familiar with some of the light gardening technology and that our recommendations in respect to equipment and methods will be helpful.

FIXTURE. The minimum effective equipment is one fixture with two 20-watt tubes and reflector. The 40-watt, 48-inch size is the most effective for the average grower. The tubes can be 6 inches apart (between centers) for the low light plants in shelf installations, but 4-inch centers may be necessary for the higher light ones.

REFLECTOR. A machine-polished aluminum or flat white reflective surface is necessary for maximum utilization of the light from the tube. Do not forget that half of the light is escaping upward and must be reflected downward.

MASKING GLARE. The curve of the built-in reflector or a valance attached to the outer edge of shelving will prevent glare.

HEAT. Heat on the plants can be reduced by removing the ballast and setting it up somewhere else nearby. Eighty percent of the heat from a fluorescent fixture is produced by the ballast.

Heat can be partially dissipated by means of fans. For single shelves the whisper type, used in electronic equipment, is effective.

TIMER. There are a number of automatic home-type timers on the market. These are flimsy in our experience and usually fail after the guaranty has run out. If you intend to garden seriously, get the least expensive of the industrial time switches made by the same firms that produce the hobby units. They're simple metal boxes with the works inside, and they last forever.

LAMPS. Since we have been practicing and writing about light gardening, we have recommended the lamps designated in the trade as Warm White (WW) and Cool White (CW) in combination. That means that, in a two-tube fixture you will use one of each. These are inexpensive, very efficient lamps.

We have never recommended any of the fancy named "growth" lamps which we consider no more effective than the WW-CW combination and far more expensive.

However, a new lamp, Verilux TruBloom, beats them all. If economy on this item is not a major consideration, this is the lamp to have. It produces more compact plants, longer-lasting bloom, and is nonglare. It is the only lamp on the market which gives true color rendition. That means that your plants don't look as if they were plastic but as they do in nature. It's the only lamp we will tolerate in our living areas. Having a longer usable life than most lamps, they are not that expensive after all. This is a definite breakthrough in fluorescent lamps for light gardening.

Incidentally, don't believe the apparent facts and figures in manufacturers' publicity for various lamps. Our measure of the value of a lamp for growth and bloom is not contained in figures and charts. These are worthless unless the lamp really produces superior growth and bloom. The Verilux TruBloom lamp does not impress us because it has the "right curve" or the "right amounts of red and blue," but for the practical reason that it does the job.

DISTANCE FROM LAMPS. If you grow just one kind of plant—a particular species or cultivar—it may be possible to work out the right distance from the lights. But there is no rule you can follow for a mixed collection even of African violets. The distance depends not entirely on the output of the tubes or how long they have been used. Length of use is an important factor too often forgotten by growers; they try a new type of lamp and imagine that there is a big improvement, when all that has happened is the replacement of an old lamp by a new one. Average humidity, temperature, fertilizer in the soil, condition of the medium, and so on, affect the way plants use the available illumination. Because pollution is heavier in the city than the country, city plants need more light to function properly.

All we can say is that the range is a maximum of 18 inches under a two-tube fixture, somewhat more under several lamps side by side. In order to make adjustments in height, plants must be raised up on pots or other supports. Some plants will have to have their tops within 2 or 3 inches of the lamps. Those that are resting need less light than those which are in active growth and ready to set bloom.

We will give approximate footcandles needed for various gesneriads, but don't take these overseriously. They are just yardsticks for the comparative needs of the different plants. Only experience and jockeying the pots around will teach you the right position for each kind of plant.

DAY LENGTH. For most gesneriads twelve to fourteen hours of continuous fluorescent illumination is sufficient to produce bloom. Formerly we recommended fourteen to sixteen hours. But, since we have used the Verilux lamps, we have cut back the time and found it quite adequate, with considerable saving in costs. Also borderline short-day plants will bloom on a twelve-hour cycle.

Most of the gesneriads are long-day plants, but we are not sure of all of them. This is a subject which has not been sufficiently studied. Our own installations make it difficult for us to maintain long and short day lengths at the same time for different groups of plants. We suspect that the kohlerias are short-day plants and that some species of other genera are also in this class. Nurserymen are no help, because their greenhouses operate with the seasons and they are primarily concerned to have bloom from springtime on. They are in no position to judge whether budding and bloom in some of their plants have been induced by short natural light days in winter (once they've started they continue to bloom), or because they are seasonal irrespective of day length.

INCANDESCENT LIGHT. For a number of reasons incandescent light is not efficient in producing bloom. There is no apparent advantage in combining fluorescent and incandescent light.

OTHER ARTIFICIAL LIGHT SOURCES. Power-twist and groove shapes add somewhat to normal output of illumination, but the normal lamps are certainly adequate for gesneriads. So-called High Output lamps are inefficient in respect to cost. Add another normal tube, and the effect is much the same at considerable saving. HID or High Intensity Discharge lamps are for large commercial installations, not for the home as yet. The fixtures are large and ungainly; the light fantastically intense and hot. The time may come when they will replace fluorescents in home growing but that is still well in the future.

To sum up. If you grow plants on the windowsill, by all means invest in fluorescent equipment. The results are so much more satisfactory in every way that it is ridiculous to struggle with the vagaries of daylight.

SOILS FOR GESNERIADS

We use the term *soil* for any medium for growing plants. It is a common fallacy to attribute to natural soils a high nutritional content. In fact it is normally very low. Even compost and humus have little free chemical content and are essentially soil conditioners. When we wish to grow large quantities of vegetables or grains, or produce big flowering plants in relatively small pots indoors, we must add high concentration organic or chemical nutrients. Under modern conditions it is the mechanical condition of the soil that has priority—its lightness and friability; a grittiness which seems to suit plants; its combination of water absorption, retention, and good aeration. For the houseplant grower, soil can be entirely sterile as long as it encourages root development and contributes to health. Growth and bloom depend on light, water, and nutrient chemicals. The chemicals to supply nutrients are always available in one form or another.

It is quite amazing what small amounts of nutrient our houseplants need to survive or even to flower. Grow gesneriads in soilless mix in which the only organic constituent is peat moss and, without the addition of chemicals, most of them will attain maturity and bloom. Considering that our water contains an infinitesimal amount of useful chemical and that the nitrogen of peat moss is notoriously low, the ability to survive at all is quite an accomplishment.

The realization that better-controlled soils for intensive commercial and home growing could be compounded from various inorganic by-products plus organic materials led some years ago to the development of soilless mixes in California. Later Cornell University added a whole series of formulas. The basic constituents and proportions are very simple, and it is with some amusement that one observes the enthusiasm with which amateurs have concocted all kinds of complex recipes, adding a little bit of this and a little bit of that and reporting just miraculous results. However, for most, the basics have proved reliable. They offer the indoor grower the advantage of sterile and efficient materials for growth. By comparison natural soils are unpredictable and must be sterilized—a messy business in the home. Humus and compost are hard to come by, and whoever has a source of really rich, light, organic woods soil can deem himself lucky indeed. The components of soilless mixes are readily available in our stores and, should the quality change or the supply dwindle, there are plenty of other alternatives which the industry can turn to as sources for acceptable material.

The components of modern soilless mixes are:

PEAT MOSS.   A brown, fibrous material from the northern bogs, it is supplied sterilized and partly cleaned in bags of various sizes. Canadian sphagnum peat moss is preferred to Michigan peat. Cornell recommends imported peat moss and may mean the German material, which is very good but not easily available these days.

PERLITE.   This is a white, gritty lava product. Medium or coarse grades are best for general potting and the fine grade, washed and sieved, for seed mixes.

VERMICULITE.   It is heat-exfoliated mica. The material should be in firm cubes. If there are thin scales, oily and mushy to the touch, it probably contains impurities which are damaging to plants and will not perform its soil-conditioning role properly. Recently there has been a drop in the quality of vermiculite and we may have to seek another material.

LIME.   The presence of lime in our mixes is to offset the acid reaction of the peat moss. Some gesneriads require more alkaline soil than others, but all are only slightly acid in their requirement. We prefer a form which releases the calcium slowly. For that reason we do not use horticultural powdered lime but either dolomite lime chips or the breakfast eggshells, dried and reduced to flakes with pestle and mortar or put through the blender. We can use more of it in the mix, and it will usually last for the life of the plant.

PROFESSIONAL AND AMATEUR MIXES.   Note that there is a difference between professional and amateur mixes. The nurseryman adds various nutrients directly to the mix, so that he does not have to fertilize during the comparatively short time the plants are on his benches. As he is growing great numbers of the same kind of plant, he can establish the correct amount of nutrient and the right kind for his needs. The amateur, on the other hand, grows plants for a much longer period and has a varied collection. Therefore he is better off with straight soil without any chemicals. Any good grower fertilizes his plants according to what he considers are their needs.

BASIC SOILLESS MIXES:

Rich Mix
3 parts Canadian sphagnum peat moss
2 parts vermiculite
1 part perlite
2 to 4 tablespoons of lime chips or ground eggshell to the quart

Lean Mix
1 part Canadian sphagnum peat moss
1 part vermiculite
1 part perlite
2 level tablespoons of lime to the quart

These are the only two mixes we use. Care must be taken in measuring out the peat moss which, unlike vermiculite and perlite, comes tightly compressed in its package. We

Ingredients of soilless mix and prop box. *Left to right:* vermiculite, peat moss, perlite The prop box has been seeded and the right side sprinkled with milled sphagnum moss.

generally break up the lumps with our hands. But if we are working with a specimen plant or making up a seeding mix, we run the material through a hardware cloth sieve. Whether the mix is heavily weighted with peat moss or not will depend on whether you measure out dry separated moss or solid masses. The former is what you want in order to achieve the proper proportions. Remember—your object with both mixes is to have nonclogging soil. An excess of peat moss will result in a solid, hard, fibrous pack. You will notice that the soilless mixes of the best nurseries are very loosely packed—almost free flowing. Good aeration is very essential to all the indoor-grown gesneriads.

CORNELL MODIFIED PEAT LITE MIX. The formula is supposed to be measured out with 6-inch clay pots. We don't all have "standard size" clay pots. Our own modification uses one-pound coffee cans.

4½ cans shredded imported sphagnum peat moss
2½ cans horticultural vermiculite, Nos. 2 or 3
2½ cans perlite, medium grade
2½ tablespoons dolomite limestone
1¼ teaspoons 20 percent powdered superphosphate
3¾ teaspoons 5–10–5 or 6–12–6 fertilizer
Peter's soluble trace elements

Examples of other mixes are the following:

8 cups sphagnum peat moss
5½ cups vermiculite
2½ cups perlite
a handful of charcoal

4 cups vermiculite
2 cups milled sphagnum moss
1 cup perlite
½ cup charcoal

OTHER SOIL MIXES.   Two other components must be considered:

GARDEN LOAM.   If it is really loam, not a clay or finely divided sand or colloidal material, this can be an excellent component of a mix. Just any dirt will not do. At least run a pH test before using. Outdoor soil must be sterilized before use.

SAND.   It is difficult to get good sand of horticultural quality. Recently we noticed that Cornell is using a sieved and washed construction sand of good quality, designated grade 4Q. Ordinary builders' sand is usually not the best. You need small- but not fine-grain, gritty material. Fine chicken grit is a good one.

1 part peat moss or humus or leaf mold
1 part garden soil
1 part perlite or vermiculite or sand, or proportions of each.

PACKAGED MIXES.   We haven't found a packaged mix yet that worked. For a while Black Magic seemed the answer, but that's changed. And we've watched for years while amateurs went overboard for one trademarked mix after another only to desert it silently within a short time. The packaged mixes may be fine for commercial use but not for the amateur. The latest ones have all been mush. One of these days . . . Here is someone's favorite:

1 quart Black Magic African Violet Mix
1 quart Baccto Potting soil
1 cup ground eggshells
1 cup charcoal

Charcoal is a harmless soil conditioner, no better than any other. It will not absorb the acids in your pot more effectively. It is simply more expensive.

The most important thing to learn about soil mixes is the "feel" of the right consistency. Get used to a light, gritty mix and observe the reactions of your plants. If you are patient, you will find out just what is right for them. Remember, every home environment varies and everybody has his own habits in treating plants. The same mix, therefore, will behave differently for you and for some other grower. No mix is a mathematical formula good for all time. Experiment with slight variations of the basic formulas, and you will have better results.

Moss as Soil

Sphagnum moss has been widely used by experts in growing epiphytic gesneriads, as a component of some regular mixes, and as an antidamping-off constituent of soil for seeding. Understand—this is not sphagnum peat moss, which is the partly decomposed product of sphagnum moss. What we are speaking of is live moss, the dried live moss, and the milled dried live moss.

We know amateur growers who live in places where sphagnum grows nearby who do not know its difference from other mosses. It is a much bigger moss than the others, growing in long strands which pack together in humps of soft greenery and have numerous branches in whorls with tiny leaves. These leaves have some cells which are empty and absorb water to twenty times the weight of the plant. Sphagnum moss is less acid than others, contains no soil when collected, is more spongy when used in potting, and has the peculiar quality of inhibiting the development of damping-off fungal diseases.

LIVE SPHAGNUM MOSS.   This will continue to grow in terrarium conditions if it is kept moist. If stored for a while, it will turn brown but soon starts to grow and green up when exposed to light. The only pests we have come across in live sphagnum moss are species of tiny snails which can be a bit of a nuisance but climb a terrarium's glass sides when moisture is high and can usually be killed off. Sometimes the sphagnum will grow faster than small plants, but can simply be pressed down out of the way. Where it does not have light, as in hanging baskets, it makes an excellent liner or the basic medium for the plants.

Live sphagnum moss is an excellent soil for tuberous and epiphytic gesneriads. Lyndon Lyon fills all his baskets with sphagnum moss and covers it with a top dressing of perlite to provide a dry surface for leaves to rest on.

Long-fiber sphagnum moss is dried and sterilized live sphagnum moss. It is a commercial product available in large sacks or small packages from variety stores. The uses are exactly the same as those of the live moss. An excellent mix for epiphytes using sphagnum moss is:

1 part sphagnum peat moss
1 part long-fiber sphagnum moss
1 part vermiculite
1 part perlite.

Two parts of the perlite also work well. This mix can be made with milled sphagnum moss, but is not as satisfactory.

MILLED SPHAGNUM MOSS. The moss is cleaned completely and dried and cut very fine so that it has the appearance almost of a dust.

This moss is so dry that it will resist absorbing water for a long time. Stirring it dry can be irritating to the nasal passages. It is best to put it in a bowl with water overnight and let it take its time.

The moss is principally used in seeding and propagating mixes. By itself it is better for cuttings than for seeding. Its use in propagation will be described in that section.

WATERING

The majority of gesneriads prefers even moisture. A few shrubby ones require some drying out between waterings. But there are also a number of refinements which may make the difference between success and failure. These will be discussed when we describe culture of the plants themselves. However, it is a warning that reliance on various automatic devices can be risky.

Some general rules of watering may be of value to the reader.

1. There is no difference between watering from above or below as long as necessary precautions are taken. From above you must be careful that any excess water passes right through the pot and that any excess accumulated in a saucer is removed. From below you must take care to see that sufficient moisture is supplied to saturate the soil. That takes a little time. But once it is completed, water in the saucer must be removed.

2. Use lukewarm water for all purposes.

3. Watch out for very rapid consumption of water during warm weather. And remember that some plants use up much larger quantities of water much faster than others. Don't expect all the plants to need watering at the same time.

4. Plants in active growth can be watered more than slow growers. If growth ceases, even temporarily, allow the soil to dry out somewhat between waterings.

5. Water more during warm than cool weather—or lower temperatures indoors. If it is cool indoors, do not add water to a moist pot.

6. With hairy, soft-leaved gesneriads do not wet the leaves and axils. A plant which can stand a misting on the leaves may rot from watering.

AUTOMATIC WATERING.   There are numerous ways to provide individual pots with automatic waterings over longer or shorter periods. Various forms of wicking and reservoir pots have their enthusiastic devotees. As a measure to prolong watering during a vacation these devices are lifesavers. But for general use they can be lethal.

No doubt there has been great success in the home with wicking, for instance. But much depends on the environment and on the particular plants involved. Users always tell about their successes but say nothing about the failures. Automatic devices may register when the soil is too dry, but they cannot observe when the plant has stopped growing. We would rather give our plants individual attention.

Such systems as Chapin Watermatic are excellent for the greenhouse, but are only a stopgap in the home. Moist sand systems are a nuisance. Probably the best of these types of moisture suppliers are the soaked plastic pads which are now being used in greenhouses. But they are only reliably effective when you have a bench with just one type of plant.

We were probably one of the first to use plastic egg crates in trays. This material is a plastic lighting diffuser about ½ to ¾ inch thick, with openings in a waffle design, much used in the ceilings of elevators. It can be cut to any size to fit trays. If water is poured into the tray to the top of the crate plants will be able to absorb it until the tray is dry. The crate offers a much more economical, adaptable, and efficient method than all the fussing with wicks and all the expense of reservoir pots.

When we are on vacation the trays are filled, garden areas covered with plastic, and the lighting period cut to eight hours. That will keep everything happy for two weeks. And, though the trays must then be refilled, at least your plant sitter will have nothing else to do and watering is not left to his or her judgment.

WATERING WAND.   The only firm we know making this kind of gadget is Tube Craft in Cleveland. It consists of a metal tube with a curve at the end, a long piece of plastic tubing, and a metal tubular wand with a spring action control. The equipment works on the siphon principle, drawing water from a reservoir when you need it. We keep a one-gallon plastic bottle on top of a tiered light unit and find the wand indispensable for individual watering of plants in the back of shelving.

HUMIDITY

Perhaps the requirement of gesneriads which is hardest to provide in the normal home is sufficient humidity. There is a big difference in the reactions of these tropical plants according to the percentage of aerial moisture. If humidity is right, flowers are larger and are produced in greater numbers; light requirements are reduced; efficient consumption of nutrients is increased.

For some of these plants only a terrarium environment meets the need. The others are somewhat subject to the law of compensation. This is our phrase for it—not a scientific term. What the law means in practice is that, if there are a number of factors required for healthy growth and bloom and you can satisfy part of these and not fall excessively short on the others, the plants will adjust.

For instance the plants *need* more light at lower humidity levels. But, if you increase the light, the humidity is no longer so important. If humidity is high, soil moisture can be relatively low. If the temperature drops, a combination of high humidity and less water will balance out. It is because of this rule that we can maintain and bloom plants very well in our living room at 30 percent humidity or less, although they would receive 50 percent or more in our plant room. The need for special treatment depends on your under-standing of the plant's other reactions. You usually can compensate.

The best way to provide humidity is a large-capacity home humidifier. These often come with built-in humidistats, but don't depend on that completely. Acquire a good separate one to hang on the wall near the garden. A humidifier, if carefully maintained, will last for ten years which means an investment of six or seven dollars a year—plus electricity, whose consumption is rather low. A humidifier is particularly advisable if you have air conditioning.

With a humidifier it should be possible to maintain a level of 50 percent throughout the year. That is what the plants really need. If you can up it to 70 or 80 percent, so much the better. We have heard claims that excessive humidity is damaging. We don't know what excessive is in terms of gesneriads. What does happen is that, during summer, growers may combine high humidity, high temperatures, and excess water at the roots of plants which are not growing fast, especially those which completed their main growth in spring. Then crown or root rot may set in.

Misting is also very helpful. However, please understand that misting is not spraying. The leaves are not drenched. Proper misting produces a very fine cloud of moisture which refreshes the leaves. It is quite possible to carry on foliar feeding at the same time.

The best and cheapest mister is the double folding metal tube used by artists for blowing fixative on their work. It is available from any art store for 75¢ or less. More expensive but worth the investment for those who want the best is the portable insecticide fogger with reservoir attached, sold through Sears and other outlets for about $50.00. Considering that poorly made plastic misters cost up to $20.00, the fogger is economical. The foggers work on house current and have a lengthy extension cord. A two- or three-second blast three times a day will make a difference to your plants. Timers can be attached which will turn the equipment on automatically for a short cycle as often as you consider advisable. For most indoor gardens the foggers may prove a better solution than the humidifier, because the moisture of the fogger is directed while that of the humidifier is easily dissipated.

A humid environment can be created in trays or beds of pebbles or in plastic egg crates (see Watering). The latter is cleaner, lighter, and less prone to harbor insects.

TEMPERATURE

Gesneriads which are not hardy Alpines can stand a temperature range of about 55° F to 80° F. They can tolerate somewhat higher temperatures under special circum-stances. The range is relatively limited for some species. Although the majority of our gesneriad houseplants is from the tropics, it is not generally understood that some grow on the sides of mountains at altitudes of 2,000 to 5,000 feet and that, even on the equator, this altitude makes a difference. So we find that some *Streptocarpus* are happiest between 55° and 70°, while a good many genera require a minimum temperature of 65°. Because most Americans maintain home temperatures with the latter minimum, these plants are usually the easiest for us to grow.

The warmer types of plants can, as we have said, tolerate higher than 80° F. But above that figure, metabolic reactions are very much speeded up, and the environmental balance must be ideal to keep them in best condition. That is why air conditioning in summer is very beneficial and fans are of some help. In our unair-conditioned apartment episcias do fine in the spring, stop blooming during a very hot spell—and are subject to stem rot at that time—resume bloom during any summer cool period, and are perfectly happy in winter as long as our superintendent maintains sufficient warmth at night during the worst of the season.

The lesson of this is that failure with certain plants may be due to temperature. If one group could be maintained steadily at 55°–65° and the other at 65°–75°, we would have few problems. A temperature drop at night is not essential. It happens naturally, even indoors, anyway. It is far more important that it not drop too much. The drop serves primarily to fix moisture on the leaves of the plants. A morning misting will compensate.

As no other absolute rules can be laid down, we will specify approximate temperature ranges in our plant descriptions.

VENTILATION

The role of ventilation in indoor growing has been greatly exaggerated. If it were so necessary, how would we be able to grow plants in terrariums so successfully? The temperature and moisture content of the air is more important by far. Polluted air is damaging, and more of it is no solution. Moving air, then, performs primarily the function of preventing temperature buildup on leaf surfaces and at the roots of plants. The breeze moves the air onward and speeds evaporation of soil moisture on the surface of pots, which causes a drop in temperature. The same effects which are beneficial at high temperatures are lethal at low ones. A plant can tolerate lower temperatures when the air is still, but will suffer if it is moving.

On this subject all we can say is that, if your plants are suffering from high temperatures, fans will help. They should not be powerful fans but, rather, gentle ones. A number of little fans work better than a big one.

FERTILIZER

We believe that it is unnecessary in this book to repeat all the detailed information which may be found in numerous publications. We all know that the basic plant needs are satisfied by nitrates, phosphates, and potash, plus trace elements. We know precious little about the specific needs of individual plants or how to produce a particular effect through the kind and amounts of feeding. Some gesneriads need a great deal of nourishment, while others get along with almost none at all.

The first question is What fertilizer? If we were to judge by the numerous articles giving forth contradictory suggestions—often complicated formulas and procedures—it would seem to be a very difficult matter. We have, from time to time, consulted commercial growers, and there are no two who use the same chemicals in the same proportions. We remember one of them recommending a lopsided proportion of phosphate and potash to nitrate, only to find, a few years later, that he was using a balanced formula. As for those private recipes given out in print by amateurs, as if they were the secret of life, not one of them has been adopted by others, and nobody who tries them seems to be able to find any substantial improvement in the plants.

One of the very common errors of growers is in failing to differentiate normal growth phenomena from an artificial stimulus. For instance, it will be reported that such and such a formula has "worked wonders with my plants," which did not respond to anything else. Diligent inquiry reveals that the magic portion was served in the spring just about the time the plants were due to get into action anyway. Or the enthusiast has just changed his old fluorescent tubes for new ones and hasn't put two and two together.

Here are a number of rules which we believe everyone should know in regard to fertilizers and their uses.

1. If you overfertilize, the accumulation of salts in the soil can cause root and crown rot. Excess fertilizer can be leached out of the soil by running clear water through the pot for a couple of minutes.

2. If you underfertilize, you may starve the plant. However, it is surprising how well some of our houseplants, including gesneriads, can do in soilless mix without any supplementary fertilizing at all. Gesneriads will stand still but rarely die from lack of fertilizer.

3. Light, soil, and moisture interacting will cause a plant to grow. If it is inactive, do not fertilize. Feeding it will not activate it. Plants which are growing *should* be fertilized as they are consuming nourishment to maintain their activity.

4. The nearer to ideal the other environmental conditions are for a plant, the more active it is likely to be. That means that it will use more fertilizer.

5. Regular, very diluted feedings at short intervals are more beneficial than a concentrated dose at long intervals of time.

6. Do not apply fertilizer solutions to dry soil. Wet the soil first then, after an interval, give the feeding solution.

7. If you fertilize with every watering, dilute the fertilizer to one-tenth the amount recommended on the label. In practice most plants are not watered daily. If you choose to fertilize once a week, dilute the fertilizer to one-quarter the amount recommended on the label.

8. A standard chemically balanced formula (such as 20–20–20) is quite adequate for all the gesneriads.

9. Terrestrial shrubby gesneriads usually require more nitrate than the others.

10. The very heavily blooming gesneriads benefit from a high phosphate-potash fertilizer, 12–36–14, for example. When bloom ceases, return to a balanced formula and reduce the dose.

11. Fish emulsion is a good alternative to the chemical fertilizers. However, we have found that if it is used exclusively there is some deterioration in the plants, perhaps because this is high nitrate fertilizer with an acid reaction. A good plan, we have often followed, is to use chemical fertilizer for a long period and then switch for a while to fish emulsion. We have used Sturdy, which is a pure organic phosphate-potash fertilizer, during periods of bloom for African violets, gesneriads, and other profusely flowering plants.

12. On the whole we find switching fertilizers from time to time helps the plants. We never like to apply any system automatically for too long a time.

Slow-release fertilizers are a case in point. We would gladly recommend them if we knew more about them. We have seen commercial growers mixing the pellets in all their soil formulations so that they would not have to fertilize from then on. No doubt this additive keeps the plants going for a time after they are sold and leads to fewer complaints from those who do not fertilize at all.

We don't like products that do not display their formulas prominently, do not state the rate of release, do not give tables of quantity, are not too sure how the pellets, capsules, and so on, should be applied. Also we do not see either savings for the average grower or increase of efficiency. Any fertilizer will affect a plant, but we don't have any idea how these work out in the long run. The slow-release fertilizers have been used commercially for a much longer time than most people are aware. We doubt that they as yet meet the needs of the amateur grower.

Foliar feeding is another matter about which we are dubious. No doubt the leaves "feed." But we are not anxious to pour diluted chemicals on the leaves of *all* our plants. We feel it will do as much harm as good most of the time. To be sure plants like a misting—any of them. Mist your plants regularly, fertilize in the ground, and stop worrying about foliar feeding.

PESTS

We almost left out a section on pests for the reason that, as far as our own experience is concerned, gesneriads rarely become infested. Our own collection of plants is not only varied but changing constantly, and we have found no way of quarantining the new ones which are being constantly added. Hence there are always some insects present. Nevertheless, the only serious infestations we have suffered have been from mealybug. Although we have had mites in the house, they have not attacked any of the gesneriads, nor have white flies or scale insects.

Dipping in a mild solution of Malathion will usually rid plants of mealybug. Although the Q-tip and alcohol pick-off method is often recommended, we have found this hopelessly tedious and inadequate.

After much experience with pests of various kinds, we suggest upending the plants and subjecting the undersides of leaves to a very strong jet of lukewarm water. If this is repeated twice a week for a period, you will usually be successful in eradicating the objectionable creatures.

As for the little woods bugs and springtails which sometimes run around in the soil scaring the lights out of growers and doing relatively little damage, a mild solution of Clorox or a standard insecticide drench will finish them off.

POTS AND BASKETS

POTS. Most indoor gardeners have switched from clay to plastic pots because they are lighter, cleaner, take up less space, and cost less. In fact much less attention is being paid to the aesthetic appearance of the container in the normal course of growing.

The plastic pots come in many sizes and in both square and round shapes. A superior quality can be had in an excellent counterfeit of brick coloring. Although a bit bulky and excessively light, Styrofoam pots have some advantages of their own, being rather cooler and allowing for some aeration. All the different plastic containers used for food packing, if of a suitable size and shape, come in handy.

We cannot recommend any particular sizes and shapes for gesneriads. Some species have very shallow roots and therefore will do best in an azalea-type pot. Others prefer deeper ones. A 6-incher is usually the top size pot we ever need for a gesneriad.

POTTING. When potting with soilless mixes, it is very important to fill all spaces in the pot but not to compact the material any more than necessary.

Because space is at a premium and indoor growing conditions make it superfluous, we do not recommend the use of drainage material in the bottoms of pots. The custom of filling the bottom with broken crock (shards of clay pots) derives from English green-house culture and is strictly passé. Pebbles or charcoal offer no advantages. Soilless mixes will drain properly and nothing else is needed. The saving in pot space is considerable.

Because of the shape of plastic pots, a special problem arises in packing the soil. A clay pot usually has a broader band at the rim but the interior is smooth. Plastic pots, on the other hand, must be reinforced by an outward bend to the last half or whole inch at the top. The peculiar effect of this design is that you can have soil well spread across at rim level yet leave gaping holes in the packing of the lower part of the pot.

This is not always immediately apparent. And, if you are watering from the top, you may be surprised to see your plant starting to sag after a few days. This is because the water is passing through the pot without moistening the soil within it. Poke a finger into the soil, and it will plunge right down.

In order to counteract this tendency, we have taken to using a potting stick. This, depending on the size of pot, can be a wooden dowel, the shaft of a houseplant shovel, or, best of all, a narrow spatula-shaped tool. With this you can force soil by leverage from the side of the pot toward the center with least damage to roots and gradually fill the gaps.

To decant a potted plant, turn it upside down and rap the edge of the pot on a hard surface while holding leaves out of the way. Contrary to some experts' advice, we always water the soil before decanting so that the mass of root and soil will come out in one piece.

In repotting, use only the next larger size. There are some exceptions among the gesneriads which need lots of room for their roots to wander, but that means intentional overpotting from the first. The majority likes only a little extra space to grow into, and for these plants overpotting is nearly as bad as pot binding.

When potting a grown plant, hold it by its root ball during repotting. When trans-planting seedlings, hold them by the leaves, not the stem.

In order to save on size of pot, we pot with the soil much closer to the rim than used to be the practice. Since no water collects on the surface if the soil has proper drainage, there is no reason to have the plant far below the rim.

Square pots take up less space than round pots as they can be set side by side forming a solid block. But, since round pots come in the larger sizes, it is easier to repot from a small round pot to a large one than from a square pot to a round one.

HANGING CONTAINERS. The business in hanging containers has grown to such an extent that they are available in every shape, size, and material. In the house, plastic baskets with molded-on saucers are the most convenient. However it is not too difficult to wire a saucer onto a container you prefer for its looks. Wire baskets and redwood baskets must be lined with sheet moss or sphagnum moss and will drip like mad. It all depends on what is convenient. If you have a tile floor, it will not matter.

OTHER CONTAINERS. Indoor growers have the advantage of being able to use any kind of water-resistant container. Styrofoam egg boxes are fine for growing the tiny sinningias, as are the little counter coffee creamers. In a pinch you can cut off and use the bottom of a quart or pint milk container. The larger fired clay saucers are fine for minia-ture gardens. Terrariums we deal with in a separate section.

Propagation

MULTIPLYING YOUR PLANTS

To the amateur houseplant grower, multiplying his plants is a means of perpetuating those he likes and producing extras to give away to friends or support a plant society or charity. Nevertheless, ease of propagation is rarely an important factor in his choices. The attractiveness of a plant is the primary incentive. But we are all ultimately dependent on commercial growers for our supply of plants, and none of these will attempt to launch volume production unless he is sure that he can multiply the plants easily and quickly. No plant can become popular without this characteristic. It may seem as if newly introduced species or hybrids fail to catch on with the public because of lack of beauty or failure to adapt. These are factors, but the most frequent cause of failure is poor propagation.

If we belabor this point, it is that it is so poorly understood not only by the average houseplant grower but by noncommercial hybridizers, which include some who are professional horticulturists. It is the reason why we have seen a hybridizer turn out dozens of new plants without producing a single one that has entered commercial channels. Although some of them were very beautiful, they all had the fatal flaw. Those who wish to be involved in hybridization should not lose sight of this fact. Their work will lead nowhere except to salve their egos, unless the resultant plants can be multiplied readily.

The African violet would never have achieved general acceptance with both amateurs and commercial florists if it had been difficult to reproduce. In fact, we can trace much of the success of the gesneriad family to its almost unique ability to propagate in many different ways. Certainly no other family offers the amateur such ease in multiplying as many attractive species and cultivars in the home.

The extraordinary developments in the gesneriad family, then, stem very largely from this marvelous quality. And it is one which guarantees an even more magnificent future as more and more selection and hybridization take place. As the matter stands today, we are reasonably certain that there is no other family of plant hobbyists as knowledgeable about and as active in propagation as gesneriad lovers.

Nevertheless there is apparent a constant need for detailed knowledge on the subject, both by hobbyists and newcomers to growing indoors. The reason is that, in spite of the simplicity of the methods, there are so many situations requiring some special kind of handling because straight procedures do not work as satisfactorily as expected. Also people are not analytical. They may catch the general idea but be unable to observe just why, in a particular instance, the method is not working. We cannot give all the answers, but we can suggest some and, in other cases, make clear the probable nature of the trouble. Any methods using organic material are compromises, variations in propagation techniques suited to particular plants. They are ideal for only a few; the rest require some modification. Bearing this in mind, we can lay down the procedures and principles underlying propagation in this family.

THE PROP BOX

We describe the prop box first because it is a basic tool in seed and vegetative propagation indoors. Its purpose is to create the high humidity terrarium conditions in which many gesneriad seeds sprout and cuttings produce roots. For instance, if we lay a number of *Codonanthe* cuttings on top of a bed of moist sphagnum moss and keep the vessel closed in a temperature range of 70° to 80° with sufficient light, we can observe, within a short time, the development of roots that reach down from every node into the moss. When the cuttings start to grow, they lift themselves, and some of the roots may become attached to the moist sides of the terrarium interior as will those of *Selaginella* and miniature *Ficus*. This environment, then, is ideal, and actually necessary for the quick propagation of the more tropical types of gesneriads.

A prop box for indoor propagation is merely a container with a transparent cover, which can be used for either stem or leaf cuttings as well as seeds. Right here we must note exceptions. A covered container is not necessary in a greenhouse, where propagation is often done in wooden flats which are quite adequate in those conditions. Also a closed container is not essential indoors if room temperature is higher than 72° F and the humidity above 70 percent. This often happens in summer. Also, we will specify more exactly further on some cuttings that are more amenable to open air treatment than others.

What the closed prop box does is ensure even temperatures for the plants and high humidity when it is not available, which is for most of the year in the northern part of the country and indoors. When conditions are perfect in the environment we do not need special care.

The size of a prop box depends on the space required to accommodate cuttings of leaf or stem—and the number you want to propagate. Thus, a 1½-inch pot becomes a prop box when a clear plastic drinking glass is upended over it. We can also use old-fashioned glasses which will hold up to eight cuttings of *Episcia* and possibly six African violet leaves. For larger cuttings and a greater number, one of the best containers is the plastic bread box, which is a foot long, the bottom part 2½ inches deep, and the clear plastic top the same. Since many vegetative cuttings and leaves need 1½ to 2 inches of medium and at least 2 inches of air space, this is just about ideal. Figure a minimum of 4 inches from the bottom to the top of your prop box. Other plastic containers, from 4-inch food storage rounds or squares to sweater boxes, are excellent, but few have the good proportions of the bread box.

Bread boxes, food storage containers, and plastic old-fashioned glasses can serve as prop boxes as long as they are transparent.

Any vessel can be turned into a prop box by stretching a sheet of plastic food wrapping over it. For the rooting of a couple of leaves or the sprouting of a few rhizomes, even a plastic sandwich bag filled with medium will do. Plastic clouds after a while from dirt and abrasion, but this is just as well when it comes to propagation, as the light requirement is comparatively low.

A cutting box does not need ventilation holes in the top or drainage holes in the bottom. Ventilation is not necessary. If the temperature of a room becomes too warm, the cover can be tilted. But if the air is cool, the holes will only let it in. Without vents the moisture and humidity will remain constant for a long time, which is what you want. We have found that holes in the bottom will tempt a nervous beginner to add water by allowing the box to soak up water. This only courts disaster. The seed box also needs no drainage holes. When you don't add water, there is nothing to drain.

If at any time you decide that some additional moisture is absolutely necessary, simply flush the water down the sidewall of the box and none of your cuttings or seeds will be disturbed.

Prop boxes which are to be used without a cover should have drainage holes either to soak up water from the bottom or to allow water from the top to pass through rapidly.

The amateur who propagates regularly is well advised to have several containers with transparent covers handy. They should be chosen with consideration of available space. The right shape and size takes up less room and fits into unused space between growing plants.

A prop box in constant use saves space and effort. As rooted cuttings are dug out, others are started. As medium is lost, it is replaced. You need not load new containers if your taking of cuttings or your seeding is timed to the removal of transplants. The production of a plastic bread box that is properly programmed is quite tremendous over a year's time.

CABLE-HEATED PROP BOXES.   Unless provided with thermostatic controls, the vaunted even temperatures offered by cables is a delusion. Modern homes are warm enough most of the year to start cuttings and seeds. In fact it is a rare day when an American home goes down below 65° F in winter. Naturally a prop box should be placed in an area where it is not exposed to open window ventilation during winter. But if it is, the cable will not do much good. Although we live in New York City, and our apartment is not ideally warm in winter, we have never found a need for cable heating of our propagation beds. These gadgets are more appropriate in England, where they are much used because homes are kept at temperatures well below 65° in winter. To an Englishman 65° F is a heat wave. That's the difference. We consider the cables superfluous.

MEDIUMS FOR ROOTING STEM AND LEAF CUTTINGS

Moist vermiculite, perlite, combinations of the two, live, fibrous, or milled sphagnum moss, and sand are all excellent rooting media. One-one-one Lean Mix is occasionally used. Potting soil, houseplant soil as bought in the stores in packages, and prepared mixes containing chemical additives are not recommended. Although we have not used sand in the past, a possible future shortage of vermiculite and perlite may make it mandatory.

SAND.   We have never considered builders' sand suitable for horticultural use. The English have the Cornish silver sands and other types that are mined for horticultural use.

Chances are that the wide use of perlite and vermiculite has discouraged the packaging of a good quality horticultural product. The fine grain sands used in most cactus mixes are of poorest quality.

On a visit to the Bailey Hortorium at Cornell University, we saw a sand being used that had the appearance and mechanical characteristics we were seeking. This, Dick Traphagen, the horticulturist, told us was grade 4Q, as sold by lumberyards for special building mixes. It is very even in texture, well sieved, and gritty. We prefer the other media, but this would do very well in a pinch. For the commercial nursery it would be impractical because pot weight would be increased, thereby raising shipping costs considerably. There are certainly smelters' waste products of a porous nature which could be pulverized to make a medium as good as the ones we have.

VERMICULITE.   We have already discussed the nature of this material in our section on the mixes and have warned against impure or inferior grades. Chemically neutral vermiculite is our preferred rooting medium for leaves and cuttings. Adherence is excellent, and the roots of the cuttings spread easily through it. Moisture is very evenly distributed and well retained. Minimum root disturbance is caused when plants are removed for transplanting.

PERLITE.   We have also described perlite earlier. As a rooting medium for cuttings, we consider it inferior to vermiculite because, when wet, it tends to be too wet, and it dries out very quickly. It is fine for those cuttings which do well if rooted in water, for the perlite seems to be nothing more than a support for the cutting when a very wet medium is used. Begonia stem cuttings, for instance, do better in perlite than most gesneriads. The combination of perlite and vermiculite offers no special advantage.

LIVE SPHAGNUM MOSS.   This is the fastest growing of all mosses. It forms thick blankets of greenery in certain types of bogs, where it can be gathered by the armful with ease. The long strands, which grow upright and tightly packed together, have innumerable branches in whorls bearing tiny leaves which absorb large quantities of water.

When you try to pack it into a prop box, you will find it so spongy that it is very difficult to compress, and the amount required is much greater than you have imagined. But it is unnecessary for propagation to have a solid mass. In fact the live moss should always be allowed to breathe, otherwise you destroy its best quality. Simply pile it in the box, being sure that it fills completely, and press down lightly. In this way it forms a moist, aerated mattress which is ideal for propagation of certain plants which form roots in the very humid spaces between the branches of moss. The material is especially suitable for epiphytic plants which require just such a spongy medium.

Sphagnum should never be soaking wet—merely moist—though a very thin film of water may be maintained in the bottom of the box. Unlike soil, the sphagnum will not become soggy. Do not fertilize at any time. Given modest amounts of light and warm conditions, sphagnum will soon start to grow and look just as fresh as in the bog whence it came. For this reason it is also very durable as a propagating material and a very attractive one to work with.

Live sphagnum is not a sterilized material and may contain insects. But bogs contain very little insect life. A more likely unwelcome visitor may be a small type of snail. If the cover is put on the box these will usually walk up the sides and can be killed off. Watch for the tiny shells of progeny when you are hunting the big ones, which are only an eighth of an inch in diameter. They do little harm.

We do not use the moss for general propagating because the mechanical nature of the material makes rowing up the cuttings difficult or impossible. We save it rather for the most difficult jobs—epiphytic plants in particular, or for the miniature sinningias—or for plants we most desire not to lose. Even when rooting doesn't take place for a long time, a cutting or leaf will rarely deteriorate.

Sometimes a cutting is merely laid on top of the sphagnum. Sometimes we will poke leaves and cuttings into the material by opening a hole with the handle of our houseplant shovel.

When leaves or cuttings have rooted, special care must be taken in removing them, because the mass of sphagnum hangs together and if you tug on the plant you may break the roots—which does not happen with milled sphagnum. What we do is to pinch the sphagnum around the roots and break the whole lot free from the rest. We do not remove the excess from the roots in potting. We place the stem and its sphagnum in the pot and pack mix in and around it. In this way the plant will have plenty of time and space to get used to the pot and gradually spread its roots through the surrounding medium.

LONG FIBER SPHAGNUM MOSS. This is the trade name for sphagnum moss that has been dried and sterilized. It is available from plant and garden supply centers in bags of various sizes. We use it for propagation if live moss is unavailable. It breaks down more quickly; is more likely to compact excessively; but is used like live moss. It is a very useful top dressing with small tender-leaved potted plants.

MILLED SPHAGNUM MOSS. This moss has been dried, cleaned, sterilized, and reduced to such short lengths that it is almost like a powder. It is so dry and light that, if stirred, it will rise like dust and be rather irritating. For the same reason it is difficult to wet. If you intend to use it damp, it is advisable to mix it with lukewarm water in a bowl or let it stand overnight. But if only a thin layer is required on top of moist soilless mix, as for seeding, it can be spread over the surface dry. Close the box containing the moist mix covered with the dry milled sphagnum, and a day later the sphagnum will be wet. This eliminates all risk of disturbing the seed by spraying or soaking.

Sphagnum moss is not only mechanically an excellent propagating medium; it is also one which inhibits damping-off fungi. The use of the moss makes it unnecessary to spray seedlings or cuttings with antidamping-off fungicides which always involves some risk. That is why we use a layer of the moss with seeds. The same characteristic makes all sphagnum moss useful as a top dressing where leaves of plants can come into contact with the surface of moist soil. When the moss lies between, rot does not take place. Newly moistened milled sphagnum moss often develops a white mildewlike growth after a few days which scares inexperienced growers out of their wits. However, this is harmless and can be ignored.

We still prefer vermiculite for cuttings, because we have little difficulty with damping-off, and the mineral has some mechanical advantages—ease of planting and removing the cuttings, for instance. However, once roots start in the sphagnum moss, they spread rapidly and cuttings can be removed with a solid ball of the moss attached to them.

WHEN TO TAKE CUTTINGS OF LEAF OR STEM

1. Whenever you have acquired a new plant try to propagate it immediately. The shock of transportation and change of environment is very great, and it may well succumb and be irreplaceable, or at least involve some trouble in replacing. A cutting, if the plant is of a type which favors this method of propagation, may guarantee survival. Also, since it starts out in your environment, in your medium, and under your care, it may well turn out a stronger, healthier plant than the parent. The possible temporary disfigurement of the original plant is not important as it will soon recover. A cutting should be tried

even if the time and conditions do not conform completely to the following rules. It's worth the risk.

2. The best time to take cuttings is when a plant is in active growth. However, you may have to act if a plant is really ill—for instance, removing healthy tissue from one doomed by fungal disease. That's a desperation action and often saves the plant. Also, if the plant was in active growth at the moment illness struck, the piece you cut off may be in perfect condition for rooting. If not, you must still try to save the healthy part by rooting it. Cuttings often take very well from plants which are in semidormancy. But, ideally, you should do your cutting during a time when the plant is particularly healthy and on the move.

3. Always use healthy tissue. Never use damaged or old leaves or stems that show deterioration. Of course, even "never" has its exceptions. If you have to, you may cut away the rotten part of a leaf or a stem and give it a try. Often as not it works.

4. Take cuttings from young mature growth. Stems with juvenile leaves have to expend energy developing them. It's the same as keeping flowers or buds on the cutting. Woody stems may "take," but they are always more difficult.

5. Spring is the best season for taking most cuttings.

6. A period of moderate warmth is best for taking cuttings. An August heat wave, if you don't have air conditioning, may rot them out. When the night temperature is above 70° and below 85° is the best time. Cool periods of winter do not prohibit taking cuttings but tend to stop plant growth. At least try to pick a humid, comfortably warm time.

LEAF PROPAGATION

Leaves of sinningias, saintpaulias, streptocarpus, and so on, are effective means of propagation. Whether or not to use them depends on the suitability of the leaf and whether it offers the quickest or most productive way, depending on your needs. A good guide to follow is a nurseryman growing gesneriads, for he *must* use the most efficient method. The character of the leaf tells us something about its ability to propagate. It is noticeable to any experienced grower that leaves which are hard surfaced and shiny are usually unsuitable—for instance gesnerias and *Aeschynanthus.* The leaves that work best are usually soft textured and often hairy or have rather thick, juicy petioles and heavy veining.

Leaves are a slower means of propagation than stems for the reason that the former must develop a plantlet from scratch while the latter, once rooted, are already partly grown plants. *Sinningia* produces only a single tuber. However, in some instances, leaves produce greater quantities of plants. Also the habit of a plant may make it easier to remove a quantity of leaves than cut a number of lengths of stem.

Leaves of *Saintpaulia* and *Streptocarpus* grow plants from single cells. This offers two advantages. The number of plants from a single leaf can be quite large—a dozen or more from *Saintpaulia,* especially if reused, and up to fifty from *Streptocarpus.* And these plants, unlike stem cuttings and other leaf rootings, have a very high rate of mutation. This is of great assistance in speeding up the improvement of the breed, especially when leaves are subjected to radiation.

Saintpaulia and *Streptocarpus* also produce many new side growths which can be separated (see section on division). Trailing types of *Saintpaulia* are candidates for stem cuttings.

We give you these examples to show you that there *are* alternatives. Nevertheless, the

Lengthwise-cut half leaves of *Streptocarpus* produce quantities of plants. *Courtesy Kartuz Greenhouses*

nurseryman usually uses leaves. This is because he removes them anyway in trimming his growing plants, and each discarded leaf can produce several plantlets.

LEAF PROPAGATION OF SAINTPAULIA

African violet leaves can serve as the model for the whole business of leaf propagation. With thousands of A. V. hobbyists and many who are considered experts, there are, as one might expect, a number of ways to handle the leaves and their pups. Though they all undoubtedly work, it would make little sense to try to list them. Those who have their own methods are not likely to change them and will not be reading this chapter for advice. Those who are less self-confident or just beginning will need an easy way that can be relied on or, at most, a choice of a few basic approaches.

It may, for instance, interest the beginner to know that an African violet leaf laid on top of or poked into any soilless mix in a container with a transparent cover and kept in a warm place with some light, will almost certainly develop roots without any further attention. A major greenhouse grower simply plunges the leaves to half their lengths in a moist mixture of perlite and vermiculite in open flats, with close to 100 percent results. Moist vermiculite, perlite, sand, fine gravel—almost any porous material will do. The leaves, in other words, are very productive and you must be really rather ingenious to kill them off. Leaves of some of the other plants, however, are rather tender and require careful handling and close watch. Here we will simply outline the steps we consider the simplest and most foolproof.

LEAVES TO USE. Since African violets are rosette plants with a single trunk, removing any central leaf will not only inhibit flowering at that point, and destroy the symmetry, but even cause the plant to branch instead of growing onward and upward. The leaves chosen for propagation, therefore, should be from the outer, or oldest, whorl. There has been talk of using second and third rank leaves, as if the outer ones were done for. They are or they aren't. If they are unblemished and vigorous and crisp, you can and should use the outer leaves. If they are discolored, damaged, or desiccated, take leaves from the next rank.

CUTTING THE LEAVES. Some people merely break off the leaves. That's fine if your nails are long and sharp. But it leads to bad habits in handling other plants. Using a small pair of scissors is foolproof. They should be sharp so that they make a clean cut. You ought not to use scissors which are grimy but, on the other hand, they need not be sterilized. With African violets we are not especially worried about viruses. Contamination is unlikely from other sources. Just cut. We make a point of this because people who consider themselves experts are always trying to fuss unnecessarily. There is no problem, so why create one?

Cut close to the stem so that you don't leave an ugly stump.

If the petiole (stem of the leaf) is long, cut it to 1 inch in length. That is the length from the bottom of the leaf blade to the end of the petiole. If, by chance, you have broken off the petiole, just make a half-inch cut with the scissors on either side of the midrib of the leaf and then cut away the two sides of the blades up to that point, leaving an artificial petiole. This is not essential because the leaf blade itself will produce pups, but the cut leaf is somewhat more tender and making the petiole will be added protection.

DIPPING. Dipping the petiole in hormone powder may or may not encourage the production of roots. It does, however, act as a fungicide. We do it just for insurance. Sulfur powder will perform the same job. Some growers have recommended Malathion. There is little point in this unless the whole leaf is soaked for a moment, and the only purpose would be to kill off juvenile insects. A half-strength solution is advisable.

Don't let the leaves lie around to harden. They don't, and you will only send them into shock. They're been through enough as it is.

PREPARING THE PROP BOX WITH GRANULAR MATERIAL. We say granular material because there is some difference, which we have already indicated above, when fibrous materials are used. Here the procedure is the same whether we use vermiculite, perlite, a combination of the two, or sand.

Our preference, and that of most growers, is for vermiculite. Fill a bread box or other container to a depth of 1½ inches with the dry material. Add room temperature water at the rate of ¾ cup to 8 cups of vermiculite. Don't worry about the even distribution of the moisture in the box. That will take place within a couple of hours after the box is covered.

Our objective in moistening the vermiculite is to achieve a soil condition which we might almost call humid, rather than moist. With the cover on, the air humidity is sufficient to keep the cuttings happy as long as the temperature is above 65°–70°. In order to continue living, the leaves are forced to put out roots. If the medium is wet they do not make this effort, but depend on the moisture available and eventually succumb to fungal diseases.

PLANTING THE LEAVES. When you are sure that your vermiculite is properly moistened you can plant the leaves. However, should the medium have become too wet, clean out the box and start over again. By the time the medium dries out sufficiently for use, your cutting would be in poor condition. You must plant promptly.

Be sure that you plant in a warm place. Remember that 65° is an absolute minimum temperature. Seventy to 80° is better.

Poke a hole in the vermiculite with a rod, pencil, or any round, narrow tool. Then stuff the petiole in the hole so that the leaf blade comes down to but does not touch the medium. You will get more plantlets if the leaf is set in deeper but you also run more risk of rotting. The leaf should stand upright. Leaves can be placed as little as ½ inch apart. Don't waste space. There is plenty of room for the little roots which will develop. Be sure the vermiculite is firm around the petiole so that your leaf won't flop over. Now put the top on the box.

Before or after inserting the leaves don't forget to label the outside of the box with the name of the plant. Peel-off labels are ideal for this purpose.

OPEN PROP BOX TREATMENT.   Anything from a 1½-inch pot, through a plastic old-fashioned glass to a large box can be used for uncovered propagation. It will work with saintpaulias though not as fast as the covered treatment. For some gesneriads, certain episcias for instance, it is just as effective.

There *should* be holes in the bottom of the open prop box, for we are not dealing here with a stable moisture environment.

Fill the container 1½ or 2 inches deep with vermiculite or other inert granular material. Water the medium thoroughly at room temperature and plant just like the closed prop box. The shape of the container will dictate the arrangement of the leaves. For instance, we always put in A. V. leaves following the circle of the rim of an old-fashioned glass, and make two or three rows with a couple of leaves in the middle for good measure.

Even more vital with open propagation is the factor of temperature because there is no protection. Keep the box where it receives no drafts and where the temperature is *always* over 70° F.

MOSS PROPAGATION.   We use moss only in closed prop boxes. Live sphagnum moss is naturally damp without being wet. It should be kept that way and should not be fertilized. Pile the moss solidly in the prop box. Poke holes in it and insert your leaves. Long fiber moss and milled sphagnum are treated much the same. The long fiber should be thoroughly moistened in a bowl, well wrung out, and fluffed before packing. The milled sphagnum should really be prepared the night before. If a cup of water is poured into a bread box of milled sphagnum, it will permeate the mass overnight.

LIGHT.   Intense light is not needed to procure satisfactory rooting with either a closed or open prop box provided temperature and humidity are right. About 150 foot-candles are sufficient. If the humidity is lower than 70 percent, somewhat more light is required. A favorite position in the light garden is at the end of the tubes about 6 inches below them—or even a few inches beyond the ends. In the window good reflected light is sufficient.

TEMPERATURE.   We have already noted the temperature range. A drop of temperature at night is no advantage to cuttings. Above 80°, mildew or other fungal rot may occur in a closed box. Open boxes, on the other hand, are more subject to these diseases if the temperature is too low or changes suddenly (drafts). If room temperature becomes very high, you will have to remove the cover from your prop box and take your chances. In summer at least, warmth is usually accompanied by high humidity, so little damage is done. Check moisture in the medium before replacing the cover on a box.

One of the best ways to deal with a bit of excess coolness is to place the prop box on a shelf over the fluorescent fixture at the point where heat from the ballast comes through. You can tell this by touch. The difference in temperature may run 10° or more and be equivalent to using a cable.

DEVELOPMENT OF ROOTING.   A. V. leaves should develop roots in two to three weeks' time. But as long as the leaves stay fresh looking don't worry about it. What you really want to see is the emergence of the first leaves of plantlets. With other gesneriad leaves you may want to test for roots. If so, give them a light tug. If they resist, they're working. Should you, by chance, pull out a leaf, just poke it back into the vermiculite again. No harm done.

Gesneriad leaves often grow considerably in the prop box becoming larger than normal. A. V. leaves often become thicker and more leathery.

FERTILIZING—OR NOT.   After you are sure that leaves are rooted, you may open the box and fertilize with a very mild high-nitrate solution. But this means doing away with the advantages of the closed box technique and makes your medium unreusable. We never fertilize. It is rather a mystery that the leaves increase in size and produce roots and pups on nothing but vermiculite, water, and rather low light—but it works.

GROWING THE PUPS.   Usually four to six weeks after rooting, the first leaves of the plantlets will appear above soil level. Don't be in any hurry to dig out the leaves. Several plantlets grow from the petiole and even from the midrib if that is buried partway. They can grow from any side of the petiole or from all of them, and each will have up to five juvenile leaves, white at first, but turning green when exposed to light.

It is important to allow the pups to develop good roots of their own, which means letting them expand until they sometimes form tight clusters just above the surface of the vermiculite.

When you feel sure that you have a number of well-developed plantlets, you can dig up the mass which you will find to be relatively extensive even if the leaves are rather closely packed together.

The plantlets can now be cut free with a razor or small scissors, removing part of the petiole in the process, or sectioning the petiole and then cutting the pups apart. Either of these methods is satisfactory. The important thing is not to damage the pups and their roots. They are very brittle at this time—especially the leaves—and must be handled with the utmost delicacy.

POTTING UP THE PLANTLETS.   The plants can now be potted up in 1½- to 2-inch pots filled with Lean Mix. Pack the moist mix firmly but not hard. The pots should be moved to good reflected light in the window or 6 to 12 inches under a two-tube fluorescent fixture. Mild fertilizing should start after a week. Keep just moist at all times. A drenching can cause the plantlets to rot.

COMING TRUE FROM LEAF.   We are all taught that vegetative propagation produces a mirror image of the parent plant. As a rule this is true. But where plants are produced from single cells as in *Saintpaulia* and *Streptocarpus*, variations do appear. Most of the mutations in African violets have occurred when a great many leaves from a particular cultivar have been rooted. Then, occasionally, a plant would appear which would differ in some noticeable way from the parent and could then be propagated on. But this also accounts for the tendency of some of the cultivars to revert. The situation therefore is by no means stable.

OTHER FIBROUS ROOTED GESNERIADS

The method is the same for other fibrous rooted gesneriads. Where it varies in detail, we will so specify in the cultural description. Most of the leaves produce single plantlet offspring. But most other gesneriads are propagated by other means.

LEAF PROPAGATION OF TUBEROUS GESNERIADS

Commercially the tuberous gesneriads are propagated by seed whenever possible because there is not a large and continuous production of leaves. But the amateur will often use the leaf method and it is necessary, of course, when the plant is sterile.

The leaves can be handled just like those of African violets. But, if the petiole is immersed in the vermiculite, a small tuber will grow at the tip which must go through a short period of dormancy before developing top growth. The size of the tuber will vary according to the size of the mature organ. The new tubers can be stored in a plastic bag or potted up and kept just slightly moist until they sprout. If the leaves are too large to handle, as with gloxinias, most of the leaf can be cut away leaving a piece no bigger than an African violet leaf.

Most growers, however, prefer rooting from leaf veins because an actual plantlet is formed and there is no dormant period. Cut the leaf into 1- or 2-inch sections, each of which includes a major vein and plant with the side facing the midvein downward in the soil. Usually only a single pup develops.

Some of the tuberous gesneriads act like fibrous rooted ones in the early stages and do not form tubers until they are much bigger.

HORIZONTAL METHOD OF PROPAGATION.   Leaves which have the ability to form plantlets easily can also be laid on moist medium, several veins cut, and treated otherwise like African violet leaves. Plantlets should develop in the slits. But in our opinion this is an expert stunt of little practical value. There are various problems involved in bringing the whole leaf in contact with the soil and keeping it from rotting. Conditions must be nearer perfect than for the other method. For these and other reasons we do not recommend it at all.

WATER PROPAGATION.   This is another stunt which has little merit. Roots are produced readily enough, but they are weak and being bare of clinging soil suffer more in the transition to a pot.

Fill any small vessel (glass or jar) with room-temperature tap water. Find a piece of flat plastic—such as the tops of coffee cans—and, with a hot icepick, make holes in it big enough to hold the petiole of an African violet leaf. Stiff paper will also do—or cardboard. Set the leaves in the holes with the petioles dangling in the water. If subjected to warmth and light, roots will develop rather rapidly.

Note that the production is of roots. True, plantlets will develop at the water level. But you are far better off to take the rooted cutting and put it in a prop box where the plantlets can grow more vigorously.

OTHER LEAF TECHNIQUES

Where required, we will discuss these along with the culture of the plants.

STEM CUTTINGS

Very few of our gesneriads are multiple branching plants, the kind which are most often used in stem propagation with other families of plants. The types of habit which are most often met up with are plants (1) with long flexible stems, (2) with single canes or relatively weak stems, and (3) with stolons. Each requires a slightly different treatment.

PLANTS WITH LONG FLEXIBLE STEMS.   These are *Columnea, Aeschynanthus, Codonanthe,* and the like. There are two types here: the leaves are closely set together with short internodes, or there are long internodes and the leaves are fewer. When leaves are close together, a length of stem is cut off, usually 3 or 4 inches long; the leaves from several lower nodes are cut away, leaving a bare stem and several leaves. The lower part is poked into moist vermiculite to a depth of 1 to 1½ inches. Several cuttings can be secured in this way from a single stem. But make sure that you always plant the end of the stem closest to the base of the plant downward. After a tip cutting has been made, it is very easy to make the mistake of reversing one of the other cuttings because the direction of the leaves on the stem cannot always be determined.

When the nodes are far apart and there are fewer leaves, it is usually advisable to have two nodes per cutting and remove the pair of leaves from the lower node.

PLANTS WITH CANES AND WEAK STEMS.   We are speaking here of plants such as *Chrysothemis,* with a strong, stiff, straight stem, or episcias, kohlerias, and the elongated stem parts of some of the tuberous plants such as *Sinningia cardinalis.* It is obvious that the single cane plants permit the taking only of the tip of the stem unless we want to divide up the whole into lengths. The tip cluster and 1 inch or 1½ inches of stem can be planted in vermiculite. The rest can be cut in lengths containing at least one leaf node and may require reducing the size of the large leaves by cutting them to a quarter of their natural length. The bare ends can then be planted. With the softer stems of the second type the method is the same, and the only difference is that, due to the slackness of the stem and natural curves that occur, they are a bit more difficult to fit comfortably in the vermiculite.

PLANTS WITH STOLONS.   The stoloniferous plants are episcias. These cordlike extensions without nodes grow from the leaf nodes of the main stems. At their tips they bear clusters of small leaves. Cut the stolon at its base and discard all but the leaf cluster and 1 or 1½ inches of stolon. The tip has a tendency to form a bend in the last 2 inches, and the cluster must often be imbedded in the vermiculite with the length of stolon extending horizontally just beneath the surface.

ROOTING THE CUTTINGS

Before being immersed in the moist vermiculite, the tips of the cuttings should be dipped in one of the hormone powders or sulfur. After planting, the top of the prop box is closed, and the box placed in good reflected light or near the ends of the fluorescent tubes in the same way we have described for leaf cuttings.

Episcia cuttings, rooted in the prop box, have been transplanted to small pots.

After about ten days, give the cuttings a tug. If they offer resistance, they are beginning to root. It is advisable to wait until removal of a cutting is accompanied by a root ball 1 inch in diameter. The cutting is then potted up in moist 1–1–1 mix and can be put out on the shelf under the lights immediately in most instances. When the plant is more tender, it may need hardening off. Put the small pots in a plastic box with cover on for a few days, then gradually remove the cover a little at a time for several days until the plant can live in the open without showing wilt.

DIVISION

We do not propagate gesneriads by division as much as by means of stem and leaf cuttings. Of course the removal of plantlets from the petiole of an African violet or *Streptocarpus* leaf is a form of division, but involves the breaking away of a whole plant. True division implies cutting a plant apart. One of the most frequently divided gesneriads is a mature *Streptocarpus* plant of the subgenus *Streptocarpus* or Wiesmoor Hybrids or 'Constant Nymph,' for instance.

These plants become tangles of leaves without any clearly differentiated clusters. As they increase rapidly, we must often break them up into small units. We try to identify sections of the plant which belong somewhat more together. Then we take a long sharp knife and drive it down between them so as to cut completely through the stem. This is done while the plant is still in the pot.

Then we decant the plant and separate the sections and their roots as best we can. All the parts are repotted. But, in doing so, we leave the wounded part, which is at the surface of the soil, free to the air by not packing soil around it. The wound is then dusted with hormone or sulfur powder. Water normally but allow the wound to air for a week. Then that part of the pot can be filled up completely. This is a good method to use with any division for, if any rotting is to occur, it will start at the wound.

Some gesneriads—*Gesneria cuneifolia,* for instance—spread by underground roots or rhizomes which appear at the surface in due time and develop into plants still attached to the parent. Branches which develop on the main stem below soil level also sometimes have their own roots. In either case simply cut the plant free, dig it up, and pot it separately. It is usually advisable to give higher humidity and low light for several days after the operation.

Mention has been made from time to time of the possibility of cutting tubers into sections, but we are not aware of this ever being successful. Scaly rhizomes are another matter. They're always breaking anyway as they are very brittle, and each section will grow into a plant.

SEED

The seed of gesneriads is exceedingly small, and the seed production even of so tiny a plant as *Sinningia pusilla* is surprisingly large. Seed culture is quite simple. What is difficult is sowing it so that the plantlets will not be too crowded.

Plant gesneriad seed as soon as possible. Some species stay fresh for up to a year; others lose viability in a few days. *Sinningia pusilla* and *concinna* seed is good for only a couple of weeks.

The principal difficulties in sowing such fine seed individually are our own impatience and a distrust of germination. This causes us almost invariably to plant many more seeds than are necessary at one time. To sow, spread the seeds on a sheet of white paper, moisten the tip of a fine sewing needle with the tongue, touch a seed and scrape it off in the soil. This is not difficult but rather nerve-wracking. The needle must be wiped clean each time. But that way you do get even distribution.

We use 1–1–1 mix, which we call Lean Mix, specially made up for the purpose of seeding. Peat moss must be sieved; perlite and vermiculite must be the smallest size. We buy small quantities just for sowing. The mix is moistened but not to the point that it becomes saturated. Then it is packed in a suitably sized propagation box to a depth of 1½ inches. Over the mix we dust a very thin coat of dry milled sphagnum moss which we buy in small packages at plant stores.

The propagation box is closed and allowed to stand overnight. The standing dampens the sphagnum moss. Then we seed as carefully as possible.

Another way of distributing seed is to take a very small quantity and mix with milled sphagnum moss. Then dust the dry material over the mix and you can close the box for good until the seed germinates.

When they have just two leaves, germinated gesneriad plants can be transplanted to another propagation box with Lean Mix by using an Opti-Visor or some other magnifier. Most of the plants will come through all right. It is also a characteristic of the gesneriads that the seedlings, once they have a few small leaves, will remain almost unchanged for months. Plantlets can be removed gradually to more spacious quarters instead of being taken care of all at one time.

When the seedlings are large enough to move to a pot, remove the propagation box top by stages so that the plants can harden off. When transplanting, hold by the leaves, not the stem.

Seedlings of *Gesneria cuneifolia* ready for potting.

TERRARIUM CULTURE

There is little point in our describing terrarium culture here in detail. Our book *Fun with Terrarium Gardening* (Crown) describes the processes step-by-step by means of text and illustrations. However, a few suggestions may be of value.

A terrarium is a transparent *closed* container that offers the advantages of very stable conditions and very high humidity—usually over 70 percent. Plants do best when the amount of moisture in the soil of the container is just right. We define this as *barely* moist, never wet.

The modern terrarium does better under fluorescent light than in a window because of the reliable daily illumination and the unchanging intensity of artificial lights. The terrarium should be set with the cover 2 to 6 inches under a two-tube fluorescent fixture.

We have introduced the method of planting pots directly into the soil. When plants themselves are rooted in the medium of a terrarium, any change of position involves disturbance of other plants and the whole design. The plants can also receive individual attention if they are separately potted.

In respect to gesneriads we have a few exceptions to the pot method. *Gloxinia sylvatica* and *Koellikeria,* for instance, require a free root run for best results. That means either trying to keep them under control rooted in the medium along with other plants in a design or, as we usually prefer, assigning them a separate terrarium container.

If terrariums are properly balanced, the chief danger to the contents occurs from temperature changes. The interior temperature should never go below 65° F or over 85° F. In unair-conditioned rooms in summer, the container may heat up excessively because of the combination of a warm day and the heat from the fluorescent fixture. It will then be necessary to open the terrarium several inches along one side or, in extreme instances, to remove the cover completely until the temperature drops down again. The moisture loss is replaced by flushing small amounts of water down the inside surfaces of the container.

All the epiphytic, rain forest, and tropical floor gesneriads from the lower altitudes will benefit from terrarium culture. This is true of both large and small plants. The distinction is only that the small plants can remain in the terrarium right through to maturity, while the large ones outgrow the container unless it is very large. Plants which suffer from shelf culture will often recover when placed in a terrarium for a period and then hardened off gradually before returning to open air culture.

In our cultural list we will mention plants that require terrarium culture to stay alive in the home.

Plant List

NAME CHANGES IN THE GESNERIADS

Changes are always occurring in the botanical names of plants for a host of reasons. For instance, it is the rule that the name must go back to the earliest mention. Researchers sometimes find out that a well-established label doesn't hold up because someone had written the plant up under a different name anywhere from a day to a century earlier. Two species may be joined together because the differences between them do not prove to be critical. Special studies of botanical characteristics may cause a researcher to transfer a species from one genus to another.

The interrelationships between the plants in some families are exceedingly complicated. Some species and genera are very stable while others display variations so considerable as to tempt taxonomists to place them in one or more separate species. The degree of variation which justifies such changes is very much a matter of individual judgment.

Taxonomists can't be constantly surveying all the species. Someone may have named a plant back in the nineteenth century and no one got around to reexamining the evidence until very much later. Also, when only a few members of a family have been thoroughly studied, especially when the plants come from widely separated geographical regions, the naming of a species and its inclusion in a particular genus are based unavoidably on insufficient information.

This being the situation in regard to a large percentage of all plants, one of the easiest ways to make a reputation among the rather small number of people really concerned with a family of plants is to do some research or exploration and start switching names around. The results are published and the botanist's name is recorded along with the genus and species name, for instance *Rechsteineria leucotricha Hoehne.* If controversy arises over the matter, so much the better. For even if the change is refuted, the one who started the fuss still gets into print, which is awfully important in these circles. As in every other field, there are solid, thorough botanists and taxonomists and also quick-study notoriety seekers. Actually the world pays no attention when the plants involved are obscure. But when they are very popular ones and a name has become a habit, the game can become both annoying and damaging.

A number of changes in gesneriad names have been authorized by the Nomenclature Committee of American Gloxinia and Gesneriad Society (AGGS) (and a considerable number rejected) in the past couple of years. I list these below. They are of two kinds. One transfers well-known and relatively unknown species from one genus to another. The other eliminates titles given to two groups of interspecific hybrids and reduces them to genus names. In these instances the transfers have been the result of exhaustive study by Dr. Carl Clayberg and Professor Harold Moore.

The changes create a problem for commercial growers and distributors of plants and even more for an author. For instance *Rechsteineria cardinalis* has been a popular plant. It is now *Sinningia cardinalis.* That's fine. But it happens that the whole group of plants familiar to amateurs by the name of *Rechsteineria* has flowers which are quite different in *appearance* from those we have always called sinningias and show at least an obvious similarity to each other. I am presented, therefore, with the choice, when comparisons are made or hybridization discussed, of lumping them all together or, for the benefit of the reader accustomed to two different kinds of plants, speaking of the "old" and "new" sinningias, or of sinningias and *former* rechsteinerias. This is very awkward but necessary until everyone doesn't have to think twice before recognizing the plants we are talking about. Sometimes that doesn't happen. For example, gloxinia persists as the name people recognize for a particular kind of *Sinningia.*

In the case of *Sinningia-Rechsteineria* the situation is not too difficult, for *both* of these genera are well known and popular. But the transfer of *Hypocyrta nummularia* to *Alloplectus nummularia* has a different wrinkle. In 1957 Professor Moore, in recording all gesneriads then in actual cultivation here, listed five *Alloplectus* and just one *Hypocyrta*. In the intervening time none of the *Alloplectus* became known to the public, while the one *Hypocyrta* has enjoyed some popularity and been joined by several others which have surpassed it in this respect. Only one of the popular hypocyrtas has been transferred to *Alloplectus,* the others ending up in *Nematanthus*—also not a widely grown genus—and this leads to considerable confusion for everyone concerned except the taxonomists themselves.

The worst of it is that these changes in labels are not necessarily for the ages. Certain botanical characteristics are considered critical at one time, but may be superseded by others at some other. Much is a matter of pure opinion, and the importance attributed by one researcher or another to likeness and differences between the parts of the plants. (There's also the matter of system. Anybody accustomed to using Gray's *Botany*—covering eastern wildflowers—will find using Dr. Small's *Southern Flora*—an enormous compendium—rather difficult because the names of innumerable plants in Gray are quite different in Small.)

Some items which may be considered critical are shape and type of anthers, stigmas, glandular structures, ovaries, habit, corolla shape, calyx, leaf texture, kinds of roots, form of capsule, form of seed, etc. If two researchers disagree on the critical part of the plant, they may come to completely different conclusions regarding its relationship with other plants—and there are many borderline cases. At this moment it is being urged, for instance, that intergeneric hybridization is critical evidence for inclusion in a genus. This kind of sexual irresponsibility occurs to a massive extent among the orchids, without the orchid taxonomists lumping the interbreeding genera together. Another critical argument is for placing all plants with stolons in one genus. In the *Saxifragaceae, Saxifraga stolonifera,* the popular strawberry geranium, has stolons and most or all of the rest of the genus lacks them. But nobody has suggested setting up a separate genus because of this variance, in spite of the fact that the species has recently been under scrutiny and a change of name has occurred (from *S. sarmentosa*) for different reasons.

So when, in the text, we speak of the "old sinningias," "old *Nematanthus*" or "old *Alloplectus,*" the reader should understand that this was the body of species before the addition of species from other genera. Or we may write "former *Rechsteineria*" or "former *Hypocyrta.*" And in some cases we will put the former genus name of a changed species between parentheses. This is for the purpose of alerting those who are not familiar with the new name as to its former identity.

We will also have to refer to the "former xGloxineras" to assist the reader in recognizing that these are not the hybrids originally called sinningias. For instance, *Sinningia* 'Dollbaby' as compared with *xGloxinera* 'Pink Petite.'

Naming Intergeneric Hybrids

For the naming of intergeneric hybrids there has been an attempt by certain botanists to treat them as new genera, combining the names of the genera involved in the cross preceded by an *x*. Thus we have *xGlokohleria, xHeppigloxinia, xAchimenantha, xMoussogloxinia* as a starter. As the crosses proliferate the new vocabulary will become impossibly unwieldy as it has in the *Orchidaceae*. The system has even been applied to the, as yet, not fully accepted realignment of *Columnea;* thus *xColbergaria* and *xColtricantha*. The advantage appears to be brevity at the sacrifice of information and the institution of a stumbling block to any amateur desiring to master the nomenclature of the family.

A far better system is to record every hybrid between genera by stating the genus and species of the seed parent, followed by the hybrid name and the pollen parent between parentheses. Such a hybrid would appear, for example, as *Achimenes longiflora* 'Flame' (*xSmithiantha zebrina*), instead of *xAchimenantha* 'Flame.' If the seed parent was a *Smithiantha* the name would be *Smithiantha zebrina* 'Flame' (*xAchimenes longiflora*). These would be true records of the crosses.

There are two major objections. It is cumbersome and hybridizers do not always wish to reveal their secrets.

The latter has happened in the *Orchidaceae*. Cumbersome or not it would have the merit of presenting a traceable recording of hybrids. As for secrecy, it is up to the recorders to decide whether to accept plants with insufficient information. Commercial catalogs could list the plant as *xAchimenes* 'Flame' or, alternatively, as *xSmithiantha* 'Flame,' eliminating the necessity of placing *xAchimenantha* or some combination of *Smithiantha* in parentheses as they now do.

PLANT SOCIETIES

African Violet Society of America, Inc., P.O.B. 1326, Knoxville, TN 37901.
Annual membership $9.00. Membership year March 1 to February 28. Five issues of *African Violet Magazine*.

American Gloxinia & Gesneriad Society. Membership secretary, Ellen M. Todd, P.O.B. 493, Beverly Farms, MA 01915.
Annual dues $7.00 includes six issues of *The Gloxinian*.

Gesneriad Hybridizer's Association. Membership secretary, Meg Stephenson, 4115 Pillar Drive, Rt. 1, Whitmore Lake, MI 48189.
Annual dues $5.00 includes bulletins.

Gesneriad Society International & Saint Paulia International, Box 549, Knoxville, TN 37901.
Annual dues $7.00, six issues *G-S-N (Gesneriad-Saintpaulia News)*.

The Indoor Light Gardening Society of America, Inc. Membership secretary, Mr. Robert Morrison, 5305 S.W. Hamilton Street, Portland, OR 97221.
Annual dues $8.00. Six issues of *Light Garden*.

TERMINOLOGY

In 1973 the Classification and Nomenclature Committee of AGGS specified the correct terminology for flower description and discarded other adjectives. Although the terms which were adopted may be perfectly correct as a norm for use in expert texts, they are inadequate and incomprehensible to the general public.

Erect, for instance, is the term chosen for a flower with radial symmetry, a regular limb or corolla tube as applied to, for instance, the florist gloxinia. Erect as regards a flower means to the general public that it simply stands straight up.

Nodding, it was decided, should indicate a flower with bilateral symmetry "with the corolla tube expanded more on the lower side, wild type." Why not cultivated type? For the public a nodding flower simply nods and the shape of the flower is not suggested by this term.

Admittedly this is a constant problem for nonscientific writers on these subjects. Personally we prefer the term bell or erect bell shape or funnel-shaped for the one, and slipper or nodding slipper for the other. They don't tell all, but at least describe a particular form to the average reader. In addition it will be necessary, here and there, to expand the adjectives to specify a shape more closely. Flower forms can be quite complicated, and this is especially true of gesneriads. All we can do in that case is to describe as well as possible in words which are understandable to more literate readers. If any word stumps you, turn to the Glossary on pages 251–54.

CULTURAL LIST OF GESNERIADS

The following descriptions follow each other in alphabetical order. However, since the Alpine gesneriads are not true houseplants, we have placed them in a group at the end, starting on page 210. These plants are to be grown outdoors or in very cool conditions. Some are winter hardy in the north.

Achimenes

Achimenes was first mentioned, according to Paul Arnold, by Patrick Browne in his *History of Jamaica* in 1756. Various interpretations have been given of the name—which sounds rather Greek—but none has been proved. The type plant *A. erecta* was brought to England in 1778. By the 1830s great interest was being shown, as evidenced by a spate of hybridizations with new material arriving from the West Indies, Mexico, other states of Central America, and northern South America.

When we examine Mr. Arnold's *Register* of 1969 we become aware that there was a discontinuity in the popularity of this beautiful plant. Up to 1875 new introductions by commercial growers were numerous both in England and on the Continent, after which there is a decline until, by 1900, virtually no names were being added. Things picked up again in 1940, and the public acceptance of *Achimenes* has increased ever since.

Most of our gesneriads are greenhouse or indoor houseplants. *Achimenes,* on the other hand, is mostly used as a hanging basket porch plant which, although finding it a bit cool in the northern states, is perfectly at home in the southern ones where it competes for popularity with fuchsias and lantanas. Compared with them it offers a much greater range of color than the former and much more varied flower shapes than the latter. The half shade of a summer porch is perfect for growing and the production of bloom is tremendous and continuous from early summer till fall.

As an indoor plant *Achimenes* has a number of disadvantages. The most popular houseplants are winter growers and its dormancy, requiring storage of the scaly rhizomes until the following spring, is rather a nuisance. The trailing habit of most *Achimenes* is hard to accommodate in the light garden. Finally, the plant is extremely sensitive to pollution and just won't flower in many of our cities.

These handicaps can certainly be overcome by systematic hybridization for qualities other than floriferousness and prettiness. Claims are made that winter bloom is possible by resting the plant early in the season, but it appears to be a stunt which works sometimes and as often not. Actual consistent results have not been achieved. Once these problems are overcome, *Achimenes* could acquire a huge new market among indoor growers.

The shape of the flower is often similar to certain *Streptocarpus*, the tube very narrow, then flaring suddenly into five rounded lobes which are fairly regular, often overlapping and not ruffled. In other words the face is quite flat except for a jutting forward of the lower lip. Size of plant ranges from a few inches to a couple of feet with many in-betweens to choose from. The color range is equally remarkable—whites, pinks, reds, blues, purples, and yellows plus interesting vein patterns in the throat. The leaves are mostly small, soft, oval-pointy like those of some roses with sawtooth edges, and clustered in opposite fours.

In our own minds the genus has a very special characteristic which it shares with petunias. Pretty as is the flower, bright as are the colors, there is something boring about the appearance of the plant, and it seems to be capable of making an impression only when massed. A single *Episcia* flower on a large plant will make a gutsier impression than a whole pot of *Achimenes*. As a matter of fact we are obliged to have a large number of *Achimenes* plants together in a pot to grow them at all effectively. The individual plants are weak stemmed and would simply sprawl without the support of the others. And that is why we see fine examples occasionally in nurseries but rarely in amateur collections. They bloom all right in a greenhouse in the country or as a basket plant in the south, but most of the time they look messy. Their prime is early in blooming when the stems are young and the first buds open. After that they go downhill. Several of the scaly rhizomatous gesneriads have this weak structure.

Achimenes require very light, loose soil. A 1–1–1 Lean Mix, using medium or coarse perlite and a good grade of vermiculite, will provide that. Lime chips or eggshell can be added at the rate of four tablespoons to a quart of mix. Don't pack the medium tightly.

The rhizomes are up to 1 inch in length and as thick or a little thicker than a kitchen matchstick. They have either been left in the pot during dormancy or kept in a plastic bag or a box with perlite or vermiculite, for it is neither desirable that they dry out or that they be subjected to any moisture during the period. It is not advisable to leave them in the pot for a second season. Rather, shake out the rhizomes from the dry soil very carefully when you are ready to repot—a procedure which will have been done in the late fall if you intended to store them elsewhere. Broken pieces will produce plants but the start will not be as vigorous.

The rhizomes start to sprout sometimes as early as April but usually during May. They may grow 3 inches in a container or in dry soil and no further unless moistened. And in this condition they can be held for a long time without damage. Even breaking off the sprout will not matter as each section of rhizome is capable of reproducing. You can wait until sprouting has begun before planting or, if the middle of May is past without action, they can usually be reawakened by a gentle amount of moisture. So even unsprouted rhizomes can be planted and the soil moistened with an expectation of action.

The rhizomes are planted horizontally ½ inch below soil level in azalea-type pots. Plant three or four to a 4-inch pot or five or six to a 5-incher. The individual plants do not grow very large and should be crowded to achieve a mounded effect. Baskets may hold as many as twelve plants.

If the rhizomes are started, once they have been planted and moistened, take care that the soil is kept constantly moist. Even a day of complete soil dryness may either kill the plant or send it back into dormancy.

Experts also agree that in the early stages you should fertilize with every watering. At the start a high nitrate solution is excellent. As buds form it may be advantageous to switch to a high phosphate formula.

As the first stems elongate up to 6 inches, they should be cut to half their length to encourage stronger stems and branching. The cuttings can be rooted easily and usually bear flowers the same season.

The temperature requirements are interesting. It appears that 60° or a few degrees lower at night are not harmful but that very high temperatures, above 80° for some species and 85° for others, can cause bud blast. This characteristic suits them very well to the conditions on southern porches, where there is half shade and plenty of ventilation. It reminds us of the needs of fuchsias and some other porch basket plants. But it also accounts for some of the problems of raising them indoors. Like fuchsias, they don't like it stuffy.

The light requirements are, for some cultivars and species, as low as for African violets. With humidity of 60° or more, 150 footcandles may be sufficient. We have seen them growing merrily under benches in a greenhouse—like other weeds. In the fluorescent light garden, you must be careful not to give them too much light for they will certainly blast their buds. This may be partly because of the increased heat with inferior ventilation close to the tubes. They can stand periods of bright sun outdoors, but are essentially a bright shade plant.

Given these conditions *Achimenes* will bloom all summer with no special attention except some judicious trimming. This requires mention of some exceptions—those plants that start blooming rather late in the season. But most of the better species and cultivars are in good bloom by the middle of July.

In late August or September the lower leaves dry up, and small, conelike, dry rhizomatous propagules may appear in the axils of the leaves, where buds and flowers have been growing. These can be removed, stored, and later planted just like underground rhizomes, except that they do not produce a vigorous plant as quickly.

When the plant becomes ratty looking, water is withheld and dormancy takes place immediately. The stems are cut away, and the pot or basket is stored away in a cellar or closet, or the rhizomes shaken out of the soil, completing the cycle. The number of rhizomes is sometimes very considerable, running to as many as ten per individual plant and fifty to a pot. So, obviously, there is no sense in trying to collect seed unless you are hybridizing.

Every scale of a rhizome is able to produce a plant. Should you wish you can separate them all from a single rhizome, dump them into a plastic bag with vermiculite and, when the slightest sign of sprouting appears, moisten the medium. Starting from so small a beginning, initial growth will be less vigorous.

One more warning. All experts agree that the first month of growth is all-important. See that conditions are ideal in May-June, that the plants have plenty of moisture, fertilizer, and proper warmth, and you can count on vigorous bloom later on. If they get a slow start, they become stringy and production is poor. Appearance suffers too.

SPECIES AND CULTIVARS

The high priest of *Achimenes* in this country is Paul Arnold of Binghamton, New York. A former Ansco executive, he has championed these plants all his life and maintains in his greenhouse the most complete bank of rhizomes in the country. In addition he has been the registrar of gesneriads for the American Gloxinia and Gesneriad Society, which is recognized as the registrating authority for all gesneriads except saintpaulias. Thus he has been responsible for the very difficult and detailed task of publishing registers of various genera from time to time. His register of *Achimenes* last appeared in the September/October 1969 issue of *The Gloxinian*.

Although some interesting strains have appeared on the market since that publication, it still remains the basic reference. Probably the most effective way we can present the *Achimenes* to you is by listing the more important species of the nineteenth and twentieth centuries and those most used in hybridization—the plants still actively grown in most instances—and then make a further list of the still popular cultivars, cultivar names actually representing species and recently introduced plants.

Professor H. E. Moore, Director of the L. H. Bailey Hortorium at Cornell University, has explored for *Achimenes* and discovered or reintroduced a number of species and their forms. Dr. R. E. Lee, also of Cornell, has been responsible for the introduction of a number of cultivars.

As the hybrids retain the basic characteristics of their parentage, the reader can get a good idea of appearance from reference to the species list, only a few of which have been used actively in cultivars that have found favor with the public. In other instances, the cultivars are only compact, more floriferous, or somewhat different color forms of the species.

ACHIMENES SPECIES

*Plants most used in hybridization.

A. andreuxii. 1839. Re-collected by Professor Moore in 1959 in Oaxaca, Mexico. Dwarf plants, 4 inches tall, branching and erect with wooly stems. Flowers about ⅜ inch across the flare (limb) on 3-inch pedicels, dark violet with white throat with purple dots. Used for miniaturization of cultivars. Now *Eucodonia andreuxii*. See "Gesneriad Update," page 215.

A. antirrhina. 1839. Re-collected in 1961 by Professor Moore. 12 to 18 inch stems and 1½-inch flowers, reddish orange with orange yellow throat. A richer red form is Dr. Lee's cultivar, 'Red Cap.'

A. bella. 1936. Stems and leaves wooly. Flowers 1 inch, pale blue, with yellow stripes inside throat.

A. candida. 1848. Guatemala. To one foot with ⅝-inch white flowers with purplish lines and dots. Similar to *A. obscura.*

A. cettoana. 1960. Collected by Professor Moore in Chiapas, Mexico. Three-whorled leaves 2 inches long. Branching stems to one foot, reddish brown. Flowers light to dark violet, 1 inch long and ½ inch across. Long blooming season.

A. coccinea. Incorrect name for *A. erecta.*

A. ehrenburgii. Now *Eucodonia verticillatta (bella)*. See "Gesneriad Update," page 215. Prostrate growth with dense white woolly reverses of the 4-inch leaves, which are glossy above. Flowers 1½ inches across the face and deeply lobed—pink lilac with purple lines.

Achimenes cettoana. Courtesy Kartuz Greenhouses

*A. erecta. Introduced to England in 1778 and the type species for *Achimenes.* A medium-sized plant with numerous vivid red small flowers, narrow leaves, and trailing stems. A natural tetraploid (n = 22). Much used in hybridization.

A. fimbriata. 1936. Reintroduced by Professor Moore in 1961. Small white flowers with purple markings.

*A. flava. 1936. Similar to *A. erecta,* but orange yellow with red dots in throat. Long trailing stems. The basic material for yellow colored plants.

A. glabrata. 1894. Weak stems to 18 inches and 2-inch white flowers flushed with lavender and streaked with yellow in throat. Fringed margins.

A. grandiflora. 1833. Stems erect to 1 foot, with red or green hairy stems. Ovate, rough, hairy green leaves, reddish beneath. Flowers on 1½-inch peduncles, deep reddish purple with pure white around throat and red dots in rows inside. Profuse in producing rhizomes. Three clones are recognized: 'Gerreri,' 'Maduna,' and 'Robusta,' collected by Professor Moore in Mexico in 1959.

A. heterophylla. 1829. Upright stems to 1 foot. Narrowly trumpet-shaped flowers, deeply lobed, and ¾ inch across. Strong red orange. Rhizomes to 4 inches long.

*A. longiflora. 1839. Trailing stems to 2 feet. Flowers up to 3 inches across. Tube bent downward. Flowers blue or bluish with white throat. *A. longiflora,* var. *alba* is the white form with touch of purple at throat, yellow below it, and faint purple spots where the corolla lobes intersect. Much used for crosses to increase the size of flowers.

A. mexicana. 1853. Upright stems to 12 inches. Velvety leaves. Large flowers for a short season. The tube broad like *Gloxinia perennis.* Various shades of violet from light to very deep.

A. misera. 1848. Trailing plants to 2 feet long with small white flowers late in season.

A. obscura. 1936. Mexico. Like *A. candida,* but has hairy stems and leaves that are prominently toothed. Trailing, with small white flowers and yellow in throat.

A. occidentalis. 1903. Short stems, unbranched, to 8 inches. Small white flowers.

A. patens. 1840. Mexico. Stems to 10 inches, bright red. Leaves opposite. Flowers 1¼ inches across, deep purple with white throat. Long spurred.

A. pedunculata. 1841. Guatemala. Tall plant to 36 inches. Trumpet-shaped flowers, scarlet with yellow limb lined with red dots.

A. skinneri. 1847. Upright plants to 15 inches with flowers like *A. grandiflora,* purplish red with yellow throat spotted with red.

A. warszewicziana. 1962. Stems to 12 inches, hairy and sticky. Flowers singly in axils, white. Yellow throat with maroon dots. Similar to *A. misera* but handsomer.

ACHIMENES CULTIVARS

Our list is made up of newer cultivars and those that have survived from our first edition. The latter we have indicated by an asterisk.

'Adelaide.' Large flowered, light blue. Profuse early bloomer.

*'Ambroise Verschaffelt.' White with a network of purple lines around the throat. An old *longiflora* hybrid. Short blooming, midseason.

*'Burnt Orange.' Reddish orange, yellow throat. Loose branching to 18 inches.

*'Camille Brozzoni.' Purple with yellow blotch, a white throat dotted with red.

'Capriola.' Compact, large flowered, violet-blue.

*'Cardinal Velvet.' Scarlet with an orange eye. Medium size. Since around 1850.

*'Cascade.' Large, trailing plants from Michelssen. 'Cockade,' deep pink, bronze foliage: *'Evening Glow,' large salmon; 'Fairy Pink,' soft pink with white eye; 'Fashionable Pink,' pink with small orchid-colored eye; 'Great Rosy Red,' deep rose, floriferous and early; *'Violet Night,' deep purple blue with yellow eye.

'Cattleya.' Large violet flowers. Basket plant.

*'Charm.' Purple-pink. An old plant similar to Little Beauty.

Achimenes 'Ambroise Verschaffelt.' Courtesy Kartuz Greenhouses

'Cornell Favorite.' Flowers purple-red. Leaves purplish.

'Cornell Gem.' Trailer. Light purple, white throat.

* 'Crimson Beauty.' Red. Lyons hybrid, compact, floriferous, late-blooming.

* 'Crimson Tiger.' Small, semidouble red flowers.

'Elke Michelssen.' Red-orange with tiger stripes in throat. Popular and different.

* 'English Waltz.' Old Michelssen hybrid. Salmon pink with yellow eye.

'Escheriana.' Red-purple with yellow throat.

'Fire Engine.' Dark red, compact foliage, trailing.

'Flamenco.' Very large orange-pink flowers. Floriferous.

'Galatea.' Large violet with purple lined lobes. Basket.

'Habanara.' Coral red, yellow eye, carmine spots on petals.

'India.' Dark veining on vivid blue flowers. Large trailer.

'Inferno.' A Worley hybrid. Big, fiery-red flowers with yellow eye and red veining.

'Jewel Pink.' Trailer with large pink flowers.

* 'Lady Lyttleton.' Hybrid from 1874 listed by Country Hills. Stiff, upright with dark yellow flowers, a yellow throat and red spotting.

* 'Leonora.' Long stem basket. Purple with yellow throat.

* 'Longiflora.' *A. longiflora* varieties go back to the 1860's and constantly reappear. A basket plant with large purple to blue flowers and white varieties. Lauray lists *longiflora* 'Chiapas.' Country Hills has revived the white form.

'Margarita.' Also a *longiflora alba* variety.

'Minuette.' Bright pink. Large flowered but compact.

'Panic Pink.' Compact, upright, reddish-pink.

Patens 'Major.' *A. patens* 'Major' from 1854. Deep purplish-red with spurs. Listed by Lauray.

* 'Peach Blossom.' 1962. Salmon with a magenta blotch.

* 'Pulchella, Jr.' Kartuz, 1965. Crimson, Early and long blooming.

* 'Purple King.' Deep reddish-purple. Compact and very floriferous over a long season. From 1936 and continuously popular.

'Quick Step.' Park. Large Blue 'Red Cap.' Bright red and yellow.

'Rose Bouquet.' Worley. Deep rose, double flowers. Dwarf, compact.

'Show Off.' Lyon's cross with red-purple flowers and petaloid throat.

* 'Tarantella.' A popular Michelssen hybrid. Free blooming salmon-red. Compact.

* 'Violacea Semi-Plena.' From 1858. Red-purple with a narrow tube. Semidouble.

* 'Vivid.' From 1875. Red with orange throat. Reported as extinct but still listed by Country Hills.

* 'Wetterlow's Triumph.' Violet-purple. Tube dark orange *longiflora* hybrid.

* 'Yellow Beauty.' An early Lyon cross. Buttercup yellow.

* 'Yellow Mist.' Vivid yellow. *A. heterophylla* variation introduced by Kartuz in 1966.

xAchimenantha, which has replaced *xEucodonopsis* as the genus representing crosses between *Achimenes* and *Smithiantha,* will be found under *Smithiantha,* page 188.

At least this is a more sensible name than the former one.

POPULARITY OF ACHIMENES

Judging by the fewer articles in *The Gloxinian* and listings in catalogs (except Country Hills Greenhouse), *Achimenes* appears to have suffered some loss in popularity,

Achimenes
'Purple King.'
Courtesy Kartuz
Greenhouses

at least in the north. That Park Seed Co. still features them indicates that they remain favorites in the south. Pollution in northern cities may be one reason for the decrease in interest; another, the fact that so many *Achimenes* are basket plants that do not bloom easily in northern windows. The long dormancy and the difficulty of growing full blooming plants except in a greenhouse is another handicap. Ultimately, intergeneric crosses may succeed in preserving the lovely shape of the flowers and the unique variety of coloration, mated to more tolerant and sturdy plants. Even dormancy may be gradually eliminated.

Achimenes
'Tarantella.'
Courtesy Kartuz
Greenhouses

Aeschynanthus

This gorgeous genus, from Southeast Asia and the East Indies, came to the attention of the public some years ago via *A. lobbianus* which was promptly nicknamed the Lipstick Vine. The spreading stems, crowded with dark green opposite leaves and tipped with clusters of 2-inch crimson flowers protruding from a long, nearly black calyx tube, make for one of the most spectacular plants in the world when well grown in a basket. The original enthusiasm has ebbed somewhat as commercial growers did not take this plant up in a big way, and the public found that they were seasonal bloomers and much too trailing for pot culture. Nonetheless, they are still displayed in the stores, and the amateur finds their foliage, even without bloom, at least as pleasing as some of the less exotic basket plants.

How such plants unwittingly deceive at first sight is of interest, because it is a problem of the whole flowering houseplant business. The visitor to a greenhouse who sees a flowering plant of *Aeschynanthus* is irresistibly attracted by it. This effect is intensified by its possessing a suggestive common name, for instance Lipstick Vine. But when the plant is brought home, the shock of transportation from one environment to another usually causes buds to blast, and there may follow almost a year of attractive but not exciting foliage. Meanwhile the plant also continues to grow and become much bigger and more space-consuming. Only then, depending on culture and luck, it may bloom. So it often goes with these beautiful species and will in the future until we select or hybridize ones that are more adaptable and continuously flowering. Although it presents problems at present *Aeschynanthus* is worth a major effort and has a great potential for cultural improvement to meet our needs.

Fortunately new species are constantly being imported, and the choice is widening. Now, in addition to those earlier plants which, beautiful as they are, have the disadvantage of blooming only at the ends of long spreading stems, we have some which produce flowers, as do Columneas, along their entire lengths. Recently we have seen a plant sent by Kew Gardens to Cornell which had light green leaves as narrow as those of a willow, instead of the usual oval-tipped dark green ones, and light-textured pink tube flowers at every node of the thin trailing stems. This hints at the existence of still other colors and forms, to be found in the tropics of the Far East, to cross with the mostly heavy textured leaves and red or orange flowers we have now.

Aeschynanthus, with about 170 species, ranges from the Himalayas to Borneo and New Guinea. They are epiphytic vines living on the trunks and boughs of trees. Growth is by means of flexible, unbranched stems growing from the base. Bloom is from the tips in clusters or several together along the stems in the nodes of the leaves. With one exception, in cultivation the leaves are opposite and with their surfaces all in one plane.

The growth habit of a plant tells us a great deal about its adaptability to culture in the greenhouse or indoors and gives us an indication as to its bloom potential. If you lay the stem of an *Aeschynanthus* on a surface, it will lie flat with all the leaves facing upward and the woody parts touching the ground. This permits the plant to send out its branches in all directions, as it does in a basket, and causes it also to contact any part of a tree in such a way that it can send out roots and anchor itself.

In our greenhouse basket the plant has nowhere to go. Its stems can elongate, but reach a limit. When flowering takes place in clusters at the tips, only a certain number of nodes can be added. When it takes place along the stem, there is a limit to the production of new buds. On the other hand, when the plant is living in a tree it finds a rooting surface some distance from the original base, establishes itself, and proceeds to start a new cycle of bloom and growth.

This being the case, bloom on the plant, as we know it today, cannot as some have claimed, be continuous for very long periods. To accomplish this we would have to change its habit either by causing the nodes to send forth many series of buds or make it branch—produce new growths—when cut back. This is conceivable with hybridization and selection.

Whether we have a very large or a small species, the problem is the same. The plant either becomes unwieldy or simply reaches the limit of its sideways growth, and, therewith, our blooming ceases. If we cut back, some new growth can be expected from the base. *A. nummularius* and, possibly, others reveal some ability to branch. But the description above indicates that our best way of continuing is by taking lengths of branch and starting new plants by rooting the cuttings. It is the same solution as with columneas which are closely related in growth habit.

The flowers are tubular in form and show considerable variation in detail. Colors are red, orange, yellow. The reds are much richer and deeper than those of *Columnea*. The long tubular calyx form of some species is an attractive and unusual feature. Anthers, often colored, protrude from the corolla, shed their pollen and, after retracting, are replaced by the maturing stigma. The seedpods are long, very narrow, and contain numerous seeds with one or a few hairs—a diagnostic feature.

It is probable that, as we come to know more about them, we will find notable differences in the culture of plants from different regions—for instance, the Asiatic mainland and Borneo. But for the present our cultural suggestions must be very much a stereotype. They all seem to come from warm, tropical regions with high humidity. The one controversial matter appears to be that of light requirement. Some growers have claimed that the plants require a great deal. And, in the greenhouse, they are usually hung high up, where they will receive maximum sun. But whether they really need that much or flower when placed in the most convenient position, where they can spread in their baskets, is moot.

Our own experience is that they need the same lighting as columneas or even less. With a plant that trails, it is almost impossible not to set the pots in a sunny position or with their tops close to the fluorescent tubes—and this may be necessary for other reasons. But we have observed that flowering can take place as much as 15 inches below the lamps and that unfiltered sunlight can burn the leaves.

Long-fiber sphagnum moss, Lean Mix, and Compost Mix packed rather loosely for aeration are all suitable for this plant. These epiphytic gesneriads are not as lime-loving as some of the others, and the medium can be slightly acid. In any event, do not add lime to the mix. We fertilize with balanced chemical formulas or fish emulsion.

The temperature should be over 65° at all times for bloom, though they will probably not suffer damage at ten degrees lower, and they seem to be tolerant of very high levels over 80°. Humidity over 50 percent and misting contribute to growth and bloom.

Most of the *Aeschynanthus* bloom sometime between spring and late fall. Whether they will prove good winter bloomers remains to be seen. Some, for instance 'Black Pagoda,' flower intermittently during the winter months but not luxuriantly as in summer. Indoor growers often find that flowers drop quickly after opening, whereas they should last as well as columneas—for two or three weeks. Excess sunlight, overwatering, lack of sufficient humidity—are all possibilities. No question that it is much easier to bloom these plants in a greenhouse and in the country than indoors in the city. Perhaps they are sensitive to pollution. We certainly do not have as yet sufficient information about the vagaries of the individual species. Articles in magazines always tell how well a plant just bloomed but hardly ever mention what is happening at other times.

Our recommendation to indoor growers is to try rooted cuttings of the larger plants, or stick to the more compact species such as *A. micranthus* or *A. nummularius* for the present. Do not attempt large hanging pots or baskets unless satisfied with the foliage for most of the year.

The above suggests to us another reason why *Aeschynanthus* has not greatly attracted commercial growers. Although the amateur may be satisfied with a rooted cutting indoors, the majority of plant buyers expect something more than that at the garden center or plant store. To grow a respectable basket plant from a rooted cutting may take more than a year; it would be worthwhile for a commercial grower only if he could secure a commensurate price. Not an easy matter.

A. ellipticus is an interesting and beautiful species from New Guinea but possibly a problem child as there are not many who have yet taken to it. The wiry stems are trailing rather than spreading and densely covered with reddish hairs. The opposite 1½-inch oval leaves are purplish at first, then turn bright shiny green. The axils of the leaves each produce several flowers which are different from other *Aeschynanthus* species we know. About 1½ inches long they start with a round bulb cradled in a short calyx with narrow green sepals. The tube then narrows and slowly expands toward the limb. It has been described as salmon-colored, but those we've seen are a rather transparent pinkish orange which is something else. The tube flares to an upper lip with two quite narrow vertical lobes, while the broadly triangular lower lobes flare widely—about ½ to ¾ inch each. The whole corolla curves out and somewhat downward.

This is a remarkably handsome shape, almost like a slipper flower turned upside down. We have usually seen it performing in summer. With a greater amount of bottom growth and a tolerance of some pruning, it would seem like a better candidate for the light garden than some of the other *Aeschynanthus*.

A. evrardii from Vietnam is also something of a switch, for it is the only one of the genus in cultivation which can be called upright in growth. This is partly explained by the fact, not mentioned in most descriptions, that the leaves are in whorled pairs, each pair being partly turned around the axis of the upright stem. That means that they also face toward the tip of the stem instead of having their one edge facing that way. This automatically creates an upright habit.

The leaves are shiny, thick, green, and 4½ inches long by half as wide. The calyx is greenish yellow, short, and bulbous, while the corolla is very narrow, 3 inches long, mostly bright orange, and with the upper lip flaring into a wide oval hood. The lower part of the tube is yellow as are the three lower lobes, and there are dark red stripes running down the tube. Stamens are dark red.

Evrardii blooms at high temperatures and humidity during the summer, with very erect clusters of ten to fifteen flowers. At least this plant suggests that we can have upright as well as pendent *Aeschynanthus*. And, though this particular one is neither everblooming nor spectacular, its combination with others may lead to plants with a greater chance of fitting into the indoor garden.

A. LOBBIANUS, PARVIFOLIUS, AND PULCHER

A. lobbianus was the original Lipstick Plant. Then new material appeared in collections which was more floriferous, somewhat more compact, and smaller in leaf, and this was identified as *A. parvifolius*. As we have only skimmed the surface of the species of *Aeschynanthus* found in Southeast Asia and the East Indies, the chances are that we will eventually discover all kinds of transitional types, so that a number of our present species may turn out to be only variations.

Aeschynanthus parvifolius, showing the true lipstick form.

Certainly the first two mentioned above are among the most beautiful exotic plants in cultivation. They have remarkable 1-inch-tube calyxes with parallel sides, very dark purple, almost black, hairy, and with very small low lobes. Only one other plant we know of, a *Bignonia,* has anything similar. The 2-inch blood red corolla projects from it in a slight downward curve. It has a narrow upper lip and short somewhat spreading lower lobes, beautifully patterned near the throat with yellow or nearly white markings. Clustered upright at the ends of the long branches, they are truly spectacular.

The stems grow to 2 feet or more in a drooping arch. The 1½-inch oval pointed leaves are fleshy, opposite, and about half as wide. They are about half the size of some of the other large basket type *Aeschynanthus.*

A. pulcher, like the other two, is from Java. The form is very similar to *A. parvifolius,* and the only notable difference is that the calyx is greenish purple-tinged, and the flowers and stalks are smoother. Flowers are a bit larger.

A. longiflorus is another of the Javanese monsters but even bigger than the previous three, sending out 3-foot stems and having larger leaves. The clustered flowers at the tips stand bolt upright and are an extraordinary mixture of red, orange, and pink purple—almost neon bright. Pink projecting stamens add to this kaleidoscope. The form of the tube is narrower horizontally and broader vertically, with the lobes of the limb curving inward, so that it is the outside of the tube which is completely displayed and offers so much color. A summer bloomer, it is a challenge for the greenhouse grower.

A. marmoratus is a large species from Southeast Asia and has the most attractive foliage of the genus and is quite widely grown for this reason alone. The long stems are lined with 3- to 4-inch opposite leaves which are thick and shiny, half as wide, and pointed at both ends. The upper surface is light green handsomely marbled with darker patches. The undersides are flushed with red. A small calyx with narrow sepals holds a 1½-inch rather thin green tube with the curve on the upper side, so that the upper lobes of the limb surpass the lower ones with little flare. This is now *A. longicaulis.*

The hybrid 'Black Pagoda,' made by Lyndon Lyon, is a fine improvement with flower clusters of deep burnt orange, more of them, and a longer blooming season. It is perhaps the most successful plant with indoor growers who also report excellent results with rooted cuttings in pots. As a foliage basket plant, with spring-summer bloom, it is a fine greenhouse subject.

A. micranthus has been reported as collected in the Himalayas, but we doubt that this fine smaller plant lives at a high elevation. But it may be somewhat more sensitive to very high temperatures than the species from further south, as our loss of plants has occurred during the heat of July and August. However it grows well and blooms at indoor temperatures of 65° to 80° rather better than any of the others—even intermittently throughout the year. Bloom is along the full length of the stems from the leaf axils. But, as with other *Aechynanthus,* we still have a problem when the stems have reached the limit of their production.

The stems are woody, trailing to 18 inches long, and, like the shiny, thick, oval pointed leaves, a rather light green. Several 1-inch narrow tube flowers, red purple in color and without flare, grow in each axil. The plant blooms in any exposure except a north window and does not need a central position under the lights. We have often placed pots with two or three branches at the side of the fluorescent fixture. It makes no great show but is pretty in bloom and is more dependable in this respect than any of the others—at least for the indoor grower.

A. nummularius, from New Guinea, is the smallest species now in cultivation, offering hope that others of pot size may be found in the future or that this little fellow will

Aeschynanthus 'Black Pagoda.' *Courtesy Lauray of Salisbury*

Aeschynanthus micranthus.

transmit its compactness to a hybrid. The whole plant is slightly velvet hairy with trailing stems loaded with opposite, almost sessile (without petioles) overlapping heart-shaped leaves ½ inch long. The flowers, which we have not seen, are described as magenta red, hairy, and about ¾ inch long. Presumably it has an urn-shaped calyx, like *A. obconicus*. Because of the small foliage the flowers are well displayed.

Growers report that it loses its leaves easily and that it is a difficult subject. We find that it behaves all right in shaded conditions, at least 15 inches from the lights, in humidity of 70 percent. This is certainly a low altitude species requiring very good warmth and humidity without any excess moisture. We found that it throve on the hottest days in our plant room, which can get to 95° under the lights. The Buells consider it an excellent plant, and we may see more of it as amateurs learn to grow it. Since the internodes are very short and the stems are only 6 to 8 inches long, it may prove an excellent terrarium plant.

A. obconicus is also no monster. *A. obconicus* is a handsome medium-sized basket plant. One problem with the *Aeschynanthus* plants is that those which are tremendous in size also have the showiest flowers. Those of *obconicus* are fascinating, but they just don't make a big display. They are distinguished by a bowl-shaped, deep purple to blackish hairy calyx, from which the red, narrow tube projects up to an inch. Both together are rich and dark but a bit lost in the foliage. There are touches of yellow and white but the description identifies it.

Stems are stiff but trailing, the leaves leathery and 3 to 4 inches long. The calyx is persistent for a considerable time after the passing of the corolla. Greenhouse growers consider this one of the most reliable bloomers, but we have not had reports of conspicuous success indoors or under lights. Flowering can last for several summer months. If the plant is cut back or stem cuttings rooted, you may have some winter bloom.

A. praelongus from Borneo has the bowl-shaped calyx with a dark red corolla hardly projecting. A medium large plant, stiffer-stemmed than *obconicus* and less attractive.

A. 'Pullobia' resembles *A. radicans*—relatively compact, similar calyx tube and leaves, and flowers having a larger yellow throat. It is reported to be more floriferous than *A. parvifolius*, but, as far as indoor growing is concerned, our own experience does not confirm this.

A. radicans from Sarawak has a long green tubular calyx streaked with burgundy and red flowers similar to *A. lobbianus* and *parvifolius*, but on a somewhat more compact plant. For some reason it is not much grown.

A. tricolor is a Malaysian plant, similar to *A. obconicus* in having a bowl-shaped calyx, but the flower as well as the whole plant is smaller. Leaves are 1 inch long. The tube-shaped corolla projects about ¾ inch, is narrow and very dark red, striped with black and yellow. The whole effect is interesting but very dark.

There are other species in collections and some hybrids or selections which do not differ notably from the plants we have described. For new developments, see "Gesneriad Update," page 215.

Agalmyla

A. parasitica is the only one of several species from the East Indies which we have seen listed and in the flesh. It is described as being similar to *Aeschynanthus*, but the plant we saw at Buell's was very different in appearance. Instead of rather waxy oval pointed leaves, it has quite normal green shiny ones, long oblong—about 6 inches long and 3 wide—pointed at the tip. The stems instead of being thin and flexible are fleshy and thick. Obviously it is a dangling vine and epiphytic. It is hardly conceivable in a basket but

Agalmyla parasitica. Photo L. H. Bailey Hortorium of Cornell University

rather as a couple of stems dangling from a hanging pot or, as we saw it, crawling around untidily in a large and deep flat.

The flowers do have some likeness to *Aeschynanthus,* being clustered, narrow, curved, long, and growing from a very narrow calyx. They are 2 inches long, scarlet, and with the narrow lobes marked with a large dark maroon spot. The general effect of the individual flower is rather shapeless but the full cluster is quite showy.

Very loose Lean Mix without lime and plenty of room for the roots to run, high temperature and humidity and even moisture are requirements of this plant of the lowland tropics. Stems probably root at the nodes, and propagation can be by cuttings. A challenging plant for the collector.

Alloplectus

Alloplectus is a genus of seventy species from tropical America which, on the basis of our present knowledge, is not going to set the world on fire. Those which have been grown by hobbyists seem to be from fairly high altitudes and require somewhat cooler conditions on average than many other gesneriads grown indoors. Due to the vagaries of taxonomy, two former hypocyrtas, *nummularia* and *teuscheri,* have been separated from seven others which were transferred to *Nematanthus,* and tacked on to *Alloplectus.* This gives the latter one moderately popular gesneriad.

The distinguishing feature of some of the "old" *Alloplectus* has been a showy, large, and persistent calyx and a short-lived rather insignificant corolla tube. The genus has a single notched gland at the base of the superior ovary. L. Easterbrook Greenhouses offer several of these plants. *A. nummularia* (formerly *Hypocyrta*) looks entirely different as our description will show. In *Alloplectus* n = 9. (Chromosome number.)

A. ambiguus is a native of the Puerto Rican forest and an epiphyte. It clings to tree trunks and creeps along boughs. It is a tetraploid having the number n = 18.

The growth is very much like some of the columneas, the stems somewhat lax, the

Alloplectus teuscheri (Hypocyrta teuscheri). A 2-foot shrub with quadrangular stems 2 feet high. Flowers are clustered thickly in the axils of the large leaves. The calyx is ¾ inch long, the sepals oblong and very leafy, brilliant scarlet and folded around the yellow tube, similar to *cristata;* with small red lobes.

Cobananthus calochlamys is a small shrub bearing attractively shaped flowers. The hairy, light orange calyx lobes are ¾ inch long and spread flat like a star, surrounding the nearly oval, very hairy, yellow tube with a narrow opening. The calyx, as in all these plants, is persistent and the effect very attractive. It enjoyed popularity for some time and deserves more attention as it is an easy plant to grow.

Corytoplectus capitatus grows to 3 feet with velvety, four-angled stems. The leaves are opposite and up to 8 inches long, a deep, rich green. Two-inch peduncles from the axils of the upper leaves carry closely massed, flattish heads of short pedicelled flowers. The prominent part is the blood-red calyx, having hairy lobes up to ¾ inch long, which is persistent for some time after the corolla is gone. The latter is a short tube, clear yellow in color. Bloom is during the spring and summer.

Corytoplectus schlimii grows at four to five thousand feet in Colombia. Thus it is a very cool grower and not suitable for the normal home environment. It is an erect shrub with leaves 3 to 4 inches long, scalloped and fringed with red hairs. Flowers have brilliant red calyx lobes. The hairy corolla is yellow with red tipped lobes.

These are all relatively cool growing plants, requiring a range from 60° to 80°. With age they tend toward woodiness and do not put out branches freely when trimmed. They object to excess moisture. Propagation is neither easy nor rapid. Although they have now been placed in separate genera these requirements remain much the same. Also, they all seem to prefer a more acid soil than many other gesneriads. Their unusual shapes and textures make them prime candidates for intergeneric hybridization if that can be done. They should do well in the Pacific northwest and Canada.

Alsobia

In 1979, Hans Wiehler proposed the transfer of *Episcia dianthiflora* and *E. punctata* to the genus *Alsobia*. The change has generally been accepted by gesneriad growers.

A. dianthiflora is very short stemmed with a terminal rosette of oval 1½-inch leaves, very soft velvety green with scalloped edges. Numerous growths and stolons are produced, so that in a shallow pot or a basket, it develops as a solid mass of greenery only 3 or 4 inches high and dripping over the edges for several more inches.

The brilliant white flowers, with a delicate spotting of purple at the throat, consist of fringed, nearly equal lobes, ½ inch long and wide. The tube is 1¼ inches long. The pedicel is very short so that the flowers seem to lie on top of the foliage. Bloom is in the warm months only, unlike many episcias that are everblooming. It is a cooler grower than some others but requires very high humidity and very careful watering. Both the habit and the way of flowering are prettier than *A.* 'Cygnet.'

A. punctata. The species was first collected in Guatemala in 1840 but, in spite of large white flowers, has never become popular.

A. 'Cygnet.' This hybrid of *A. dianthiflora* and *A. punctata* made at Cornell University and introduced in 1967 is far superior as a houseplant to both its parents. From *A.*

Alloplectus calochlamys.
Photo Frances Batcheller

Alloplectus cristatus.
Species collected by
the Elberts in St. Lucia,
West Indies. Not in
cultivation.
Remarkable for the
beauty and size of the
frilly pink calyx and for
the thick, large yellow
tube. *Photo by authors
in St. Lucia, West
Indies*

punctata it seems to have derived its woodier stems and the long-petioled crenate leaves plus the purple dots. From *dianthiflora* it inherited smaller leaves and lower stature. But 'Cygnet' is a much freer bloomer and can be counted among the truly everblooming gesneriads. It is also more tolerant of different environments than the others. We can, therefore, recommend it unequivocally for lasting pleasure, provided that our trimming instructions are followed. The feature of this plant is that its stem growth allows us to keep neat plants much longer than any other episcias and to train them to very attractive shapes.

A. 'Cygnet' has 2-inch-long scalloped rhombic leaves, on 2-inch petioles, which are velvety light green and not especially good looking. Starting with a rooted cutting in the normal course, we have a little plant, no more than 2 or 3 inches high with a stem that is stiffer than other episcias and a rosette of leaves at the top. Flowering, usually a couple of blossoms at a time, starts immediately and, if the environment is kept fairly stable, will continue right through the life of the plant.

If stolons are religiously removed whenever they appear, flowering is much encouraged, and new growths will start up from the base of the stem. In this way, within a relatively short time, you will have several stems which will grow very slowly and produce an endless series of flowers. An older plant in an azalea pot will be no more than 4 or 5 inches high. The stems in time will curve over on themselves and create some odd figures, but you will never have the untidy trailing which would have taken place had the stolons not been removed.

The flowers last only a couple of days each but are larger than any others except *E. lilacina.* The tube is directed forward and is over an inch long. The five lobes spread out evenly to a width of 1¼ inches, are pure white, beautifully fringed, and prominently dotted with purple in the throat.

With *Alsobia* 'San Miguel,' Bartley Schwarz has improved on *A.* 'Cygnet,' with larger flowers, brighter spotting, and a more compact habit. It has rapidly become deservedly popular.

Culture is easier for the hybrids of *Alsobia* than for most episcias. Light requirement is 250–300 footcandles. Use ordinary Lean Mix with lime, and, contrary to the episcias, keep it *very wet* at all times. However, the temperature must be above 60°. Almost any houseplant fertilizer applied regularly will suit it. No insects come to dinner, and the plant is less subject to fungal rot than most.

Propagation is very easy from single stolons allowed to root in the soil. By fixing them with hairpins in a nearby pot of vermiculite, they can be induced to root more rapidly. You can also use the stolons you remove in the course of trimming.

Bellonia

At first sight no plant could look less like the gesneriads to which most of us are accustomed than *B. aspera.* There are many small and large shrubby members of the family, but the large ones are too big for the house while the more compact species have not been popular in cultivation because of their slow growth. Nevertheless the little shrubs deserve our attention for, if we have a bit of patience, they are among the most rewarding. The gesneriad family has plants which are often rather insignificant in appearance but rarely lack some appealing trait. So, even when the plant is woody and small leaved, as is *B. aspera,* something quite different and more attractive may greet our eyes.

The plant develops its bushy aspect very early in its growth, the stems and branches rapidly becoming woody. The feature which, at least for us, makes it an outstanding small foliage plant rather than a flowering one is the charming appearance of the leaves. These are 1 inch to 1½ inches long, very sharply toothed, prettily veined and thin, hard, and absolutely oily, which makes the whole plant gleam with reflections. Also the new leaves are yellowish with rosy tints so that there is something jewellike in its aspect.

Very little attention is usually paid to the attitude of leaves. It is not a matter that arouses great interest in botanists except in unusual instances, and growers hardly notice it. But, whether leaves are horizontal, point upward, hang downward, overlap, are whorled in one way or another is a very important feature of appearance and often makes the difference between homeliness and beauty in a plant. Leaf arrangement is also related to the climbing, upright, trailing, or spreading growth of a plant and to the placement and visibility of flowers.

Sometimes an incongruity develops between the leaf arrangement of a plant and other features. The foliage of *A.* 'Cygnet' is not as colorful, interestingly textured, or shapely, as that of other episcias. But when the plant is quite small and the leaves are arranged almost in a rosette, it is a fine sight indeed. On the mature plant the wrong leaf is placed in the wrong position, held too high or hanging downward in an irregular way. One sees this sort of thing more often in hybrids.

Our reasons for reacting in a certain way to natural formations is probably no different from our judgments of ornamental art. Our eyes seek patterned arrangements and reject those which are not obedient to some rule, not botanically, but visually. Our sense of beauty is guided by different criteria from botanical reasoning. No doubt the leaves of 'Cygnet' are related just as logically in space as those of plants whose foliage pleases us more. But that is not the way it looks to us. And that is why our method of trimming that plant (see p. 105) makes sense, for it is an attempt to force it to make rosettes and thus improve its appearance to some extent.

The leaves of *Bellonia* tend to grow vertically, and, when the plant faces a source of light, that side becomes the viewing angle as the leaves all turn that way. By this means the leafage looks right and matches the growth of the branches in a way that those of many other shrubs do not.

The flowers, appearing in the spring, are an inch across and distinctly lobed, with an extremely short tube, and opening flat, like a white African violet. In the center is a cone of bright yellow stamens and the area around it is also flushed with yellow. The fallen flowers have a distinct hole in the center. They open vertically, facing the same way as the leaves and make a very pretty picture.

The flowers last several days each and bloom goes on for a couple of months or more. Plants have a more spreading than climbing tendency and rarely grow over a foot in height in the house.

The culture of *B. aspera*—and *B. spinosa* (see below)—is very simple during the growing and flowering stage. Potted in Lean Mix with lime, they can be kept moist and fertilized like other gesneriads. But once flowering is over, it is necessary to be very careful not to water excessively. In fact this is one of those instances, so often proved wrong regarding houseplants, where drying out is advisable between waterings. Otherwise the leaves dry up and drop off and the stem will die, probably as the result of strangulation of the roots or fungal activity there. If the soil is too dry, the leaves will drop off too, but the plant will revive if it then is moistened. It is a ticklish matter, and one reason why *Bellonia* has not become more popular.

Too many people try, but never report their failures. We are sure that many have had their troubles with this plant because the exact watering procedure it requires was not followed. We do not claim to be certain of our ground, as there has not been much experience to draw on, but we feel sure that for most of the year *Bellonia* can survive in dry conditions. We know that it comes from arid regions of the Caribbean islands— usually the south side which is hot and dry. But many plants grown in the house, which have a similar or even more desiccated habitat, require good watering. And it should never be forgotten that a pot is not a dry hillside or cliff. There are sources of moisture hidden in the earth which do not exist in a pot. Pots dry out infinitely faster, and only we can supply the water. It is for this reason that we never advocate totally dry conditions indoors unless a plant goes into definite dormancy. Perhaps the best plan is to allow the pot to soak up a normal pot-sized saucer of water once a week. That way the danger of under- or overwatering is greatly lessened. Keeping the pot on moist, not wet, pebbles will also do. This procedure has been successful with many "dry" plants.

In any event be careful that your soil has excellent drainage. *Bellonia* seems indifferent to humidity and will therefore behave well in the dry air of a living room under lights. Twelve hours of light daily at 250–500 fc. is sufficient. We do not advocate fertilizing more than once a month during the growing season and not at all after growth slows up. The plant can be pruned to branch more and assume a bushier shape.

Cuttings do not root with facility indoors. Hand pollination is your best bet, and growth from seed. However, you should try, during the growing season, to remove only very young growth and plant it in slightly moist vermiculite in an open pot. Cuttings subjected to high humidity immediately dropped their leaves. *Bellonia* is also tolerant of temperatures down to 55° or even 50°.

B. spinosa grows to a 4-foot shrub on its native heath. Possibly *B. aspera* does the same. The distinction of this plant is the spininess for which it is named. The thorns, growing in the axils of the leaves, are an inch long. Leaves are smaller, narrower, and less attractive than those of *B. aspera*—less toothed, less shiny, and rather dun. The flowers, though somewhat smaller, are similar. Culture is the same. *B. spinosa* has been recommended because of its spines, the only ones recorded for a gesneriad. But this strikes us as an odd virtue, to be appreciated only by collectors. In euphorbias or cacti it's more appropriate. *B. aspera* is the more attractive plant and the one to grow—if you can.

Besleria

The genus contains a large number (170 or more) of species which are rather coarse shrubs with fibrous roots. Mrs. Batcheller reports that *B. maasii*, a compact plant with orange flowers, has good horticultural potential.

Boea

Boea is a genus from Malaysia, the East Indies, and Queensland, Australia, of which the only species in cultivation is *Boea hygroscopica*, a very pretty and not especially difficult plant and one particularly suited to a terrarium.

Mr. G. Herman Slade wrote about it in *The American Orchid Society Bulletin* and Mr. and Mrs. Wm. H. Hull, Jr., quote a significant passage in *The Gloxinian* as follows:

"*Boea hygroscopica* is a plant which is quite like a delicate *Saintpaulia;* they are both *Gesneriaceae*. It grows on bare conglomerate rocks where no rain falls for six full months, on the road between Port Moresby and Sogeri at the Rouna Falls. The plants look like pathetic rolled-up herbarium specimens during the dry period, but the first of the monsoons brings them back to miraculous life. They then become rosettes of soft green leaves, surmounted within a few days of the monsoons, with purple flowers. A dried up piece, placed in a polyethylene bag and moistened, changed overnight in its fantastic way to green loveliness. One could never believe the transformation without seeing it." A mention in GSN is: "The genus is quite widespread occurring from sea level to at least 7,000 feet."

We asked Michael Kartuz, who grows and supplies *Boea*, about this miraculous characteristic of transformation. He said it didn't work. And, when we mentioned our two references he laughed and told us that when he dried out the plants they died—but definitely.

Boea hygroscopica.

We are reminded that most growers of *Gesneria cuneifolia* are not aware that these little plants growing, similarly, on cliffs in Puerto Rico, dry up completely during the summer season. In midwinter with the rains they come to life again and bloom. But nobody has been successful in letting them dry out completely for even a couple of days.

Taking into account the remarkable unreliability of reports (stated as firsthand fact when often merely oft-repeated hearsay), there is a possibility which most of us have not considered. And that is that both *Boea* and *Gesneria* will, indeed, give up the ghost if dried out at any time during most of the year. But perhaps the plants will survive if the drying takes place at exactly the time when they are triggered to do it in their natural environment. We know that this is the problem with certain plants. We would be very interested if any reader is able to demonstrate the truth of either of these stories with exact dates and with photographs. In any event we suggest that nobody let this plant go dry for a single day if he wishes to keep it alive in the foreign environment of his home.

As with each gesneriad introduction, *Boea* was greeted with enthusiasm, and the most extravagant claims were made for its future potential, even to the point of rivaling the African violet. What was overlooked, of course, is that *Boea* is a pretty stable plant, while *Saintpaulia* is an extremely variable one. Too often the descriptions of these plants were made by growers who rushed into print as soon as they had a flower and before they had acquired any knowledge of its habits at other times of the year. Unfortunately, since we can't grow everything, we sometimes find ourselves dependent on accounts which are our only accessible source but of whose reliability we have some doubt.

In spite of these questions *Boea* remains a plant well worth growing, extremely attractive and very possibly a candidate for much greater popularity.

The foliage grows in a low rosette, consisting of opposite oval leaves about 3 by 4 inches on short petioles. This means that they overlap. They are very handsomely covered with small puffs or pimples, the spaces between the intricate veining soft in texture and hairy. The color is a fine jade green. The nodes intervals are so short that it rarely grows higher than 4 or 5 inches. In other words the leafage is much more compact than *Saintpaulia* and quite different in appearance.

Each leaf axil produces a peduncle which lengthens to about 2 inches and produces ten to fifteen ¾-inch, very deep blue purple flowers. These have almost separate petals like *Saintpaulia* (in other words, a very short tube). The upper two lobes are shorter and broader than the lower ones, and they tend to curve inward somewhat rather than remain flat like *Saintpaulia*. This gives them also a somewhat irregular look.

Pot the plant in Lean Mix with lime. Keep the temperature above 65° F and keep the plant very well watered at all times. Humidity should be a minimum of 50 percent. Fertilize, however, very sparingly—perhaps once a month with high phosphate formula. Terrarium conditions suit it as long as there is no excessive heat buildup. Spraying or misting of leaves is beneficial.

A plant rarely lasts more than a year or eighteen months indoors. However, growth from the base and side shoots can be removed and rooted. Leaf propagation is possible but not as satisfactory. And seed is difficult to come by.

Dr. B. L. Burtt reported finding *Boea lanata* growing on cliffs near Kuala Lumpur in Malaysia. It is a plant with white wooly leaves and magenta flowers. He stated that they grew so close to sea level that they must be able to withstand salt spray. Other boeas with light blue flowers were also observed in great profusion on *limestone* cliff faces. These had grayish felted leaves. Dr. Burtt also described *Boea havilandii* as a woody plant, 6 feet high. We look forward to the introduction of more smaller species.

Capanea

Central and South American scaly rhizomatous shrubs usually of large size. The flowers are up to 2 inches, borne in clusters. *C. grandiflora* is in cultivation.

Chirita

Although a number of discoveries and rediscoveries of New World gesneriads indicate that we have a long way to go before we close the book on them, we have the feeling that we are far more familiar with that group than we are with the plants of the Old World. When we read that a genus such as *Chirita* has over ninety species, of which only two are in general cultivation in this country—and these are rather different and beautiful plants—we can't help wondering about all those others. Exploration and discovery in many cases took place a long time ago, and our growing conditions have changed so very much that plants which were forgotten or discarded then as being unsuitable as houseplants might, on a second try, turn out very differently.

We find it hard to believe that *Chirita sinensis* was not even listed as in cultivation in Dr. Moore's work of 1957. In 1970 Frances Batcheller listed it along with five other species. But neither *C. barbata* or *C. hamosa*, described by Dr. Moore in 1961, was mentioned. The coming and going of these plants and other similar situations are typical of the fate of plants which never find a commercial sponsor or, having found one, are dropped because of lack of public interest. They are just too much bother or do not multiply quickly or are not easily grown under home conditions. If the plant is unusually beautiful or attractive in some other way, it sometimes continues to hang on to a limited public interest and remains in cultivation by specialists, but is not generally available to the public.

Most of the chiritas are herbs, growing at most 3 feet high and living throughout the regions from the Himalayas to Southeast Asia. A good many seem to be cool-growing plants, rather unhappy in our hot summer temperatures. Those that have been introduced here are at least not Alpines. The genus contains the only two gesneriad annuals in cultivation.

Didymocarpus, from the same regions, resembles *Chirita* so closely that one day, no doubt, a taxonomic storm will burst out in the Old World as it has in the *Sinningia-Rechsteineria* tangle in the New World. The decisive difference appears to be that *Chirita* has a lobed stigma curved over like a fishtail—which is rather unusual—while *Didymocarpus*'s stigma is more upstanding. We doubt that it matters much and suspect that the taxonomic wars will look pretty silly at some future date when biologists find some aspect of the molecular structure of cells that establishes more reliable criteria for the classification of plants than the current, often very superficial ones.

C. sinensis is at the present time the one plant which continues year after year to attract hobbyists. *Chirita sinensis* is quite an interesting subject. For one thing it came in from Hong Kong in 1846. The leaves, which form a rosette, do not grow in a whorl as with *Saintpaulia* but are a tight decussate arrangement—opposite pairs—on such short internodes that the pattern is symmetrical-flat when seen from above.

The leaves, individually, are truly remarkable. About 6 inches in length and half as wide, with a 1- to 2-inch-thick petiole, they are a regular oval in shape, curving to the tip and much the same at the other end. They are very thick, leathery, and heavily veined, causing them to appear quilted.

There are two forms of the leaf. One is dark green with a complex network of veining broadly toned in pure silver. The other is green throughout.

The matter of the two types is rather sketchily discussed by growers for the apparent reason that nobody seems to know why or how the difference occurs. When we've seen plants at nurseries, the green form usually looks more vigorous and rather less flat. But the silver form is so much more beautiful that there is no comparison. It is only because of this spectacular form that the species attracts so many hobbyists, for there is nothing quite like it among the gesneriads or, for that matter, in any other family. We have compared these leaves to some beautifully tooled and dyed piece of leather inlaid with a pattern of silver.

We have wondered why amateurs took such pride in blooming this plant. For, aside from the fact that it is not very easy, it hardly seems worthwhile. The flowers are carried on petioles 1½ inches long arising from the axils of the leaves. They are reputed to be 1½ inches long but have never appeared longer than an inch or a little more, to us. The

Chirita sinensis.

broad tube, or almost bell flower, is nodding, little flared, and slightly jutting below—like some smithianthas. The color is a pale lilac with light orange flush in the throat.

We have never bloomed *C. sinensis* and are not very concerned to do so, being happy if we can grow a long-lived plant with a perfect rosette of the spectacular leaves. This, too, is not that simple. Overwatering causes the edges of the leaves to brown, just as with begonias. Although the plants like misting, they are subject to water spotting. Temperatures above 85°, even with high humidity, can be lethal.

We use Lean Mix with an overdose of perlite and some lime chips, pot in 4-inchers and arrange so that the water drains right through the pot. This is another one of those plants which objects to wetness and should be allowed to dry out somewhat between waterings. We usually keep them in a position 6 inches under the lights and in bright reflected light in the window. We figure 500 footcandles for good maintenance. The coolest place in the light garden, near the floor, suits it best, for it seems happy down to 55° F, and the risk seems greater at the upper end of the thermometer.

Leaves of *C. sinensis* propagate fairly readily. We cut them in half in the middle and make a wedge out of the upper part. Seed is usually available from AGGS.

C. asperifolia is less well known than *C. sinensis,* but we have even greater hopes for this plant from Indonesia. It is a far finer flowering plant and has an excellent habit— actually far better than most of the sinningias. However, growers have, as yet, too little experience with the plant to come to any definite conclusions regarding its ease of culture under normal home conditions.

Although *asper* means rough, the leaves are not noticeably so. In fact they are rather soft, nicely diagonally veined, and a good green. They form a long pointed oval 1¼ inches wide by 3 to 4 inches long on 1- to 1½-inch petioles.

The flowers impress because they are rather like those of *Sinningia eumorpha* but more attractive and borne in much greater numbers. About 1½ inches long, they have a very waxy substance. The short calyx is tubular and fused, constricting the broad round tube of the limb so it appears somewhat longitudinally crimped. The color is a bright, rich true blue purple—sapphire—and the tube flares to bright white lobes about an inch across with the throat showing purple.

The plants are very floriferous over a long period and may turn out to be everbloom-

Chirita asperifolia. Courtesy Buell's Greenhouses

ing under lights. New growths appear spontaneously from the base, which is good reason to use rather large azalea pots—6-inchers for a moderate-sized plant. Light requirements appear to be no more than for African violets but, like most of the chiritas, temperatures above 80° can be harmful.

This plant needs further testing, but it is certainly worth an effort to discover the best culture indoors.

C. lavandulacea is an annual best grown from seed, which the flowers produce spontaneously. It can be seeded any time of the year, grows rapidly, and blooms readily. Of the cotyledons (the pair of starter leaves), only one develops and grows so fast that it makes transplanting a bit difficult. But, once that stage is passed, it produces a straight, sturdy though juicy-looking green stem which is unbranched. At intervals, of an inch or so, broad 4- to 6-inch leaves, velvety bright green, arch out opposite each other. It is from the axils that the light lavender flowers rise on one inch pedicels. They are about 1½ inches long, broadly tubular, with a slightly flared mouth and a sort of wide-eyed look about them. They last only a couple of days but are produced profusely.

The charm of this plant is in its straight growth, the broad hanging leaves, and the neat placement of the flowers. The leaves at the bottom are the largest, and they grow smaller progressively toward the top, forming a triangle and fitting well in between other plants in an indoor garden.

C. lavandulacea shows its temperature preference by its manner of growth. When the thermometer registers over 80°, it becomes a 3-foot plant—perhaps owing to overstimulation. Keep it within the 55° to 75° range, with a drop at night, and it will remain much more compact and bloom for a longer time. A 3- to 4-inch pot is ample for a single plant in Lean Mix. Keep moist and fertilize regularly along with your other plants. Higher humidity prevents browning of leaves. Except for temperature it is not at all fussy. Just have plants coming along from seed.

C. micromusa is a somewhat smaller plant with similar stems and leaves. Also an annual, it grows rapidly from seed to a height of 1 foot. Seven to twenty flowers bloom successively from the leaf axils. These are deep yellow and rather like small *Episcia* flowers, the lobes more flared than in *C. lavandulacea* and the bottom lip juts forward.

It is a spring bloomer requiring high humidity and cool house temperatures like some other chiritas. The narrow 1¾-inch seedpods are freely produced.

C. elphinstonia is very similar but a smaller plant.

For indoor growing annual plants are not as desirable as perennials, but at least the chiritas can be grown at any time of the year. In parts of the country where homes are very warm in summer, they will do much better during the winter season.

Chirita elephinstonia. Photo Frances Batcheller

Chrysothemis

At last a genus with a civilized name, for Chrysothemis was the gentle sister of Clytemnestra. Of the "half a dozen or so" species from the West Indies and Central America, just three are in active cultivation here. The first to be introduced was *C. friedrichsthaliana,* which was soon ousted from hobbyist favor by *C. pulchella.* Now we are beginning to become acquainted with *C. villosa,* which is the most likely to succeed. All three have very similar flowers, so a choice between them is based on foliage, habit, and performance.

C. friedrichsthaliana, so similar to *C. pulchella* that it needs no special description, lost out to the latter because the persistent calyxes—the chief attraction of the flower—were green or yellowish while those of *pulchella* are orange. Both plants have a fault which we describe below.

We tried growing *C. pulchella* for some time and found that it responded well and soon flowered from all the leaf axils. However, it was not long before the leaves developed a blight which invaded them with large brown patches of dead cells. Since every plant we grew had this tendency, we gradually, and regretfully, gave up the battle.

As we are busy with many other plants besides gesneriads, we are by no means always the first to hear of novelties or changes in the family. On a visit out of town we noticed a beautifully grown plant of *C. pulchella* which had totally dark bronzed shiny leaves instead of the green ones of the plants with which we were familiar. We asked for, and received, a cutting through the generosity of its grower, Mrs. St. Lawrence. About the same time we noticed a brown-leaved variety listed in Mr. Easterbrook's catalog and had him send us a plant. The two proved to be identical. They gave no trouble at all and were altogether sturdier, more resistant plants than the green-leaved form. It is true that it is also considerably larger, but since the foliage is far more colorful, this, in many situations, is a plus rather than the contrary. It has been labeled forma 'Woodsonii' but the name seems to have no validity.

The incident points up the variability of the gesneriads. As many of them have a wide range in Central and South America—and elsewhere—variations often turn up. Most of these are not for the better, but superior clones (an individual plant and its vegetative progeny) do appear from time to time in the botanical material. It is reasonable to believe that many opportunities have been lost for the improvement of some of the newer plants due to nonrecognition and nonevaluation of these variants. Greenhouse growers, especially commercial ones, have entirely different criteria from indoor growers, and it is up to the amateurs to select better plants in most cases. Without having had the experience with the form of *C. pulchella,* we could not have included it in this section as a recommendable plant.

Our description therefore is of the bronze-leaved form of *C. pulchella.* It grows mainly in Trinidad and the West Indies. The stem is square, consisting of four fluted sections as if tied together in a bundle. It grows a foot high though we suspect that, given a big enough pot, it can become considerably larger. The leaves are oval pointed and toothed, up to a foot long, the part toward the stem tapering gradually for the last 3 or 4 inches. It is an extraordinary leaf, finely hairy, intensely dark bronze and very shiny-oily in appearance. The purplish underside is heavily and prominently veined. The arrangement of the leaves is opposite-alternate (decussate) and they stand out stiffly from the stem. The petiole on either side has an extension which embraces the stem, meeting in the center.

Peduncles about an inch long appear in the axils, bearing four to eight flowers. First to show color is the calyx which is ¾ inch long with triangular lobes and a bright orange color. The corolla is only exerted a short way, has five lobes, and is soft yellow with red

Chrysothemis pulchella, dark form.

lines in the throat. The corolla lasts only a few days but the calyx remains fresh and colorful for weeks. Thus, a plant which is well grown may have a dozen or more of these orange clusters in the axils.

Not right away, but when partially grown, *C. pulchella* develops a tuber which can grow to several inches across. Under indoor growing conditions and with fluorescent light, there is no dormancy as long as the plant is moistened regularly. When old stems are removed, new ones rapidly take their places.

C. pulchella should be potted in Rich Mix with lime. Do not compact the soil. Provide a temperature of 65° F or higher and 50 percent humidity. It likes even moisture and dislikes heavy watering, especially on cool days. Sensitivity to cultural treatment is much greater before than after a tuber is formed. Incidentally, the tuber lies naturally with its top even with the surface of the soil. If removed, it should be replanted in the same position. Being a rather large plant it should soon be moved to a 4-inch and then a 6- or 8-inch azalea pot. This is not one of your low light requirement gesneriads. Even when quite small, it should be kept within 4 inches of the tubes, for the flowers develop when the plant is only 3 inches high, and it is very desirable to maintain close internodes. If these can be kept to an inch, the plant will have a fine appearance.

As with so many of the gesneriads, we have not collected seed but depend on cuttings for propagation. Not only can the stem be cut in sections with a leaf attached—the leaf can be cut down in size for convenience—but excess growths from the tuber can be removed and potted up. Often they have a piece of root attached. It would be interesting to let these growths from the tuber all grow together and have a cluster of *Chrysothemis* stems in a suitably large pot. If you have the room, the effect may be striking.

In short, the bronze form of *C. pulchella* is a handsome foliage plant which compares well with its relatives the *Nautilocalyx*.

Chrysothemis villosa has long velvety green leaves tapering at both ends and a deep orange calyx. The growth is smaller than the two other plants, and it may, therefore, make a better subject for the indoor garden. For further comments, see "Gesneriad Update," page 215.

Codonanthe

Codonanthe is a small genus which inhabits low altitude forests from southern Mexico to southern Brazil and Peru. The plants are generally reported to have been found growing on anthills.

The known species are branching, trailing plants which spread into colonies by means of roots from the leaf axils. Most flowers are white and tubular in form, with short flaring lobes. A peculiar feature is the way they are cradled by the calyx, with one sepal curling up behind the short, knobby spur, and the rest supporting the flower in a horizontal position. Flowers are short-lived and followed by colorful fruits.

A definite symbiosis with ants is indicated by the presence of nectaries on the lower leaf surfaces, in the axils of leaves, and at the base of sepals. As these would be of little interest, and inaccessible, to flying insects we must assume that ants also carry on the function of cross-pollination. This is the only genus of gesneriads whose seeds are enclosed in an aril—a fleshy tube arising from the seed stem (funicle). Since such arils in other families serve the purpose of seed distribution, notably by ants, this is probably its role in *Codonanthe*. Incidentally, the red spots, which are the indicators of the nectaries on the leaves, suggest insect or fungus infestation. They have caused anguish to many an amateur experiencing *Codonanthe* for the first time. But the presence of these dots is a sure indication of the genus.

Tropical anthills consist of compacted granules of soil which provide a very loose, well-aerated medium and relatively stable moisture. One purpose served by the plants

Codonanthe gracilis. Not yet in amateur collections. There are a large number of gesneriads, identified and unidentified, flowing in from tropical sources, which often differ only in details from the better-known plants. *Photo L. H. Bailey Hortorium of Cornell University*

which are "gardened" on these mounds may be to anchor the soil during the rainy seasons. The regions where *Codonanthe* grows have high mean temperatures and humidity the year round. Anthills are on the ground, often shaded by the trees of the forest. Thus we have an excellent indication of how to grow these attractive plants indoors. Our warm house temperatures, porous soilless mixes, and relatively low-intensity but continuous light sources fit the picture very well. Our main concern, then, will be to maintain high humidity for these plants.

No hybrids of importance to indoor growers have been reported in this genus.

Codonanthe carnosa is a good example of the continued state of flux among gesneriads in cultivation. Two others, *C. macradenia* and *C. crassifolia,* have been most favored by amateurs, but *C. carnosa* appears to be well on the way to superseding them. The reasons are the same that underlie our reactions to any set of relatively unknown species. We try out those that are first available and, if they have some merit, we grow them for a while. But, among the gesneriads, where there is such a wealth of species material, much of it new to amateurs, commercial distribution depends on a number of practical and chance factors. In this case the better plant came along later, and the amateur will find even greater and longer-lasting pleasure growing it.

Although both *C. macradenia* and *C. crassifolia* flower more easily indoors than many of the more spectacular gesneriads, they have the disadvantage of blooming for only a day, or two at most. The colored berries, which are an attraction, do not occur with any frequency except in good greenhouse cultivation. Also these plants possess an untidy trailing habit. On the other hand *C. carnosa,* although possessing a flower less than half as large as theirs, has all the advantage. Flowers remain open for several days at a time, so that there is an accumulation of blooms well distributed over the whole plant. They are, moverover, of simple, classic shape and stand out more from the foliage and are delicately perfumed. The habit is neat and symmetrical, and there is no tendency, as with the other two, for the branches to become excessively long and straggly. Hence it is unnecessary to grow it in a hanging pot or basket. Having these excellent characteristics, plus ease of cultivation, it has taken its place among the "miracle gesneriads."

Originating in southern Brazil, from Rio de Janeiro to Santa Caterina, *C. carnosa* is a small plant spreading in cultivation rarely more than 16 inches. The growth is essentially shrubby, as it sends up stems that eventually develop very short woody trunks which branch in every direction. The branches are wiry and undivided, some 6 to 7 inches long, green but soon turning brown. The opposite leaves are on very short thick petioles, curved upward and outward from the stem. They are ½ inch long, nearly round or oval, slightly pointed at the tip, and quite thick. The whole plant is very white fuzzy, giving a grayish sheen to the deep green leaves.

An attractive feature of the foliage is the way it grows out quite flat, the stems being stiffish, slightly arched, and dangling only at the young tips. The leaves face upward on the sturdy upturned petioles. Although nectaries are noted in the axils of the leaves, they are not prominent on the underside as they are with *C. macradenia* and *C. crassifolia.*

The flowers are borne on short pedicels in the axils and above the foliage. The calyx is tiny and the whitish corolla flares broadly instead of being preceded by a long tube as in other species. It is about ⅝ inch long. The five lobes are clean cut, kidney-shaped, and the three lower lobes jut forward. Thus the form is similar to that of some of the sinningias (*S.* 'Freckles' is a good example, but without the long tube). The fruit is orange and about ⅓ inch in diameter. It has not been produced spontaneously for us, and attempts to pollinate did not produce consistent results. But this fruit should be an attractive feature if it can be induced reliably and easily.

Our experience is that *C. carnosa* blooms chronically throughout the year, being prolific in the production of new branches as the old ones die off.

We pot *C. carnosa* in Lean Mix with lime, fertilize with high phosphate formula, and provide constant moisture. Temperatures should be above 60° F and humidity 50 percent or higher. It grows well on the edge of a fluorescent light stand, hung with the branches projecting 3 or 4 inches below the lamps. In a window it should have good indirect light, but periods of gray days will inhibit bloom. It is our impression that it will bloom at 60° F, but we would not advise lower temperatures. High summer heat does not bother it, and pollution is not a serious problem, though it may shorten the life of the flowers. Tip cutting encourages new branchings from the base or trunk.

When the plant has grown rather woody at the base and has several of its short trunks, it can be divided and, in fact, should be in order to prevent degeneration. In very high humidity, as in a terrarium, white aerial roots are developed at the leaf axils. Cuttings can then be planted and will root immediately. Under normal conditions, branch cuttings root easily in moist vermiculite. A 4-inch pot is ample for this small plant at maturity.

C. crassifolia and macradenia we treat together here because, as cultivated houseplants, they are nearly indistinguishable. In fact nurserymen and amateurs have consistently mislabeled them. Since *C. crassifolia* is a variable species, some plants may look more, some less, like *C. macradenia*. *C. crassifolia* is probably the most widespread plant of the genus—from southern Mexico to southern Brazil and Peru. *C. macradenia* is found from southern Mexico to northern Colombia.

For the amateur the chief difference between the plants is that *C. crassifolia* shows a red midrib on the underside of the leaves and redness toward the tip. It also sets seed spontaneously, while *C. macradenia* requires assistance. The fruit of both plants is red or pinkish. The botanical description notes that *C. macradenia* has the larger flowers and the smaller leaves, but considering variability this is not very helpful.

The plants are more trailing, the stems more lax, and the base less woody than in *C. carnosa*. The opposite leaves are about an inch long and shiny green. Underneath there are a number of regularly spaced red dots which indicate the nectaries.

The flowers on short pedicels in the axils are white and ¾ to 1 inch long. It is our impression that those of *C. crassifolia* are definitely the narrower tubed of the two. They are not showy, for the tube is thick and the flaring of the lobes is not sufficient to give the effect of petals. Also the tube is sinuous, with a hump in the middle so that it has a somewhat ungainly appearance.

These two codonanthes may trail well over a foot and have solid overlapping masses of greenery. Culture is much the same as for *C. carnosa*. Both seem to react favorably to high humidity terrarium conditions, producing flowers and aerial roots. Their chief advantage is that they bloom throughout the year and are of easy culture.

There are a number of *Codonanthe* species floating around in the nurseries, some of them recently imported and not yet labeled.

Since our first edition, *Codonanthe* has remained a favorite of gesneriad enthusiasts without achieving any notable increase in popularity with the public. It makes a nice pot plant in spite of its trailing habit, flowers rather consistently throughout the year, and the blooms emit a faint perfume. It is easy to grow and propagate and is an excellent terrarium plant. In short, it is a charmer that is almost ideal for light gardening. Whether *Codonanthe* will ever find its way into public recognition as a houseplant remains doubtful.

The genus has been subjected to a degree of botanical scrutiny that is remarkable considering that, except for a span in size between short cupped tubes (½ inch) and long tubes (1½ inch), there is not a great deal of visible difference between the flowers, in a genus that covers such a vast geographical range. In order to separate the species it has been necessary to go into minute detail. See "Gesneriad Update," page 215.

Columnea

Columneas demonstrate especially well the late arrival of many gesneriads in cultivation and the speed with which they have been adopted by growers everywhere. It is no exaggeration to say that the gesneriads, more than any other tropical plants, have inaugurated a new era in greenhouse and indoor growing.

The genus was named by Linnaeus in 1753, but it was not until 1953 that any of these plants were offered on the American market. The whole development of this plant in cultivation in this country is due to the explorations and hybridizations of Dr. Robert E. Lee and Dr. Harold E. Moore of Cornell University. They were almost the sole cause of the subsequent popularity of columneas, and there are probably few incidents in history of greater individual contributions to horticulture. Within fifteen years *Columnea* has become a very popular and important commercial plant.

Columneas occur all through the American tropics, in central and northern South America and the West Indian islands. They are epiphytic—that is to say, like most bromeliads and many orchids, they grow on trees—spreading their roots through the spongy masses of live and dead ferns and mosses which decorate the boughs. There are more than 125 species, and exploring botanists are still reporting new ones. Undoubtedly some switching of species from one genus to another will take place with time, for though there are numerous plants which unmistakably belong together, as usual in a large genus, there are a number that are borderline cases with other genera.

Columneas have two-lipped tube flowers with four oblong anthers united in a square or rectangle. The filaments are also united together and to the corolla tube for a short distance from the base. The anthers dehisce (open) by a lengthwise slit. Style and anthers are often longer than the tube, the stigma being club shaped or two lobed. The fruit is a smooth, somewhat flattened, round berry, often ivory white, and filled with small smooth seeds. There is a gland at the base of the ovary or five equally spaced around it.

The most characteristic form of the flower is the one which has earned it the name of the goldfish plant. The upper lip of the tube is much extended and somewhat downcurved at the end. The two upper lobes are merely indicated by a notch and the sides of the lobes are a continuation of the upper half of the tube. The lower lobes often separate halfway down the tube, the side ones spreading more or less horizontally and the center one, being longer and strap shaped, often being reflexed. The effect of a swimming, or flying, fish is more striking when the flower is held horizontally or erect than when, as is too often the case, it angles downward.

The coloring is predominantly red and yellow with occasional rather uncertain pinks. So far there is none of the variety of coloring found in *Achimenes, Saintpaulia,* or *Streptocarpus.* On the other hand the coloring is often very brilliant, the hairy textures impressive, and the length—up to 3 inches—quite spectacular. Once the flowers of a genus have evolved beyond the primitive form of equal distribution of the parts, considerable variability can be expected. This is true of *Columnea* which shows an extraordinary range of shapes. The appearance in Lyndon Lyon's greenhouses of a plant with a definite horn on the upper part of the tube is a most unusual development. Still more extraordinary is the fact that it proved a mutation transferrable to its progeny. Thus a flower of a new type was created, and one with considerable promise of great popularity.

The calyxes are also extremely varied, some being simple and small and others leafy, even ferny, or covered with masses of very long upstanding hairs. Most *Columnea* flowers grow on short pedicels, but a few, including the brilliant *C. erythrophaea,* have long ones which suspend the flower well below the branch.

In respect to habit there are two principal kinds. There are some with very lax stems that trail straight down from a pot or basket and to a length of 6 or 8 feet. The other type is arching/upright in growth, with woodier stems. One must mention still a third kind which has still thicker stems and great coarse leaves, usually covered with hair.

The leaves are opposite, smooth or hairy, and usually a long oval, tapering toward the petiole. A few are heavily quilted. Some are think textured, others rather fleshy.

Floriferousness is tremendous in the better species and cultivars. A basket of columneas with a cascade of 6-foot strands of leaves may be aflame with hundreds of flowers each of which can last up to a month! In the newer hybrids, bloom can be continuous summer and winter.

CULTURE

That *Columnea* is found over such a wide geographical range tells us that complete uniformity of culture cannot be expected. The majority of the plants in cultivation come under the rule that temperatures should never go below 65°, yet there are several species and cultivars which will not bloom unless they are subjected to cooler periods. Also we have noticed a high sensitivity to extreme heat in most of the plants. This varies to such an extent that it is difficult to specify exactly. However, if you can keep the plants in an environment between 65° F and 85° F, they will be relatively safe.

What happens when the temperature is too warm is that any overwatering produces stem rot with astonishing speed. This seems almost a contradiction in terms but does occur with other gesneriads. Light gardeners are well advised, if they do not have air conditioning, to put the lamps on a five- or six-hour cycle during hot spells in July and August. The plants will not be harmed, and the reduction in temperature will be considerable.

We pot the plants in Lean Mix without lime. As epiphytes their pH does not run to neutral but to mild acidity. We also find that they do well in long-fiber sphagnum moss.

Watering is the ticklish problem. In general it should be kept to a minimum. We have not yet killed a *Columnea* through underwatering although that is of course possible. But what it indicates is that, in a situation where careful attention to moisture needs is normal, *Columnea* can be maintained in a relatively dry state—just moist is the proper condition. This is particularly necessary during winter coolness as well as in the above-mentioned heat of summer. The requirements of seasonal bloomers, which are not in active growth in winter, are particularly demanding during that season.

In spite of this problem, growers rarely have much trouble with columneas. If stem rot does set in, prompt cutting of healthy stems and rooting in moist vermiculite will soon replace the damaged plant.

The light requirements of many of these plants are quite low—about the same as for African violets. We have found that 150 to 250 footcandles can be quite sufficient. But this varies, and you must find out for yourself where the plants are happiest—in the window or under lights. On the whole, however, you can count on good reflected light (at the side of a window) or up to 15 inches from the lamps. Large baskets are another matter and are simply hung up in the greenhouse where they get light.

We fertilize with high phosphate formula during active growth and bloom and not at all when the plants are standing still, which they have a habit of doing for long periods.

The columneas have enjoyed remarkable popularity in spite of a hanging or spreading habit. They are of course ideal in baskets in a greenhouse. But the greenhouse population is a minority. In the home they present problems. The true trailing types can be grown as juveniles in pots if they are put on a shelf under the lights or suspended in a window. They will never put on the big show of the basket plants, but the large size of the flowers can make a pretty imposing appearance on a small plant that is kept trimmed. But, even then, we can't expect very long continuation of good performance, for most of the columneas are not branching plants and growth from the base is poor. You just have to start new plants from cuttings from time to time.

Every effort has been expended to produce plants of the upright type which are good bloomers in pots. This has been relatively successful in a number of instances. With the plants having a heavier stem structure, a good way to achieve a handsome effect is to plant five or six equal-sized cuttings in a 6-inch azalea pot to produce a relatively symmetrical plant for a relatively short time. For the woodier plants often do branch, but irregularly and unsymmetrically. Columneas in pots just can't be left without attention or trained to good looks without a bit of ingenuity. The minor differences in habit between the species and cultivars are innumerable and require slightly varied treatment in each case.

SPECIES

Reference is made here to use of species in producing the famous Cornell series of hybrid columneas which were the starting point for our present crop of fine improved plants. Regarding synonyms, see ''Gesneriad Update.''

C. affinis grows at from 1,500 to 5,000 feet altitude in Venezuela. Long thick stems covered with reddish purple hairs. Upright growth. Leaves unequal, the larger up to 9 inches long and 2½ inches wide, dark green. The flowers arise from orange bracts in the axils. The hairy calyx is orange. The narrow tube flower is 1¼ inches long, yellow covered with a dense coat of orange hairs. Very small lobes hardly spread. Parent of 'Campus Favorite.' Tendency to everbloom. (*Dalbergaria aureonitens*)

C. allenii is sometimes confused with *C. arguta*. However, leaves are a broad oval, while those of *arguta* are a narrow long-pointed oval and smaller.

Thin hanging stems and broadly oval leaves distinguish this Panamanian plant. They are about ¾ by ½ inch. Flower red varying to orange and yellow, the upper lip well extended and coming to an abrupt squared tip, the middle lobe of the lower lip very narrow, emerging less than halfway to the tip of the flower. Seasonal bloomer. Spring-summer.

C. argentea, not frequently grown at present, has ''silky, silvery, long, and narrow leaves, lemon colored flowers and white berries.'' Presumably seasonal.

C. arguta comes from Panama. Long slender stems, red hairy. Leaves equal, overlapping, sharply pointed narrow oval. Calyx very hairy, ½ inch long. Corolla 2½ inches long, slightly hairy, orange red with yellow at the throat. Upper lip short and round lobed. Lower lip, the lobes broad and almost even. The limb emerging from the narrow, slightly hairy tube, is therefore relatively more symmetrical than most columneas. Parent of 'Campus Sunset.' Flowers in the fall on older stems.

C. crassifolia is the parent of several of the Cornell hybrids. Has large, narrow, shining leaves and large orange red flowers in the spring with orange yellow at throat and a coat of stiff red hairs. Apparently an upright grower.

C. dissimilis, a recently introduced plant, can be secured from gesneriad nurserymen. The stems are thick and woody, the habit spreading to upright and somewhat branched. Leaves are large, hairy, and thick. The flowers are remarkable in being nearly cleistogamous (closed). It arises from a densely hairy deep orange calyx—like a large ball of fuzz—and the very hairy orange tube is thick at the start, then tapers to a round point that zones into yellow. It is about 2 to 2¼ inches long. A spring and summer bloomer which has presented problems to growers. Requires rather high light conditions. A very striking plant, but too large for pot culture. (*Tricantha dissimilis*)

Columnea dissimilis. Courtesy Kartuz Greenhouses

C. erythrophaea is the most interesting of the new species introductions. It attracted immediate attention and won a best of show in Philadelphia in 1974. The plant is not upright but a half trailer, with rather sturdy stems capable of extending out from a pot or basket without trailing. The leaves are small, oval, pointed at both ends and a little over an inch in length. The flowers hang below the branches from 2-inch-long pedicels and make a right turn to the horizontal. The calyx is leafy and orange colored—with about ¾-inch lobes—and the tube flower is 3 inches long, narrow in all its length and an interesting burnt orange color. There appear to be clones with a showier, brighter orange and some with a very much broader upper lip, like a hood. In any event the plant has already been used in some fine hybrids bringing out stronger color to a flower, which, because of its size and the way it is separated from the horizontal branches, makes a very showy effect. It is nearly everblooming but a bit sensitive to sudden temperature changes and overwatering.

C. flaccida has been listed as having trailing stems, small pointed leaves, and red flowers in summer.

C. glabra comes from Costa Rica. Erect, small-leaved plant with large scarlet flowers in early spring.

C. gloriosa is a somewhat variable Costa Rican species which has been much cultivated. The leaves are oval—about an inch long and half as wide—and very hairy. Flowers from a small hairy spreading calyx are 3 inches long. The upper and two side lobes form a definite helmet form opening below to release the narrow middle lobe. The color is scarlet except for a yellow patch at the throat. The white berry is over an inch wide. Parent of 'Ithacan' and many other cultivars. Blooms chronically during the year.

C. harrisii has large velvety leaves and red yellow foliage.

C. herthae. Spreading, trailing habit. Hairy leaves. Clusters of small yellow flowers with orange calyxes. (*Tricantha herthae*)

C. hirta is an epiphytic shrub with short stiff very red hairy stems and hairy leaves to 1½ inches by ½ inch. Orange red flowers in the spring, almost two inches long. Upper lip forms a helmet and side and middle lobes are narrow.

Columnea gloriosa. Photo Mildred
Schroeder

C. hirsutissima is described as a basket plant with gray green leaves and arching stems. Long pink flowers in winter.

C. illepida's origin is uncertain. Rough, hairy leaves, opposite and unequal, with red blotches beneath. The thick stems are brown and hairy. Tube flowers, several successively in leaf axils, dull lemon yellow striped with longitudinal maroon lines. All parts of the plant are hairy. Flower about 1½ inches long and individually striking.

C. jamaicensis is listed by Kartuz. Small glossy leaves, wiry stems. Clusters of small tubular yellow and orange flowers all year. (*C. repens*)

C. lepidocaula, the parent of 'Ithacan,' is an erect shrubby plant with stout succulent stems to 18 inches. Glossy, green leaves 3½ by 1¼ inches, smooth above, hairy below. Solitary flowers. Calyx green to 1 inch. Corolla about 3 inches, orange shading to yellow at throat. Covered with pale long hairs. Upper lip helmetlike, same length as the tube and blunt. Upturned triangular side lobes. Lower lobe slender and short.

C. linearis is an upright shrub with branches to 18 inches. Leaves narrow, 3½ inches by ½ inch. Opposite and equal. Calyx with green lobes ¾ inch long, bent outward. Corolla 1¾ inches long. Slender upper lip and lateral lobes bent backward. Hairy pink flowers for most of the year. This is the source of pink color in many of the hybrids. Originally from Costa Rica.

C. magnifica comes from Costa Rica and Panama. Slender hairy stems with opposite equal leaves to 3½ inches, broader toward the tip. Flowers solitary, scarlet, on pedicels ½ inch long. Calyx green, hairy, ½ inch long. Corolla hairy to 2½ inches, brilliant scarlet. Tube 1¼ inches long and broad, the helmet of the same length. Narrow lateral lobes and lower lip to 1 inch.

C. microphylla, another Costa Rican plant, a favorite basket species, is remarkable for the smallness of the leaves in relation to the very large flowers (hardly distinguishable from *C. magnifica*). Leaves are at a maximum ½ inch long, arranged opposite and close together on the lax, long thin, pendent stems. Flower to over 3 inches. This is the most striking display plant of the species, but strictly for basket culture under greenhouse conditions. The stems may trail to 6 or 8 feet. Color is red with yellow throat. Bloom in spring.

C. minor (Tricantha minor). See *C. teuscheri.*

C. moorei is a short-stemmed trailer, almost a miniature. Thickish succulent stems with tiny, round, waxy leaves. The 1–1½-inch flowers have a yellow tube with an orange limb. Spring bloomer. There is a variegated form. (*Tricantha moorei*)

C. mortonii, a basket plant with wiry stems and overlapping large fleshy leaves, has large and red flowers. (*C. hirta*)

C. multiflora has been listed. Possibly a cultivar.

C. nervosa. (*Pentadenia nervosa.*)

C. nicaraguensis, a parent of 'Harvard Window,' 'Katsura,' 'Onondagan' is an epiphytic shrub from Costa Rica with brownish-hairy stems to 2½ feet high. Leaves opposite, very unequal, the larger 5 inches by 2 inches. Flowers 1 to 3 in the axils, with red limb and yellow on tube and throat. Calyx 1 inch long, white hairy with narrow lobes. Upper lip 1¾ inches long. Lateral lobes ¾ inch attached to the helmet. Lower lobe narrow and reflexed.

C. oerstediana is not in cultivation here. Hairless stems, small fleshy leaves and 2½-inch scarlet flowers.

C. percrassa was described by C. V. Morton in 1959. Fleshy, trailing, olive green stems with thick fleshy hairless leaves. Small, narrow tubular flowers, 1 inch long, scarlet with orange and red tube and yellow line in throat.

C. pilosissima has small downy leaves, large orange flowers. It resembles *C. hirta,* according to Kartuz. "Blooms all year."

C. purpureo-vittata (Ital.) is a new species from northern South America. Coarse, woody plant with interesting 6-inch, narrow leaves, strongly quilted and hairy. Pendent flowers to 2½ inches, yellow with longitudinal maroon stripes. Can be pot grown because of strong upright growth.

C. querceti comes from Costa Rica. Sturdy, upright branching plants have brown scaly, hairy stems. Unequal leaves, the largest 2¼ inches by ⅝ inch and pointed at both ends. One to three flowers in axils, reddish orange to light orange.

C. salmonea was described by Marcel Raymond in 1961. Arching stems becoming gray hairy with age. Leaves opposite, 1 inch long. Flowers 2½ inches, salmon colored and hairy, with triangular reflexed lateral lobes.

C. sanguinea is a stiff trailer with hairy stems 4½ feet long. Leaves unequal, the larger up to 12 inches by 4¾ inches. Two or three pale yellow flowers borne in the axils. Corolla up to ⅞ inch long, hairy, yellow. Leaves red spotted beneath.

C. sanguinolenta, a parent of 'Campus Favorite,' has long arching stems with glossy leaves. Calyxes fernlike and clasping the tube. The tubular flowers covered with pale hairs, dark red "blending to strong red in center and ending strong reddish orange at the tip." Limb is vivid yellow with lobes outlined in red and a red line at the center of each lobe. Suffusion of red on two upper lobes. (*Tricantha sanguinolenta*)

Columnea purpurea-vittata. Courtesy Frances Batcheller

    C. schiedeana, although originally popular in greenhouses, is rarely seen nowadays. From Mexico, it is a coarse subshrub with stems 3 feet long and hairy unequal leaves. The larger ones reach 5 inches by 1½ inches. Flowers on red hairy pedicels often hidden by leaves. Calyx red, downy, and short. Corolla soft hairy, 2–2½ inches long, the helmet 1½ inches long. Lateral lobes ½ inch. Lower lip very narrow and reflexed.

    C. teuscheri has been called *C. minor* and *Tricantha minor*. It has an extraordinary flower and is nearly everblooming with ideal warmth and watering but is a difficult subject indoors.

    From Ecuador. It has very thin wiry lax trailing stems with unequal leaves, the smaller one being almost invisible. Nodes are widely spaced. Larger leaf dark green and

Columnea scandens. Another of the innumerable attractive, still untried, gesneriad species. *Photo by authors in St. Lucia, West Indies*

about 2 inches in length. Flowers two inches long. Calyxes bristly, red haired like a ball of fuzz. The narrow tube is dark purple expanding into small oblong lobes, the upper two purple, the lower yellow. There is no overhang of the upper lip, all the lobes being in the same plane and slanted slightly backward and upward. The effect is very curious and attractive—almost like an artistic mask. A very different species.

C. translucens comes from Panama, described by M. Raymond in 1961. Shrub with short horizontal branches with orange to red hairs. Unequal leaves, the larger four times the length of the smaller. One to three flowers in an axil on 2-inch pedicels. Corolla 2 inches long, translucent, orange.

C. tulae is the source of most of the yellow cultivars. The plant has two distinct botanical forms differing only in respect to flower color. *C. tulae* cv. 'Flava' is pure yellow. (*C. scandens* var. *tulae*). *Columnea tomentulosa* (Urban) appears to be a more hairy plant.

Hairy stems bear opposite leaves to 1¾ inches by ¾ inch. Leaves are densely hairy. Flowers solitary on bracted pedicels ½ inch long. Flower 2 inches long, the calyx short leafy, the tube narrow. The short helmet is blunt and the lower lip narrow and only ¼ inch long. The habit is much like *C. linearis.*

C. urbanii.

C. verecunda many times is listed as *C. verecunda* 'Florence Carrell.' Shrubby with stems to 2½ feet. Leaves very unequal, the larger being 4¼ inches long and 1¼ inches wide, smooth green above and burgundy below. The smaller leaf is ¼ inch long. Flowers 1½ inches long, yellow or pale red. Calyx about ⅝ inch long the segments very narrow. The upper lip very much extended over the lower. Bright pink berry. From Costa Rica.

C. warszewicziana. Now *C. anisophylla.* Stems and leaves pale green. Flowers red. Difficult to bring to bloom. Apparently requires low temperatures. From Costa Rica.

We should not finish this section without acknowledging that the late Mrs. Maude Cogswell of Whistling Hill Nursery, Hamburg, New York, a commercial grower, has been responsible for importing a number of species as plants or seed which were later identified by the staffs at Cornell and Montreal.

The following species came to our attention through catalog listings after the above more basic record was compiled. The information here is from Mrs. Frances Batcheller.

C. raymondii, an upright grower from Costa Rica, resembles *C. nicaraguensis.* Very large red flowers.

C. subcordata, this large, shrubby plant from Jamaica, has yellow flowers.

C. zebrina is a shrubby, big-leaved plant from Panama. Flowers yellow with maroon stripes.

Such species listings change from year to year depending on the receipt of plants from students and explorers. For clarification of disputed names of genera and species, see ''Gesneriad Update,'' *Columnea.*

CULTIVARS

Using plant material in the collection of the Bailey Hortorium at Cornell University, which consisted partly of columneas discovered at a much earlier date and partly of recent discoveries and imports by himself and others, Dr. Robert E. Lee developed fourteen hybrids which he started to distribute to amateurs and the trade in 1963. Up to this time, although known in Europe in the nineteenth century, columneas had been largely neglected by hobbyists and commercial nurserymen. In our general list of modern cultivars, there are only two entries by a European breeder.

These fourteen hybrids gave an enormous impetus to interest in the genus. Although they are mostly large basket type plants more suitable to greenhouse culture than indoor growing, they continue to be carried by nurserymen in spite of the numerous hybrids developed since that time. Most important they demonstrated that hybridization was not difficult and that characteristics could be combined in a systematic way to produce plants with new and superior qualities.

We are going to list the Cornell hybrids first and separate from our general list because as a group of first-time hybrids they are unique and because so many of the more modern cultivars have developed from them. The whole concept of everblooming columneas—realization that this was possible—derived from Dr. Lee's plants. The current popularity of the genus is largely due to his creative contribution.

THE CORNELL HYBRIDS

C. 'Aurora.' Upright plant with arching stems and large leaves flushed with red below. Produces clusters of yellow flowers of modest size, striped with red. Chronic bloomer.

C. 'Campus Favorite.' Vigorous grower, with spreading stems and drooping long oval 4-inch leaves, glossy above, and irregularly spotted with red. Flowers red with fuzzy ball-shaped red calyx. The appearance is more truly shrubby than most columneas. Spring bloomer.

C. 'Campus Gem.' Partially bushy half trailer. Soft small leaves. Medium-sized orange flowers in spring.

C. 'Campus Queen.' Small trailing growth suitable for hanging pot or small basket. Deep pink small flowers. Blooms chronically but may do so at any time of year.

C. 'Campus Sunset.' Vigorous bushy trailing plant with small pointed leaves. Flowers are of medium size, yellow with red edge. Fall bloomer.

C. 'Canary.' Spreading to upright plant of medium size. Bright yellow flowers in clusters chronically during the year.

C. 'Cascadilla.' Vining, trailing plant with very large (2½–3-inch) deep red flowers. Leaves dark green. Relatively easy to grow.

C. 'Indian Summer.' Small-leaved trailer. Long-tubed flowers verging from orange to red with yellow in throat. Not one of the favorites, and a shy bloomer.

C. 'Katsura.' A difficult plant to flower. Spreading somewhat shrubby habit. Flowers are pink; leaves variegated white and light green. Tendency to stem rot at high temperatures. A cool grower.

C. 'Oneidan.' Very trailing plant. Vigorous grower with large red flowers. A chronic bloomer but not an easy plant to maintain.

C. 'Onondagan.' Spreading plant. Red flowers but shy bloomer. For various reasons it has not been a popular plant.

C. 'Orange Beauty.' Bushy plant with spreading habit. Clusters of orange flowers of medium size. Hardly everblooming as claimed.

C. 'Red Arrow.' Bushy trailer. Bronze leaves. Large red flowers. Superseded by superior red columneas.

C. 'Tiogan.' Slender trailer. Smallish pink and yellow flowers in late winter-spring.

It should be noted that, except for 'Campus Favorite,' all these plants have leaves arranged rather evenly along the spreading to trailing stems and that these are no more than 2 inches in size, usually pointed at both ends.

Other hybrids were produced at Cornell, and some of these are listed in the following collection. None of the Cornell plants has been successful in indoor growing, mainly because of their rather pendent or large spreading habit. However, they are still much grown in greenhouses, and those that have large flowers are very showy. A good portion, however, has flowers at the most 1½ inches long.

CULTIVARS—GENERAL LIST

Efforts of hybridizers since the appearance of the Cornell series have been primarily directed toward producing more compact, bushy, upright plants which are everblooming and toward increase in the size of flower and variety of coloring. The *Gesneriad Register* of 1963 listed a number of hybrids besides the Cornell plants, all of which have disappeared from cultivation except 'V. Covert' and 'Stavanger,' 'Evlo,' originally considered a challenging plant, is perhaps still grown by a few hobbyists. These have all been succeeded by greatly improved plants mostly developed by Eyerdom, Kartuz, and Lyndon Lyon.

Saintpaulia and *Episcia* have long ago reached the stage where slight changes in form or color have been named and issued as original plants, resulting in whole categories of look-alikes. *Columnea* is still in a state of flux. And, though there are a number of near repeats the list of active cultivars has not grown as yet to unwieldy proportions. We think the following list is quite representative of the current crop of plants. We have not, and could not, grow them all and are therefore dependent in many instances on catalog descriptions. However, the more popular plants are specially noted, and we have several recommendations in the text of plants with special merit for indoor culture.

OLDER CULTIVARS

C. 'Alpha' (Lyon). Recognized as the best of the yellows. Compact branching growth and profuse production of canary yellow flowers, 2½ or more inches in size, and with the hood greatly overreaching the lower lobe. Seen direct on, it is a broad diagonally flattened flower of great substance. Will bloom on rooted cuttings and is virtually everblooming.

C. 'Betty Stoehr' (Lyon). An early cross of great beauty. Described as upright but does trail as stems lengthen. The red flowers face outward, being held erect, and the lobes of the flower are relatively regular. There are two forms, the other having a yellow flushed throat. Hardly everblooming as claimed but does produce chronically.

C. 'Bonfire' (Lyon) (*C.* 'Fang' x *C. erythrophaea*). Vigorous branching plant with 3-inch flowers on 2-inch dangling pedicels. Leafy orange calyx. Flowers yellow and crimson. More brilliant than *erythrophaea* but retaining its sturdy characteristics. Everblooming.

C. 'Brighter Dawn' (Eyerdom-Granger). Bronzy foliage, good-sized yellow flowers with red suffusion.

C. 'Butterfly' (Lyon). Trailer with small pointed foliage. Yellow flowers touched with orange. Nearly everblooming. Basket plant.

C. 'Butterball' (Kartuz). Upright shrubby plant with bright clusters of yellow flowers. Leaves reddish beneath. Chronic bloomer.

C. 'Calypso' (Eyerdom-Granger). Bronze leaves. Orange and red flowers.

C. 'Cayugan' (Cornell hybrid). Three-inch red flowers. Wiry-stemmed, vigorous trailer. Chronic bloomer but a fine show plant.

C. 'Chanticleer' (Kartuz). Light green velvety leaves and shrubby, compact habit with considerable branching. Flowers 1½ inches and light orange. Although not a spectacular plant, this is the one we would choose for any beginner because of its vigor and tolerance. Easy to grow in pots under fluorescent lights. As a houseplant this is the best of the columneas.

C. 'Cherokee' (Kartuz). Semiupright plant with glossy tapered foliage. Deep orange and yellow flowers. A recent introduction.

C. 'Chippewa' (Easterbrook). Waxy green foliage. Large orange and red flowers. Seasonal.

C. 'Chocolate Soldier' (Eyerdom-Granger). Unfortunately the same name as a very popular *Episcia*. Described only as chocolate red leaf and red flower.

C. 'Christmas Carol' (Saylor). Trailing plant with closely set small leaves and large, deep red flowers. Named for Bill Saylor's (see *Nematanthus*) wonderful wife, Carol.

C. 'Christy' (Wyrtzen).

C. 'Constant Flame' (Eyerdom-Granger). Trailer with closely spaced leaves. Red flowers.

C. 'Cornellian' (Cornell Hybrid). Erect, branching habit. Narrow leaves with red reverses. Clusters of deep orange, yellow-throated flowers. Profuse seasonal bloomer.

C. 'Crimson Banner' (Kartuz). Small dark foliage with medium-sized deep red flowers.

C. 'Eagles' (Kartuz). Dark waxy leaves on spreading, trailing plant. Medium-sized light golden flowers.

C. 'Early Bird' (Lyon). The most popular of the houseplant type columneas. Very compact, with spreading stems closely packed with small waxy pointed leaves. Flowers orange streaked with yellow and with yellow base to the tube. Broad open helmet shape. Size 2½ inches and carried quite erect. Excellent year round bloomer and quite tolerant. A beauty!

C. 'Evlo.' Cross between *C. gloriosa* and *C. nicaraguensis* made by Miss Genevieve Boggs in 1957/8. One of the first. Very choice plant with dark, coppery leaves and vining stems. Bright large red flowers. It has always been considered a difficult plant but is magnificent when culture is right. Cool growing.

C. 'Fanfare' (Saylor). Semitrailing with small satiny leaves. Pink calyx with ferny sepals. Flower tube red with yellow face.

C. 'Fang' (Lyon). Flowers with broad hood, orange red with yellow throat. Yellow hump above side lobes. Probably halfway to 'Horned.'

C. 'Firechief' (Easterbrook). Huge red flower. Everblooming?

C. 'Flamingo' (Kartuz). Clusters of light yellow small flowers changing to white-bordered pink. Narrow dark green leaves, spreading habit. Chronic bloomer. Some similarity to 'V. Covert.'

C. 'Gold Rush' (Eyerdom-Granger). Stiff trailing stems. Yellow flowers with touches of orange.

C. 'Gold Spice' (Lyon) (C. 'Giant Horned' x C. 'Horned'). Large yellow flowers with cinnamon-colored horn rising from the tip of the hood. Dark glossy foliage. Everblooming. We ought to call the horned plants the "Rhinoceros series."

C. 'Great Horned' (Lyon). Large orange red flower with large horn on top of helmet. Spreading habit. Fantastic!

C. 'Horned' (Lyon). More compact form of 'Great Horned.' Good houseplant and a chronic bloomer.

C. 'Magic Lantern' (Kartuz). Semitrailer with deep rose pink flowers. Small dark green leaves. Probably supersedes Mary Ann.

C. 'Mary Ann' (Kartuz). One of the most popular columneas for the house. Deep pink flowers throughout the year. Narrow dark green leaves. Compact spreading, trailer.

C. 'Mia.' Large trailing plant with tiny leaves like *microphylla*. Large brilliant red flowers held upright.

C. 'Moonglow' (Lyon) (C. 'Great Horned' x C. *erythrophaea* x self). Buttercup yellow flowers with long tube and open face borne upright. Surface covered with red hairs. Good everblooming pot plant.

C. 'Orange Fire.' Large upright orange flowers. Pendant stems. Small opposite leaves. All year.

C. 'Orange Zing' (Lyon). Slender trailer with small leaves. Medium burnt orange flowers.

C. 'Ramadan.' Deep red flowers lined with yellow.

C. 'Red Ball' ('Evlo' x 'Red King).' Red flowers. Not easy.

C. 'Red King.' A selection with large upright red flowers. Trailing.

C. 'Robin' (Kartuz). Small, dark, closely set leaves. Trailer. Large red flowers. Everblooming?

C. 'Sea Gull' (Kartuz). Another "improved" selection. Probably replaces 'Flamingo.' Yellow changing to near white. The whites on these columneas are a new development but look more like bleached yellow and are not brilliant. Flowers in clusters.

C. 'Snake Charmer.' Slender wiry stems, tiny leaves. Very large flowers. Chronic bloomer.

C. 'Stavanger.' A famous early cross made in Norway by Magne-Haualand. Huge flowers red with yellow in throat. A very cool growing plant and unsuitable for most greenhouses except on the west coast. Very vigorous and makes a gorgeous basket plant. Still occasionally grown.

C. 'Sunny' (Saylor). Short trailing stems. Leaves unequal. Calyxes feathery. Flowers medium—canary yellow with red splotches on upper lobe.

C. 'Sunset' (Lyon). Very large orange flowers. Small coppery leaves. Everblooming.

C. 'Sylvia' (Kartuz). Semitrailer, compact. Light pink flowers.

C. 'V. Covert.' Cross made by Mrs. Kenneth Covert of Amsterdam, New York, and developed by Lyndon Lyon. This is the first of the compact pinks. Still a good, bushy plant, very upright and with many small pink flowers for a long period of the year.

C. 'Yellow Dragon.' Yellow flowers have touch of red. Red-flushed leaves. Strong-growing branching and trailing plant.

C. 'Yellow Gold.' Trailer. Yellow, flushed with orange.

NEWER CULTIVARS

'Aladdin's Lamp' (Schwarz). Big, deep red flowers all year according to Kartuz. Best red.

'Autumn Leaves (Saylor). Trailer with orange flowers.

'Autumn Mist' (Lyon). Orange-tipped, yellow dangling flowers all year.

'Bill Saylor.' Upright, spreading. Red flowers veined with yellow.

'Boheme' (Bona). 'Chanticleer *x erythrophaea*). Two-inch long pink to reddish-orange flowers.

'California Gold' (Schwarz). Big golden flowers edged in red. A trailer.

'Campfire' (Saylor). Trailer with red flowers.

'Cho Cho San' (Bona). Orange flowers with yellow.

'Dragon Fire' (Lyon). Slender trailer. Large upright flowers.

'Early Sunrise.' Large orange and yellow flowers. Trailing everbloomer.

'El Dorado' (Saylor). Small-leaved with large yellow flowers. Everblooming.

'Fledermaus' (Bona). Sport of Cho Cho San. Everblooming trailer for a basket.

'Inferno' (Lyon). Clusters of yellow flowers, tipped orange. Red-backed leaves.

'Julia' (Strickland). Everblooming scarlet. Bright green leaves. Trailing.

'Kaye' (Becker) ('Mary Ann' x 'Constant Flame'). Large red flowers. Everblooming.

'Maarsen's Flame.' Small, variegated leaves. Large red flowers. Trailing.

Columnea 'Red King' (Lyndon Lyon).

'Madame Butterfly' (Schwarz). Orange and yellow flowers. Pendent stems.

'Magic Lantern' (Kartuz). Rose-pink flowers on a semitrailer.

'Midnight Lantern' (Strickland). Yellow and orange flowers. Coppery leaves. Everblooming.

'Multiflora' (Granger). Very large orange-red flowers. Small leaves, trailing, compact.

'Musetta' (Bona). Yellow flowers, tipped with orange. Hairy leaves, red beneath.

'Nelly' (Becker) (Butterball *x erythrophaea*). Stiff, spreading stems. Yellow flowers with bright orange-red edging. Everblooming.

'Orange Princess.' Red-edged, yellow flowers. Trailing.

'Pink Wink' (Arndt). *C. linearis* hyrid. Pink flowers in winter.

'Purple Robe.' *C. linearis* sport with slender rose-pink flowers and purple calyces. Purple-backed leaves. Everblooming.

'Rising Sun' (Schwarz). Very large red flowers. Dark green, compact plant.

'Shalimar' (Schwarz). Big, bright red flowers. Trailing. Everblooming.

'Top Brass' (Schwarz). Big yellow flowers. Everblooming trailer.

'Tosca' (Bona) (Chanticleer *x erythrophaea*). Shrubby growth, branching, with red flowers.

'Traviata' (Bona). Same cross as above. Very long, reddish-orange flowers. Shrubby.

'Turandot' (Bona). The same cross. Deep red, large flowers. Shrubby. Prolific.

'Waterfall.' Large yellow-orange flowers. Trailing.

'Wonder.' Bronze leaves, dark red flowers.

'Yellow Bird.' Upright yellow flowers. Trailing. Everblooming.

In this more recent crop of hybrids there are some interesting developments. Although trailers continue to be in the majority, some are more compact and efforts continue to produce shrubbier plants on the model of *S.* 'Chanticleer' but with larger, brighter colored flowers. Leader of this movement is Ted Bona with his Opera series. Notice also the development of more pinks through use of 'C. V. Covert.'

NOTE: The reader will quickly note the "look-alikes." In the whole list there are perhaps a dozen or fifteen real changes in form and flower. The rest are plants which repeat those of the previous year but are "selected" and renamed. Growers' catalogs are notably lacking in information about actual size of flower or some precise description of the differences. A series like that starting with the beautiful 'V. Covert' and continuing with other shrubby pinks is pretty obvious. The same applies to many of the oranges and reds. The main difference to watch for is not flower but culture. Pick the plants which are easiest to grow. The rest are for those who revel in problems.

Diastema

The diastemas are small herbs from Central and South American mountainous regions which accounts for the difficulties experienced with them by the average indoor grower. The temperature range is lower than the maximum levels achieved in summer in most homes. Difficulties start at 80° and the ideal range is 55° to 75° F. This accounts for the species not being especially popular in spite of reiterated recommendations on the score of ease of culture. Plants are lost in the heat of summer through rot, and that is also our own experience.

Many people do have the right conditions for these plants. An air-conditioned room with supplementary humidity or a cool cellar in the country is what it needs.

Diastema also has the handicap of being sensitive to pollution. We find it annoying when experts growing in the country assure us that such a plant presents no difficulties for a competent amateur. It turns out that they have greenhouses, live on the northwest coast, or have a country cellar. They should try to grow these same plants in a city apartment, as we do, and find out the difference. And a lot more people *are* growing that way these days. On the other hand, country growers do not achieve such continuous bloom in their greenhouses and often find certain plants a problem which are no trouble at all in our warm, stuffy city homes—with pollution.

We would also like to tuck in here an observation which should not be given too much prominence in a book on the "Miracle Family." We are describing a great many species, quite a number of which are not particularly attractive, because they are blood cousins of the real beauties. But the reader who specializes exclusively in gesneriads should realize that the tropics are full of little green plants with pretty flowers like those of *Diastema* and that there is really nothing very special about such plants except the fact that they are gesneriads. Even in Florida we could name at least a dozen plants with similar tubular flowers and coloration which might, if anybody were interested to try, make just as good or better houseplants. We like diastemas, but we also know that they belong to a genre of plant which is by no means uncommon in the warmer regions.

Diastemas are low, compact plants with attractive foliage and charming little flowers. Alas, they also have scaly rhizomes and go into dormancy, though this lasts a shorter time than for some of the other plants of this type.

There being considerable similarity between the species in cultivation, *Diastema quinquevulnerum,* which has been the most widely grown, may serve as model for the whole group.

Diastema quinquevulnerum, for the relatively small plant it is, has a very sturdy growth, with thickish central stem, well branched, up to 6 or 8 inches high. The leaves are opposite-alternate (decussate) clustering at the tips of the branches, 3 inches long and 2 wide, roughly oval with short stiff hairs. The edges are coarsely dentate, the points facing upward toward the tip and the deep paired veins creating strips of puckered quilting between.

Diastema quinquevulnerum. Photo L. H. Bailey Hortorium of Cornell University

The thickish short peduncles at the tips of the branches produce up to twelve flowers, each of which lasts only a couple of days. The pedicels are short. The tube of the corolla has a little round bulb which nestles into the cupped calyx whose pointed lobes do not clasp, but stand away from it.

Above the bulb the tube narrows slightly and is oval in shape for ½ to ¾ of an inch up to the lobes. Of these, two are nearly erect and three jut slightly forward. They are white with a splotch of violet on one or sometimes all. The throat of the flower is yellowish.

Here we can digress to note that the shape of the corolla flare and of the tube in cross section gives the flower its broad appearance seen from in front. The tube opening is an oval *on its side,* and that is the shape for most of its length. This broadening of the flower through a flattening of the tube is typical of some *Streptocarpus* and other gesneriads. The effect is to spread the two side lobes of the bottom three and make even quite small blooms appear a little more showy than a completely circular shape or a vertical constriction. Altogether it is likely that the exact shape of the tube of the gesneriads of this type has much to do with the angle of the lobes of the limb, forcing them into position.

Accustomed to a shady place in nature, *Diastema* will bloom with no more than 250 footcandles of light on a twelve-hour day. Give it Lean Mix with lime and do not pack tightly, nor is a tight-fitting pot advisable. Most scaly rhizomatous gesneriads like to roam.

We will note this root habit again in *Koellikeria* which is particularly resentful of tight potting. In fact, all the scaly rhizomatous gesneriads share the same peculiarity to a greater or lesser degree. This is understandable, since the storage organs, instead of being concentrated in one place as a single tuber, are numerous and grow attached to the finer roots. To accomplish this there must be space for each cluster to develop. It is also evident that, as the roots have the task both of supplying the plant with moisture and nutriment, when building supplementary storage vessels, they must draw on a greater area of soil.

We are not attempting a scientific explanation, but ours does suggest at least a possible reason why all these plants need rather large, though not necessarily deep, pots in relation to their aboveground size. The growth is not very deep but is spread sideways.

This is also a reason why they require particularly well drained and friable soil. The roots burrow outward, and there is no point in making the task more difficult.

For the same reasons, moisture should be even during the growing period and there should be no standing water. All the diastemas prefer humidity above 50 percent, which is an important fact in making them bloom. Fertilizing can be as for African violets—mild solutions with each watering or weekly.

Although the individual flowers do not last long, branching and blooming can continue for ten weeks or more, after which there is a letup, water is gradually withdrawn, and the foliage will die down to the ground. It is quite possible to leave rhizomes in the pot to be put aside in a coolish place (55°–60° if possible) until they sprout again. But this is not generally advisable. The accumulation of rhizomes during the season is such that, if they all start to sprout in the same pot, the space will be inadequate.

This is a further demonstration of the space habits of the plant. For, in nature, it obviously spreads out underground from a central point and, in doing so, by geometric law, the area covered increases very rapidly. As we grow the plants in normal pots, we rarely permit sufficient space even with the best intentions, and so the rhizomes tend to concentrate more in one place than they probably do in the plant's habitat.

Therefore, it is better to wash off the soil from the roots, remove the small rhizomes carefully, and store them dry in a plastic bag with some peat or vermiculite. Dormancy usually lasts three months but is irregular, so keep an eye on the situation and check every week after the first month.

Cuttings root with comparative ease, and seeds can be produced by hand pollination. However, the rhizomes are a sufficient source of new plants—and cuttings can be taken in an emergency.

Diastema vexans is a small plant growing no more than 4 inches high so that the short internodes, compressing the leaves, give the effect of a rosette. Leaves are a longish oval to 3 inches, with long petioles. The flowers grow in the leaf axils on upcurved pedicels ¾ inch long and tend to hide under the leaves. The flower tube is ½ inch long, and the lobes measure only ⅛ inch, each with a purplish spot near the throat.

Diastema maculatum, from Peru, has lavender corolla lobes and narrow toothed leaves, olive on the surface and reddish on the reverse. The tube is whitish yellow and each lobe is provided with a darker spot.

Diastema longiflorum is much like the others. Foliage has a doubly serrated edge and the two upper lobes of the corolla are pink with the lower ones white. The throat is yellow. As with *D. quinquevulnerum,* flowers arise from a terminal peduncle.

Diastema rupestris is a little trailing plant much like the others, with 1-inch leaves.

Diastema urticaefolium was described by Dr. Moore as a creeper with hairy leaves, 2½ inches long. The flowers are carried on peduncles at the tips of the stems and are ½ inch long, pale violet in color. The leaves are dotted with pale spots.

Didymocarpus

There are over one hundred species, native from the Himalayas to Malaya, and so similar to *Chirita* that they are not only often confused but the question arises whether they ought not to be one genus, as some botanists insist. The flowers are tubular, funnel-shaped, or campanulate, white, blue, and sometimes yellow. *D. podocarpus, vestitus,* and *aurantiacus* have been mentioned, but we have never seen them in cultivation.

Diastema maculatum. Photo L. H. Bailey Hortorium of Cornell University

Drymonia

Drymonia includes about thirty species of shrubs and vines from Central and South America. The first seeds were offered here in 1948. Although grown on and off by nurseries specializing in gesneriads, they have enjoyed no popularity with greenhouses or indoor growers because of their large size, usually less than brilliant coloring, the short-lived flowers, and difficulty of propagation. All these objections are legitimate, and the plant hardly meets a single one of our specifications for a good houseplant. We might well have passed up mention of this genus if it were not for one species with which we have had considerable experience and which we think may be a rewarding one for those who want a long-lived if rather large specimen.

We are among the very few, we suppose, who can claim a plant of *Drymonia stenophylla* at least five years old. We acquired it perhaps from Easterbrook nurseries as a rooted cutting. After being acclimated at home, it accompanied Jinny to her office where it lived for at least two years. It stood in a north window behind green tinted glass and under ceiling fluorescent light. The office was air conditioned but in winter over weekends the temperature could drop to 60° or lower. There it languished for quite a while and then in spring started to grow and produce additional canes from the base. Nipping made it branch low down, but after that the stems simply continued to grow slowly.

One day it decided to bloom, and we were disappointed to have the flower drop off at the end of a single day. But it turned out that new blooms appeared regularly in the leaf axils and even on wood at the nodes which had already lost their leaves. We have long lost count of the production per node. The surprising thing was that it never did stop blooming. Eventually it was brought home to an entirely different environment. No air conditioning, uncertain temperatures in winter, and intense heat at times in summer. It lives now on the edge of a chest of drawers close to a window, but receiving no direct sunlight at all, and continues to bloom and be a very beautiful plant. Now it is a good

93

Drymonia stenophylla.

2½ feet above the pot and arching with six long stems that must be attached to stakes. It receives a minimum of attention.

As we have pointed out, the great merit of the gesneriads is their ability to bloom constantly under artificial lights. With the exception of *Saintpaulia* and *Columnea*, they will not do so in a greenhouse. Only *Saintpaulia* will bloom continuously in a window, and then only if there are no long spells of cloudy weather. Nevertheless there is some factor in the genetic makeup of this family which causes the everblooming characteristic to crop up in the most unlikely places. Wherever the trait can be transferred through hybridizing, it confers on the cultivar a special distinction. For ability to bloom consistently is a greater factor in popularity than even the showiest of bloom which is seasonal. For this reason our *Drymonia* should be better known, and some attempt made to produce plants with more persistent flowers and a more compact growth.

Drymonia stenophylla has brown woody canes up to 3 feet long that bear unequal opposite leaves. The longer ones are up to 6 inches by 1½ inches. The shorter ones are 1½ inches long. They are long tapered ovals with red petioles and midveins. The flowers grow in the axils on very short shiny reddish pedicels, and the calyx, about ½ inch long with broad lobes, is shiny reddish. The flower is 1½ inches long, clear yellow in color with a rather thick round tube curving down and then up to the limb. The lobes of the limb are broad and spreading, the lower one fringed and tending to turn upward and close the throat of the tube. As the flower ages it becomes slightly flushed with red. It lasts only a day but new ones are produced from the axils over a very long period. New flowers are produced every day somewhere on the plant.

The habit means that when the plant is small, the production of flowers is not as constant nor as plentiful as when it is taller and has many nodes. It is therefore one of those rare plants which can be maintained for a long time and actually improves in appearance as it grows to a 2- or 3-foot size, although it may need support. The long, shiny leaves, leathery in texture, face one way and overlap. Even as a foliage plant it is

Close-up of Drymonia stenophylla.

superior to many others. Certainly not ideal for the normal light garden, it is a fine window plant. Incidentally, it has at no time attracted insects.

Drymonia spectabilis is still in cultivation. It is reputed to be a vine but is actually rather sturdy stemmed and produces growths from the base. In its branching it is somewhat similar to *D. stenophylla.*

Stems are green, turning tan with age. Leaves are 5 inches long by 2 inches, pointed at either end with short but sharp toothing. The reverse is flushed with red. The flower is remarkable for the leafy calyx which may be 2 inches long, very leafy and toothed. The corolla is 2½ inches long, white striped with soft bands of red and with a fringed lower lip.

Drymonia turrialvae is from Panama and Costa Rica. The stems are squarish, reddish, turning brown. Difficulty of propagation in all three drymonias seems to be due to the very pulpy-woody texture of the stems. Only the very new growth seems to root a little better. This is also the reason, no doubt, why even when rooted the cuttings take so long to get going and are meanwhile subject to fungal disease.

The big broad oval pointed leaves make one think of a *Nautilocalyx* or the bronze form of *Chrysothemis* more than of the other drymonias. They are up to 12 inches long and 8 inches wide, bright shiny green, scalloped along the edges. The veinings are depressed and strongly marked in darker green. The reverse is pale green with reddish veins.

The calyx is deep purple with sepals ¾ inch long and leafy. The 2½-inch flower is waxy white, similar to *stenophylla* in shape, becoming pink-tinged with age. The flowers grow in clusters on a red peduncle.

In cultivation the plant can be tip pruned to maintain more compact growth, and leaves do not grow larger than 6 or 8 inches as long as the plant is kept rather potbound.

Three other drymonias are worth mentioning:

D. macrophylla also has very large calyx lobes, leafy and toothed. Flowers are yellow. The plant grows to 6 feet!

D. mollis is described as an epiphytic vine with yellow flowers.

Our lengthy description of *D. stenophylla* suggests the type of plant represented by more recent introductions, some of which bid fair to attract more attention with time. See "Gesneriad Update" under *Drymonia*.

Episcia

Episcia is a small genus of about ten species ranging from southern Mexico to Brazil. It is principally remarkable for the varied beauty of its foliage and the brilliance of its small flowers which, in the principal two species, are abundantly produced.

All those which have been widely cultivated are creeping, trailing plants with soft textured leaves and are different from other genera in producing great numbers of stolons. These are long flexible stems without nodes, which bear at their tips a whorl of leaves. The *Episcia* is a shallow-rooted plant which, by means of the stolons, extends its territory, the leaf clusters of the stolons rooting readily wherever they come into contact with soil. The stolons of the strawberry geranium (*Saxifraga stolonifera*) operate in the same manner and have the same purpose. Those of *Episcia,* however, are thicker and can grow to a foot or more in length.

There have been a number of species classified as episcias which do not possess stolons. Their status came into question, and these plants have recently been reassigned. Although the matter is of interest to only a few academicians and may or may not stand up with time, it will be necessary to list the changes as follows:

Episcia melittifolia becomes *Nautilocalyx melittifolius.*
Episcia ciliosa becomes *Paradrymonia ciliosa.*
Episcia decurrens becomes *Paradrymonia decurrens.*
Episcia lineata becomes *Paradrymonia lineata.*
Episcia lurida becomes *Paradrymonia lurida.*
Paradrymonia is a new genus invented for the occasion.

Episcias have achieved widespread popularity among both greenhouse and indoor growing hobbyists. Magnificent leaves in a great range of colors and textures complement the glowing colors of the flowers. The trailing growth is at present no great handicap because of the popularity of foliage basket plants. Interest in other gesneriad trailers must depend on the flowers, and only *Columnea* meets this test. No doubt if some means could be found to achieve a more upright growth in episcias, so that they would be easier to manage in pots, the commercial development would increase greatly. Nevertheless, it cannot be said that these plants are lagging seriously in public esteem for we see them constantly gaining new converts.

There are at present partial solutions to the problem created by the trailing habit. In some cultivars the stolons can be removed, and the stems strengthened or supported. We discuss this under the headings of E. 'Moss Agate' and 'Cygnet.' The same method can be applied to some of the other cultivars.

The two principal *Episcia* species are *E. reptans* and *E. cupreata.* Their variations and the hybrids between the two are responsible for the vast majority of plants grown by amateurs today. This is only possible because we are dealing here with two highly variable species which seem capable of continuous modification. Yet they are very much alike and, due to hybridization and selection, few growers have seen typical plants of the species. Nor are we quite certain that there is a typical form. However, botanists have specified their differences, and we list these on the following comparative table.

Note: *E. dianthiflora,* 'Cygnet,' and *punctata* transferred to *Alsobia.* See "Gesneriad Update," page 215.

EPISCIA REPTANS   *EPISCIA CUPREATA*

Hairy plant with short central stem, numerous
red or green stolons.

LEAVES

2–5 inches long.

1½–2½ inches wide   1–3 inches wide

Broadly elliptic   var. *cupreata*

Deep or bronze green with pale green or   Deep copper or bronze green, often varie-
silvery variegation along the midrib and   gated with silver or bright green, strongly
lateral veins.   embossed and covered with erect, darkish
                                                 hairs. Reddish, with erect hairs below.

                                                 var. *viridifolia*

                                                 Clear green, sometimes variegated with
                                                 pale green or silver. Slight embossing with
                                                 short whitish hairs. Translucent green
                                                 with sparse hairs below.

FLOWERS

From very short peduncles.   Calyx green inside, sometimes flushed red
                                                 outside. Narrow, hairy, not toothed (en-
3–4 together on pedicels   tire) pointed lobes about ⅜ inch.
¾ to 1 inch

Calyx dark green inside, flushed red out-
side. Oblong hairy lobes about ½ inch.   Corolla. Hairy, tube about 1 inch long.
More or less spread and more or less con-   Gradually widened and angled upward
spicuously toothed.   with a rather prominent swelling below
                                                 the throat.
Corolla. Hairy tube about 1½ inches long,
gradually, only slightly, widened toward
the throat.

Outside of tube pale rose red. Inside   Outside of tube reddish above, yellowish
blood red, densely covered with translu-   with red markings below. Inside yellow
cent papillae at throat, giving the appear-   with red spots and densely covered with
ance of a white "eye."   translucent papillae giving appearance of
                                                 a white "eye."
Lobes. ⅜–½ inch rounded, spreading,
toothed. More equal than *cupreata*. Pale
red outside. Blood red inside.   Lobes. Orange red. Upper ⅛–⅜ inch long
                                                 and broad, bent backward. Three lower
3–4 together on pedicels   lobes longer and more or less at right an-
¾ to 1¾ inches   gles to the tube.

Innumerable crosses have been made between *E. reptans* and *E. cupreata* and between *E. cupreata var. cupreata* and *var. viridifolia.* The resultant plants vary in a number of ways. For instance floriferousness is very great on a few and very difficult to come by on others. Considering the attractiveness of the flowers, it does not appear to us that the foliage types will remain long in cultivation. They are still around mainly because amateurs, in purchasing from the catalogs, are unaware of the difficulty of securing bloom on these plants, and it takes a while before the information gets around. They will never be a factor in the mass market.

Generally speaking the orange, red, tomato flowers of *Episcia* cultivars are so brilliant that, if reasonably floriferous, size makes little difference. The contrast with the leaves is startling, and a very few light up the whole plant. The pinks are often larger in size but less noticeable. The yellow in 'Tropical Topaz,' an interesting sport, is rather dull.

The leaves resulting from the crosses are mostly of two kinds. The one, represented by 'Colombian Orange,' is velvety-downy and bright Kelly green—a most unusual texture and color. In improved cultivars, there is a silver midrib. The second type is less hairy, usually, and heavily patterned. This is the result of the spaces between subsidiary veins of the leaf, which form an overall network between the oblique veins and the midvein, being depressed, causing the leaf to have a quilted appearance. These domed areas are often of a different color from the surface of the veins themselves. The major forms are those with brown quiltings and green or silvery green veining, the darker or lighter color occupying different amounts of area and forming different patterns on the leaf.

Other variations of this form are more or less overall brown with pinkish veining or bright green with silver or whitish veining. These are all combined in different ways in certain complex cultivars and result in quite fascinating and altogether unusual designs.

It is difficult to judge the actual appearance of a plant from color photographs in catalogs and magazines. Juvenile plants often look quite different from adults. We have occasionally been tempted into buying a plant with striking markings only to find out later, after it had grown a bit, that the colors graded off and became disappointingly uninteresting. Accidents of culture also have a good deal to do with these rather sensitive tints and textures. Under different conditions leaves are larger or smaller, more or less richly colored, or display a different texture. In addition cultivars are often issued without sufficient stabilization and soon revert to a common type. Those which require great care in cultivation to show their finest hues will be rather disillusioning for an average grower. For that reason we recommend sticking to well-established, thoroughly tested plants.

CULTURE

FERTILIZATION.   The pollen ripens in 75 to 80 percent humidity and minimum 65° F.

SEEDING.   See general cultural section. Seed germinates in about three weeks.

VEGETATIVE PROPAGATION.   Tips of stolons root easily in moist medium at about 75° F with 70 percent humidity. This is the best way for indoor growers to multiply their plants. Treat like ordinary stem cuttings. Leaves will also root but the process is slower. The procedure is the same as for African violet leaves.

SOIL.   Lean Mix with lime or live or long-fiber sphagnum moss. Use a top dressing of sphagnum moss or perlite to protect the leaves. Soil should be quite loose in the pot.

TEMPERATURE.   It is an interesting fact we must never lose sight of that our warnings about low temperatures should always be mated with equal calls to caution above 80° F. On both ends of the thermometer, keeping the plants relatively dry is the preventive for the same trouble—stem rot. The difference is that below 60°–65° dryness may not always cure, while above 80° episcias become quite tolerant as long as the soil is not soggy. There is no contradiction between this and the rule that gesneriads usually like even moisture. A very porous soil will accomplish this objective automatically. 'Cygnet,' 'Frosty,' *E. punctata, E. dianthiflora,* 'Star of Bethlehem,' 'Chocolate Soldier,' and 'Cameo' are among those which stand up well in heat. *E. lilacina* requires high temperatures and humidity at all times in order to bloom.

HUMIDITY. Episcias benefit very much from high humidity and suffer from a lack of it more than most other gesneriads which do not require terrarium conditions. Fifty percent as an average is required for most of them, and higher levels are better. High humidity never killed an *Episcia.*

They respond very well to misting and foliar feeding.

LIGHT. There have been very misleading indications from experts that episcias require even less light than African violets. If we grew them only for their leaves, this might be true but, since we want flowers, considerably more light is needed. The confusion results from a difference between indoor and greenhouse growing. Commercial growers sell their episcias as leafy-rooted cuttings, usually without flowers, and these are grown at bench level shielded from intense light. However, you will notice that the baskets of blooming episcias are grown high and close to the panes, not so much for hanging room—for they can be set much lower—but to receive maximum light and humidity.

The majority of episcias require 500 to 800 footcandles for good flowering under fluorescent lights. We keep them within 6 inches of the lamps and find that dropping them further stops bloom. With very high humidity, these figures might be shaded a bit.

FERTILIZER. Episcias have a big appetite—partly a product of their small roots being obliged to support a big plant. So, either fertilize lightly with every watering or once a week with a stronger solution. We use high phosphate formula alternating with fish emulsion which is weakly acid. This regimen seems to suit them particularly well.

POTTING. Shallow pots are better than deep ones. The roots like to spread through a very light medium close to the surface. Keep them there by allowing plenty of room to spread. Episcias don't like pot binding.

TRAINING. A problem with episcias is dealing with their long, prostrate branches that are thicker than those of columneas and do not hang down nearly as far, but are difficult to confine to a pot. In addition, there are the stolons that, however useful to the plant as a means of propagation, are unsightly. In the early days of *Episcia* culture, hobbyists produced enormous specimen baskets by planting them with a number of rooted cuttings, trimming branches so that they just hung over the edges, and removing stolons wherever they were visible. In the long run this proved too specialized for most indoor growers who had neither space to hang such giants nor the time for meticulous training.

Gradually, through selection and hybridization, the more compact plants of today were developed. They are better suited to pot culture and the new miniatures eliminate the difficulties almost completely.

To cope with the needs of the larger-leaved plants, amateurs more and more use containers only a maximum of 3 inches in depth and of various diameters. They are quite adequate because of *Episcia*'s shallow roots. Also, the shallow containers are easier to cover with a plastic dome when terrarium culture is advisable.

Plant one or more rooted cuttings in the center of the container and, as stolons develop, pin them down around the mother planting. In due time the whole of the surface will be evenly covered with leaves. Rooted and freshly grown stolons are cut as well as the tips of branches that have invaded too much territory. In this way you can grow a fine specimen plant under fluorescent tubes. When the original planting ages, it is relatively easy to replant by removing the older parts and rearranging.

OTHER SPECIES

In 1979, H. Wiehler proposed the establishment of the genus *Alsobia* to accommodate two *Episcia* species, namely, *E. dianthiflora* and *E. punctata,* principally on the
basis that *Episcia* produces two stolons per node, whereas *Alsobia* produces "1 stolon
per node in alternating leaf axils." This change, like those of Dr. Moore and Dr. Skog,
is likely to hold up better than some others. Even to an amateur, *E. dianthiflora,* which
was the better known species, must seem very different from other episcias, in leaf, in
habit, and in the form and patterning of the flowers.

E. *fimbriata* seed was available for a short time here but has apparently disappeared
from cultivation. The plant is a native of Peru and has white flowers resembling
E. dianthiflora. However, the leaves are described as small, narrow, and pointed with a
narrow silver tree pattern in the center.

E. *lilacina* is probably given a lengthier description than is warranted by the number
of amateurs growing, but that is simply because we admire it greatly. The lavender blue
flowers are the largest and handsomest of the episcias and resemble some of the African
Streptocarpus more than the New World *Achimenes* or *Sinningia.* It is deplorable that it
should be so difficult to bloom indoors and has a very short season. In compensation, we
feel that the foliage too is the finest of all. For that alone (in spite of our bias for flowering
plants), we consider it well worth growing.

This is a species from Central America which varies somewhat in flower color and a
great deal in leaf pattern and color. There is a variation which has dark green leaves. But
the real beauty is one which somehow picked up the name 'Mrs. Fanny Haage' during its
introductory period. Some of the other variations also have been named, but only this one
has been widely grown.

The habit of this plant—weak stem, oval leaves, numerous rhizomes and flowers
arising in the axils on short pedicels—is no different except in minor details from
E. cupreata and *E. reptans.* Only the flower and the rich patterning and texture of the leaf
distinguish it.

The leaf shape is typical for *Episcia,* about 4 inches long by 2½ inches wide. It has
the appearance of being very thick. A broad area along with the midrib is a strangely
beautiful glowing silvery light green which also extends into the finer six to eight pairs of
side veins. The border is a green so dark as to seem nearly black and so puckered and
apparently hairy as to have the aspect of toweling.

It is most revealing to examine the leaf under moderate magnification. Then we see
that the lighter area is indeed green with very superficial small irregular areas of pure
silver which are very reflective and covered with very slightly raised pores, each with a
fine white hair. When we move our lens into the darker section, we notice that it is a
pattern of plateaus, each with several prominent nipples close together rising from it and
with the finer veinings between. Each nipple has just one hair, and the toweling effect is
not produced, as we might have imagined, by the hairs, but by the massive character of
the irregular nipples.

It is only along the finely toothed edge that the short white hairs increase greatly in
number. The whole leaf is domed—that is to say, the edges are turned downward so that,
upside down, the leaf forms a shallow boat. The texture is seen to be extremely thin but
the combination of nipples and shape produce the seeming thickness. The reverse is
veined and suffused with burgundy red. It should not be overlooked that nature often
comes up with very subtle effects. The upper surface owes its peculiar richness in no small
degree to the glow of red from below.

We have seen *E. lilacina* growing in greenhouses in very high humidity and blooming in late spring. We have also bloomed it under lights in November-December. In the greenhouse it sprawled in an untidy manner, and we suspect that it is even more difficult to develop as a neat basket plant. A number of attempts to grow it in the house produced fine foliage for a while, but the stem was very weak and, sooner or later, we had to cut off a large part of the main growth which left us with a rather unsightly mess. So we concentrated on developing fine small plants with healthy foliage. We used both Rich and Lean Mix without any notable success.

Finally we tried the plant in live sphagnum moss and kept it moist, in 50 percent or better humidity and temperature of 70° or higher. This time the stem was thicker, the leaves grew more luxuriantly. Because of the sturdy stem and relatively short internodes, we were able to stake the plant. In this state it looked very handsome and soon put out buds and its magnificent flowers which lasted only two or three days each. The display lasted for two months and then stopped. Our light cycle was a fourteen-hour day, and the location was to the side of the main bank of lights where it received about 500 footcandles, at the top of the plant.

Several flowers grow from each axil, one at a time, on pedicels about an inch long. The calyx is greenish with hairy lobes. The tube of the flower is slender, over an inch long and white. The upper lobes are angled backward and the lower ones forward on a flat plane. The total width is 1½ inches. The color is an enchanting soft lavender blue with a touch of pale yellow around the throat. The back of the limb is white.

Professor Moore gave the name *E.* 'xWilsonii' to crosses between *E. cupreata* and *E. lilacina.* The resulting flowers have not retained the large and unusually shaped flowers of *E. lilacina.* All that has been accomplished is a thicker texture in the leaf. *E.* 'Pinkiscia' is credited with being intermediate between the parents, but those plants we have seen in cultivation are nothing of the sort. The *cupreata* influence is certainly dominant. As for *E.* 'Ember Lace,' the rather ugly pink variegation of the leaves seems to owe nothing to either parent. The medium-sized flowers, however, are pink. It is hard to believe that this unattractive mongrel is rather popular. Apparently, any kind of variegation will do.

E. melittifolia. This plant has been transferred to *Nautilocalyx.*

E. punctata. The species was first collected in Guatemala in 1840 but, in spite of large white flowers, has never become popular. This has been transferred to *Alsobia.* It is a parent of *A.* 'Cygnet.'

The thick main stem is 6 inches high with numerous stolons. The fleshy toothed green leaves are 3 inches long and margined with a flush of red. Flowers on short pedicels grow in the leaf axils. The tube of the corolla is an inch long, yellowish white with purple spots. Corolla lobes are up to ⅜ inch long, heavily spotted with purple, toothed, and irregularly fringed.

EPISCIA LOOK-ALIKES AND CULTIVARS

An effect of the great popularity of gesneriads with hobbyists and the general public is an enormous increase in the number of cultivars within a short time. The variability of some genera is the major contributor. Nurserymen find, when they grow large numbers of saintpaulias, episcias, columneas, streptocarpus, etc., that often, in spite of vegetative propagation, a sport occasionally turns up. The greater the number of plants grown, the greater the likelihood. In addition, fertile hybrids are regularly crossed by amateurs and nurserymen.

Faced with the constant thirst for novelty from hobbyists, who are by no means satisfied to keep on growing plants of proved merit, nurserymen have been virtually forced to issue new lists every year. This is most striking in *Saintpaulia* and but little less in the others. In his register of *Episcia,* published in 1968, a compilation of names accumulated between 1963 and 1966, Paul Arnold included 50 percent more names, not counting rejected names which were even more numerous.

The result of all this activity has been a very few really interesting changes and a great number of look-alikes.

It is true that if you put two look-alikes side by side there is usually some difference between them. But if they are separated—sold for instance in different nurseries—they become simply different labels. Furthermore the rate of reversion to type is quite common. A "new" plant simply reverts to an old plant when subjected to a different cultural regimen or environment. Thus the public is faced with hundreds of names which have little real meaning, and buying a plant becomes strictly buying a pig in a poke.

The other problem which runs through this whole matter of gesneriad listing is that the quality of the plant and its size and ease or difficulty of culture are almost never touched upon. Orchid dealers are guilty of the same fault, and their catalogs tell you the color of the flower and nothing else.

There is a further consequence involved in the confusion of names. What if a very fine cultivar is produced which, for reasons of lack of promotion, immediate availability, or being superseded by another label, simply disappears after a single catalog listing? We are inclined to think that this often happens. Such a plant does not undergo a thorough test and, therefore, nobody ever finds out whether it is a really superior plant or not.

In November 1973 *The Gloxinian* published a short list of look-alikes made by Jane Crandall. We reproduce it here as it illustrates what we have discussed above. But it is only the tip of the iceberg. In all fairness we must add that the same situation prevails in other families.

THE LOOK-ALIKES

Cultivar of Episcia	Year Introduced	Hybridizer	Parentage	Description (Dealer)
E. 'Yoer's Beauty'	1965	Unknown	Unknown	Bright green leaf, chocolate edge, red flower.
E. 'Daisy'	1967	Unknown	Unknown	Dark pebbled edge, silver leaf, red flower.
E. 'Topsy'	1968	Easterbrook	Unknown	Slender, silver leaf, chocolate edge, red flower.
E. 'Green Haga'	1958	Unknown	Unknown	Several shades of green leaf, pink flower.
E. 'Golden Embers'	1964	Easterbrook	Unknown	Two-toned green gold leaf, pink flower.
E. 'Red Corduroy'	1957	Unknown	Unknown	Greenish bronze leaf, green midrib veins, red flower.
E. 'Green Corduroy'	1961	Unknown	Unknown	Quilted leaf, silver veins and netting, red flowers.
E. 'Moss Agate'	1955	Unknown	Unknown	Bright green leaf, silver laced, red flowers.
E. 'Shades O' Erin'	1966	Easterbrook	Unknown	Bright green leaf, silver lace pattern, red flower.
E. 'Canal Zone'	1955	Unknown	Unknown	Smooth green leaf, chocolate margin, red flower.
E. 'Jade'	1963	Mari Figgee	Unknown	Green foliage, touches of darker color, red flower.
E. 'Painted Warrior'	1939	Hazel Harmon	'Canal Zone Hybrid'	Silver leaf flushed pink, dark green edge, orange-red flower.
E. 'Purple Glory'	1961	Unknown	'Ember Lace' × 'Silver Sheen'	Silver center, dark green edge, purple red overlay, red flower, yellow throat.
E. 'Tinted Silver'	1971	Betty Stoehr	'Antique Velvet' × 'Cleopatra'	Silver shading to rose, pebbled edge, red flower.
E. 'Ebony'	1963	Mike Kartuz	Unknown	Glossy, dark brown leaf, orange red flower.
E. 'Laquer Lady'	1965	Unknown	Unknown	Glossy, lacquered effect dark leaf, red flower.
E. 'Adam's Rib'	1966	Easterbrook	Unknown	Olive green leaf, green midrib, red flower.
E. 'Chocolate Shine'	1970	White/Hazel Harmon	Unknown	Blackest leaf, reddest flower.

E. 'Olive Lawson'	1970	Olive Lawson	Same 'Canal Zone Hybrid' seed that gave 'Painted Warrior'	Silvery green leaf, pink blush on leaves.
E. 'Rosewood'	1972	Grace Arndt		Shiny leaf, rose colored, brown edge, red flower.
E. 'Cameo'	1964	Mike Kartuz	A variety of 'Pink Acajou' selfed	Metallic rose-red leaf, dark green edge, orange red flower.
E. 'Ruby'	1964	Mike Kartuz	Sister seedling of 'Cameo'-different color	Deep rose red leaf, dark green edge, red flower.
E. 'Velvet Brocade'	1965	Mike Kartuz	Sister seedling-'Cameo' more intense color	Deep rose pink leaf, dark green edge, red flower.
E. 'Cleopatra'	1964	L. Easterbrook	Sport of 'Frosty'	Pink leaf, green oak leaf design, white halo, red flower.
E. 'Pink Brocade'	1965	Ann Buymak	Seedling-'Sun Gold'	Pink, green white foliage, red flower.

EPISCIA CULTIVARS

The following list is necessarily a very selective one and not altogether on the basis of our own judgment of merit since we have not been able to grow all of the episcia cultivars ourselves. We have included old favorites as well as a few recent introductions which may prove of value.

E. 'Acajou.' An early cultivar which must be very close to the wild brown *cupreata* species. The 4-inch leaves have a broad leaf pattern of silvery green over a dark tan border. The modest-sized flowers are red orange. A number of other named cultivars are merely slight variations on 'Acajou' and almost indistinguishable from it.

'Acajou' continues to be a popular plant because it is everblooming, of easy culture, and attractive. Although a few of the look-alikes have more brilliant or larger leaves and flowers, the difference is not that great, and there seems to be no improvement in floriferousness. This is an excellent plant for the beginner, and its smaller size is an advantage under lights. It is really a toss-up between 'Acajou' and the very different 'Moss Agate' for the honors of being the "easy" *Episcia*.

E. 'Annette.' One of the early miniatures with small, pink, silvery leaves and bronze bordering. Red flowers. A Kartuz cultivar best grown in a terrarium. This is listed here to fill in for *E.* 'Amazon White,' which no longer appears to be in cultivation.

E. 'Antique Velvet.' "Silver pebbled leaves, raised dark edges, red flowers."

E. 'Cameo.' Popular Kartuz cultivar from 1964. Glossy leaves, rich metallic rose, edged dark green. Compact but many stolons. Bright orange red flowers.

E. 'Chocolate Soldier.' A very early introduction by R. G. Wilson and a *cupreata* variation. Large dark chocolate-colored leaves with silver midrib. *Cupreata* red flowers. It has retained its early popularity and is everblooming.

E. 'Cleopatra' and 'Pink Brocade.' There are no other gesneriads in cultivation quite like *E.* 'Cleopatra' and 'Pink Brocade.' We suspect that 'Pink Brocade' is the same plant although we have noticed that it has a tendency to revert. In any event we're 'Cleopatra' rooters. According to Mr. L. Easterbrook it turned up in his greenhouse in 1962 as a sport of *E.* 'Frosty.' Variegation, due to cellular structures without chlorophyll, has not turned up frequently in the gesneriads as they have in some other families. *E.* 'Cleopatra' makes up for this omission by making such a spectacular show with its foliage that the bright red flowers look strangely mismatched.

The leaves are typically quilted and turned down at the edge. They show a broad, leafy pattern of light green all the way up the midrib, surrounded by a "halo" of white. The spaces between veins from there to the edge of the leaf are a soft true pink in color and irregularly quilted. The leaves are only sparsely hairy and when well grown have a very crisp appearance.

How this kind of extreme variegation can come about may be of interest to some readers. Although the chromosomes carry the principal hereditary signals, plastids are structures outside the nucleus which also play a part in inheritance. They too are divided along with the cell. Usually the carry-over of protoplastids is in the cytoplasm of the egg, and color variants are due to changes within the plastid itself which can be inherited solely through the maternal side. Chloroplasts sometimes mutate so that the capacity to develop pigment is suppressed or is achieved only in the presence of a certain maternal or paternal genome. An egg cell may contain therefore plastids, some capable of developing chlorophyll and some not. Cells then occur which contain wholly pigmented plastids while others contain only the unpigmented sort. Variegated forms arise in this manner and also from viral infection. The odd light veinings in some episcias may indicate that the plants have the tendency which, in an extreme form, produces an *E.* 'Cleopatra.' Whew.

'Cleopatra' would need no further discussion if it were not that it is somewhat more difficult to grow than some other episcias yet so desirable that many people want to try it. Also, being a slow grower, it remains an expensive plant and not one you want to lose once you have it in your possession.

We have had no difficulty managing it in our plant room where a humidity of 50 percent or better and a temperature of 65° or higher is maintained. The plant is sensitive to anything over 85° but will tolerate 55° for a short period if kept fairly dry. Water sparingly at all times. As it is slow growing, it is not advisable to soak the plant. Keep it just moist. In fact, like most other episcias it will tolerate some drying out. Lean Mix should be lightly packed to give it maximum aeration and it prefers a 4-inch pot for a single stem to allow plenty of root space. Fertilize with balanced solutions along with your other plants.

The light requirements are slightly higher than most other episcias and we rate it as

Episcia 'Cleopatra.'

750–800 fc. and a position 4 inches under a 50-inch two-tube fixture.

For those who cannot provide high room humidity, the only solution is a terrarium. Most people grow the plants in medium-sized plastic ones. Keep the temperature between 65° and 75°. Long-fiber sphagnum moss can be used as an alternative medium.

'Cleopatra' produces stolons like other episcias, and these can be fixed with hairpins into the medium surrounding the plant. Leaf cuttings take best in moist long-fiber sphagnum moss at about 80°.

E. 'Colombia Orange.' This attractive plant belongs to the green-leaved *cupreata* type. It is distinguished by small, smoothly plush, Kelly green leaves, bright orange flowers of moderate size and a very trailing habit with many stolons. It is one of the easier cultivars to grow and bloom. We think it is best treated as a small pot plant, the stolons removed, and tips of branches nipped, to form a mound of greenery with some overhang.

E. 'Ember Lace.' This is another of the variegated sports (like 'Cleopatra') which appeared among seedlings of a cross made between *E. lilacina* cv. 'Cuprea' and *E. cupreata* at F. M. Haga & Son in 1955. The medium-sized brown leaves are irregularly blotched with areas of white and pink. It is a shy bloomer but has been popular because of its rather chaotic coloration. Prolific in the production of stolons, it is not a neat plant, but a rather easy one to maintain. The flowers are pink.

E. 'Fire n' Ice.' Kartuz plant with "Icy silver leaves bordered light green with contrasting red flowers."

E. 'Green Haga.' Originally from F. M. Haga & Son. Leaves are a mixture of greens. Pink flowers. 'Pink Haga' has brown leaves and pink flowers.

E. 'Jinny Elbert.' Not registered and noncommercial but, taking an author's privilege, just about the best clone of a brown-leaved *Episcia* we've ever come across. Few stolons, compact habit, and endless red flowers displayed in clusters *above* the leaves. Performs superbly under fluorescent light, blooming when it has only a few leaves.

E. 'Jade.' Jade green foliage with pink veins. Orange flowers.

E. 'Moss Agate.' This is, along with *E.* 'Jinny Elbert,' 'Acajou,' and 'Cygnet,' the best of the episcias for growing indoors, especially under lights. It differs from the other three in being very large leaved and enormously vigorous. But, because of its thick stem, it can be trimmed of stolons and supported with a stake, thereby becoming a very beautiful pot plant.

The leaves are a rich green and up to 5 inches long. The texture is thick, and the whole surface is a remarkable network of quiltings with silver veining. The flowers are orange red, fringed, and a good inch or more across. Of the "easy" episcias, this is certainly the handsomest all-around plant.

E. 'Noel.' Bright green leaves, red flowers.

E. 'Painted Warrior.' Kartuz. Zone of metallic pink between the silver center and the dark green border. Orange red flowers.

E. 'Pinkiscia.' Another *cupreata-lilacina* cross with pink flowers. The medium-sized leaves are a deep bronzy green. We have grown 'Pinkiscia' but still can't account for its popularity, which is considerable.

E. 'Red Flair.' Peterson. Rich green leaves overlaid with lacy veining. Red flowers.

E. 'Shimmer.' Large-leaved *E. reptans* variation with velvety texture and silver in center with chocolate margin. Red flower. A very handsome foliage plant and a good bloomer.

E. 'Silver Sheen.' Similar to 'Shimmer' but less silvery. Also an excellent performer.

E. 'Star of Bethlehem.' A pink star on yellow background makes this the only bicolor flower to date. The plant has continued to be very popular but many find it difficult to bloom. Compact.

 E. 'Sun Gold.' Coppery green leaves, creamy yellow flowers, and deep yellow eye. An improvement over 'Tropical Topaz.'

 E. 'Tri-Color.' Leaves white, light green, and dark green brown pattern. Orange flowers.

 E. 'Tropical Topaz.' A sport which was the first of the yellows. Light green leaves and small flowers. Blooms with difficulty indoors.

SURVIVORS AND NEW CULTIVARS

 Episcias maintain their popularity with hobbyists for the combination of richly patinaed leaves and glowing flowers is irresistible. In achieving greater public recognition they have been handicapped by an inability to stay in prime shape for long in flower shops and garden centers. They deteriorate rapidly when exposed to dry air, underwatering and low light. Too many have also been basket plants, requiring several cuttings to a container and perfect condition of all to make a fine show.

 The new hybrids have been innumerable but with many look-alikes. Normally they seem to be very different leaves in a juvenile state. But, as they mature, their resemblance to related hybrids increases and hobbyists report having difficulty telling some plants apart, even when grown in their own collections.

 Nevertheless, there has been progress. The uniquely beautiful *E. lilacina,* which has many variations, has been selected and hybridized for sturdier growth and deeper blue-colored flowers. And, in the latest crop, we are seeing a whole line of new minis: plants with much smaller leaves, shorter or no stolons, and full size flowers.

Episcia 'Jinny Elbert.'

PLANTS WITH BLUE FLOWERS

'Blue Nile.' Velvety, blue-green and bronze-green leaves. Flowers blue, fringed.

E. hirsuta. Emerald-green leaves with silver midrib. Light blue flowers. Does not trail.

E. hirsuta 'Bronze.' Dark bronze leaf variety of above. Long, light blue flowers.

E. lilacina 'Selby's Best.' Downy, soft green leaves. Eggshell-blue flowers.

E. lilacina 'Shaw Gardens.' Large, lavender-blue flowers.

COMPACT PLANTS

'Annette' (Kartuz). Silvery-pink leaves, bronze edged. Red flowers.

'Longwood Gardens.' Almost black leaves. Red flowers. Compact.

'Moss Brocade.' Large red flowers. Leaves bronze and silver.

'Rose Gold Mist.' Light red flowers. Velvety copper leaves with gold veining.

'Ruby Red Dress.' Silver leaves with pink veins. Flowers light red.

'Schizophrenia' (Freiling). Broad, short, silver-veined leaves. Orange flowers.

'Singing Sands.' Miniature with ''bright mosaic leaves.''

'Sun Gold.' Dark coppery foliage. Large creamy yellow flowers.

'Toy Silver.' Silvery-green leaves, red flowers.

For other newer hybrids, see ''Gesneriad Update,'' page 215.

Gesneria

Gesnerias seem only to have waited until Professor Moore finished his book before invading the United States in force. This happened because Dr. Thomas E. Talpey—also responsible for the great hybrid, *S.* 'Cindy'—happened to be living in Puerto Rico at the time. He started to explore for the genus on the island, sending plants and seeds to hobbyists in the continental U.S. and describing them in *The Gloxinian.* Puerto Rico is particularly rich in members of the genus which is indigenous to the West Indies. His initiative led to a search for plants on other islands, so that we now know of a considerable number and some of these are being grown by amateurs.

The genus *Gesneria* was described originally by Linnaeus, consisting of about thirty-five species. A very few species may also grow on mainland Central America. There are both herbaceous plants and small and large shrubs.

One of the primary reasons for our interest in writing this book was our affection for *G. cuneifolia.* But we do acknowledge that it is a bit ahead of its time. Its fame, no doubt, is sufficient to guarantee a considerable demand if it were not so difficult to acquire the plants. This is because there are problems in both growing and shipping which have made commercial growers shy of attempting to raise *G. cuneifolia* in quantity. We believe that improved methods of packing and shipping will soon be available, and we have no doubt *G. cuneifolia* will then be tops in popularity for light gardens and terrariums. It needs a minimum of attention once established and will last for several years. No other plant, including the African violet, is so positively everblooming.

A good many of the plants described by Dr. Talpey and others are of little interest to anyone but a specialist. The only one we *can* recommend unreservedly is *G. cuneifolia.* On the other hand, some of the others are so exquisite that we are hopeful that further experience will teach us how to grow them successfully. The best are naturally small and suited to light gardening and terrarium culture.

Gesneria cuneifolia is a variable species growing in Cuba, Puerto Rico, and other West Indian islands. It is, at the start at least, a ground-hugging rosette plant with dark green shiny leaves, spatulate (spoon-shaped), dentate, veiny, and growing eventually to 6 inches in length. Hairy green thin pedicels grow from the axils, the calyx is small and green, and the flower a 1-inch narrow red or orange red tube with very shallow lobes.

The form, 'Quebradillas,' has a yellow tube with orange lobes, on longer, more erect pedicels. Form 'El Yunque,' of catalog listings, has heavily veined leaves, a broader calyx and larger flowers, orange red, flared, and fringed much like an *Episcia*. Dr. Laurence E. Skog has renamed this plant *Gesneria reticulata* (Grisebach) Urban. A third form which we have grown has darker leaves that are more upright, dark maroon calyx and pedicels, and a heavier textured tube flower with red and burnt orange longitudinal stripes. We have not seen it lately and hope it turns up again as it was superior to normal *G. cuneifolia* in its ability to bloom outside of a terrarium. (Author's Note: It has!)

G. cuneifolia and *G. cuneifolia* cv. *Quebradillas* are extremely floriferous and under fluorescent light will bloom without missing a day throughout the year. Leaf nodes seem able to produce a considerable number of flowers even long after leaves themselves have dropped. Although it grows upward at an extremely slow rate with close internodes, it does develop a fairly thick, woody stem that may reach a height of 6 to 8 inches. The flowering on a larger plant is incredible. Nothing like it is known in the houseplant repertory. We have had plants blooming steadily for four years on end, and the number of flowers has been so great that, as the stem grows, it leaves behind a mass of dried pedicels that looks like a hedgehog.

G. 'Lemon Drop.' Although this is a sterile hybrid, made by Michael Kartuz, between *G. cuneifolia* and *G. citrina*, its behavior and appearance are so closely related to the first parent that it belongs in the same group. The habit is, in fact, much the same, but the flowers are a pure rich yellow. The floriferousness, believe it or not, is even greater than *G. cuneifolia* and the lasting qualities the same. A fertile *G.* 'Lemon Drop' would be the nearly perfect houseplant, for it does not require terrarium culture.

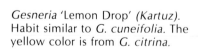

Gesneria 'Lemon Drop' *(Kartuz).* Habit similar to *G. cuneifolia*. The yellow color is from *G. citrina.*

The only distinction in culture between these plants is that normal *G. cuneifolia* definitely does better in a terrarium while 'Quebradillas' and 'Lemon Drop' can manage very well on a shelf. However, this still means a humidity of 50 percent or better for the latter, while the former is happier at 70 or 80 percent.

The temperature should be a minimum of 65°. Use Lean Mix with a heavy dose of lime chips. These plants grow on limestone cliffs, and you won't be overdoing it if you add four tablespoons to the quart.

During the dry summer season in the islands, these gesnerias dry down to the roots. But don't try this indoors. We have found that they require constant wetness. We are not speaking here of equal moisture in the same sense that we have used it with regard to other gesneriads, but of actual wetting down. When a well-established plant is in full bloom even a small reduction in the water content of the soil can cause flowers to drop. Keep them wet all the way and every day. We use high phosphate fertilizer almost exclusively.

The light requirements are about the same as for African violets and depend in the same way on the degree of humidity, varying from 200 to 500 footcandles. Unless there is a stretch of unusually sunny weather, your plants will not bloom continuously in a window. Of course they should only be in good reflected light, but a series of gray days proves inadequate for their needs.

G. cuneifolia, if given sufficient pot space, will put forth underground runners which surface around the parent plant and can be separated and potted up. In the case of 'Lemon Drop,' we are almost entirely dependent on this means of propagation. Leaves will sprout in moist vermiculite or sphagnum moss but only after weeks and sometimes months. With mist propagation systems, this can be speeded up.

To secure seed, squeeze the tube gently when mature and pull off without damaging the stigma. Flowers often self-fertilize, and the capsules can be collected when the calyx has spread and reveals a domed area at the top. The seed is then dried and shaken out of the capsules. Seed germinates easily but takes a long time to develop into a good-sized plant under normal cultural conditions . . . at least three months. But flowering will begin with four or five leaves.

If the plant develops an unsightly stem after a year or more of growth, just set it in a deeper pot so that the rosette is on the surface. Use very light, airy mix as a top dressing.

G. acaulis, christi, and *pedicellaris* are plants similar to *G. cuneifolia* in habit but with flowers on short pedicels which are more or less erect. All are red orange or red. Culture is the same as *G. cuneifolia.* They are pretty plants but decidedly less floriferous.

G. citrina is a shrublet which takes a long time to grow 6 or more inches high. The much-branched little plant, which preserves a quite narrow profile, has leaves no more than ½ inch in length and toothed at the ends. The slender pedicels curve over and suspend ¾-inch tubes of purest yellow. This is a stylish little plant which makes a natural blooming bonsai.

Bloom is in the winter, and culture is terrarium with attention that just moist conditions—unlike *G. cuneifolia*—are maintained. Very temperamental, it is no plant for a beginning grower. Seed is produced in great quantity spontaneously and all germinate. If you have patience and skill, these are splendid plants to grow for small terrariums.

G. pauciflora was found by Dr. Talpey in the mountains of Puerto Rico. We have never seen it and don't know if anyone is growing it. But his description is so tempting that we would certainly like to see more of it. It is a shrub with slender woody stems and oblong leaves 4 inches long and 1 inch wide—in other words, much like those of *G. cuneifolia.* The flowers are bright orange and an inch long. Seed has been difficult to obtain, and it may be some time before it is available for cultivation.

Gesneria christi.

Gesneria citrina.

Gesneria saxatilis is not in general cultivation but deserves to be. Actually the *Gesneria* shrublets make beautiful bonsai and can be used for that purpose. This one will grow to 15 inches, much branched, with hollylike leaves ¾ of an inch long, very shiny and toothed. The flowers are set charmingly here and there in the axils, growing nearly upright on short pedicels. They are about ¾ of an inch long and a particularly rich shade of scarlet. Presumably it grows in more exposed and less moist conditions than the rosette-leaved group and therefore requires more light and less moisture.

Gesneria saxatilis (pulverulenta).　　　　　　Close-up *of Gesneria saxatilis (pulverulenta).*

Gloxinia

Until recently *Gloxinia* was a genus whose principal claim to fame was the mistaken use of its name for *Sinningia speciosa,* the florist gloxinia. *Gloxinia perennis* is occasionally cultivated by hobbyists, and *G. pallidiflora* has sometimes been mentioned in the literature. Now, as the result of action by the AGGS, the two former seemannias, *sylvatica* and *latifolia,* have been recognized as one and renamed *Gloxinia sylvatica. Seemannia gymnostoma* becomes *Gloxinia gymnostoma.* In addition, our old friend *Kohleria lindeniana* is now properly labeled *Gloxinia lindeniana.* That raises the power of *Gloxinia* considerably. These are all plants from central and northern South America, and all are scaly rhizomatous. All are also moderately difficult to grow indoors and require some skill and experience. Hybridizing programs are in process which may lead to more adaptable plants.

Gloxinia perennis. The real *Gloxinia* will never match its common namesake in popularity but is a plant which hobbyists will probably continue to grow because of its largish bell-shaped bluish flowers and its similarity to some of our outdoor garden perennials. It entered cultivation long before *Sinningia speciosa,* seeds having been sent to England as early as 1739. It is a native of Colombia and Venezuela, where it grows at moderate elevations.

Although usually smaller in greenhouse and home, *G. perennis* can reach a height of 2½ feet. The opposite leaves are broadly oval and heart shaped, averaging 5 inches long by 4 inches wide, with a wavy edge, green and slightly hairy above, flushed red below.

111

Gloxinia perennis. Photo L. H. Bailey Hortorium of Cornell University

Flowers grow singly from the axils on short thick pedicels. The calyx is peculiar, the tube being heavily grooved and the sepals about as long as the tube—½ to ¾ inch—the spread segments leaning forward. The corolla tube is 1½ inches long and very broad from the start, widening somewhat at the bottom before narrowing slightly upward toward the limb. We would hardly call it pouched as have some writers. The throat is wide open and the lobes broad, rounded, and somewhat overlapping. The two upper ones lean backward and are more conspicuous than the lower ones which carry the tube forward and then curve slightly down or outward. In other words this is a very stubby-looking flower verging on a bell shape. It is about 1½ inches long. The color is lavender with a darker spot at the base of the lower lobes.

The height and sprawling habit make this a difficult plant to tame. Pinching will produce some branching, and since the plant starts to bloom before reaching maximum height it may look very pretty for a while. The problem arises as it continues to age.

Rich Mix with lime and ample potting are advisable. Temperatures should not exceed 85° or go below 65° F. Keep moderately moist. The light requirements are about 500 footcandles. During growth use a high phosphate fertilizer.

Flowering is in June-July followed by gradual return to dormancy. Medium-sized scaly rhizomes are produced in quantity. Revival is usually late April or May.

G. sylvatica (SEEMANNIA LATIFOLIA and SYLVATICA). In 1957, when Dr. Harold E. Moore, Jr., wrote his book *African Violets, Gloxinias and Their Relatives, Seemannia* was not included. It turned up about 1968, having been collected in Peru, and immediately attracted enthusiastic attention, being dubbed the gesneriad of the future. The question is which future? For, in 1976 *Seemannia* is still being grown by relatively few people. Such expectations have greeted a number of other gesneriad species and innumerable cultivars, which have dropped into obscurity leaving hardly a trace.

Having developed an affection for this plant, we hate to see it lose even its familiar name. Now it is *Gloxinia* and our old *Seemannia latifolia* is *Gloxinia sylvatica.* It takes an effort to make the switch.

By and large, neither botanists nor expert amateurs seem to have any real grasp of what makes a plant truly popular, as we have pointed out in our introductory remarks. New plants are like inventions: they can be just right from the first or definitely flawed. And there is a third category of those which come before their time—in other words are dropped from consideration without adequate trial or before some technological or cultural development makes them easier to grow.

G. sylvatica is an altogether beautiful plant and now deserves and should enjoy a happier, somewhat more popular future.

The story of the plant and its problem can be summed up by the example of a lady who was particularly successful in growing them. She planted individual rhizomes in small plastic cubical terrariums and grew them on to bloom beautifully in this confined space. Her creations were truly exquisite as they flowered when quite small. But friends to whom she gave these planters found that the plants stopped flowering after a short while, the leaves rotted away, and all that remained were a few straggly stems and spindly growths from the rhizomes in the soil. The difficulty was really lack of space, for the container was inadequate for this plant. Like most rhizomatous gesneriads, *G. sylvatica* must roam.

This limits its usefulness no doubt, but it is such a regal plant that we can allow it a larger home of its own. And, when we do that, we discover that we have a plant which will grow and bloom continuously for months on end. With terrariums so popular, this is a natural for ones somewhat larger than those required by *Koellikeria.*

G. sylvatica leaves are 3 to 5 inches long and at most an inch wide, very gray green, somewhat velvety, with a depressed midrib. They are whorled on the stem, and the flowers grow in large numbers in the axils. Note that the stems are thin and brittle and stand upright only if supported by other stems with their clusters of terminal leaves. This weakness is also partly due to the rhizomes being very near the surface, small and weakly rooted so that the stems are poorly anchored. Either the soil must be mounded around the base of the stem or several rhizomes grown close together. Sometimes an interesting effect can be secured when several stems straggle over a rock in a terrarium with their rosettes close together and forming a mat.

The flowers are carried on wiry pedicels 3 to 4 inches long rising from the new short leaves of the rosettes. The calyx is green and spiky with crisp spreading thin lobes. The flower is no more than ¾ of an inch long, a rich velvety tomato red shading sometimes to deep orange. Pouched for most of its length, it narrows somewhat toward the front and then expands into five tiny crisp triangular lobes which are dark red. The throat is yellow with red glands.

A most peculiar impression is produced by the stigma, which is yellow, thick, and projects out from the roof of the tube with an anthropomorphic mouth and tongue effect. When carefully grown, the whole plant has a very neat appearance in spite of the trailing habit. The leaves dispose themselves evenly and are overlapping, and the flowers stand out stiffly in a crown of color above them. This is very different from the spectacular but rather stuffy look, say, of *Sinningia cardinalis* which has short pedicels and leaves that are rather frowzy. Indeed, *G. sylvatica* has a very aristocratic air, and a few flowers light up a large plant as do those of the finest episcias.

The longer it blooms, the longer grow its grayish stems which curve along the top of the soil ending in the close-packed whorl of leaves with their flowers. The whole trick with it is to give so much room that it can be manipulated. A healthy plant soon grows many scaly rhizomes which, in turn, send up their shoots. In a terrarium these can be pinned down, and the tops will automatically stay erect. By shoving things around a bit, a large surface can be covered by leaf and flower in a more or less symmetrical arrangement. A terrarium rock landscape in a five gallon tank with a small fern or two in the corners soon affords a striking scene, and the bloom goes on and on.

This kind of arrangement must be fussed over a bit and trimmed of course. Straggly young growths can be pulled out along with their rhizome and potted up separately. But, even if a piece breaks loose, nothing is lost, for that, too, can be propagated very easily in Regular Mix in terrarium conditions. In this way the scene will change but always remain neat—one of the more spectacular gesneriad arrangements.

To have everbloom requires something more than just space. The Rich Mix with lime must be very loose and not compacted at all. The rhizomes are set just below the surface and later on often grow lying right on it. Moisture, humidity, and temperature must be nicely balanced. Just moist for the soil, 70 to 80 percent humidity, and temperatures of 65° to 75°. The cover of the terrarium should never be entirely closed. Leave about an inch open on one side in winter and 2 inches in summer. There should never be standing water in the container. Use fish emulsion fertilizer every month.

The light requirements are about 500 footcandles—rather higher than for African violets. This means that the fluorescent fixture must be within a couple of inches of the top of the terrarium on a 12-to-14-hour day.

Rhizomes can be removed and stored in slightly moist peat moss but will usually sprout immediately. They can be fattened up and will stay semiquiescent for quite a while until you are ready to pot them.

Former *Seemannia sylvatica,* with yellow flowers, is now joined with *Seemannia latifolia* as *G. sylvatica,* as we have noted. This means that the yellow-flowered plant is recognized as only a form of the species. Culture is the same.

G. gymnostoma is the former *Seemannia gymnostoma.* The flowers are purple pink with lighter specklings.

G. 'Chic' is Lyndon Lyon's hybrid with deeper red flowers and a somewhat more tolerant habit. He has been growing it as a basket plant in the greenhouse. It may be more suitable for "on shelf" growing. This is devoutly to be hoped for.

Gloxinia lindeniana (Kohleria lindeniana) we leave till the last description of this pretty species. The shuffling around of the species makes an alphabetical arrangement within the genus unsuitable for the moment, as we want to separate the newcomers from the older members of the genus. Some of the confusion in species and genera has undoubtedly arisen because of the sudden influx of new plants within a very short span of years. *G. lindeniana* is an example because, though it turned up in Belgium in the 1860s and its presumed habitat is Ecuador, it did not reach our shores until the early 1950s and was offered at that time as a *Gesneria.* It was not until there had been a number of explorations, discovering still more new plants or relocating old ones, that it became possible to make those comparisons on which a reasonable classification can be based.

When it was still a *Kohleria,* we liked this one best of the genus not for its flowers, which were not easy to come by, but because its foliage is so neat and beautifully patterned. It is a scaly rhizomatous plant, as are both *Kohleria* and *Gloxinia,* producing single stems that may reach a foot in height and with good culture can be made to keep an erect

Streptocarpus x Cyanandrus.

Streptocarpus 'Tina.' Courtesy John Innes Institute. *Streptocarpus* 'Netta Nymph.'

Agalmyla parasitica. Courtesy Bailey Hortorium.

Sarmienta scandens. Courtesy Bailey Hortorium.

Chrysothemis villosa. Courtesy Frances Batcheller.

Gloxinia perennis. Courtesy Bailey Hortorium.

Nautilocalyx lynchii. Courtesy Bailey Hortorium.

Titanotrichum oldhami. Courtesy Bailey Hortorium.

Aeschynanthus obconicus.

Diastema vexans.

Episcia 'Cygnet.'   *Episcia lilacina.*

Episcia 'Jinny Elbert.'

Columnea teuscheri.   *Kohleria eriantha.*

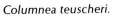

Gesneria cuneifolia cv. *Talpey.*

Columnea 'Moonglow.' A Lyon cross.

Phinaea multiflora. *Nematanthus perianthomegus.*

Nematanthus 'Green Magic.'
A Saylor cross.

Sinningia 'Cindy.'

Sinningia pusilla.

Saintpaulia 'Lisa.'

Sinningia 'Rex.' A Lyon cross.

Bellonia aspera.

Florist Gloxinia. A Buell cross.

Smithiantha.   *Gloxinia* 'Chic.' A Lyon cross.

Gloxinia gymnostoma. Photo Pam Provost

posture. The whole plant is softly short hairy with an appealing velvety quality. Leaves on 1-inch petioles are heart shaped, up to 3 inches long, the parallel veining clearly marked against a background of dark reddish brown and depressed so that stripes of the darker color are created which meet with the midvein. The edges are evenly toothed. The underside is lighter and flushed with red under the darker portions of the upper surface. The arrangement is decussate (alternately opposite).

Gloxinia lindeniana.

The flowers are on long erect pedicels, one or more to a leaf axil, the calyx hairy and star-shaped. The corolla is almost a pure bell, hairy, white, the tube about ½ inch long and as wide, the lobes of the limb spreading almost evenly. The interior of the tube is yellowish, and a lavender to violet zone at the throat extends partly outward onto the white lobes which are nearly as long as the tube.

The flowers bloom usually in the fall, though we have seen them on plants as early as late July. Bloom does not usually last for more than a month to six weeks. Dormancy is from late September till the following spring. The rhizomes can be left in the pot, and, if kept moist, some will sprout promptly. Better results are obtained if there is complete dormancy, and they are stored in a plastic bag with slightly moist peat moss. We find it best to grow individual rhizomes in pots rather than mass them in baskets, where they make an untidy effect. The culture is very much the same as for the former *Seemannia— Gloxinia sylvatica.*

Hypocyrta

Of the original approximately twenty species of *Hypocyrta* from tropical America, about eight have been in cultivation here among hobbyists. Two have been recently transferred to *Alloplectus* and five to *Nematanthus*, leaving just one in peace—at least we think it is.

H. selloana is a stout small shrub with leaves 4 inches long, narrowed at both ends, very hairy and with a toothed margin. The flowers are narrow tubes about 1½ inches long, narrower at the bottom than the top and very hairy, obscuring the orange pink color

Hypocyrta selloana.

beneath. The opening of the tube is very small and lobes are hardly apparent. Culture is the same as for *Nematanthus*.

That is all of the familiar plants of this genus which once included all of this type of pouched gesneriads.

Although we give the full list of species reclassification on pp. 45–46, the following may be useful in reminding you of the disposition of these species.

H. *nummularia* to *Alloplectus nummularius*
H. *teuscheri* to *Alloplectus teuscheri*
H. *strigosa* to *Drymonia strigosa*
H. *fritschii* to *Nematanthus fritschii*
H. *radicans* to *Nematanthus gregarius*
H. *hirtella* to *Nematanthus hirtellus*
H. *nervosa* to *Nematanthus nervosus*
H. *perianthomega* to *Nematanthus perianthomegus*
H. *strigillosa* to *Nematanthus strigillosus*
H. *wettsteinii* to *Nematanthus wettsteinii.*

Koellikeria

Koellikeria erinoides is an exquisite, long-blooming plant, unique among the gesneriads for producing a multitude of spikes or racemes with little flowers borne well above the attractive foliage over a long period. Unfortunately it goes into dormancy for an indeterminate period, and best culture requires virtually exclusive use of space in a terrar-

Koellikeria erinoides.

ium. Once this characteristic is understood and accepted, *Koellikeria* could well become very popular, for it does flower easily and with very little attention. As new growth rhizomes *do* sprout, it may be possible through selection to develop clones capable of near-continuous blooming.

The plant was originally brought to Kew gardens from Colombia in 1845 but has only entered general cultivation here since Dr. Henry Teuscher, of the Montreal Botanical Garden, brought back plants from Venezuela in 1951. There are just two other, very similar, known species, but the plants are found growing over a wide area in Central America and much of South America, usually at low altitudes.

Leaves are oval dentate, hairy, and with red veining. Scattered on the surface are small silver spots which those unfamiliar with the plant often take for an insect infestation at first sight. The size, depending on culture, is 1 to 4 inches long by ¾–2½ inches wide. The arrangement appears as a flattish rosette at first but, as the stem grows, it is seen to be a whorl.

The flowering stalks (peduncles) arise, one to several, from the axils of the leaves and are 9 to 12 inches tall. Flowers are held free of the stalk by inch-long pedicels. About ½ inch long, they consist of a short fat tube, two short deep pink upper lobes, and three white larger lower ones which jut forward and are toothed. Each flower lasts several days so that a number are usually present on a spike at any one time.

Culture has been described as easy with the proviso that sufficient humidity be provided. The matter is not that simple, at least for indoor growers, who have found *K. erinoides* by no means foolproof. In fact, its culture requires certain special conditions for maximum results. Numerous growers have reported difficulty which can be easily avoided.

Like *Sinningia pusilla* (and some others) it seems to grow best in a relative humidity of well over 50 percent. It blooms at a temperature of minimum 65°. Also for blooming two 20-watt fluorescent tubes should be not more than 6 inches above the top of the plant. The medium should be very porous and not compacted. Finally, it objects to drenching and soggy soil. Contact with wet soil will rot bottom leaves. The mix, therefore, should be just barely moist.

These conditions can be met indoors only in a terrarium. In fact the environment just described is virtually the ideal one for closed containers. However, there is a further condition. *Koellikeria* dislikes root restraint, especially in a lateral direction, and flourishes when its lower extremities can wander at will. (See *Diastema.*) Although a small plant, it does spread and, ideally, it should have a terrarium with a minimum of 8 inches in diameter and a height of 10 to 12 inches at its disposal. A five-gallon fish tank is ideal. If it begins to outgrow its home, rhizomes around the edges can be removed. You can leave dormant rhizomes right in the terrarium.

We pot in Rich Mix with lime and set the rhizomes horizontally just below the surface of the soil. We fertilize with high phosphate formula once or twice a season.

The scaly rhizomes are narrow and about 1 inch long. They are produced freely and, as older rhizomes go dormant, often start up on their own. However, it is noticeable that these new rhizomes will usually produce flowering early in the blooming season only—in other words not later than the dormancy of the earliest to enter into this state. Toward the end of the period, growth is weak, and it is generally advisable to let all the rhizomes in a planting go dormant for a period by removing top growth and reducing moisture and light. A three-month dormancy is usually sufficient—at any time of year indoors. Rhizomes locked in porous slag for a whole year in a perfectly dry state responded promptly when brought to light and moistened. But safer storage is in slightly moist soilless mix, moss, or peat.

In the home, seed is not produced spontaneously, and we have depended on rhizomes and cuttings of young growth which root easily in moist vermiculite.

Although the conditions we have mentioned are somewhat demanding if an attempt is made to grow these plants on the shelf, they are quite easy to achieve in a terrarium.

Koellikohleria rosea. A hybrid between *Kohleria spicata* and *K. erinoides* has been created by Hans Wiehler at Cornell University. It is a larger, more vigorous plant with pink flowers twice the size of *K. erinoides* and, instead of a single flower, up to four from each bract on the peduncle. Also new shoots continue to be sent up, lengthening the flowering season. However, the culture is pretty much the same as for *K. erinoides* and the new plant is rather large for most terrariums. Growing it to perfection, therefore, is not easy. In a greenhouse 70 to 80 percent relative humidity is no problem as it is in the house. So this is probably more suited to growing under glass than indoors. We believe that *K. erinoides* will continue to be the more popular plant.

Kohleria

Our critical remarks below regarding *Kohleria* seem to belie in several respects our descriptions of the plants themselves which follow. Here are gesneriads with unusually beautiful leaves and flowers whose merit as houseplants we belittle. We assert that they sprawl, yet in at least three instances we list species with sturdy, upright growth.

The contradiction here is between the plant as it grows in the wild and its behavior in our own garden. Much depends on its original location and the environment to which it is transported. We have a clue to the problem when we learn that *Kohleria* comes from the highlands of Colombia. It is also significant that it has been much more popular in Europe than here. The Colombian environment and that of Europe, especially English greenhouses, have one thing in common—coolness in summer and a rather sharp drop in temperature at night.

We now know that many greenhouse (and outdoor) plants that do well in England cannot be adapted to our environments as effectively. And it is our belief that *Kohleria's* bad habits are at least in part due to a need to be grown in a temperature range which is difficult to maintain in this country in average indoor environments. We believe the plant needs temperatures of 50°–60° F in winter and does better after a period of real dormancy. In spring and summer the temperature level should be 60° or higher but not over 80° for long and with a normal 10° drop at night.

In other respects it can be treated like most of the rhizomatous gesneriads. But the sprawling habit of which we speak is certainly due to weak growth arising from chronic failure to provide proper conditions. We have rarely seen really well grown kohlerias even in professional greenhouses, and this, or something similar, must be the reason. Readers who live in the country and have cool cellars with fluorescent lighting and those living in the Pacific northwest may grow these plants with more confidence. Since we, ourselves, on a couple of occasions have had perfectly beautiful plants (a big *K. eriantha* was particularly memorable), our criticisms are not meant to prevent you from attempting them but to warn that success is not automatic and that we really do not know for certain just where the trouble lies.

Thare are about sixty-five species with scaly rhizomes growing in central and northern South America. They are generally hairy with large broad leaves in whorls of three or four. Flower shapes are rather uniform, being thick tubes with two small and three larger roundish lobes, the center one jutting a bit forward and larger than the others. The pedicels angle upward, and the flowers hang directly down. Thus there is no slipper effect (partially a product of being held horizontally and partially the way the lobes are spread), as the throat is quite open and rounded and the lobes stand out rather straight. Lobes and throat are covered with a pattern of spots in a more intense or contrasting color. There are usually five glands to the disk. Fertile stamens are four, joined at the tips as in many other gesneriads, and the style is two lobed and mouth shaped.

K. amabilis. In 1957 when Professor Moore's book *African Violets, Gloxinias and Their Relatives* was published, kohlerias were in the ascendancy, and *K. amabilis* was reputed to be one of the most popular and a good terrarium subject. Now it has largely disappeared from amateur collections as it has a poor habit and is impossibly disorderly in a terrarium.

The stems, up to 2 feet long, are weak and usually prostrate. The whole plant is hairy. Dark green leaves with purple veins are 4 inches by 3 inches, becoming smaller toward the end of the stem. The flowers on 3-inch erect pedicels are held vertically. The small calyx is star shaped and the corolla tube is 1 inch long and ½ inch wide, expanding and curving downward on the lower side. The lobes are rosy pink with a pattern of purplish red dashes and dots, and the inside of the tube is spotted with brick red. The plant is sensitive to summer heat and soggy soil.

K. bogotensis. This is a Colombian species which grows to a height of 2 feet, with velvety leaves, lighter veinings, and flushes of brown. Pedicels are 2 inches long, and the flowers typically nodding and 1 inch long. The tube is red above, turning yellow below, and swells below the throat. The upper lobes of the limb are smaller, red with darker markings, and the three lower lobes are yellow dotted and dashed with red as is the inside of the tube. The 1-inch length of these flowers may suggest that they are small. But they do not create this effect because the tube is swollen, the lobes of the limb very conspicuous, and the coloring so rich over the whole tube and limb that it glows intensely. This is true of almost all kohlerias.

K. digitaliflora. True to its name the flower reminds one of a hairy digitalis with its lower lobe jutting forward more than in most other kohlerias. Growth is similar to the others, but the plant is larger with leaves nearly 8 inches long. The flowers are borne on hairy peduncles and are heavily wooly, white with a rose flush. The limb has short rounded lobes, light green with fine purple spots. A Colombian species.

K. eriantha. This very handsome species is probably still the most popular in spite of its height. The stout stem, like the rest of the plant, is reddish hairy and can grow to 4 feet, though it can be easily kept to 18 to 24 inches by underpotting. The scalloped, thick hairy leaves are up to 5 inches long, green with a distinct band of red along the edge. The flowers come three or four to an axil on 4-inch reddish pedicels. The hairy corolla tube is 2 inches long. The base color is a rich burnt orange with the lower lobes of the limb spotted with yellow. The description does not do justice to the beauty of the very hot coloration. The whole plant is a handsome sight when in bloom. It has flowered for us in late spring, but it is by no means an easy subject indoors.

K. lindeniana. This is the most different of the species with its violet coloration and it is not surprising that it has recently been transferred to the genus *Gloxinia.*

KOHLERIA HYBRIDS

Kohlerias, which have been in cultivation in Europe for over one hundred years, have been actively hybridized. The strains have been categorized as "Amabilis Hybrids," "Bogotensis Hybrids," and "Eriantha Hybrids." One group with the jawbreaker name of 'Sciadotydaea Hybrids" is presumed to be a series resulting from crosses between *K. digitaliflora* or *K. warszewiczii* and unknown species. Occasionally imported seed of

Kohleria eriantha x hirsuta.
Courtesy Kartuz Greenhouses

European strains of these attractive plants are offered. But in reality none of these hybrids can be found in wide cultivation. Lengthy discussion is therefore unnecessary.

Of more recent interest are the hybrids 'Connecticut Belle," developed by Dr. Carl Clayberg, Mrs. Frances Batcheller's 'Rongo,' and *K.* 'Longwood.'

K. 'Longwood' was propagated by Longwood Gardens from a plant imported from "a Portuguese botanic garden." This is a large, hairy, sprawling plant with very fat, large

Kohleria 'Rongo' (Batcheller)

bright deep pink flowers with an exquisite pattern on the lobes. Although a more or less constant bloomer on the bench in a greenhouse, its habit is unsuitable for indoor growing. Tip cutting will make it shorter but hardly improves its general appearance. It has not caught on with the public.

Dr. Clayberg's more compact 'Connecticut Belle' has 3-inch hairy leaves, flushed with red beneath. The flower pedicels are erect and carry inch-long bright red tubes covered with white hairs. The broad limb is rich purple on the upper lobes and light pink on the lower, dotted and lined with dark purple. It blooms for three months at a time, usually spring-summer.

Mrs. Batcheller's 'Rongo' completes our list with the most popular *Kohleria* in cultivation. A sturdy plant, reaching no more than a foot in height, it has 2-inch magenta flowers gorgeously veined with white on the shapely lobes. This is certainly the most adaptable cultivar yet developed. See ''Gesneriad Update,'' page 215.

Lietzia

Here just for the record, quoting Mrs. Frances Batcheller. One species, *L. braziliensis,* a tuberous, tall erect plant with a wide mouthed yellow green flower.

Lysionotus

From much the same habitats as *Petrocosmea*—the Himalayas, China, and Japan—comes this genus of only three species. The one which has been cultivated by a few amateurs in this country is *L. serratus.*

L. serratus was very carefully described in *The Gloxinian* of September/October 1967 by Iris August. Unfortunately the photograph accompanying the article was drastically retouched.

Kohleria 'Longwood.'

The plant grows to 10 or 12 inches and is compactly shrubby. Leaves are whorled in threes and are 2 inches by 1 inch with dentate edges. Peduncles 1 inch long bear first five blooms, then two. The flowers are 1½ inches long, pale lavender, striped on the upper side of the tube with dark lavender. The shape of the tube is curiously fishlike, with a narrow tail, swelling in the center, flattened on top and with the two upper lobes of the limb hardly separated and arching upward. The lower lobes open like a mouth and the throat is deep yellow. According to Mrs. August, "two bright yellow 'stripes' run down the inside lower portion of the tube. (On inspection these resemble thickened veins, or tubule-type structures, commencing about halfway up the tube, coursing downwards for about ½ inch to within ¼ inch of the edge of the lobe; on some flowers they are adherent to the tube their entire length; on other flowers they are raised, slightly above the lower attachment, forming a small loop."

Culture is much the same as *Petrocosmea.* Mrs. August thought that the plant might need a period of high humidity and low light before setting bloom. Graf's photo in the *Brooklyn Botanic Garden Handbook* shows peduncles with many flowered cymes. The plant looks more diffuse than Mrs. August's description and the mouth of the flower much more open. We suspect that, like *Petrocosmea,* it needs rather cool conditions.

L. pauciflora is a Japanese semihardy Alpine much appreciated in England. It is a small plant with holly leaves, shiny above and white hairy below. Trumpet-shaped flowers are 2 inches long and borne in profusion in the upper axils. The color is cream white with three purple lines in the throat.

These plants are for the cool greenhouse or cellar garden.

Monophyllaea

About eight species come from Southeast Asia and the Philippines. They have a single leaf, usually nearly round, with a sharp indentation at the joining to the stalk. As in *Streptocarpus* the flowering stalk rises from the base of the leaf and is a compact raceme.

Monopyle

There are several species from Central and South America. *Monopyle* has unequal leaves, the flowers in a terminal inflorescence, and the corolla campanulate.

Nautilocalyx

We have always looked upon *Nautilocalyx* (eleven species from northern South America) as closely related to *Episcia,* in fact like a nonstoloniferous, erect section of that genus. Recently the transfer of *Episcia melittifolia* to *Nautilocalyx* as *N. melittifolius* proves that botanists, too, have been a little up in the air as to what constitutes a classifying difference. The suggestion has now been made that the stolons are critical. Stolons equals *Episcia;* no stolons equals *Nautilocalyx.* As a filing system, taxonomy is useful. As a science, it is about as valid as mesmerism.

Decoratively they are foliage plants, although the flowers are not without their charms. Unfortunately this is hardly a great recommendation, since they are hidden under a bushel (or leaves) and are very short lasting. Their great vigor, easy culture, and really handsome textures and coloration place them on an equal footing with the many other very handsome richly colored foliage houseplants now available to the amateur.

N. bullatus.   This is a stout plant growing 2 feet high with stiff thick stems. Descriptions of the position of the leaves state that they are opposite. This, as with all plants of the type, is quite misleading. *Columnea* leaves are also opposite, but they are all in the same plane. The feature of most erect plants is that leaves are usually whorled—in which case they circle around the stem as they move upward—or whorled and opposite, which means that each pair shifts its position in spiral motion up the stem or, very commonly, they're decussate. This is a sad word, but we have no other, to describe a very simple arrangement. Each pair of leaves is at right angles, or nearly so, to the preceding pair. These descriptive terms make a big difference in our vision of a plant. As far as we can remember, from the last time we grew *N. bullatus*, it was decussate.

Anyway, the leaves are crisp, shiny, sparsely hairy, 5 to 9 inches long, oval pointed, and somewhat winged at the lower end. They are also heavily quilted and veined, with the edges rolled downward giving them a substantial look. As with some episcias we find, when we turn the leaf over, that the midvein is very prominent and the texture is really very thin, the minor veins standing out to create symmetrical leaf surfaces with overall quilting. The color is dark green, becoming olive with age, and the reverse is lighter.

Flowers appear in spring, 8 to 10 clustered in the axils. First to appear are the large (1-inch) hairy, leafy calyxes. These are followed by a thick vaselike tube, an inch or more long, pale yellow and covered with white hairs, which expands into five low roundish lobes. The expanded lobes and the throat are deeper yellow.

The blooming period can continue for eight weeks or more as new leaves expand. As leaves get smaller and flowers fewer, the top of the stalk can be cut down. Usually new growths will have started from the base. Once these are well on their way, the rest of the original stem can be cut down.

In the window, flowering may be inhibited by stretches of cloudy weather or coolness, but under lights it is easily achieved and, if the plants have had good care, new stalks may be in flower before the old ones go. Nevertheless, it is not advisable to compromise the handsome appearance of the plant. Only enough stalks should be allowed to grow to make a bushy specimen. Repotting becomes necessary as the root structure grows.

Eventually in such plants the old roots degenerate. It pays to divide them up or start new ones from stem cuttings, which root quickly in open containers of moist vermiculite in a room maintained at 70° or higher.

Use Rich Mix with lime and allow plenty of room for root growth. Eventually a deep 6-inch pot will be necessary. If you want bloom, give 50 percent or higher humidity, but for foliage alone 30 percent will suffice. Do not overwater. As with so many foliage plants, overwatering produces a drying of leaf edges. Underwatering makes the leaf go limp and may indeed be followed by drying of the tip or edges, but that is another matter. Even moisture is desirable. Temperature should be 60° or higher. We do not advise much fertilizing. It will only lead to excessively large leaves and long internodes. Better a bit of starvation, for the plant will look and bloom just as well. Give it twelve hours of 250 footcandles daily.

N. forgettii is the handsomest *Nautilocalyx* in cultivation. Very much the same as *N. bullatus* in habit, the leaves are extraordinary for their rich brown color and often reddish veining. They are less quilted and toothed than *bullatus,* and the reverses are reddish purple. Flowers are similar to *bullatus* except that the calyx has a reddish tone. Culture is the same.

N. lynchii's principal difference is in the leaves, which are dark maroon in color.

N. melittifolius (Episcia melittifolia) is an upright branching plant with 6-inch shiny

Nautilocalyx forgettii. Photo L. H. Bailey Hortorium of Cornell University

puckered leaves and small rather open-faced magenta flowers, ½ to ¾ inch across, clustered in the axils and partly hidden by the leaves. Grown in Europe since the middle of the last century, it was not introduced here until the 1960s by Easterbrook Greenhouses. It is a rather coarse herb, occasionally producing tubers but without stolons. Culture is like *Nautilocalyx*.

N. picturatus is a quite different plant which grows low and compact like a very long cluster-leaved *Episcia*. The leaves are 6 inches long and 3 wide, the broad mid- and side veins light green and the rest green black with the heavy granulation or puckering of some episcias. The edges, which are closely and shallowly scalloped, are turned downward. Flowers are very hairy, pure white outside and the lobes spreading. The tube is lined with long purple stripes. The texture is very similar—oddly thin and lax, as in *N. villosus*. Culture the same as *N. bullatus*. Season short.

N. villosus, the whole plant of which is covered with white hairs, looks almost like a fungus growth. The habit is shorter than *bullatus* and taller than *picturatus*, the stem being less stiff than the former. It reaches about a foot in height. Leaves are 6 inches long and 3 wide, bright green with a dense cover of the white hairs. The flowers are clustered in the axils as in the other species but are much larger, being 2 inches long, white, with small purplish blotches in the throat. The texture is amazingly thin, so much so that the lobes have difficulty remaining erect for even a short time. In spite of their size they do not make an attractive impression and each one is finished in a day or at most two. Culture is as for the others.

*Nautilocalyx picturatus.
Photo L. H. Bailey
Hortorium of Cornell
University*

*Nautilocalyx picturatus.
·Photo L. H. Bailey
Hortorium of Cornell
University*

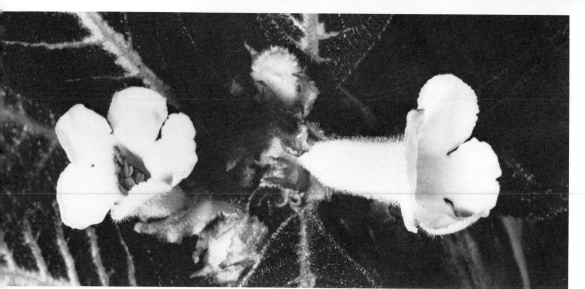

Nematanthus

There used to be about six species attributed to *Nematanthus*—all natives of Brazil. Now, as the result of the action of the Nomenclature Committee of AGGS, a number of former hypocyrtas have been transferred to it, including *H. nervosa, perianthomega, radicans, strigillosa,* and *wettsteinii*—the most popular plants of that genus. Thus what the public has looked upon as a visually homogeneous group of pouched flowers on short pedicels has been moved to a genus which has consisted of tube flowers, dubbed "thread flowers" because they are pendent from branches by long pedicels—an exclusively distinctive feature. It is this latter type—the original *Nematanthus*—that we will discuss first. Growth habit is very similar to *Columnea.*

N. fritschii (N. fluminensis) has numerous arching stems up to 2½ feet in length with opposite shiny green leaves, 3 inches long by 2 inches wide, oval pointed, on ¾-inch petioles. The undersides are flushed with red which is more intense along the veins. Hairy threadlike pedicels up to 5 inches long hang from the axils. The calyx, facing directly downward, has narrow sepals ¾ inch long, while the tubular corolla hangs almost at right angles. The tube is 2 inches long, broadening and somewhat crimped toward the front. The limb consists of five lobes so sharply curled back that they usually appear shallow and squarish, the lower one being almost tucked under the tube. The color is a bright, rich pink. Although the flowers are quite unsymmetrical, the effect of several of them dangling from their branches on such long pedicels is very showy.

Nematanthus longipes is the better-known species and very similar. Leaves are 4 inches long and 1½ inches wide on shorter pedicels and with paler green reverses. The corolla is scarlet, more than 2 inches long and more funnel-shaped than *fritschii.*

Obviously these two are large basket plants and cannot be considered for pot culture. They are seasonal bloomers in spring and should receive the same warm, moderately moist, and highly humid conditions as the more difficult columneas. In other words these are greenhouse plants but can be grown on a moderately sunny porch in the south.

N. 'Stoplight,' like all *Nematanthus* are of relatively recent date in cultivation. It wasn't until the late 1960s that crosses between species were attempted. The first one, by Professor Robert E. Lee of Cornell University, was between the above two species and produced 'Stoplight.' It has proved an excellent combination of the virtues of both parents. The flower color is that of *N. longipes,* and the colored foliage of *N. fritschii* is retained. There is much more new growth from the base, and the more slender canes do not become woody as rapidly as the parents. Flowering is prolonged. In fact, under lights—if you can fit it there—it may be nearly continuous. The only trouble is that it is still a big plant for blooming indoors.

Nematanthus 'Stoplight' (Lee).

Nematanthus
'Stoplight' (Lee).

The following species have been long familiar to us as hypocyrtas. These are trailing plants with small, shiny green opposite leaves and flowers, in shades of orange to red, or more stiff stemmed and hairy leaved. The word *pouched* fully applies to these flowers whose short tube is bloated and the throat closed like a purse, until it is only a tiny hole with almost inconspicuous lobes. This peculiar form, found so rarely in the floral world, is extremely pretty and amusing and, since the contrast in coloring is sometimes very apt and the flowering profuse they can be very showy plants indeed.

N. gregarius (Hypocyrta radicans) has leaves that are shiny dark green, about 1½ inches long and opposite on trailing green stems. The calyx is broad, leafy and light orange in color. One-inch flowers are orange with the small limb yellow. In most of the hypocyrtas, the pouch takes a sharp dip at the bottom and then comes up to meet the straight upper side of the tube so that the limb is directly in front or, as with this plant, the lower side cuts back slightly producing a pursing effect, and the limb looks as if it were set a bit back of the frontal bulge and more "on top."

N. nervosus (Hypocyrta nervosa) is a spreader with dark green foliage consisting of 2-inch oval leaves with a pointed tip. Flowers are an inch long with a yellow green calyx. The beginning of the tube is narrow and in sight, so that the bright red 1-inch flowers are more shortly and acutely pouched with the limb facing forward at the tip. It is less floriferous than *N. gregarius.*

N. perianthomegus (Hypocyrta perianthomega) is the most robust of the former hypocyrtas, with stiff, woody horizontal branches and thick, dark shiny leaves 4½ inches long. The calyx is yellowish orange. The feature of the flowers is that they are upside down in relation to other *Nematanthus,* for the swelling is on the top rather than the bottom. About an inch long, they are yellow with horizontal stripes in maroon. These flowers are quite remarkable close up but do not form a sufficient contrast to the foliage to be

Nematanthus nervosus.

conspicuous. Thus *N. perianthomega* is one of those large basket plants which the collector grows more as a curiosity than anything else. As a greenhouse plant it has the advantage of blooming most of the year with flowers which last sometimes for weeks.

N. strigillosus (Hypocyrta strigillosa) is a species in which the oval leaves are small, hairy, and set closely on the trailing stems. The calyx is green and the 1-inch-long red orange flowers are similar to *N. gregarius*. Not the most floriferous of the group, but the rich coloring of the flowers in contrast to the softer colored foliage is very attractive. It is less adaptable to pot culture than *N. wettsteinii* or *N. radicans*.

N. wettsteinii (Hypocyrta wettsteinii) is nicknamed the candy corn plant, this is by far the most popular of all the genus because of its exquisite foliage, floriferousness, and wonderfully contrasting colored flower with the typical amusing pouched form.

The stems are thin and, when long, hang straight down from pot or basket. The ¾-inch leaves are thick and firm, oval, and a magnificent dark green jade with a high polish. They are opposite and produced in great numbers and close together on the stems. The calyx is small, yellowish, and with narrow sepals. Flowers are tomato red with the somewhat projecting narrow limb shading to yellow. They are at most an inch long and similar in form to *N. nervosus,* but they are produced in much greater numbers, last longer, and are present almost throughout the year.

N. wettsteinii is more adaptable to pot culture because it blooms easily indoors and when the stems are quite short. By means of trimming it can be kept quite shrubby. But a large basket with solid masses of stems all around, the deep green leaves forming a tight pattern and the whole interspersed with spots of bright orange red, has made it a sensation at flower shows. Until a really popular hybrid comes along, it will continue to be the most satisfactory in this group.

THE SAYLOR HYBRIDS.   Shortly after he had built a small greenhouse in 1965,

William Saylor of Brewster, Massachusetts, became fascinated with gesneriads and began attempting to cross the then hypocyrtas. It must be remembered that many of these gesneriads had only recently become available to hobbyists, and no previous hybrids within the genus *Hypocyrta* had been recorded. In 1969 Mr. Saylor was able to report on his successes and failures with combinations of the then known range of the genus. In the succeeding years he has continued his researches and widened them to include crosses between *Hypocyrta* and *Nematanthus*. It was largely as a result of the successful mating between members of the two genera that the decision was made to reclassify a number of hypocyrtas as members of the genus *Nematanthus*. As another result, his species crosses in *Hypocyrta* became *Nematanthus*—for instance *Nematanthus* 'Tropicana' instead of *Hypocyrta* 'Tropicana.' Likewise *xHypotantha*, representing a cross between the two genera, is replaced by simple *Nematanthus* followed by the cultivar name. All the following cultivars are Bill Saylor's.

N. 'Rio' (*N. gregarius* x *H. selloana*) is an erect plant with soft green short-petioled leaves and single orange to vermilion pouch flowers growing from the axils on short pedicels. This is a very pretty plant but a rather shy bloomer—mainly in spring.

N. 'Tropicana' *(N. perianthomega* x *N. gregarius)* has dark glossy green leaves, purple stems and petioles, much like some of the columneas in habit. Leafy calyx dark orange, pouched flowers dark yellow, striped with maroon. Very floriferous but chronic bloomer. Nicely compact.

N. 'Butterscotch' *(N. stigillosus* x *N.* 'Tropicana' *)* has buttercup yellow flowers on a plant similar to *N.* 'Tropicana.' Untried by us at time of writing.

N. 'Bijou' *(N. wettsteinii* x *N. fritschii)* is of trailing habit, the leaves small and red beneath. Flowers pink on pendent pedicels. For the form, see *N.* 'Green Magic.'

N. 'Castanet' *(N.* 'Black Magic' x *N. perianthomega* x *N. fritschii),* a compact, bushy plant, has pendent pouched flowers. Untried by us at time of writing.

Nematanthus 'Castanet' (Saylor).

N. 'Green Magic' and *N.* 'Black Magic' (*N. wettsteinii* x N. 'Stoplight') are plants that have been in cultivation somewhat longer than 'Bijou' and 'Castanet' and represent the type produced when the long-pediceled *Nematanthus* are crossed with the former hypocyrtas. The distinction here is in the color of the leaves—those of 'Green Magic' being appropriately green and those of 'Black Magic' very dark. The size is about 1½ inches and pointed oval in shape. The flowers hang from the axils on 1½- to 2-inch pedicels and are shorter, fleshier forms of 'Stoplight,' with the color shading from yellow to tomato red along the tube. Especially 'Green Magic' is a very pretty plant. Growth, trailing but relatively compact on wiry stems. The flowering cycle indoors is still uncertain, but in the greenhouse they bloom in spring and summer and occasionally in winter.

The culture of *Nematanthus* is so much like that of the warm-growing columneas that it is pointless to repeat the details, and the reader is referred to that genus. There is the same need for very porous mixes, for moderate watering, and the same sensitivity to extremely high temperatures. *Nematanthus* loses leaves rapidly at high temperatures and with overwatering, both over 80° and under 65°. Propagation methods are exactly the same.

The best of the *Nematanthus* species and cultivars are not yet as everblooming as the best of the *Columnea.* But they are plants of great promise, and perhaps one of Bill Saylor's new cultivars will make the breakthrough to give us a near everblooming plant with more tolerance.

Niphaea

Of this small genus native to Mexico and Guatemala only *Niphaea oblonga* is in cultivation. A rhizomatous plant, it produces rhizomes not only underground but, like *Achimenes,* occasionally in the axils of the stem.

Niphaea oblonga.

The 8- to 10-inch high single stem bears a few leaves in pairs, each about 4 inches long with toothed margins, coarsely veined in dark red, and turned down at the edges. Flowers grow several to an axil on long red pedicels. The corolla is flat, about an inch across, pure white and with even rounded lobes. An attractive feature is the bright yellow of the protruding anthers.

This is a pleasant, quite neat plant, suitable for the light garden but unlikely to become a leader in popularity. Blooming periods are relatively short, after which dormancy sets in. The rhizomes, about an inch long and rather solid, can be stored in a plastic bag with dry or slightly moist peat moss or vermiculite until they sprout the following spring.

Use Lean Mix with lime and provide even moisture and regular feeding. Minimum night temperature is 55° to 60° F. We grow *Niphaea* about 4 inches under a two-tube fixture. Otherwise a partially sunny east or west window will do.

Paliavana

Tall shrubs from Brazil. Wide funnel-shaped flowers are greenish. Two species.

Paradrymonia

In 1975 the Nomenclature Committee of the AGGS accepted various transfers of *Episcia* species to the genus *Paradrymonia*. The species involved are:
Paradrymonia ciliosa (Martius) Wiehler
Paradrymonia decurrens (Morton) Wiehler

Paradrymonia ciliosa. Photo Frances Batcheller

Paradrymonia lineata (Martius) Wiehler

Paradrymonia lurida (Morton & Raymond) Wiehler

For further information on *Paradrymonia*, see ''Gesneriad Update,'' page 215 under that heading.

Pearcea

Pearcea hypocyrtiflora, from northern South America, has been known for a long time but has only recently been introduced in this country. It is a scaly rhizomatous plant of unusual charm. We saw it blooming merrily in June at the Bailey Hortorium of Cornell University and, since it seems to have been receiving much the same treatment as the other plants there, we would guess that it is no more difficult to bloom than, say, *Gloxinia sylvatica.* A small plant is doing well in a terrarium, and we would not be surprised to see it flower this or next season. However, two good growers have warned us that it is a difficult plant.

There is one advantage in trying out rhizomatous or tuberous plants for the first time. No matter how severely they suffer from a change of environment, even if they die down to the ground, there is always the long-lasting root to fall back on. With a fibrous-rooted plant, once it dies down to the ground it is finished. As long as your rhizome or tuber is healthy, you can store it until it sprouts and give it another try when it revives.

Pearcea is low—not more than 6 inches high—producing a number of stems from its underground rhizomes. The leaves, reminiscent of episcias, are 3 inches long, generally oval—broad at bottom and pointed at tip—very dark, almost black velvety green, with major veins forming a very light, almost white thread design. The flowers growing on pedicels from the axils are weird. They are nearly round bubbles of velvety, fiery red, ½

Pearcea hypocyrtiflora.

inch in diameter, with a small opening surrounded by tiny lobes facing upward. When several of these are on the plant the effect is curious and unique. The inflated form is the reason for the species name; but shouldn't it be changed now to *Pearcea nematanthiflora?*

Presumably it is a summer bloomer and goes partially dormant like *Kohleria.* We have observed that when the main stem fails to grow, new shoots appear within a short time. The flowers are much more showy individually than the former hypocyrtas and equally or more amusing on a more compact plant. Only further growing can reveal the full potentiality of this plant.

Petrocosmea

These are good examples of plants which have a number of counts in their favor but are unlikely to become popular as houseplants because they require cool temperatures. This used to be a recommendation in the days of uncertain central heating in homes during winter, which also coincided with the vogue for sun porches. The petrocosmeas might conceivably become the cool growers' African violet, but, as long as our homes continue to range from a low of 60° upward, it will be neglected by most. Those who have sun porches will enjoy growing it.

The genus is native to the mountainous regions of Southeast Asia where they are accustomed to average cool temperatures at night. We give them Rich Mix with lime and a summer temperature which does not exceed 80° for long. Ideal would be a maximum of 75° F. In winter, day temperatures of maximum 65° and night of 55° is the only way to keep these plants really happy and blooming. They will tolerate coolness down to about 45° like some of the Chilean gesneriads. The light requirement is about 500 footcandles, which is more than that of saintpaulias, plus humidity of at least 50 percent and even soil moisture without soaking. So you can see that this is a troublesome plant for city dwellers or people who like their homes warm.

Petrocosmea kerrii is the most interesting of the species in cultivation because of its yellow color. Tempted by the similarity of *Saintpaulia* and *Petrocosmea,* amateurs have attempted to cross the two with the objective of introducing yellow into the African violet repertory. It did not work, partly because of the difference in chromosome numbers.

Petrocosmea kerrii is a very hairy plant forming a flat rosette that develops with age into a stem. The leaves are thick, oval, about 4 inches long and 2½ wide. As the peduncles are rather short, the flowers are often hidden by the foliage as in *Episcia.* There are usually three to a stalk, each about ¾ inch in diameter, the upper lobes erect and narrow, the three lower ones broader and more rounded at the tips, therefore spreading wider. Seen from certain angles, the flower looks like one of our wild species of blue lobelias. The color is white with yellow around the throat and splotches of the same color on the upper lobes.

Petrocosmea nervosa is rarely seen. The rosette is similar to *P. kerrii* but even flatter, and the new leaves are silver, so covered are they with brushed white hairs. They are 2 inches in length. The flowers, otherwise similar to *P. kerrii* are purplish blue.

Petrocosmea parryorum differs in having a stem which is very thick. The leaves are 4 inches long and scalloped. Flowers are purplish blue and of the same size and general appearance as *P. kerrii,* though the lobes tend to curve inward. They bear up to twelve flowers.

Petrocosmea parryorum. Photo Howard Conrad

Phinaea

Almost as small as *Sinningia pusilla, Phinaea multiflora* is also a terrarium plant with the difference that there is no way at present of keeping it from going dormant. The ½-inch-long pink scaly rhizomes, hardly thicker than cotton string, do not look as if they

Phinaea multiflora 'Tracerie.
Courtesy Frances Batcheller

135

could preserve their internal moisture for months on end, but they do. We do not know how to readjust the time clock in these small, and apparently simple structures, but no doubt the secret will be revealed to research in due time. It is a pleasant prospect to consider for, although anything but spectacular, *Phinaea* is an unusual-looking and charming little plant.

The ability of the rhizome to revive is astonishing. We remember receiving our first one in a small plastic bag, and it was so like a piece of dirty string that we thought it was a hoax and never for a moment believed it could survive if it wasn't. It sat on a shelf for at least three months until we finally became impatient and decided that it would have to do something or be thrown out. We therefore put a drop or two of water into the bag— a measure we would not in the least advise others to follow. But we suppose that our action by pure chance was well timed (or the rhizome heard us, as the authors of *The Secret Life of Plants* would have us believe), for, lo and behold, a week later there was a touch of green at one end.

So we filled a 1½-inch plastic pot with limy soilless mix and just covered the rhizome, which we planted horizontally like *Achimenes*. It sprouted nicely and the pot then went into a plastic bread box providing terrarium conditions under fluorescent light. In a surprisingly short time, perhaps a month, there was a rosette of very hairy, short-petioled, 1-inch leaves. In another couple of weeks, buds appeared on surprisingly thick, very straight up, short pedicels, the hairy calyx segments, very much like miniatures of the regular leaves, cupping the white bubble of a bud in its center. Instead of opening immediately, however, the flowering was delayed until the pedicels had grown an inch in height. So when the flowers opened, they sat perfectly erect on top of the pedicels, as if they were pedestals. Pure white, they were just like little cups, so closely were the lobes pressed together and slightly curved inward. Each flower lasted only a few days, but new stems and buds kept coming on continuously for six to eight weeks with very little noticeable increase in the size of the plant. Eventually the bottom leaves reached their full inch in size, shaped very much like small *Episcia* leaves.

We allowed this first plant to ripen and found the thick capsule jam-packed with tiny seeds. We collected these, planted them promptly, and had a good crop of new plantlets in about eight weeks. Growers advise not allowing the plant to set seeds as this shortens its active life and may cut down on rhizome production. On the other hand, the seed, which is viable for only a short time, is the only way of achieving more than one blooming a year. With fluorescent light, you can have a triple flowering with seed. And with plants maturing at different times, it is possible to have a continuous succession of bloom if the plantings are judiciously spaced. This does mitigate the problem of dormancy, but you must like the plant rather well to go to the trouble.

If, on the other hand, you clip off the pods after blooming and develop rhizomes in greater quantity, you must wait until the plant, having finished flowering, gradually dies off aboveground. The rhizomes are then either left in the ground (in a terrarium for instance) or stored in a plastic bag until they choose to show signs of life again. You can, of course, compromise on the issue by allowing only one flower to go to seed. No damage is then done, you will have ample seed and the best of both situations.

Phinaea, like so many of the tuberous and rhizomatous gesneriads, does not like its surrounding soil to be very wet; it does not like coolness or low humidity. Its proper environment is 65° to 80° F at all times, very good drainage in lightly packed soil which is just moist, and humidity of over 60 percent. Fertilizing is hardly necessary at all. Perhaps more sturdy, floriferous plants can be achieved by using a very mild solution of high phosphate–potash fertilizer twice during the growth period. As for light, we calculate that 125–200 footcandles will be sufficient for a terrarium.

Rechsteineria

This tuberous genus of about seventy-five species, with a range from Mexico to Brazil, comprised a few popular species. In 1974 and 1976, the Classification and Nomenclature Committee of AGGS accepted the proposals of Dr. Harold E. Moore to transfer a number of species to the genus *Sinningia*. We list these changes below.

Sinningia aggregata. The plant we illustrated and described as *R. pendulina* should have been *R. aggregata*. *R. aggregata* having been transferred to *Sinningia*, the name should read *S. aggregata* 'Pendulina.'

Sinningia allogophylla was *R. allogophylla.*

Sinningia canescens. This was formerly known as *R. leucotricha,* changed to *S. leucotricha,* and finally settled in for good, we hope, as *S. canescens.*

Sinningia cardinalis is the former *R. cardinalis.*

Sinningia claybergiana replaces *R. lindleyi.*

Sinningia cooperi replaces *R. cooperi.*

Sinningia macropoda replaces *R. macropoda, R. cyclophylla,* and *R. lineata.*

Sinningia macrorrhiza for *R. macrorrhiza.*

Sinningia magnifica for *R. magnifica.*

Sinningia tuberosa replaces *R. tuberosa.*

Sinningia verticillata replaces *R. verticillata.*

Sinningia warszewiczii replaces *R. warszewiczii.*

Requiescat in pacem.

It must be said that Dr. Moore's changes make sense. Only later on did the situation get somewhat out of hand.

Rechsteineria pendulina. Courtesy Kartuz Greenhouses

Sinningia aggregata 'Pendulina' (*Rechsteineria pendulina*). Because, in our revision, the text of genus *Rechsteineria* became obsolete, whereas practical considerations required filling this space, we are maintaining here our description of a plant that we still rate highly.

S. aggregata is tuberous, of course, as are all of the genus. Here the tuber is orbicular, usually shows above soil level, and is covered with crumpled velvety scales almost carnelian in color. On close examination a number of small green growths are revealed, indicating an ability to produce several stems. The tuber may also be divisible into several "eyes" for propagation.

The whole plant is minutely hairy. The stem is stiff, narrow and woody, with many branches, and up to 18 inches high if not trimmed. The leaves are oval-pointed, 1 to 1½ inches long and crisply, rather deeply toothed. The flowers, produced from the axils in great numbers on long pedicels, are over an inch long, narrowly tubular with a short flare and bright red. They stand out well from the foliage, which grows in threes with long internodes.

The plant has another, unique, form in which the tube is uniformly split into five segments for its entire length. As the substance is very thin, they tend to curl in a ragged manner. Nevertheless, the apparent size of the flowers is increased at least three-fold. It is a phenomenon we have never seen elsewhere in the gesneriads. This variation has been available from Kartuz as *S.* 'Red Feather.'

The fault of *S. aggregata* 'Pendulina' that has hindered its popularity is probably the difficulty of propagation. Unfortunately, commercial growers must abandon any plant that is not capable of easy propagation. That, however, should not deter gesneriad enthusiasts. We have found that neat heel cuttings from young branches placed in sphagnum moss under terrarium conditions respond sufficiently to satisfy an amateur's need for plants. It would be a shame to see this fine plant disappear from cultivation entirely.

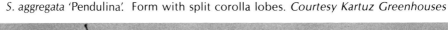

S. aggregata 'Pendulina'. Form with split corolla lobes. *Courtesy Kartuz Greenhouses*

Rhabdothamnus

There is one New Zealand species. A small shrub with campanulate orange or yellow flowers. *R. solandri*, like most New Zealand plants, prefers cool growing conditions as in our Pacific northwest.

Rhynchoglossum

There are about fifteen species in *Rhynchoglossum,* formerly called *Klugia,* from East Asia and Central and South America—the only example of a genus from both the Old and New Worlds. They seem to be herbs of moist warm places.

We have seen *Rhynchoglossum notonianum* at the Bailey Hortorium of Cornell University. It reminded us in leaf and growth of a somewhat larger, more spreading *Streptocarpus holstii.* The flowers are the most two-lipped we have seen in the *Gesneriaceae.* They are about 1¼ inches long, with a narrow white tube opening up into a short white upper lip which is reflexed and an unlobed, spade-shaped lower lip as long as the tube, rather flat but curving downward. The color of the lower lip is bright pure blue. They grow on one-sided racemes opening a few at a time and are not very conspicuous. Nevertheless a pretty plant. It is fibrous rooted. This is now *Rhynchoglossum gardneri.*

Rhytidophylum

There are ten or so species of *Rhytidophylum*—shrubs from the West Indies. They are related to *Gesneria* but have greenish, inconspicuous flowers. The plants are usually large.

Saintpaulia

The most popular of all gesneriads, the African violets, will not receive in this book the amount of space proportionate to their importance and popularity because there are so many other sources of information in print. The Helen Van Pelt Wilson books cover the subject more than adequately. *African Violet Magazine* and GSN deal with every aspect in their issues. The following, therefore, is meant to be of interest principally to those who are meeting up with these wonderful plants for the first time.

In spite of their great popularity, or perhaps because of it, we have often heard houseplant growers depreciate African violets. Others, in spite of their superb record in cultivation, report that they are unable to grow them well. To us it is almost inconceivable that anyone would not want these plants or, if having difficulties, not persist in growing until they knew how to deal with them. There is no question that, in respect to floriferousness, variety, ease of culture, and overall beauty, they surpass any other houseplants we have today.

Because of our broad interests in plants, we do not collect many different kinds of African violets. But we have always had a substantial proportion of our gardening space devoted to the cultivars we like best. And this is facilitated by the fact that, living in an apartment and depending for flowering on our fluorescent light gardens almost exclusively, African violets are the only plants which will bloom throughout the year in a window—interrupted only by prolonged periods of cloudy weather.

They are the only ones which are not demanding of high humidity, do not go to pieces in summer heat, and will tolerate some coolness without wilting. None of the other actively blooming plants can remain almost completely dry for a week without visible damage or take an occasional excessive soaking without rotting—though this is the greater danger to African violets. As for insects, for which gesneriads as a family do not seem to be the most appreciated hosts, African violets appear to be regularly subject only to rather severe visitations of mealybug.

Except for the period when it became a fad to hybridize and grow plants of monstrous diameters—cartwheels as big as Swiss cheeses—African violets have always had a habit and size which suited them ideally to the window or fluorescent light garden. What other plant permitted one to grow so many of rather uniform height and constant bloom and variety within so little space?

It is true that they need constant attention to achieve fine bloom and form. The idea that they can be just set out to pasture and that nature will care for them is erroneous. They do need fertilizing and regular watering for best results. They do age moderately quickly and must be replaced. Beyond a certain point, repotting no longer results in handsome, well-shaped plants. But, in compensation, they are among the easiest plants to propagate.

Much of the difficulty with African violets has been due to poor hybrids which have been tossed in great numbers on the market because of peculiarities—often hideously ugly—of leaf and flower. Sometimes the largest- and handsomest-leaved blooming plants are difficult to grow and have all kinds of faults in cultivation. Commercial growers have reacted to a constant thirst for novelty rather than quality by giving the customer what he or she wanted. The newcomer to African violets is easily misled into imagining that failure with these wretched individuals is typical of the plants in general. On the contrary, African violets do not act at all alike and only carefully selected plants will fit perfectly into a given environment. If you have failed with one plant, try another.

There is an amusing aspect to this business of choosing the right plant. As a generally good rule, do not consult an African violet "expert." These are usually much too concerned with winning prizes at shows with novelties or with growing some gorgeous but faulty plant to perfection, to give sound advice to a novice. You are better off with a friend who has a small collection and some experience and can tell you which ones have really done well with normal care. If you're not growing for show, you want regular performance, not novelty.

Equally unreliable is the nurseryman. He is impelled to promote his most recent "list" rather than dredging up some good plant of the past. When you visit a real African violet nursery, the effect is overwhelming—a kaleidoscope of plants of different sizes and flower shapes that is enough to turn one off. Choices become matters of momentary caprice, some plant name one has heard somewhere or the chance that one set of plants is in better bloom than the others—which has nothing at all to do with quality or beauty. In this situation the novice is helpless and it is pure luck if the plants purchased turn out to be decent ones.

Don't think we're immune. Often we have looked for something "really new" and have found a plant with a most attractive color—a shade or a shape we had never seen before. Almost invariably these plants turn out to be duds from the word go. A pure waste of time and money.

Let us explain that we consider these warnings an essential aid in growing African violets. The lesson is that there are good and bad plants. If you don't have a good one to start with, your chances of success are poor.

Happily there are some very fine plants and we think the *African Violet Magazine* Honor Roll on pp. 148–49 is an ideal guide to the best. If a plant can stay popular for five years, it has to be a good one.

If you have never grown a flowering houseplant, this is where to start. Recently very superior African violets have been carried by florists because of the development of the 'Rhapsodie' and 'Ballet' strains. These plants, tolerant, durable, naturally of good habit, present few problems for anyone. The returns in long-lasting flowering are incomparable. Later on you can go on to the trickier plants, but start with a good African violet. It is the greatest blooming indoor plant in history.

MINI-HISTORY

We cannot resist spelling out the name of the discoverer of *Saintpaulia* in all its magnificence. He was Adalbert Emil Redcliffe Le Tanneur von Saint Paul-Illaire. A name like that is no doubt a spur to heroic deeds. He found his plants in 1892 while governor of the German colonial province of Usambara, a district in Northeast Tanganyika. The seeds he collected in two locations were sent to his father, a prominent official in Fischbach, Silesia, who was an amateur horticulturist and promptly sent plants to the famous Herman Wendland (there are quite a few species named *Wendlandii*), director of the Royal Botanical Gardens at Herrenhausen. Wendland named the genus in honor of its discoverer. Friedrich Benary of the world-renowned seed house of Ernst Benary, Erfurt, was the first to grow them commercially.

There are now twenty recognized species of *Saintpaulia*. The seeds sent back by Saint Paul were apparently of two species, and fortunately one of these was *S. ionantha* which has proved one of the best sires. One of the original lots was collected at only 150 feet above sea level and the other at maximum 2,500 feet—not, as often reported, in caves but in shaded situations. The low altitude at which they grow makes the African violet particularly suited to the warm conditions of our homes, unlike some collections of other genera made at high altitudes and better adapted to English growing conditions.

In the Benary nursery, mutations soon began to appear, starting with a pink shade and then a white. Since then, African violets have shown an extraordinary ability to produce mutants in respect to leaves, flower form, and flower color, which has reinforced the efforts of hybridizers so that the range of differences is endless.

Saintpaulia plants grown in Europe were for a long time species or mutants. The plants were latecomers on the scene, many other gesneriads having been discovered and commercially grown much earlier. For instance *Streptocarpus rexii* was found in 1818 and *Sinningia speciosa* around the same time. Before it came to our shores, the African violet was just another houseplant enjoying less popularity than the *Gloxinia* or *Achimenes*.

Commercial interest developed in the United States only after 1927 when Armacost & Royston of Los Angeles, California, imported German seed and introduced the plants to the trade. Development of the hobby was slow until the 1930s and the African Violet Society of America was not founded until 1946. Anne and Frank Tinari had already started to produce African violets exclusively a short time before. Lyndon Lyon started in the 1950s and made tremendous progress with the finest double pink-flowered plants in 1954. Henry Peterson in Cincinnati was another pioneer. These growers and Hugh Eyerdom of Granger Gardens introduced many cultivars which resulted in all the fine colors and interesting shapes of the modern plants. After this beginning, the spread in popularity was rapid. Today it is stated that the African violet is the largest cash flowering plant crop in the country. Although the gesneriad societies, including those devoted exclusively to African violets, remain relatively small, the number of amateur growers can be counted in the millions.

In spite of the worthless crosses and false starts, a fine repertory of plants has been created. Our illustrations reproduce the basic modern forms of flower and leaf. The colors are white, pink, blue, red, and even green. A yellow African violet is still to be achieved.

THE SPECIES

The similarities between *Saintpaulia* species are so great that someone may eventually throw them all in the same pot. The flowers are remarkably alike, consisting of two small upper lobes and three lower ones, as separate in appearance as petals, a flat face, and a very short tube. Peduncles from the leaf axils bear two to ten flowers. Two fertile stamens bear oval yellow anther sacs which split to release the pollen, though, if you want to do some hybridizing, you may have to help the process by slitting or squashing them. The style and stigma stick out rather conspicuously from the side.

The flowers, as we know, are very long lasting and the peduncles will often produce more buds if the first bud is removed.

There is an obvious division of the genus into two types of plants. The one has roundish leaves and a trailing manner of growth with the leaves arranged alternately on the stems. These include *S. goetzeana, amaniensis,* and *magungensis.* The rest are all rosette-type plants, nearly stemless, with oval, somewhat pointed leaves with one side of the blade often larger than the other. Until recently the rosette type was developed exclusively, but now plants have been crossed with the trailing species to produce more variety. The other differences between the plants of each species have in some instances been reduced to a question of long or short, sparse or plentiful hairs.

The present known species are:

S. amaniensis
S. brevisepala
S. confusa
S. difficilis
S. diplotricha

Saintpaulia diplotricha. Photo L. H. Bailey Hortorium of Cornell University

Saintpaulia grandiflora. Photo L. H. Bailey Hortorium of Cornell University

S. goetzeana
S. grandifolia
S. grotei
S. inconspicua
S. intermedia
S. ionantha
S. magungensis
S. nitida
S. orbicularis
S. pendula
S. pusilla
S. rupicola
S. shumensis
S. teitensis
S. tongwensis
S. velutina

We have derived a great deal of pleasure from growing some of these species, all but two of which are said to be in cultivation in this country. They cannot compare in size of flower or brilliance of coloring with the modern hybrids but have all the virtues of wild flowers—simplicity, undisciplined growth, delicate colorings. We have what must be quite an old type hybrid with small, semidouble nice blue flowers, very compact and wonderfully adaptable. It is quite close still to the wild ones and a relief from some of the stiff, artificial-looking plants we often see today. It's good to see what nature did before man "improved."

Saintpaulia grotei. Photo L. H. Bailey Hortorium of Cornell University

Saintpaulia magungensis occidentalis. Photo L. H. Bailey Hortorium of Cornell University

Saintpaulia pendula. Photo L. H. Bailey Hortorium of Cornell University

*Saintpaulia rupicola. Photo
L. H. Bailey Hortorium of
Cornell University*

Saintpaulia tongwensis. Photo L. H. Bailey Hortorium of Cornell University

Saintpaulia velutina. Photo L. H. Bailey Hortorium of Cornell University

THE HYBRIDS

There are three types of standard African violet plants—rosettes, minis, and trailers. The first continues to be by far the most popular. Minis are charming but tend to sucker and be less easy to bloom. The trailers are basket plants unsuitable for many uses but having the advantage that they grow in a free manner and get away from the "bridal corsage" look of the others. Those not really familiar with plants in general may easily be misled into thinking that a totally artificial symmetry is desirable in plants. Nature has its own symmetry. A trailer or a mini allowed to produce some suckers and develop into a bunchy plant can, with judicious trimming and training, assume many beautiful shapes when in flower and far surpass the geometric monstrosities which win the prizes at the shows—marvels of care and culture but all looking distressingly alike, and dull. These are plants for people who settle into an unvarying pattern of living and want their plants to behave like model children—something no child or plant should ever be. Happily African violets don't have to be that way. Up with African violet lib!

We have already mentioned the Honor Roll of African Violets which is compiled by Mrs. M. G. Gonzales of San Jose, California, and published by the *African Violet Magazine.* We print this below. Any beginner would be wise to start with a plant from this list. It contains all the African Violets which have been consistently popular over a period of five years, and it is sufficiently selective to have found that, in the year 1972, none had met the exacting requirements.

Saintpaulia 'Rhapsodie Gisela' (HR). Pink flowered. *Mildred Schroeder*

HONOR ROLL OF AFRICAN VIOLETS

by
Mrs. M. G. Gonzales
Best Varieties Compiler

1965

Isle of Dreams No. 1187 (Lyndon Lyon)
Jubilee (Naomi)
Lilian Jarrett No. 1060 (Tinari Greenhouses)
Richter's Charm Song No. 1137 (Richter's Greenhouse)
Shrill (Lyndon Lyon)
Smoke Rings (Vallin)
Ulery's Trifari No. 1234 (Ulery's Greenhouses)

1966

Bloomin' Fool No. 1473 (Richter's Greenhouse)
Blue Chips No. 1340 (Naomi's African Violets)
Fandango No. 1782 (Granger Gardens)
Flash (Lyndon Lyon)
Fleet Dream No. 1131 (Select Violet House)
Glad Rags (Lyndon Lyon)
Granger Garden's Angela No. 1210 (Granger Gardens)
Granger Garden's Blue Modiste No. 1449 (Granger Gardens)
Granger Garden's Fair Elaine No. 1217 (Granger Gardens)
Granger Garden's Snow Ballet No. 1219 (Granger Gardens)
Hi Hopes No. 1303 (Lyndon Lyon)
Oriental Red No. 1304 (Lyndon Lyon)
Richter's Green Dawn No. 1138 (Richter's Greenhouse)
Richter's Red Crown No. 1180 (Richter's Greenhouse)

1967

Delft Imperial No. 1326 (Granger Gardens)
Granger Garden's Fury No. 1216 (Granger Gardens)

Granger Garden's Never Lovelier No. 1213 (Granger Gardens)
Granger Garden's Sweetheart Blue No. 1225 (Granger Gardens)
Granger Garden's Top Sail No. 1212 (Granger Gardens)
Paul Bunyan (Lyndon Lyon)
Sea Grape (West)

1968

Christmas Holly (Reed)
Champion's Water Lily No. 1289 (Champion's African Violets)
Silver Crest No. 1161 (Mrs. Duane L. Champion)
White Perfection No. 1471 (Lyndon Lyon)

1969

Tommie Lou No. 1744 (Oden)
Peak of Pink No. 1467 (Lyon)
Master Blue No. 1465 (Lyon)
Candy Lips No. 1461 (Lyon)
Clipper No. 1724 (Lyon)
Crown of Red No. 1462 (Lyon)
Plum Tip No. 1468 (Lyon)
Leawala (Lyon)
Full Stop (Lyon)

1970

Strawberry Shortcake No. 1509 (Taylor)
Jolly Giant No. 1549 (Lyon)
My Darling (Luciano)
Purple Choice (Lyon)
Red Honey No. 1551 (Lyon)
Cousin Janet No. 1547 (Lyon)
Icy Peach No. 1642 (Lyon)

1971

Lullaby No. 1783 (Granger)
Pink Jester No. 1598 (Granger)
Prom Queen No. 1533 (Granger)
Henny Backus No. 1725 (Lyon)
Hello Dolly No. 1641 (Lyon)
Tinted Frills (Lyon)
Red Cavalier (Lyon)
Janny No. 1527 (Granger)
Happy Time No. 1866 (Lyon)
Wrangler No. 1731 (Lyon)
Magnifica No. 1643 (Lyon)
Alakazam No. 1723 (Lyon)
Cochise (Lyon)
Emperor No. 1597 (R. J. Taylor)
Ruby (Lyon)

1972

No African violets qualified.

1973

Autumn Russet No. 1777 (Granger Gardens)
Charm Glow No. 1779 (Granger Gardens)
Granger Garden's Pied Piper No. 2021 (Granger Gardens)

1974

Ann Slocomb No. 1907 (Lanigan)
Blizzard (Lyon)
Bullseye (Lyon)
Creekside Moonbeam (Bea Mills)
Dazzling Deceiver No. 1865 (Lyon)
Rhapsodie Claudia (Holtkamp)
Rhapsodie Gisela (Holtkamp)
Rhapsodie Elfriede (Holtkamp)
Triple Threat No. 1989 (Lyon)

1975

Brigadoon No. 1014 (Granger Gardens)
Butterfly White No. 1983 (Lyon)
Blue Reverie No. 2013 (Granger Gardens)
After Dark No. 2117 (Richter's Greenhouse)
Firebird No. 2018 (Granger Gardens)
Granger's Carefree No. 2221 (Granger Gardens)
Jingle Bells (Richter's Greenhouse)
Rhapsodie Gigi (Holtkamp)
Rhapsodie Ophelia (Holtkamp)
Courtesy *The African Violet Magazine.*

When we examine Mrs. Gonzales's honor roll we readily observe that Richter and Tinari were important hybridizers. Tinari's 'Lillian Jarrett' remains one of the greatest of

Saintpaulia 'Lullaby' (GG). Lavender flowered. *Mildred Schroeder*

Saintpaulia 'Tommie Lou' (Oden.). Beautifully variegated type. *Mildred Schroeder*

all African violets to this day. Then, except for a group from Mrs. Duane L. Champion, it is all Hugh Eyerdom of Granger Gardens and Lyndon Lyon. Lyon has been undoubtedly the hybridizer of genius in this field. Finally, along with Lyon appears the name of Holtkamp.

The Holtkamp plants are from the 'Rhapsodie' series which has been augmented lately by the 'Ballet' series, each being a group of African violet plants representing a good range of color and form. Certainly 'Lisa,' one of the Ballets will be on the list in the near future, for this is the most reliable single-blooming pink we have ever known. This development is in a different direction from the earlier hybridizing.

In 1967/68, at one of the last International Flower Shows in New York, we almost stumbled on the floor of the exhibition hall over a mass of blue African violets the likes of which we had never seen before. One look and we exclaimed, "This is what good African violets are supposed to be." They belonged to a German hybridizer (possibly Englert) who was just off the boat and didn't even have a booth to show them in. That was the beginning.

Without Lyon and Granger, it couldn't have been done. But the German hybridizers concentrated on producing commercially viable plants of the type that could be sold through florists—possessing good shelf life, tolerant of neglect, very strongly blooming on stiff peduncles, flat leaves, long-lasting flowers. And here they were. We all know that these plants have almost monopolized florist business in African violets across the country and deservedly so. We have been told that there are much "better" plants than these. If there are, we haven't seen them. More interesting, yes. Larger-flowered, yes. More exciting and odder colors, yes. But, as all-around plants these are incomparable. And the reason of course is that they have not been created to satisfy the hobbyists but the general public. Through the work of these hybridizers, the plant has finally achieved mass distribution which was altogether impossible with the earlier ones. No doubt we will become bored with them and some will be failures. But the trend is right. The best plants are the

Trailing African Violet (Lyndon Lyon).

Miniature African Violet (Lyndon Lyon).

most popular ones—the easiest to grow at the nursery, to ship, to hold for sale, and to make the transition unhurt to the average home. It is the choice between satisfying 20,000 hobbyists or millions of people who are starving for colorful plants in their homes. We opt for the majority. For the Honor Roll 1976–82, see "Gesneriad Update," page 215.

CULTURE

LIGHT.   African violet cultivars are not a monolithic tribe of plants with the same cultural needs for all. In regard to light the variation can be considerable. As a general rule four or five hours of sunlight a day, or twelve to fourteen hours of 500 footcandles under fluorescent light, will produce maximum bloom. But there are hybrids which need more light unless the humidity is over 60 percent. And there are others which will bloom like mad with half the light intensity in the fluorescent light garden and fewer hours in the window.

It is always assumed also that light is an absolute factor. It is not. The amount of light required for good bloom for each plant varies according to the temperature, humidity, watering regimen, and fertilizer. Concentrate on just one cultivar and carry on comparative tests with hundreds of plants and you will be able to nail down the exact needs. But when we speak of hundreds of cultivars, not individuals of the same kind, the story is altogether different. The point is that with the maximum light requirement shown above you can win almost all of the time. But with certain ones you are going to have problems unless the other factors are adjusted. And nobody can tell you just how to handle the situation in each case. That is where experience and your personal observation count.

In any event African violets are not the shade-loving plants some would have us believe. They need a healthy amount of light, and they must have it pretty much day after day. The light from overcast skies is not enough to do the job. In the city figure on 30 percent less light on average than in the country. That is why apartment dwellers, even with southern open exposures, are unable to bloom the plants at some times of the year.

Your best assurance of bloom comes with fluorescent light culture combined with good warmth and humidity.

TEMPERATURE.   The only way to guarantee continuous bloom is with temperatures year-round of 65° or higher. Saintpaulias are not as sensitive to temperatures over 85° as some of the other gesneriads. Newly repotted plants do suffer at these high levels.

HUMIDITY.   African violets will bloom in quite low humidity if the light intensity is 500 footcandles or higher. But the plants will flourish far better with humidity over 50 percent. At 60 percent humidity some clones need only 150 footcandles to bloom.

WATERING.   Keep them just moist most of the time. Crown rot, a common problem with African violets, occurs when there is overwatering at temperatures of 60–65°. The plants do not like a soggy soil at any time. Nevertheless wick watering and the use of Aquamatic planters and similar systems have been very successful with the plants. If you do use this method, keep the temperature up. Use lukewarm water.

MISTING.   The plants benefit from misting—not spraying.

SOIL.   Rich, very porous compost or soilless mixes. They'll do very well on average with Lean Mix too. Lime is advisable at the rate of two tablespoons of chips to the quart of mix.

In other words, African violets, for normal results are very little different in their needs from a number of other gesneriad genera.

PROPAGATION.   See pages 27–41 which covers this subject in part.

PROBLEMS.   Crown rot. Save what you can of healthy parts of leaves and propagate them.

Stem growth. When a plant develops a stem and becomes unsightly, you can decant it, trim the roots, and repot lower down in the soil. But, as we've pointed out before, this is a temporary measure until young plants come along. The plant rarely recovers its original vigor. Too woody.

PESTS.   African violets are attacked occasionally by mites, more commonly by mealybugs. More and more we are eliminating the use of pesticides ourselves. We find that persistent washing under a jet of lukewarm water will eliminate these and other pests. Even violets will not suffer too severely from this method if you hold the plant upside down and work the water into the axils turning the plant slowly. None of the pests can stand up against this treatment for very long.

We've tried Q-tips and alcohol and found it far more tiresome. Malathion is effective against mealybugs but is awful to work with, whatever its efficacy. In our opinion the water does a good job.

We do use a pesticide soil drench for little soil insects. And, of course, for nematodes you have no choice except Nemagon or throwing the plant out. We don't try to cure nematodes. They are the one thing that will cause us to destroy a plant.

Sarmienta

We have never grown *Sarmienta repens,* and we have seen only one small plant. Dr. Henry Teuscher, former director of the Montreal Botanical Garden, who has introduced so many gesneriads to cultivation and has been a constant contributor of information through horticultural magazines, wrote a description in *The Gloxinian* of July/August 1967. It was mouth-watering, but the fact that, up to now, this species has received little further attention is evidence that the relative unpopularity of the cool growing plants holds in spades for this one. It is a mountainous dweller from Chile and would have been included with our section on Alpine gesneriads if we had not considered the subject of some interest for indoor growers, if only as a warning.

Accompanying Dr. Teuscher's article were two black-and-white photos. The one showed a large azalea pot with a plant growing therein which had sent out a myriad of long pendent stems lined with small leaves and reaching down as much as 12 or 15 inches below the rim. This plant was without a flower. The other photograph showed part of a plant close up, and these same branches almost hidden by scores of long hanging bell flowers—the shape like an upside-down vase—each with two stamens issuing as far out from the throat as the length of the corolla itself.

We quote from Dr. Teuscher's description. ". . . they adjust themselves very readily to the reversed seasons of the northern hemisphere. All that is required is that during our winter they should be given a cool resting period of 3 to 3½ months at 40 to 45 degrees F. When, after this period, they are returned to a greenhouse with 65 to 70 degrees F., they flower readily and abundantly."

He then refers to the two photographs. "One of the plants has been kept continuously in a warm greenhouse (65 to 70 degrees F.) and has never flowered for over 4 years. The other plant was placed this winter in a cool greenhouse (40–45 degrees F.) for 3½ months, from the end of November to early March. Within 2 weeks after it was returned to the warm greenhouse it burst into bloom as shown, covering itself with bright salmon-colored, elongated hanging bells. A glorious display which at this writing (end of May) is still continuing."

We do not know whether another *Sarmienta,* namely *S. scandens,* is in cultivation.

Sarmienta scandens.

Close-up of Sarmienta scandens.

Sinningia

After *Saintpaulia* the sinningias are next in popularity. Gloxinia, the common name for the showiest member, became a great gift plant in Europe and the United States long before *Saintpaulia* was introduced and eventually overtook it in public esteem. The slipper gloxinias (*S. speciosa, regina,* and variants) are also beautiful plants. *S. pusilla* and *concinna,* extraordinary plants in their own right, have, since 1950, spawned hybrids with *S. eumorpha* and other *Sinningia* species. These have gained more and more adherents among indoor growers. The recent addition of some fine former rechsteinerias to the genus has further increased its importance. The long term prospects of *Sinningia* are even better than *Saintpaulia*'s, for the future will certainly bring many more fine, everblooming cultivars.

It may be instructive to compare the very different qualities of *Saintpaulia* and *Sinningia.* The former are fibrous-rooted plants with only about eighteen species, all quite recognizable at first sight. For, although the limbs are fused, the tube is very short, and the lobes of the corolla look, at least in the species, like petals. Also they are all open faced and the difference in leaves is only between round and oval forms and in growth between a rosette and more trailing habit. This suggests that, although there will always be novelties in color and form, we may be rather close to the limits of the genus at this time.

The species sinningias, on the other hand, show great variation. For instance *S. hirsuta* is similar to *Saintpaulia* in flower but is immensely hairy. *S. regina* displays beautifully veined leaves and showy slipper flowers, while *S. speciosa,* in the form of the florist gloxinia, has spectacular flowers of great size in a magnificent color range. *S. pusilla* and *S. concinna* display miniaturization to its best advantage. *S. barbata* is in the form of a Dutchman's pipe. The addition of *Rechsteineria* species introduces pure tube shapes. Thus there is a broad spectrum of plants with which to carry variation and adaptation to new heights by means of selection and hybridization.

JOINING *RECHSTEINERIA* TO *SINNINGIA.*   The hybridizing work of Dr. Carl D. Clayberg demonstrated that rechsteinerias could be crossed with sinningias. As a result, a number of *Rechsteineria* species have been transferred to the genus *Sinningia.* This leaves about sixty-five species of rechsteinerias which have not been tested in this respect and, therefore, until there has been further study, these remain in limbo. In other words they continue to be rechsteinerias under suspicion of being switched at any moment—a very disturbing situation for any self-respecting species. And, of course, *Sinningia,* a genus ranging from Brazil to Mexico, with about fifteen species may not just receive the ten we list below but end up greatly outnumbered by the transferees.

RESEMBLANCE OF *RECHSTEINERIA* AND *SINNINGIA.*   Despite differences in flower shapes there are a number of structural similarities between *Rechsteineria* and *Sinningia.* Both have a disk at the base of the ovary with two to five glands. Both have half-inferior ovaries. You will notice this in the florist gloxinia, where the ovary does not stand up fully outlined once the limb is removed, but is half imbedded, and the calyx and tube are attached at its middle. In both, the four anthers are united at their tips and are heart-shaped. A recount of chromosome numbers also indicated that most of the important rechsteinerias had the same count, $n = 26$, as the sinningias. So the differentiation into two genera was largely based on the appearance of the flowers, which has proved a less and less reliable criterion for labeling gesneriads—though a very convenient means of recognition for the amateur.

Thus *Sinningia* has grown in importance and offers future hybridizers a wide-open field for exotic combinations. The only tuberous everblooming plants under indoor conditions (except perhaps a couple of the tuberous oxalises) are sinningias, and it has been proved that this quality is dominant in crosses between *S. pusilla* and *concinna* and other sinningias. Undoubtedly many beautiful and useful houseplants will emerge from any future activity involving these plants.

CONFUSION BETWEEN *SINNINGIA* AND *GLOXINIA*.   The story of the mix-up between *Gloxinia* and *Sinningia* has been recounted *ad nauseam* but can't be avoided for the reader still unfamiliar with it.

The trouble arose because the botanical name of a plant must always be the one applied to it for the first time in print. Thus there are numerous instances of names that have been accepted for many years being changed because further research digs up the fact that the plant had previously been mentioned under a different label. Whatever confusion this may temporarily cause, it is the only rule which prevents chaos.

Sinningia speciosa was brought to Europe in 1815 under the name of *Gloxinia*, a title already published for another genus of gesneriads. By the time, in 1825, that Christian Gottfried Nees von Esenbeck (1776–1858) applied the name *Sinningia helleri* to a tuberous Brazilian plant, gloxinia had come into general use for the funnel-shaped flower forms of *Sinningia*. So now the situation is that gloxinia is the common name for the large florist sinningias and the genus name for a number of other gesneriads. *Sinningia* is the correct botanical name for the florist gloxinia and for the original sinningia species plus any additional plants included in the genus.

A PECULIAR CUSTOM.   For the fun of it we would like to lodge a protest against the fuss always arising over the individual after which a genus or species is named. Wilhelm Sinning, 1792–1874, was the horticulturist of the Royal Agricultural College in Bonn, Germany. On the other hand the texts rarely do honor to the explorers and botanists who actually discovered, researched, or named the plants. Sinning is a minor figure compared to Nees, John Lindley (1799–1865), and many others. Though Gesner was an important figure he had nothing to do with gesneriads, while there are dozens of other scientists after whom no gesneriads are named who really advanced the knowledge and cultivation of this family.

DEPENDENCE ON ORIGINAL SPECIES.   As hybridization and selection develop apace in cultivation, the origins of the plants decline in interest for the average grower. Hybrids are crossed with fertile hybrids, and in mass growing "superior" plants are selected for further development. The original plant material from the wild no longer figures in the breeding patterns. And what often happens is that the native plants are either neglected or so destroyed by human encroachment that nothing is left.

In itself this may seem of little importance since we have our much more highly developed commercial plants, in comparison with which the natural ones seem most uninteresting. But, when species in nature are wiped out, we lose the ability to redirect the development of plant breeding. We are forced to depend on the genetic stock of the plants we have. In the case of *Saintpaulia*, in spite of enormous hybridizing activity, the species plants are still available and contribute to the development of new forms. Disappearance of the species seems very unimportant in the short run but may be of great significance with the passage of time. Our needs and tastes are not immutable and the plants which satisfy one generation and environment may be totally unsuitable to the tastes and requirements of another. In the long run, if we are to get "new blood," it must be from normal or unusual wild plants which carry different genetic codes.

PRESERVING WILD PLANTS.   Botanists are concerned about the wild species preserved in botanical gardens and private collections, since the conditions are so different from the habitat and, after a number of generations, they no longer resemble the true wild stock in certain possibly important respects. We see the need for changes of direction when we have become surfeited with one "official" form of a plant, or taste has changed, or the horticultural environment is readjusted. Everybody assumes that a gloxinia must look just so, that it may change coloring and marking and size but be always essentially the same. That is not true, especially so in such a variable genus as *Sinningia*. The loss of wild variations is, therefore, a very serious matter for the future of horticulture.

Sinningia speciosa, which includes all the large-flowered slippers and funnel-shaped florist gloxinias, is still the most important species in commerce, it is the one we will describe first.

S. speciosa has been in cultivation since 1817 and, having achieved early popularity, and being extremely variable, the original form of the plant has become difficult to trace as the flood of sports, selections, and hybrids has increased. Of course there are still wild slipper gloxinias in Brazil, which may or may not represent the clones originally imported into Europe. It really doesn't matter anymore as far as the general reader is concerned. But, for the sake of clarity, we will follow Professor Moore's arrangement of the species into three groups, the first of which he calls *Convariety speciosa* or the *Speciosa* group, representing the presumed wild type. *Convariety maxima* includes the improved slipper gloxinias up to the present. And *Convariety Fyfiana,* or the *Fyfiana* group covers the funnel-shaped florist gloxinias.

The *Fyfiana* group is named for John Fyfe, a Scottish horticulturist, who is only one of several apparent discoverers of the first funnel-shaped florist gloxinia. We would have preferred to call this the *Peloric* group (see *S. cardinalis* 'George Kalmbacher'), for it is this recessive mutation from slipper form to rotate form which characterizes these plants.

Sinningia speciosa, Convariety Speciosa, the wild *S. speciosa,* is a tuberous plant with short stems and leaves reaching 8 inches in length and 6 in width, scalloped along the edge. Height may reach 12 inches. Stem and leaves are hairy. The reverse of the leaves is often paler or flushed with red. The flower is nodding and about 1½ inches long, often with a ridge or angle at the top and rounded underneath. The two upper lobes of the limb are erect, and the three lower are somewhat broader and thrust forward. The anthers of the four stamens are united.

The hairy green calyx consists of five lobes up to ⅞ inch long, broad at the base and attenuated toward the tip. We describe the calyx last for the reason that the position of the nodding flower in relation to the calyx is different from that of an erect flower. When the tubular flower is in a nodding position, or at right angles to the calyx, the opening at the base, which permits the entry of the anthers and stigma, or rather surrounds them, is not at the end of the tube but under it. The tube is usually supported in this position by the two lower lobes of the calyx; two stand erect on either side; and one is forced backward or curls over the end of the tube. In erect flowers the relationship is symmetrical, the sepals evenly clasping the tube and the hole being at the end. It is this way in the funnel-shaped flowers of the florist gloxinia.

Even in the wild state *S. speciosa* shows considerable variation in coloration and form. The color may be violet, white, pink, or red, with yellow flushing the inside of the tube or white spotted with red, depending on the base color.

Professor Moore recognizes the following typical forms:

S. Speciosa. Typical with short stems and violet flowers.

S. Albiflora. White flowered and almost exactly like *S. eumorpha.* The flowers have, however, 5 glands instead of 2, and there are no spots in the corolla tube.

S. Caulescens. Described as a plant with elongate stems—to 12 inches. None of the slipper gloxinias is acaulescent (without a stem), so this is presumably merely a less compact form.

S. Macrophylla. Characterized by large leaves, marked with white about the veins.

This variety is often confused with *S. regina* when the flowers are purple, especially in the hybrids. The distinction between the leaves of *regina* and this form of *S. speciosa* is, apparently, difficult to describe accurately in words—white and silver in such plants being almost interchangeable. But *regina* leaves are notably more elegant in form and in brilliance of marking.

S. Menziesii. Flowers white or ivory with purple tinge, the throat much spotted with purple.

S. Rubra. The red wild slipper sinningias.

These species forms are of no importance whatsoever in trade and are not grown by amateurs. They do appear in botanical collections and are a bank of natural forms to draw on for the creation of new hybrids or backcrossing of the modern highly complex ones.

Sinningia speciosa, Convariety maxima. This is the designation for selected and hybridized slipper type gloxinias. Since 1838, when the famous English garden architect Joseph Paxton listed a "hybrid" between two forms of *S. speciosa* of the slipper type, there have been innumerable selections and "hybrids" improving the size of flowers, shape, size of plant, and coloring up to the present day.

When we approached the writing of this section we imagined that there would be much to report and many plants to list. But the more we looked into the matter the less we found. The whole history of the larger sinningias is dominated by the simple fact that the funnel-shaped florist gloxinias have always been very much more popular with the public and the trade, to such an extent that commercial growing of the slippers has never been carried on, at least in this country, on a large scale. A number of firms which formerly grew and advertised the plants have curtailed production and no longer make offerings. Even *S. regina,* which is also a slipper flower, has been grown more consistently.

There is an evident logic behind this development. The major business in the florist gloxinias has been for the gift and holiday plant trade. They are temporary, seasonal bloomers which most people toss away when dormancy sets in. Though some did carry the plants over, this represented only a small part of the market and would never have justified mass production. Possessing the same fault of dormancy, the slipper gloxinias are less adaptable and produce fewer blooms in a smaller range of colors over a shorter period.

Whereas the florist gloxinias hold their flowers in a vertical position for all to see, the slipper gloxinias nod and, when placed on a table, show only the tops of the tubes. The florist gloxinias also were bred to produce circles of leaves with a solid mass of bloom at the center, like African violets. This was never successfully accomplished with slippers and, if it were, no doubt the effect would have been unattractive. Finally, interspecific *Sinningia* crosses have seemed to offer a more hopeful line of breeding.

The result has been, recently, a number of attempts to introduce interesting slipper gloxinias and each one has proved abortive. For instance, the November-December 1973 issue of *The Gloxinian* announced a "Best of Show" won by Al Buell's *Sinningia speciosa* 'Lela,' a beautiful open-faced trumpet, white with a strong suffusion of rose red on the lower lobes except for the edge which was lightly and irregularly scalloped. The plant was also recommended for its vigor. A number of similar *S. speciosa* cultivars were produced during this period but, in spite of all the admiration they aroused, none has held on. The following few listings are an indication of the present situation.

S. SPECIOSA CULTIVARS

Buell's Greenhouses. Strains of slipper gloxinias have been maintained for a number

Sinningia speciosa 'Laurentian' (Buell).

of years. Two named varieties are 'Laurentian,' with white 2-inch nodding flowers of graceful form with a deep purple splotch in the front of the throat, and 'Mont Royal,' which is of the same size but has a red splotch in the throat. Both are stable from seed, outstandingly pretty, and well worth growing. However, leaves are 6 or more inches long and the blooming period is relatively short. Similar in size and habit are some pure pink and white slippers.

In addition, Buell has had an unnamed mixed seed line of larger flowered plants of the type in which the throat widens almost regularly, with broader overlapping lobes in various colors with much speckling and flushes of yellow. Named varieties are 'Midnight Queen,' dark purple; 'Red Empress,' dark red with upper lobes lighter; 'Ruffled Queen,' pink; 'Snow Queen,' pure white; 'Striped Corsage,' pink with white throat. These are offered as tubers.

Fischer Greenhouses formerly offered 'Blue Blaze,' 'Blue Flicker,' 'Royal Blue,' described as having 2-inch flowers. No longer offered.

Kartuz Greenhouses still offers *S.* 'Florence K.,' a Peggie Schulz plant of 1959. It has leaves with silver veining and red slipper flowers. This is a compact plant and very floriferous—quite possibly the best of the lot for the average grower. The flowers are about 3 inches long and held more horizontally than most.

Lyndon Lyon turned out cultivars of the slipper gloxinias for a number of years. As recently as 1974 he offered 'Elfin,' described as peach colored, upcurved tube, with white ruffled limb and pink splotch on the floor of the tube. The face, as we remember it, was very wide and open. No plants have been offered recently.

Easterbrook offered "Slipper Type Miniature Gloxinias" but we suspect these are xGloxinera types.

S. 'Paschia' was offered originally by F. Jank, Hamburg, West Germany, in 1956 and

Sinningia speciosa 'Red Slipper' (Buell).

Sinningia 'Florence K' (Kartuz).

Sinningia speciosa double (Lyndon Lyon). A relatively dwarf plant.

then listed for many years by Geo. W. Park Seed Co. It was claimed as a bigeneric cross between *Kohleria* and *Sinningia* but seems to be a normal *S. speciosa* with 1½-inch slipper, red with white inside the tube, and 2 inches across the face. It has not proved a particularly satisfactory plant, but leaf spread is a bit more compact than the type.

Sinningia speciosa, Convariety Fyfiana. The florist gloxinia. As we've already noted, the wild *Sinningia speciosa* is a small slipper flower which shows considerable variability. Earliest improvements in the breed involved increasing the size and the range of colors and markings. John Fyfe, a Scottish gardener, is usually credited with originating or discovering the florist gloxinia in 1845. The seed, of unknown parentage, produced upright instead of nodding flowers with equal lobes instead of a pair of upper and three lower ones of different size and shape. On the other hand, it might have been created in France by Georges Rossiaud, chief gardener of the Count Talleyrand. Perhaps it's a matter of patriotism on both sides.

The new flower might have been put down as a simple case of *peloria*. However, the flower did differ in one other respect from the normal. The fifth stamen, normally vestigial in the slipper gloxinias, was fully fertile and united with the others to the side of the style. You can notice this in your home-grown gloxinias. Also the plant produced a stem. Naturally this upright flower had a calyx which gripped the tube evenly on all sides in contrast to the nodding slipper which was cradled.

This striking change in appearance made gloxinia's fortune, as the upright blooms were far showier than the normal species.

Many other flowers have been admired and attempts made to improve and vary them with limited results because the species belonged to a type which remained stable. Fortunately the funnel-shaped gloxinia was not only very fertile but proved extremely variable and breeders had a field day with it.

Most of the great classic plants were developed before 1900. After that there was a gap until the 1950s when both European and American firms became active in the development of new plants. In this country Antonelli Bros., Alberts and Merkel, Buell, Lyon, the firm of Earl J. Small, and Peggie Schulz, have produced interesting new plants. The principal recent developments have been in the area of doubling the flower and reducing its size. Doubling had a short, brilliant, success followed by a setback. Part of the problem is the added weight of the flower which tends to nod. The other was that the cultivars had a habit of not coming out of dormancy. There has been steady improvement by commercial growers recently, and we may expect another burst of doubles interest.

Other nurseries have concentrated on producing larger and larger flowers in a greater range of colors. The results are an enormous number of art shades and tigrina, or spotted, flowers. Some of these are huge, and blooms 5 inches across are now common. Leaves are correspondingly tremendous in these strains. Most of these plants do not come true from seed but are produced as mixtures from which occasional plants emerge with truly extraordinary beauty. Mr. & Mrs. Wm. Hull used to display such monsters and Buell's have been particularly active in producing them. To list these plants would be hopeless as they change from year to year. Readers are referred to the annual catalogs.

The sale of gloxinias to the florist trade may, for all we know, be as large or even greater than ever. With a growing population and the greater interest in houseplants generally, this seems likely. But, relatively, the large gloxinias are meeting resistance. The enormous size of the leaves, their brittleness, and the difficulty in packing and shipping have made florists chary of carrying them, and large nurseries, of growing. Amateurs, who, in the sixties grew them in great numbers, having discovered that they responded well to artificial light, object to their great spread monopolizing bench space. Their short period of bloom, magnificent as it is, is not sufficient compensation. So, lately, there has been far more effort expended to develop smaller plants with good flowering characteristics. In 1975 Park's catalog, for instance, lists a Danish strain of more dwarfed plants which are recommended for "smaller, shorter, and more flexible leaves which bend without breaking." Floriferousness is just as great. Earl J. Small, the Florida growers, advertise such plants wholesale. Miniaturization is probably written into the future of the florist gloxinia.

FLORIST GLOXINIA CULTIVARS

There are three types of florist gloxinias offered the American public. One consists of new hybrids and selections from nurseries such as Kartuz, Buell, and Lyon, plus occasional individual creations like those of Peggie Schulz. Secondly, there are the old plants from the 1890s, such as 'Emperor Frederick,' 'Emperor William' or Wilhelm, 'Etoile de Feu,' 'Prince Albert' (the original form), 'Blanche de Meru,' and 'Waterloo,' which are classics, still favorites with florists and the public as gift plants. Finally, there is a mixed and constantly changing flow which strikes the catalogs, consisting of various selections from offerings of dealers and growers in Belgium, Denmark, Switzerland, and Japan. These are plants of indifferent to very superior quality. Antonellis Bros., on the west coast, and Earl J. Small in Pinellas Park, Florida, are two of the few offering their own productions to the trade.

It must be understood that the majority of plant, seed, and bulb mail order houses do not grow their own stock, in spite of the publicity they make for their "gardens." For instance much of the F1 (first generation) hybrid annual garden flower seed is grown in Costa Rica. The firms, however, do contract for growing and do set the terms in respect to quality of the plants they are to receive. The naming of the plants is largely capricious and, except for the classics, the same one may receive ten different names in as many catalogs.

The florist gloxinia has, at this stage, been hybridized, selected, and bred to such an extent that true differentiation has become as impossible as with African violets. The doubles which are on the market now, after the disappearance of some abortive breeds, are partly from original European stock but developed and possibly grown here.

It is obvious that if we speak of the importance of a plant we must think in terms of commercial and public popularity. The gloxinias which really count are therefore those which are offered in the mail order catalogs of the larger firms and distributed through garden centers and florist shops. They are also, by and large, the best buys in terms of price and quality. They have to be reasonably dependable in every respect and are chosen for appealing form and color. In this lottery the old classics continue to be the real leaders in spite of "improvements." Item after item comes from the period of the beginning of this century. Many of the others are developments from these plants. In the list which follows, the only rather distinctive plant offered by Park for instance is 'Libelle,' a Swiss import.

The products of the smaller nurseries are, in some instances, more spectacular, but they rarely receive the test of mass distribution and are replaced almost yearly by new varieties. A major smaller nursery, famous for introductions, does a much larger business serving the wholesale trade with plants from foreign bulbs or seeds that are uniform and of sturdier growth. The major possibility we have seen is the recent development of a still more dwarf strain than that of Ohlsens Enke of Denmark by Lyndon Lyon. That, however, is in the works and the plants are still uneven—mostly doubles. Plants which skip dormancy and produce a series of new growths would also be desirable. The Buell Greenhouses continue to turn out plants with simply enormous flowers—probably the largest anywhere.

There are two mutually exclusive situations in growing such plants as gloxinias. You can hybridize, service the hobbyist, and sell in small quantities. Or you must have the very large quantities available for delivery to the great mail order catalog firms and national distributors. These are the true developers of new plants in most cases, turning out massive editions of their older plants while working constantly to produce new and improved plants for eventual distribution. By and large the Europeans have a far larger market of this kind than we have, and the world-famous firms have been largely instrumental in developing the best of our commercial flowering houseplants.

This is the reason why it is often so difficult to do justice to the very fine plants offered by the smaller nurseries which may be very innovative but whose listing may have disappeared long before this book gets into print. For instance, of a fine group of slipper gloxinias developed by one hybridizer a number of years ago, not a single one is available today. Where are Mr. Casalese's beautiful hybrids which were once so highly regarded?

Therefore our list has to consist overwhelmingly of standard listed plants which have some hope of continuance. To be sure, if a new strain comes on the market from Europe, all will be changed immediately. But it is unlikely that anything startlingly new will develop except more dwarfing and better-shaped single flowers. It is hard to conceive of more beautiful plants than the classic ones and we would be happy to grow them all the time if we had the space. It is the lack of this commodity that is making dwarfing necessary, and we can, therefore, expect that gloxinias will become smaller and the problem will disappear. Watch for real dwarf and miniature florist gloxinias within the next ten years. We hope.

LIST OF FLORIST GLOXINIAS

Since 1976 there has been some decline in the popularity of gloxinias. They still appear in the shops for a short season. Hybridization has slowed down considerably. Nevertheless, this revised listing contains a number of changes.

Blanche de Meru. An old Belgian hybrid still available in the trade. The flowers are white with a rose throat.

Benary's Giant. The famous firm of Ernst Benary, Erfurt, Germany. This is one of a series of selective groups of improved gloxinias sold in the U.S. under original or various names as seeds or tubers.

Blue Chips. Park from seed. Deep royal blue.

Buell's. Buell's Greenhouses, Eastford, Connecticut, has become the main source for esoteric gloxinias, both peloric and slipper type, in the last ten years or so. The flowers are of huge size—5 inches across in some instances—and cover a wide range of colors. Much of the stock varies in coloration from plant to plant and is catalogued by number. Also doubles.

Crispa Meteor. Park. Described as large scarlet, beautifully ruffled and fringed. Crispa, as a name, goes back to 1908 to a label for Jank's 'Meteor.' Perhaps this is a similar plant.

Delight. Park from Ohlsens Enke, Denmark. Dwarf white with red throat.

Diana. Park. Pink with rose throat. A name often used for gloxinias in commerce as early as 1893 and by Park themselves for an Egger (German) hybrid in 1965. Many of such plants are little changed from the old hybrids. Blossfeld used the name for his best rose or pink.

Double Gloxinia. All the major growers offered double gloxinias between 1960 and 1970, when the vogue faded. Apparently commercial dealers experimented with American hybrids of this type but ultimately found that the novelty wore off and that European hybrid seed and tubers were more reliable.

Dwarf Gloxinias. Dwarf gloxinias have been offered since 1965 mainly through the hybridizations of Paul Rockelmann for Fischer Nurseries, Lyndon Lyon of Dolgeville, N.Y., and Ohlsens Enke, Denmark, as carried by Park. The Fischer dwarfs faded out in the early '70s. Best of these was 'Tom Thumb,' a fine small double red with white border. The Ohlsens Enke plants are listed here. Mr. Lyon's efforts have remained largely confined to the hobbyist trade. His crosses have been smaller than those from Denmark.

Emperor William. "By any other name" it's usually the same. Spellings vary from German to French with frequent gibberish. Originally this was 'Kaiser Wilhelm,' of course. The plant goes back to Albert Schenkel, 1899, and has become one of the standard and truly great florist gloxinias. This is a gorgeous plant with large flowers a rich, dark violet with white border, very uniform and symmetrical. A lasting favorite.

Emperor Frederick. Originally Kaiser Friedrich. A match for Emperor William. Red flower with white border. Any idea that this is a disappearing strain is vain. Another of the great standard gloxinias. Reliable grower and bloomer, clearly and handsomely colored and marked, these early plants are the best of the large gloxinias and have never been superseded as gift plants.

Etoile de Feu. Scarlet flowers in a very compact mass. This is also one of the early greats. It is still listed by Park and others. Probably of Belgian origin.

Fire King. Roi de Feu, Feuerkoenig are synonyms. An old dark scarlet ruffled plant; one of the first of this type, and still listed as seed and tuber.

F-1. T. Sakata, Yokohama, Japan. Stable seed-producing early bloom with 6 to 8 lobed flowers in vivid colors. Widely listed. The products of this nursery are of very high quality.

Gloeckner. The firm of Fred C. Gloeckner & Co., seed wholesalers and importers in New York City, are suppliers of many of the mail order seed and bulb firms. The latter have been buying gloxinia seeds and bulbs under various descriptive names, usually unrelated to any recognized strains, and putting their own fanciful names on them. Caveat emptor. The amateur can do no more than go by descriptions. Many of these seeds and bulbs are undoubtedly from fine sources and are actually standard gloxinias. But which?

Hollywood. Park. Pale violet.

Jack O'Diamonds. Scarlet double flower with white edge. A hybrid or selection of Peggie Schulz from 1958. A most successful double which has been widely grown commercially. One of the first doubles of this type.

Kegeljani. A strain developed by Mr. Ferdinand Kegeljan, Namur, Belgium. Large flowers in various colors. The bulbs and, perhaps, seeds are still being imported, and the pure white single-flowered type is listed by Park.

Libelle. E. and M. Keller, Switzerland. White flowers with patterned large splotch of red on lobes, like chevrons. Offered as seed by Park. This is a very interesting plant, demonstrating the possibility of patterned markings like those of some *Streptocarpus.*

Light Touch. Park. Cream flower with suffusion of pink. A double which is rather dull. Offered as seed with prediction of 50–75 percent double flowers, the rest single flowers.

Monte Cristo. Park seed. Swiss origin. Double deep scarlet.

Prince Albert. Early, 1858. Magnificent blue with white throat. The equal of the emperors and a classic.

Queen Wilhelmina. Various plants in pink, purple, or violet flowers have been listed under this name.

Roi des Rouges. Vilmorin. Red flowers. A famous plant that is still offered.

Tigrina. A designation applied to numerous plants with flowers that are spotted or netted with blue, pink, red, etc., on white ground. Probably started by Ernst Benary. Buell has developed many fine tigrinas.

Waterloo. A great old plant from Benary—1905. Still very much alive. Small, deep red flowers in a solid cluster.

The following are relatively recent cultivars from outstanding hybridizers or offered by nurseries without mention of their origins. Most of these plants are more compact than the older ones and some have nodding flowers. Ted Bona has been developing outstanding gesneriads for years. Recently he began to produce compact bell-flowered plants.

Claire Roberts. Pink and white bell flowers.

Claire Roberts x Lavender Queen. Low growing. Violet lobes, an ivory throat.

Don D. Rosy bell flowers, coppery leaves. Very compact.

Marty Mines. Dark pink flowers.

Mini Regina. Small Regina-type plant.

C. A. Cruikshank Ltd. of Toronto offers three double florist gloxinias.

Lyndon Lyon, in addition to his outstanding African violets, has many fine bell-flowered sinningias to his credit.

Double Delight. Upright, large, blue ruffled flowers on a dwarf plant.

Double White Swan. Bright white, double flowers. Dwarf.

Pink Dandy. Ruffled double pink, edged white.

Tickled Pink. Upright, large double pink flowers. Dwarf.

Earl J. Small of Pinellas Park, Florida, has been supplying nurserymen with an extensive line of single and double florist gloxinias of high quality and compact habit. A number of these are two-tone, with colored lobes and white throats like the finest of the older cultivars. They also have a complete line of super compacts. This and the following firm are the only sources at present that we know of for superior gloxinias in quantity.

Southern Floral Company, Houston, Texas, offers 'Bridget's Best' florist gloxinias in all the standard colors.

SPECIES SINNINGIAS

Sinningia aggregata (Rechsteineria aggregata) was transfered to *Sinningia* after having been crossed with *S.* 'Dollbaby' to produce 'Iduna' and with *S. eumorpha, richii,* and 'Ramadeva.' See *Rechsteinerias*, page 137.

Stem 2 feet tall. Leaves 4–5 inches long, 2–2½ inches wide, on ½-inch petioles, toothed, velvety, and strongly scented. Flower 1 inch long, single or in pairs from the axils. Tubular with small lobes. Reddish orange with yellow orange in the throat. Not a commercial plant.

Sinningia allagophylla. (Rechsteineria allagophylla). Dr. Clayberg hybridized this plant with *S. hirsuta, richii, concinna,* and *speciosa.* As the corolla is only ½ inch long, it has little interest for the amateur except as hybridizing stock.

S. barbata's flower is the most curiously and amusingly shaped of the genus. The calyx even is extraordinary, being leafy and covering the rear part of the tube rather untidily. The pure white, very hairy corolla starts out as a vertically descending tube, grows horizontally as it widens out in all directions like a bagpipe, is crimped and narrowed into a neck as it curves upward and finally opens up into five fairly equal short, rounded lobes. A comparison of this 2-inch flower to a Dutchman's pipe is inevitable.

This very different *Sinningia* has a strong square stem and large leaves which rise stiffly, arching outward as in *Nautilocalyx.* They are shiny green, burgundy below, and somewhat folded over the midrib. The flowers appear in clusters in the axils. The plant will grow up to 4 feet high and develop a tremendous root system without tubers or with an occasional irregularly shaped one of small size.

Because of its odd growth, *S. barbata* is only worth growing as a very large specimen plant or dwarfed by trimming. Propagation is best by means of stem cuttings, leaf cuttings with heels, or leaves. With a humidity of 60 percent or better, a light intensity of about 800 footcandles, and continuous warmth over 70°, rooted cuttings will bloom quite rapidly. Under lights it is advisable to keep the plant potbound and, if it starts to grow upward, to nip it so that it branches. Fertilize with high phosphate formula. It is quite possible to bloom *S. barbata* in small pots, and this can be very rewarding for the amusing flower alone.

Old roots deteriorate after the blooming season, but new growths appear from the base or from branches brought into contact with the ground. This is probably the easiest way to propagate for the amateur.

S. cardinalis (Rechsteineria cardinalis), an easily grown and attractive gesneria, has been declining somewhat in popularity due to the improvement in the repertory of columneas which often resemble it in flower and are not subject to vegetative dormancy. Its attraction is in its very intense red coloration, rich texture of the flower, and relatively compact growth. It certainly belongs in the collection of anyone who regularly grows gesneriads and does not mind the fact that it must be put aside for many months at a time.

The tuber of *S. cardinalis* is very similar to that of *S. canescens* and the other sinningias. But, though it is usually paired with *canescens* in the lists, its growth pattern is quite different.

The tuber, usually in spring, produces one or more stems which soon grow 4-inch, soft hairy, rich green leaves in a whorl, with the result that each series overlaps to a certain extent, giving the plant a compact look. Shortly, round buds appear in the axils, followed by the flowers which are 2 inches long, with a short clasping calyx and an upper lip projecting ½ inch over the short lower one. The shape is much like that of a *Columnea* without the side wings and the drooping lower lip. But the texture is very hairy and the

Sinningia cardinalis.

color a much richer blood red than we encounter in *Columnea.*

Under ideal conditions *S. cardinalis* will bloom constantly for about three months, elongating in the process and usually requiring staking. It may eventually reach almost a foot in height, though that is unusual. But the loss of lower leaves at this time does not improve the appearance.

Eventually growth stops, water is withheld, and the plant goes into a dormancy lasting until the following year, although occasionally reviving earlier and setting up a shorter, less seasonal cycle.

In 1968 Dr. George Kalmbacher, taxonomist at the Brooklyn Botanic Garden, reported flowering a peloric *S. cardinalis* from seed imported from France as being from normal stock. In fact, all the other plants from the shipment produced regular *S. cardinalis* flowers. Dr. Carl D. Clayberg of the Connecticut College of Agriculture then reported in *The Gloxinian* that he had been successful in producing the peloric plants from seed of self-pollinated plants. He named the variant *S. cardinalis* 'George Kalmbacher' in honor of the original grower.

Peloria occurs when a plant, which normally produces unequal-lobed flowers, grows one whose lobes are regular—in other words have equal-sized lobes. It turns up occasionally in the plant world and is recognized as a recessive mutation—in other words, reversion to a simpler flower form. The most famous case of peloria was the occurrence which produced the florist gloxinia from normal slipper-shaped flowers. We have often experienced peloria with 'Doll Baby' and similar *Sinningia* hybrids. But production of seed that repeats the process is very rare. A peloric flower is not necessarily an improvement in its appearance. Certainly 'George Kalmbacher,' with a plain straight tube ending in little points is neither as large nor as handsome as the species. Seen in this light the beauty of the florist gloxinia is a unique event. The flowers of 'George Kalmbacher' sometimes have five, sometimes six, lobes. The same variability occurs in the florist gloxinia.

Tubers of *S. cardinalis* should be planted with the upper surface even with, or slightly above, soil level, in Rich Mix with lime. The bottom of the tuber is usually smoothly rounded and the upper part bumpy. After planting, culture is much the same as for African violets except that *S. cardinalis* needs somewhat more light. Three to five hundred footcandles are required for bloom, with humidity over 50 percent, and with temperatures over 65°. Watering, as with all these plants, should be continuous but sparing—even moistness being the objective. Excessive standing water may cause rotting of the bulb. If

Sinningia cardinalis 'George Kalmbacher.'

the temperature drops below 60°, the soil should be allowed to dry out between waterings. Early growth should be encouraged by high nitrate fertilizer and flowering, later on, by high phosphate formula.

S. cardinalis 'Innocence.' In 1967 Geo. W. Park Seed Co., introduced seed from Denmark of an *S. cardinalis* which was pure white and, in 1969, the variant was named 'Innocence.' These plants have been regularly available from the trade. Park used the genus name *Gesneria* for these plants.

Sinningia claybergiana. When *Rechsteineria lindleyi* was transferred to *Sinningia* by Dr. Moore in 1973, a new species name was required by the fact that there was already a *Sinningia lindleyi* (Lindley was a most influential nineteenth-century botanist and horticulturist), even though the latter was not in cultivation. The plant was renamed *Sinningia claybergiana* in honor of Dr. Carl D. Clayberg. This same plant has been listed in catalogs as *Rechsteineria sellovii*. It is purely a collectors' item, described as having stout stems to 4½ feet, with flowers in clusters, a little over 1 inch in length, pale red outside, almost white inside with red spots. Dr. Clayberg reported a cross with *S. tubiflora*.

S. concinna was, as late as 1964, being described by Dr. Clayberg in *The Gloxinian* as a rare species. A few popular gesneriads have been around well over a century. It took that length of time to learn all there was to know about growing them and to metamorphose them from simple wild flowers into the highly adaptable and gorgeous plants we see today. Certainly the recent great influx of plants opens a new era for the gesneriads, but it may take many years more to master them. *S. concinna* is still a novelty for many in spite of its having played an important part in hybridization when scarcely known even to hobbyists. No doubt it will continue to retain an importance in the houseplant world out of all proportion to its small size.

This tiny plant, suitable only for terrarium culture, is an everbloomer in spite of its

Sinningia concinna.

tuber—an invaluable quality which we discuss under the heading of *S. pusilla.* Like *pusilla* this characteristic has been dominant in crosses with much larger species, and along with it has gone a dominance of its small size which has reduced that of the joint progeny.

Hybrids have been made with *S. aggregata* ('Tinkerbells'), with *S. allagophylla, S. eumorpha* ('Cindy'), *S. hirsuta* ('Freckles'), and *S. pusilla* ('Wood Nymph'). Also, by way of S. 'Freckles' and 'Dollbaby,' it has provided the rich purple and the spotting to *S.* 'Stuck Up.' All of these plants are everblooming under fluorescent lights. All have inherited the rich coloring which is absent in *S. pusilla.*

Leaves and growth habit of *S. concinna* and *S. pusilla* are so much alike that, unless you see them side by side, you would be hard put to tell the difference. The flower of the former, however, although of approximately the same length, is differentiated by the rich purple of the lobes and the speckling of the throat. The limb is somewhat larger and squarer and the lobes broader. *Concinna* has a disk with five glands, while *pusilla* has two glands with three others which are vestigial or lacking.

Although the cultural directions for both plants are the same, *S. concinna* is the more difficult plant to grow well. This is because its leaves succumb more easily to fungal diseases and all the tolerances are narrower. It must be kept in Lean Mix with lime, very lightly packed for maximum aeration in a terrarium with minimum 60 percent humidity and a temperature range of 65° to 80° F. The light requirement is a bit higher than *pusilla*—300 to 400 footcandles. The terrarium must be balanced in respect to moisture and should need watering only at long intervals. Fertilizer is unnecessary but does no harm. Long-fiber or live sphagnum moss is an alternative medium. Dormancy occurs only if the cultural environment is unfavorable. The means by which *S. concinna* is everblooming are discussed under *S. pusilla.*

One reason why *S. concinna* is not grown as much as *S. pusilla* is that it does not produce seed spontaneously. A persistent humidity of about 70 percent and temperature of about 70° are required for the ripening of seed, and hand pollination is usually necessary. However, leaf propagation is not difficult in propagation boxes with moist vermiculite.

The simplest way to pollinate is, after the flower has fully developed, to hold the calyx gently and lift the tube of the flower slowly upward, pulling at the same time, so that it comes off without ripping out the stamens. This will leave both the anther and the stigma free. Test the anthers with the tip of a finger for pollen. If none appears, try the following day. Once a fine dusting appears on the finger, touching the stigma of the same or other flowers will fertilize them. Sometimes the anthers do not split and pollen is not shed. In that case it may be necessary to remove them with scissors and flatten them out on a white piece of paper. The breaking of the pollen sac should scatter the pollen which can then be picked up with the tip of a finger or a fine brush. These two methods work with many other gesneriads.

S. cyclophylla (Rechsteineria cyclophylla) is a synonym for *S. macropoda,* which see.

S. discolor was described by Dr. Clayberg, in *The Gloxinian* Jan/Feb, 1967, as about what one would expect from a wild form of *S. speciosa.* The leaves are narrower and turned slightly upward on either side of the midvein. The flowers are bluish purple on very long petioles—up to 4 inches—and are 1½ to 2 inches long, the lower lip jutting forward. But the lobes of the evenly expanding tube are shallow so that the effect is quite bell-like from the front. A pretty plant, it would seem, which has not entered general cultivation.

S. eumorpha. It is always with a little shock of surprise that we learn how recently some gesneriads, now thoroughly familiar to us, have made their appearance in cultivation. *S. eumorpha,* for instance, was virtually unknown before 1950. Since it was first

Sinningia eumorpha.

imported it has not captured the public imagination nor become a commercial plant. But, in that short time, it has been one of the parents in many potentially rewarding crosses.

Eumorpha has the advantage of being intermediate in size of leaf between the miniature sinningias and the florist gloxinias. Even more to the point, it has proved receptive to the pollen of the little fellows.

It is a modest plant with shiny dark green, heart-shaped leaves no more than 4 inches long and a more upright growth than *S. speciosa.* The corolla is up to 2 inches long, usually 1 inch wide, with an inflated, saclike tube, white with yellow suffusion or lavender spots in the throat. The flower hangs vertically from the arching pedicels.

Culture is exactly as for *S. speciosa.* However, dormancy is shorter and two to three relatively short flowering periods a year are possible.

Botanically *S. eumorpha* differs from *S. speciosa* in possessing two rather than five glands on the disc. *S. eumorpha* 'Pink' is an attractive color variation. Paul Arnold lists the following interspecific hybrids: *xS. cardinalis* ('Bernice,' 'David,' 'Velvet Charm'); *xS. concinna* ('Cindy'); *xS. leucotricha* ('Ramadeva'); *xS. macropoda* (*S. xrosea,* 'Clarice T,' 'Rosabelle'); *xS. pusilla* ('Dollbaby,' 'Tetra'). 'Dollbaby' and 'Cindy' have become among our finest everblooming houseplants.

S. guttata, a curious *Sinningia,* was transferred from *Gloxinia* (the genus) to *Sinningia* in 1954. It appears to be a fibrous-rooted plant with a strong stem growing to a height of 1½ feet, with opposite velvety leaves. The calyx is tubular (fused) and the flower is pale green with the limb and throat dotted with purple. Not presently available in cultivation.

S. hirsuta might at first sight be taken for an African violet because of the way the flowers are held and the open face of the corolla, although it is a taller plant when mature. Actually there is a longer tube behind the lobes and open throat, and the flowers are smaller than most of our new hybrid saintpaulias. Also the whole plant is incredibly gray-hairy, and the calyxes are a mass of fuzz that almost hides the form of the lobes. The thickish, 4- to 6-inch leaves, dull green with red reverses, form a large overlapping rosette

Sinningia hirsuta.

Sinningia hirsuta.

with the numerous flowers clustered in the middle. In addition it has a round, flat tuber like other sinningias.

The extraordinary feature of this plant is its floriferousness. Once it starts to bloom, the foliage is virtually hidden by masses of white flowers with a purple throat, and the show can go on for months. This immense fecundity of bloom is not unique with *S. hirsuta.* It turns up in *G. cuneifolia* and the hybrid 'Lemon Drop' and, of course, African violets. But it is difficult to think of any other plants which can compare. If this characteristic could be passed on by *S. hirsuta* to hybrids along with the everblooming of *S. pusilla,* we would have a new ideal compact houseplant to rival the African violet. Such things are possible but take time and an enormous amount of experimentation.

The culture of *S. hirsuta* is, in general, the same as for *Gloxinia.* But the plant is considerably more touchy. This is largely due to the late formation of tubers, which is noticeable also in a couple of other gesneriads. During the early rooting period before the plant is established, it is very sensitive and will react badly to overwatering and excessive temperatures. During this period do not let the temperature go below 65° F nor above 80°. Leaves, low at that time, are subject to rot from contact with moist medium. Good light—500–600 footcandles—is required, and the humidity should be maintained near 70 percent for best results. Once tubers are well formed, the problems disappear and the growth from tubers coming out of dormancy develops normally.

Large-sized plants with 3-year or older tubers are hard to come by. In fact plants sent from nurseries are usually lacking in any tuberous growths. It is difficult to see how this can become a popular plant considering the difficulties in propagating and maintaining it in the early stages. Seed is usually available from the seed fund of AGGS, and germination is satisfactory. But it is a long haul to good blooming condition. Leaves will sprout in a combination of moist vermiculite and perlite but there is a good deal of wilting. Tubers sometimes produce side growths which can be separated and grown more easily than leaves.

The species has not been available for very long and we can hope that improved methods or more resistant plants will be developed with time.

S. canescens. Unless they are induced to produce large, showy flowers such as those of the florist gloxinias, the other gesneriads with tubers and a dormancy period will never be really popular. The whole trend in indoor gardening is toward plants which have some sort of display all year long or, if it is of short duration, at least can be replaced rapidly from cuttings or seed. It is unlikely that *S canescens* will change this habit—that we will find some sport which has the ability of an *S. pusilla* to bloom constantly. If we hybridize it, we will not be able to preserve the unique coloration and texture which make it desirable. In the florist gloxinia the prospects are better because there a particular shade or zoning of the flower is not that important. There will undoubtedly be research into ways of restimulating a dormant tuber, and this may eventually be accomplished by short periods of temperature change or by chemical treatment.

This would be particularly welcome in *S. canescens* because it is a very beautiful and aristocratic plant, different in appearance in some vital aspects from any other gesneriad. It used to be argued that the tuberous plants are so coded in regard to dormancy that this period is necessary to survival and that continuous growth would be deadly. This is pure nonsense as tubers increase in size throughout the blooming period and have plenty of energy left for further production at the time the plants go into dormancy. Besides, we have the evidence of *S. pusilla, concinna,* and a number of hybrids that this theory is exploded along with a number of other prophecies of doom which used to be the stock in trade of horticulture.

The tuber of *S. canescens* is rounded at the bottom and flat or with a shallow depression on the top. This top surface is planted even with the surface of the soil. In

Sinningia canescens.

spring—usually March or, at the latest, April, growths appear in the center. From a large bulb—2 inches across or more—several stems may be allowed to develop but, for best results, all but one or two should be nipped off at the base.

Each stem grows vertically and quickly reaches a thickness of ¼ to ⅜ of an inch in diameter, with four young leaves, their tips cupped at the top. When the stems are 2 inches or more high, the leaves are an inch long, without apparent petioles, and a cluster of tiny buds fill the center.

The extraordinary appearance of the plant at this stage is due not only to the form of the stem and leaves but even more so by the texture and color. All parts are evenly coated with silvery white hairs which have a brushed appearance like a long-fibered fine felt. For instance, those on the stem are brushed horizontally and both cling to and circle it. The hairs on the leaves are brushed to follow the direction of the veining. A soft glow of green penetrates the coating of pure silvery white. The leaves which are turned down at the edges and rhombic in shape appear, because of the hairy covering, to be thicker than they are. It is this stage of growth which probably inspired Mr. A. B. Graf of Exotica fame, its introducer from the State of Parana in Brazil, to call it Brazilian edelweiss. In Brazil the common name is Rainha do Abismo or Queen of the Abyss.

In themselves the flowers are by no means remarkable. The short, fuzzy calyx extrudes a tube, ¼ of an inch wide and 1¼ inches long, almost even for all of its length and slightly flared at the tip with tiny unspread lobes. They are a soft pink covered with brushed white hairs. But they appear in a solid cluster and, against the silver of the rabbit fur ears they make a combination which anyone familiar with art recognizes as rococo—the silver and pink decorations of rooms in this French period and the painting of Fragonard.

After this first burst which lasts for weeks, the leaves expand until they are up to 6 inches long and 4 inches wide. They now appear thinner; the hair is less prominent; and the color is silver gray. A rather woody stem develops, thin and twisted, and the big cluster of leaves sags. But the plant still looks quite decent for a while, Then, toward the end of summer, water is withdrawn, and the tuber goes into its long sleep until the following year.

Culture is as for the florist gloxinia except that *S. canescens* is less demanding in

Sinningia canescens.

respect to humidity and watering. It will bloom satisfactorily also on an east, west, or south windowsill. Keep just moist most of the time and do not push hard with either watering or fertilizing during the original growing period. The tuber is best left in its pot and, if moved, just placed in a larger one the following year with extra soil added. We have grown tubers as big as small turnips. As they get older, they lose their flat shape and can become almost round.

S. macropoda (Rechsteineria macropoda, R. cyclophylla, and *R. lineata)* has for several years bounced around the market and was described in articles under all three names between the parentheses. Finally, in 1973, Professor H. E. Moore joined *R. macropoda* to *Sinningia* and eliminated the other epithets. It has been grown a good deal by amateurs but has never been actively cultivated in the trade. This is due to a rather untidy habit, no doubt.

S. macropoda has, when mature, a large round, bumpy, rough tuber with the upper side somewhat flattened and depressed. It can grow up to 2 feet high but usually spreads out to about 18 inches. This is a plant that usually throws up several hairy thick, but not very strong, stems with long internodes between whorls of leaves arranged in threes. These are round, small-toothed, velvety, about 4 inches in diameter. Three-inch peduncles bear six to fourteen pendent flowers, blooming usually in clusters. They are bright red, 1½ to 2 inches long (about ¾ inch wide in the tube) and, though two-lipped, have shallow, nearly equal, lobes. The lower three lobes are speckled with purple. The plant has been crossed with other sinningias. Culture is the same as for *S. cardinalis* and *gloxinia.*

Great floriferousness typifies this plant. The fact that its peduncles produce so many flowers should encourage crosses which might produce a plant with that quality plus a better habit.

Sinningia macrorrhiza (R. macrorrhiza). Rechsteineria in limbo. Red-flowered large-tubered plant similar to *S. cardinalis,* growing over 3 feet tall and with flowers at the tip less than 1 inch long.

S. pusilla. In 1957 Dr. Moore commented that *Sinningia pusilla* " . . . is not a difficult subject and should receive wider attention." Well, it has, and for a multitude of reasons. No other miniature flowering plant grown indoors is as popular. The only thing standing in its way is the unwillingness of nurserymen to grow it in sufficient quantity to meet the demand. That is because it is such a tiny plant and people who do not know it well are hesitant to pay a reasonable price for it. It should cost as much as the larger gesneriads not only because it takes just as much time and care to grow from seed to bloom but also because of the rich dividends in plants which it seeds itself.

The importance of *S. pusilla* in the horticultural world is out of all proportion to its size because, in addition to the beauty, which it shares with many other houseplants, it has one unique characteristic. As this is a matter which underlies the promising future potential of many gesneriads, we want to deal with it before describing other aspects.

Like all sinningias, *S. pusilla* has a tuberous root. This is a swelling at about ground level—in nature it is not usually buried much below its top surface. This may be thought of either as a thickened stem, similar to plants like Jatrophas, where it lies normally well above ground level, or as a thickened root. Finer rootlets grow out from it.

In either case the purpose of such structures is water storage during a season of the year when nearly complete dryness prevails. Members of the lily and amaryllis families have bulbs that serve the same purpose.

When the dry period commences, the green parts of the plant die down to the ground. Moisture is preserved in the tuber through a period of nearly complete inactivity called dormancy. Any untimely moisture will invariably cause the tuber to rot. When the normal period of dryness nears its end, the tuber puts up a sprout whether it is moistened at that time or not. If the rainy season is late, the sprout will cease to grow until it comes. Just as the plant needs water to grow and flower, it must have none at all during dormancy.

All the sinningias go into dormancy which is more or less protracted. *S. leucotricha* revives in the spring and keeps its leaves through part of the summer, then goes dormant. *S. speciosa* has a relatively short flowering period and may go into dormancy for only three to five months so that it can bloom occasionally twice in a year. It is not quite so certain of its needs. In other words the time clock is not immutable in all of these plants so that, if the temperature remains unchanged—a factor which may help trigger dormancy and revival—the seasonal change may become irregular.

Sinningia pusilla (and to a slightly lesser extent *S. concinna*) is the only gesneriad which under proper conditions has no dormancy whatsoever, so that it is in the true sense an everblooming plant. We draw a distinction with *S. concinna,* because *S. pusilla* is a very much easier and more reliable plant. Thus little *pusilla* goes counter to one of the basic laws of plant growth—a possibility not conceived possible even a short while ago. An everblooming tuberous plant was formerly considered a contradiction in terms.

When a leaf cutting of *S. pusilla* roots or a seed starts to grow, a tiny tuber is formed almost immediately, just as it is on a larger scale with *S. speciosa* where it can be observed as an enlargement of the tip of the petiole of the leaf or at just below soil level in a young seedling. Gradually the rosette of leaves is formed and the tuber enlarges, eventually becoming as big as a small pea. No taproot is formed. Only a fine network of roots emerges from the bottom surface of the tuber and always remains very short.

Flowers are produced from the base of the petioles as with African violets and, as successive leaves appear, a short, very thin stem is formed. When only an inch high, it becomes weaker—incapable of supporting leaves and flowers—and often succumbs to a fungal disease. In the normal course of events, this should signal the onset of dormancy. That is certainly what happens in its native land, where it must disappear from sight without leaving a trace. It may be that dryness is not the only climatic change, and one suspects that humidity drops and temperature rises.

Indoor growing revealed that this plant could be induced to skip dormancy in spite of time of year or duration of bloom. In all probability the time and bloom triggers are not dominant in *S. pusilla* and, if we do not provide one of the other working signals, dormancy does not occur. In practice our measures are positive. All we do is treat it like most of our other gesneriads in terrarium conditions. Temperatures are maintained above 65° and below 90° (the tolerance may be somewhat lower), humidity of 60 to 70 percent but not much higher, even soil moisture and a day length of twelve to sixteen hours. These conditions are possible in the open indoor light garden but can be provided much more easily in a terrarium to which the small size of the plant is especially suited.

What happens is that, while the original rosette comes to the end of its flowering cycle, a new rosette develops on the surface of the tuber and takes its place, so that there is often no break in flowering between the passing of the first rosette and the blooming of the second. So *S. pusilla* continues to bloom throughout the year.

From personal experience we have not been able to ascertain the normal life-span of the tuber. We suspect that it reaches a certain size, becomes woody, and succumbs to rot—like most others. There is, in any event, another feature of the plant which has prevented us from making this observation. Seed is produced spontaneously, and small plants usually appear in great numbers around the parent. The seed is viable only for a short time—a few weeks at most under ideal conditions. But, of course, when it self-seeds, germination is assured.

These new plants soon replace the older one, and so it becomes a bit difficult to keep track of the age of the plants. One other peculiarity can be mentioned here. Almost invariably a very fine growth of moss surrounds the base of an *S. pusilla* plant.

S. pusilla forms a very flat rosette of ½-inch hairy leaves with a distinct short petiole. From the center, on threadlike but stiff stems, rise the flowers—¾ of an inch long, the tube ⅛ of an inch wide. Of the five flaring lobes the two upper are short and erect and the three lower ones jut forward—altogether like a miniature *Streptocarpus* of the 'Constant Nymph' type. The color varies in different strains from violet to lavender, with some plants showing almost solid color and others a combination of a zone of white on the lower half and lavender or violet at the top. The mouth of the tube is often white. Flowers last a week or more and are produced rarely more than three or four at a time.

A sport, *S.* 'White Sprite,' is pure white, and *S.* 'Snowflake,' originated by Dr. Clayberg, is white with fringed lobes. The last is a less reliable plant. *S. pusilla* has been used as one of the parents in innumerable crosses with *S. eumorpha, S. cardinalis,* and *S. leucotricha,* creating some plants to which it has imparted its everblooming characteristic.

The culture of *S. pusilla* is the same as for *S. concinna* and *S. speciosa,* except that it requires terrarium conditions. This simply highlights the importance of humidity over 60 percent and even, warm temperatures and controlled moisture. Since the plants are so small and usually seed themselves in the immediate vicinity, they can be left undisturbed in plantings for a long time. But they are easily transplanted as the need arises. Under ideal conditions the light requirement can be as low as 150 footcandles—in any event as low as that for the best African violets. For this reason it can be planted low down in a terrarium garden as much as 18 inches from a two-tube fixture.

S. regina has often been confused with variations of *S. speciosa,* and doubts remained as to the existence of a true wild species until a Mr. Mulford Foster (according to Professor Moore) rediscovered the plant in Brazil. As striking as are the differences in the leaves of *S. regina* and other sinningias, they are hardly more so than between different strains of *S. speciosa.* The flowers are much the same shape.

The most noticeable features are the rich purple, heavily textured flowers and the deep, opulent green of the leaves, 6 inches by 2½ inches, oval and a little toothed, which are broadly veined in white. It is a smaller species than *S. speciosa.* The flower is usually less than 2 inches long and a little over an inch in diameter across the limb. The tube is rather straight above, but, as in so many slipper flowers, expands and then narrows upward from below. The lobes are rather even except for the lowest one which is orbicular, larger, and juts forward. In other sinningias it is usually rather narrower than the others. The pedicels arise in pairs.

Beautiful as is *S. regina,* purple selections and hybrids of *S. speciosa* seem to be more common in collections and trade. Nevertheless *regina* is by far the most aristocratic plant and of better, truer purple color. Culture is the same as for *S. speciosa.*

S. richii was discovered in Mexico some ten years ago and published by Dr. Clayberg in 1968. It suggests that there may be many more of the genus to be found as plant explorers go farther afield. The collection was made by Frank Rich, Jr., in the province of Veracruz on limestone outcroppings. It is a trailer with very large opposite leaves—up to 10 inches long and 5 wide, and very hairy. The root is equipped with underground stolons bearing small tubers, like *S. tubiflora.* One or two flowers grow from each axil on 2-inch peduncles of which there are several. The calyx is hairy and star-shaped. The 2-inch, pure white, hairy pendent tube (½ inch in diameter) becomes fat in the middle like the belly of a fish, then narrows slightly before opening into two distinct lips with the upper lobes quite broad and the lower short, jutting, and spread flat. A very attractive flower. The disk has five separate, white glands. The plant flowers in the late spring and continues till fall.

The large size of the leaves and recumbent habit make it a plant suitable only for a trough or large shallow container, which should contain very well drained Lean Mix with lime chips. It blooms well under lights, indicating that it is not a short day plant. Dormancy follows, and the medium can be allowed to dry out completely. It is not wise to transplant. Except for use as a hybridizing sire, this plant must remain a curiosity and a challenge for the expert amateur, mainly because of its extensive and spreading habit.

S. schiffneri is a fibrous-rooted, evergreen *Sinningia* with straight, hairy, woody stems up to 3 feet tall. The leaves are opposite at intervals of a couple of inches, are oval pointed, 4 inches long by 1½ inches wide, toothed, velvety above, and hairy below. The lower ones are lost as the stem grows upward. The flowers are on 2-inch pedicels clustered in the axils. The narrow-tubed purplish or white flowers are less than an inch long with narrowly flared lobes. The disk has four glands.

S. schiffneri can start blooming when under 10 inches high, and with judicious pruning can be maintained as a small plant. Although popular in Europe after its discovery in 1908, it is carried by only a few nurseries and collectors nowadays. It does not compare in attraction with some of the other sinningias.

S. sellovii (Rechsteineria sellovii) is not in cultivation. However, plants are offered from time to time under this name. They are usually the present *S. claybergiana.*

Sinningia xStreptocarpus, the so-called *Stroxinia,* has been reported on a number of occasions as a spectacular breakthrough in intergeneric hybridizing. Plants have been sold under cultivar names as of this origin. However, the existence of true hybrids between the two genera remains to be proved. The purported crosses were peculiar but not especially attractive, being probably varieties of the *Maxima* type.

S. tuberosa (Rechsteineria tuberosa) is a transferred *Rechsteineria.* It has one or two nearly 10-inch leaves growing directly from the tuber, plus several much smaller ones. Corolla is red with yellow-flushed throat, the upper lobes projecting over the lower ones. Not commercially grown.

S. tubiflora is the tallest of the sinningias, having thin branching green stems up to 3 feet, requiring support. The leaves are relatively small—3 inches by 1½ inches with scalloped edges. Long bare racemes are one sided with the pedicels opposite. The flowers are 2 to 3 inches long, pure white, very narrow tubed with an abrupt and wide flare of the lobes which soon recurve so that the limb has a squared or pentagonal appearance. The flowers are *sweetly scented.*

Sinningia schiffneri.

The plants develop underground stolons with numerous tubers. One or more of these should be potted up in early March. Growth is rapid, and the first flowers appear in April and the last in August (according to Ted Bona). Watering and fertilizing should continue thereafter until dormancy sets in. Then the tubers should be stored until the following spring in plastic bags with peat moss or perlite. High humidity and gloxinia light are required.

More compact plants can undoubtedly be achieved by early nipping to produce some branching. Until now *tubiflora* has been little grown because of its size and dormancy. However, it is worth attempting to select smaller clones from seed-grown plants or learning to train the plant. Its perfume and charming flower shape are the great assets of this very different *Sinningia.*

Sinningia verticillata (Rechsteineria verticillata). Few gesneriads have gone under as many species names as this one. *R. purpurea* has been the favorite, but recently we bought seed labeled *R. doeringii,* and there have been several other titles. Originally it wasn't even considered a gesneriad and was described in 1926 as an *Orobanche.*

Some surprise has been expressed by hobbyists that it has not become a more popular plant considering that it possesses an unusual and attractive appearance and is easy to grow. The explanation is simple enough. It isn't until the third year that it begins to produce flowers in quantity. Recently planted seed produced nice growths, and we now have a bunch of tubers, ranging in size from a pinhead to a small lima bean, which are dormant and will have to be revived twice in separate years before we can have flowers. In respect to popularity, that is a handicap a plant is unlikely ever to overcome. However, we have seen plants in bloom and they are worth the effort for a true hobbyist.

When mature, *S. verticillata* has a large tuber producing up to three stems, each 1½ feet high. The leaves are somewhat heart-shaped, about 3½ by 6 inches on 2-inch petioles. The surface is velvety dark green. Up to twenty flowers grow from a terminal pair of leaves. Each consists of a tube 1½ inches long, tannish pink distinctly spotted with dark red—sort of tiger spotted. The flare of the lobes is pretty and equally spotted, the ones on the lower lobe developing into streaks.

In the first year a few pairs of leaves are produced. In the second year you may have a couple of flowers. But it is only from the third season on that real flowering starts. One advantage is that the plant is pretty durable, and the tuber, growing in size each season, can last for years.

Culture is as for other rechsteinerias and sinningias. *Verticillata* likes a very light porous soil, warmth, and high humidity. But it is rather more tolerant than some of the others and requires less light than the florist gloxinia.

Sinningia warszewiczii (Rechsteineria warszewiczii), was transferred to *Sinningia* by Professor Moore. This is a Mexican species introduced in 1955 which has been hybridized with *S. tubiflora* and *S. speciosa.* Described as having "silver green leaves about 2 inches apart on 2 foot stems. Bright orange flowers" (Cogswell). (Now *S. incarnata.*)

CULTIVARS DERIVED FROM CROSSES BETWEEN S. PUSILLA, S. CONCINNA, AND "ORIGINAL" SINNINGIAS

Cultivars resulting from interspecific crosses within the original *Sinningia* genus (not including former rechsteinerias) are of two kinds. The first, between the two minisinningia species *pusilla* and *concinna,* are a little larger in size than the parents. The much larger second ones are crosses between *S. pusilla* or *concinna* and either *S. eumorpha* or *S. hirsuta.* Except for Dr. Nixon's *S.* 'Poupee,' all are fertile and all posses the outstanding feature of everbloom.

The discovery in *S. pusilla* and *S. concinna* of plants with tubers capable of continuing to bloom under unbroken daily periods of light, even temperature, and humidity is unique in the plant world. Furthermore, if the conditions of culture do not meet the needs of these plants in a number of respects, they do not, as do fibrous-rooted plants, die out but merely go dormant for a relatively short period of a month or so. The everbloom is the result of the production of new crowns as the old ones reach maturity. Under proper conditions, the removal of a flowering rosette induces prompt replacement with another one.

The effort to use this outstanding quality in the production of more varied hybrids, also evident in the former xgloxineras, which mated the two *Sinningia* species and their hybrids with former rechsteinerias (now sinningias), produced less satisfactory results. For the present, the old *Sinningia* crosses are among the most satisfactory of all blooming indoor plants. A great deal of work can and should be done along these lines.

S. 'Bright Eyes' is Dr. Clayberg's 1964 cross of *S. pusilla* x *S. concinna* which is only slightly larger than the parents but produces more flowers at one time. The pedicels are an inch high and the flower about an inch long. The tube is narrow (⅛ inch) and widens to lobes that are similar to those of *S. concinna.* Those we have grown have been whitish on the lower three lobes and light purple above and in the throat. Although possibly fertile, ours has not set seed for us. Paul Arnold describes the plant as "face purple, slightly darker at edge and throat." The name 'Bright Eyes' seems to suggest a lighter coloration although there is probably some variation in the plants. In any event, the throat is unspeckled.

The habit is the same as the parents', and it is very floriferous, producing crowns readily under terrarium conditions.

S. 'Cindy' *(S. concinna* x *S. eumorpha),* a cross made by Dr. Thomas Talpey in 1965, but it was not very widely grown though the most beautiful of all the *cocinna* hybrids. It has the usual problem—sterility—the inability to set fertile seed. And leaf propagation of these small plants is a rather long process. In 1971 C. William Nixon, by means of colchicine treatment of the tuber was able to produce a self-pollinating tetraploid which is called *S.* 'Cindy-ella.' Hopefully the plant will now become better known to the public as it richly deserves.

The plant is tuberous, of the rosette type, with heart-shaped 2-inch-long leaves on 1-inch petioles, with scalloped edges. The surfaces are less oily looking than 'Dollbaby'. Flowers on 2-inch pedicels are characteristically slipper shaped, up to 1½ inches long, the tube and upper lobes bright purple, the bottom of the tube and lower lobes white. Deep purple dots in regular lines extend from near the edge of the lobes into the throat. The flowers owe their great charm to the deep color of the dots, their symmetrical pattern, a very shapely form to the expanding lobes, and an erect almost horizontal habit. Bloom is continuous. As older rosettes develop a stem, new growths appear promptly to replace them. The flowers and leaves of 'Cindy-ella' are the same form as 'Cindy' but somewhat larger. The former sometimes grow a full 2 inches long and in a terrarium are very showy.

If, for any reason the two Cindys go dormant, keeping the soil just moist at 80°–85° F usually induces a quick return to activity. Plant in Rich Mix with lime and give it 250–500 fc. illumination. Keep evenly moist and fertilize with fish emulsion or a balanced fertilizer.

Although the Cindys are easier to maintain in a terrarium and flower more profusely, they can be kept on the shelf with 50 percent humidity and above 65° F temperature.

Sinningia 'Bright Eyes' in a little terrarium.

We consider 'Cindy'-'Cindy-ella' the finest of all the miniature sinningias and one of the most beautiful of flowering houseplants.

S. 'Dollbaby' *(S. pusilla* x *S. eumorpha)* is the most successful of the small *Sinningia* crosses in public favor. We can attribute this partly to the early date when it was converted from a sterile to a fertile plant. The original cross was made by Mrs. Ruth Katzenberger in 1963. Later (there are a number of claimants for the honor), a fertile plant was developed which is true from seed and behaves like a tetraploid. The flowers are somewhat larger than the sterile form. But this is academic since the fertile plants, by now, have certainly replaced the sterile ones everywhere.

They are rosette plants with tubes, the leaves are heart-shaped, oily-hairy, about 1½-inch long on ¾-inch or longer petioles. The leaves and petioles are very brittle. Flowers on 1½-inch pedicels are 1½ inches long, irregularly lilac purple to bluish suffused over white. There is considerable variation in the strength of coloring, depending on culture. The shape is that of a trumpet or slipper with projecting lower lobes and graceful form.

Culture is as for 'Cindy.' This is another true everbloomer, very easy to maintain on the shelf or in a terrarium. It produces seed spontaneously, and it is not too difficult to propagate with leaf cuttings.

Sinningia 'Freckles' *(S. concinna* x *S. hirsuta)* is a remarkable combination of everbloom of *concinna* with some of the hairiness of *hirsuta.* At the same time smallness has been preserved, and of all the terrarium plants except *S. pusilla* this is the least temperamental and the most floriferous.

The ½- to 1-inch long soft hairy leaves are on thin petioles. Beginning as a rosette plant, it soon develops a stem which can grow 3 or 4 inches tall without completely toppling over. The flowers, on 1- to 1½-inch pedicels, are produced in great quantity and continuously. They are quite similar to *concinna* but shorter tubed and with more white

A cross by Lyndon Lyon utilizing *S.* 'Cindy.'

showing, though the throat retains the purple spotting. New growths appear from the tuber as the flowering stems age.

'Freckles' does quite well on the shelf at 50 percent humidity, with moderate watering and 250–500 footcandles of light. In a terrarium it needs no attention at all. We rarely fertilize this plant. Although it is sterile, it is very popular and can be propagated by both stems and leaves. The tubers are very long lived. We have some which have kept going for four years without increasing excessively in size or losing their ability to produce stem after stem of these fine flowers.

Sinningia 'Grace M' (*S. eumorpha* x *S.* 'Dollbaby'). The plant (James Wyrtzen, 1971)

Peloric form of *S.* 'Dollbaby.' Occurs occasionally but is not persistent.

resembles a 'Dollbaby' with larger flowers and a more pouched tube, the limb whitish with a lavender blush. In other words, a whiter 'Dollbaby.' Culture is the same.

Incidentally, readers should not be misled by color photographs of bluish plants which look pink or even reddish in the illustrations of magazines. Due to the vagaries of photographic film and printing, it is very difficult to represent a true blue flower. And those that contain an admixture of red almost always photograph with a much stronger red tinge with the blue almost suppressed. Thus pale blue, lavender, lilac, or violet may be bright pink in a picture.

S. 'Hircon' (Nixon, 1973), a presumed tetraploid of 'Freckles,' it is fertile and uniform. Plants and flowers are larger. Presumably it will supersede 'Freckles' in the trade provided the other good qualities are preserved—in spite of its name.

S. 'Poupee' (*S.* 'White Sprite' x *S.* 'Dollbaby'), a cross made by C. W. Nixon in 1971, it is presumed to be tetraploid but is sterile. A similar plant to 'Dollbaby' but smaller. The tube is ⅝ inches long, and the limb as much in diameter. The general tone is light lavender with ivory and pinkish streaks. Each lobe has a purple stripe and the edges are toothed. The form is attractive and flowering, two or three flowers at a time, is fairly extended. Tubers recover quickly from dormancy. Because of a rather flat, open face, delicate coloring, and fine details of form, this is a remarkably pretty plant. It can be grown either on the shelf or in a terrarium.

S. 'Snowflake' (*S.* 'White Sprite' x unnamed *S. pusilla* mutant) (Clayberg, 1967). Flowers like 'White Sprite,' but lobes are fringed and notched. Breeds true from seed. According to most growers, culture is more difficult than *S. pusilla* or 'White Sprite.' It's just more temperamental, it would seem.

S. 'Stuckup' ('Freckles' tetraploid x 'Purple Dollbaby') (Sonja Cuneo, 1973). In habit and appearance like a considerably larger 'Freckles' with richer purple markings. The sense of size in the flower is increased by the flatness of the limb almost as large as 'Cindy' and more open. Flowers are 1½ inches long and 1 inch wide across the limb, reddish purple with speckled throat. Leaves similar to 'Dollbaby' but more hairy and up to 2 inches across. The plant is everblooming, producing multiple crowns, and it tolerates relatively low humidity. However, it appears to be sterile. Leaves root easily.

S. 'Tetra' (*S. epumila* (*S. pumila* x *S. eumorpha*) by use of colchicine) (Carl Clayberg, 1960). Rosette plant with ⅝-inch tube and ½-inch limb. Light purple shading to deep purple in throat. True breeding from seed.

S. 'White Sprite' is an albino sport of *S. pusilla* raised by Ruth Washburn, Ohio. Pure white form of *S. pusilla* breeding true from seed.

Sinningia 'Wood Nymph' *(S. pusilla* x *S. concinna)* (Lyon 1966) has plants of the same size as *concinna* and *pusilla* with flowers reddish purple with white spotted throat. More like *concinna* in color and shape. Everblooming and fertile like its parents.

In 1969 Mr. Lyon produced 'Wood Nymph Improved,' resulting from the cross of 'Wood Nymph' with *S. concinna.* This strengthened the purple coloring. There is considerable variation in the seedlings, and Mr. Lyon is now (1976) working on improved selections. The logical objective is a richer-colored, slightly larger flower, and greater fertility; a more floriferous plant and a less temperamental one than *concinna.*

HYBRIDS BETWEEN SINNINGIA AND FORMER RECHSTEINERIAS AND OTHERS

All hybrids between *Sinningia* and *Rechsteineria* were called xGloxineras until Dr. Moore, in 1973, included them all in *Sinningia* as a result of Dr. Clayberg's studies of intergeneric crosses. The history of the xGloxineras is peculiar. The principal hybridizers

Sinningia 'Poupee' (Kartuz).

have been Mrs. Frances Batcheller, Mrs. Katzenberger, Ted Bona of Reading, Pennsylvania, and Dr. Clayberg. Of the various hybrids only 'Pink Imp,' 'Pink Petite,' and 'Little Imp' of Clayberg and 'Krishna' of Mrs. Batcheller have achieved any degree of popularity. This was largely due to crosses with *Rechsteineria* failing to perpetuate the everblooming characteristic of *S. pusilla* and *S. concinna.* All the plants went into dormancy.

Mr. Bona produced an astonishing range of plants with which we had some experience. These were plants with leaves often similar to *S. cardinalis* or to those of *S. speciosa* or *eumorpha.* The flowers too had the medium narrow tube, usually nodding and of the same texture. The range of coloring was extraordinary and very beautiful, from vibrant tans to the richest and oddest pinks and reds. They were also very floriferous, producing greater quantities of flowers than *S. speciosa.*

They were widely distributed for test by amateurs. In our own case, much as we admired them, and in spite of considerable care, they simply died off after a while, of a number of ailments, and often so suddenly that we failed to take leaf cuttings to start new plants. A common failure was an inability to come out of dormancy the second time around.

We consider it to have been a serious loss that none of these plants has come into wider cultivation. And it would seem that one problem was that they were never grown sufficiently long at source to discover their peculiarities. That being the case, the amateur who received the tubers for test had no guidance as to their special needs. We heard all about their form and color but nothing about their culture. Also, for the amateur who had a great many gesneriads, there was little inducement to propagate plants which came without any assurances regarding their tolerance and adaptability.

Some of Mr. Bona's plants from the late 1960s are still around, cherished by a few growers, but we would very much like to see them reach a wider public. By this time, those who grow them must have sufficient experience to advise us on culture and on the relative merits of different plants. There were literally dozens of different plants, and we wonder today how many clones are still in cultivation.

A sad feature of this type of hybridization is that it seems to be carried on only for the enjoyment of the specialist and without the slightest understanding of the needs of a mass market, which is the only way a plant comes to be widely known and grown. Ultimately, of course, all experimentation with plants can lead to some good results. The type of plant developed by Mr. Bona, if it had some everblooming quality, would be highly desirable and a truly significant expansion of the gesneriad repertory.

We have listed a few of these plants in the following section, along with Mrs. Batcheller's and others. In doing so we are surprised at their small number after combing the catalogs and records fairly diligently and having grown a large number of them ourselves.

Bee Dee Hybrids.   The name applied by Ted Bona to a number of his hybrids: 'City of Reading,' 'Esther Bona,' 'Maude Cogswell,' 'Glox News,' 'Mrs. B.,' 'Frances Batcheller,' 'Hazel Deschenes.' Some of these were of the type described above. Produced around 1964.

S. 'Benten' (S. barbata x S. 'Ramadeva'). Frances Batcheller. Hairy plants with reddish erect stems and olive green leaves, somewhat narrow and pointed—3 inches by 2 inches—with red reverse. Flowers 1¼ inches long, the bent tube pale purple at base and white hairy, turning upward at the end. Very little flare. Tuberous. A sterile triploid.

S. 'Bob W.' Ted Bona, 1969. Compact floriferous plant like a small S. regina. Narrow tube purple with deep purple throat.

S. 'Connecticut Hybrids.' Dr. Carl Clayberg, 1964. A group of small plants with nodding flowers and darker eye, deriving from selected tetraploid xGloxinera hybrids, involving pusilla, eumorpha, and cardinalis. The large trumpet flowers are attractive, but the leaves are brittle and the plants often fail to revive after dormancy. They became famous for demonstrating the possibility of interspecific and intergeneric crosses but have been superseded by superior performers.

S. 'Coral Baby' (C. W. Nixon) (S. cardinalis 'George Kalmbacher' x 'Modesta'). Continuously flowering plant with 1-inch tube flowers in a deep yellowish pink. Recovers easily from dormancy. Has been listed commercially from time to time.

S. 'Cupid's Doll' (S. 'Ramadeva' x 'Dollbaby') is very similar to 'Dollbaby' with a red purple spot in the throat and the lobes white along the edges. Difficult to distinguish unless the two plants are set side by side. Occasionally listed.

S. 'Iduna' (Sterile diploid 'Dollbaby' x 'S. aggregata'). F. Batcheller. Stemmed plant with thin green leaves 2½ inches by 1¾ inches. Flower tubular, lavender pink, nearly 1 inch long.

S. 'Kore' (S. 'Ramadeva' x S. 'richii'). Mrs. Frances Batcheller. A sterile plant with oval, bright green leaves 2 inches long and 4 wide, forming a flat rosette. The flower is 1 inch long, narrow, widening to an open throat and held horizontally. The lobes red purple.

S. 'Krishna' (Tetraploid sport of S. 'Ramadeva' x 'S. leucotricha'). Plant similar to 'Ramadeva' though slightly larger and the color a stronger pink. In our opinion an improvement over 'Ramadeva.' Dormancy is usually short. Seeds come 90 percent true.

S. 'Little One' (S. eumorpha x S. eumorpha x S. verticillata). Peggie Schulz, 1963. Stems and petioles maroon; leaves shiny, oval. Narrow flower tube is 1½ inches with ½-inch diameter limb. Color, white with pinkish flush and purple lines in the throat. Grows to 8 inches tall.

S. 'Little Imp' *(S.* 'Pink Petite' x *S. pusilla* x *S. eumorpha* x *S. cardinalis)* Clayberg, 1962. A smaller plant than *S.* 'Pink Imp' (which see). Flower less than an inch long and flare ⅓ inch across. Tube lavender pink with dark magenta lobes. Fertile.

S. 'Maude Cogswell' *(S.* 'Velvet Charm' x Bona hybrid). Bona, 1962. *S. speciosa* slipper type producing fifteen to twenty fringed flowers at a time. Tube 1¾ inches long, strong red. Flaring lobes ¾ inch wide, pale pink. This effect of dark tube and lighter limb is typical of many of the Bona hybrids.

S. 'Minarette' *(S.* 'Modesta' x 'Little Imp'). Sonja Cuneo, 1973. Pink nodding flowers. Everblooming (?).

S. 'Modesta' *(S.* 'White Sprite' x *S. leucotricha)* N. P. Bernard, 1972. Slightly hairy leaves 1½ inches long, 1⅛ inches wide. Flat rosette growth. Tube 1¼ inches long, limb ⅝ inch wide. Coral pink. Reported as everblooming but sterile.

S. 'Patty Ann' *(S.* 'Modesta' x *S.* 'Little Imp'). Peduncles bear two or three 'Little Imp' type flowers which bloom continuously. Lobes crimson with magenta spot on lower lobe.

S. 'Pink Flare' *(S.* 'Ramadeva' x *S.* 'Pink Petite' x *S.* 'Dollbaby'). Erwin Rosenblum, 1966. A plant very much like *S.* 'Dollbaby' except in minor details, however the color is rose pink. It has not been widely distributed probably because the pink color is not sufficiently different and culture is somewhat less easy.

S. 'Mod Imp' *(S.* 'Modesta' x salmon selection of *S.* 'Patty Ann'). Frances Batcheller, 1973. Flower similar but larger than *S.* 'Modesta' with salmon color. Fertile version of 'Modesta.'

S. 'Oengus' *(S. concinna* x *S. schiffneri)* x *S.* 'Krishna'). Fertile tetraploid with ovate leaves 1¼ inches long, ¾ inch wide, green hairy with maroon reverse. The horizontal tube narrow, spreading, about 1 inch long and ⅝ inch across the lobes. Tube dark purple, upper lobes reddish purple and lower lobes lighter. The leaves are raised. Plant is compact and of good habit. Not available in the trade.

S. 'Pink Imp' *(S.* 'Pink Petite' x *S. pusilla* x (F2 *S. eumorpha* x *S. cardinalis*). Dr. Carl Clayberg, 1962. A tetraploid with stable seed. Forms a very flat rosette of 1-inch leaves. Usually flowers with three or four blooms at a time. Tube slender, 1 inch long, lavender pink. Limb ½ inch across, reddish purple with dark spot on lower lobe.

This is a popular small plant that produces seed freely which is highly viable. Flowering is nearly continuous, and dormancy, if it occurs, of short duration. As with most of these hybrids the leaves have a tendency to curl and have a rather contorted, unattractive appearance. The flowers, however, are charming and this makes an excellent shelf or terrarium plant.

S. 'Pink Petite' *(S. pusilla* x *S. leucotricha).* Carl Clayberg, 1963. Fertile tetraploid induced by colchicine. The rosette of maximum 2-inch long leaves is very flat and does not develop a stem. This is not a greatly floriferous plant but blooms for a considerable period, has a short dormancy if any, and produces plenty of seed which germinate quickly and rapidly grow into a blooming plant. This is the best of the pink-tubed miniatures and is widely grown.

S. 'Ramadeva' *(S. pusilla* x *S. leucotricha).* Frances Batcheller, 1963. Plant somewhat larger than *S. pusilla* with leaves 1¼ inches long by ¾ inch wide. Nodding tube, narrow, scarcely swollen, ¾ inch long, white and hairy. Limb narrow, reddish purple. Said to be everblooming. Diploid, pollen sterile.

S. 'Robinhood' *(S.* 'City of Reading' x *S. cardinalis).* Ted Bona, 1970. An 18-inch-high plant with leaves 6 inches by 4½ inches on 3-inch petioles. The tube is 2½ inches long and the limb 1¼ inches wide. Red color slightly ruffled. Goes dormant.

S. 'Tinkerbells' *(S. concinna* x *S. aggregata).* In habit the plant is similar to *S.* 'Freck-

Sinningia 'Tinkerbells' (Elena Jordan).

les,' but the flowers are deep carmine with a narrow tube flaring to ⅜ inch across. Leaves are dull green, hairy, red underneath, 1⅞ inches long, ⅞ inch wide. Stems may reach 12 inches and trail. Sterile. The flowering period is very long, and dormancy, if it occurs, quite short. The stems root in moist vermiculite. A showy little plant quite different from the others in this list because of the intensity of color. It has become popular rather rapidly. It was hybridized by Elena Jordan.

S. 'Velvet Charm' *(S. eumorpha* x *S. cardinalis)*. Peggie Schulz. *S. cardinalis* type leaves with raceme of tube flowers, vivid pink with mauve inside. Narrow regular limb.

CULTURE

MEDIUM.   Long-fiber or live sphagnum moss is probably the safest medium in which to grow the miniature sinningias. In any sort of transparent container, the moss, properly moistened but not dank, does no harm to the leaves and seems to provide just the right humidity and root conditions. On the shelf, sphagnum moss provides ambient humidity which is very helpful for the plants. This is a little strange, since they are not epiphytic, and the moss is rather acid in reaction.

Second best we rate Lean Mix with the peat moss well fluffed, so that the proportion of perlite is correct and very much in evidence. This provides the necessary aeration for the fine roots.

TEMPERATURE.   The normal correct temperature seems to be around 70°. Below 65° F buds may not set or may blast. Leaves also become subject to fungal diseases, especially if the moisture is too high. Between 80° and 85° F, activity is speeded up, and in this range some of the largest blooms and best growth occur but, unless humidity is also high, damage can be done. Over 85° is definitely injurious.

LIGHT.   The requirements are somewhat higher for the large than the small minis and both together require more light than *S. pusilla.* About 250 footcandles are about right as long as humidity is high. Keep a foot below a two-tube fixture. 'Dollbaby' and 'Cindy' may need to be a bit closer.

HUMIDITY.   Should always be over 50 percent whether on the shelf or in a terrarium. The 70 to 90 percent of a terrarium is superior as long as the temperature is maintained in the 65°–85° F range.

MOISTURE.   The true minis are more sensitive to overwatering than the larger plants. Even moisture is what they want.

FERTILIZER.   The true minis need none and the larger ones can be treated to high phosphate formulas. Once a month is ample.

Smithiantha

Smithiantha, named after Miss Matilda Smith, a botanical artist, has been in cultivation since the middle of the last century. A small genus from Mexico and Guatemala, it is very floriferous and decorative. Scaly rhizomatous, it goes through a period of extended dormancy like *Achimenes.* Its popularity has never been very great but it has always attracted attention. Thomas Butcher of Shirley-Croydon, England, formerly grew it in quantity as a holiday gift plant, and it must be said that there is not a more spectacular one around. Beautiful as to foliage, it throws up a spire which bursts into a magnificent mass of rich red and yellow bloom. Park has listed it for years, usually as *Naegelia,* a name which has been abandoned for a long time.

Although it does not always go into complete dormancy, *Smithiantha* is a short season plant. For us it has bloomed around Christmastime, which suits it for that kind of trade, and no doubt with a bit of manipulation it can be made ready for Easter or some other occasion. The flowers themselves are long lasting but come out in rapid succession. This is, of course, one reason for its great beauty and is an advantage for a gift plant. The houseplant grower, on the other hand, must wait all year for this single burst. It is a plant preferably bought in bud and we would be grateful to anyone who would produce them for market, where they would hold up well in competition with florist gloxinias, calceolaria, cyclamen, and azaleas.

Smithiantha cinnabarina is a red hairy plant 1 to 2 feet high with a stout stem, the leaves up to 6 inches long and 5 inches wide, heart-shaped, neatly scalloped, velvety, on 3-inch hairy petioles. The whole leaf has a bloom of red over the green, while the reverse is paler.

All the smithianthas have beautifully shaped and colored leaves. Superficially the description above may sound much like the leaves of former *Rechsteineria cardinalis.* The difference is that they are arranged in a regular whorl around the stem, are held out horizontally, and are cleanly shaped . . . all of which the *Rechsteineria* leaf is not. The texture is a softer velvet without quilting, and the scalloping is very regular. The colors are rich and where there is a suffusion of another tint, as in this species, it is not blotchy but spread evenly. Words cannot fully do such refinements justice, but it is of some relevance that many people have grown smithianthas just for their leaves alone.

The spire which rises from the whorl of leaves is naked except for the flowers, which are like those of *Digitalis* and other prized perennial plants of the garden. *Rehmannia* is the closest gesneriad in this respect. The flowers are whorled all the way up this stem, the stiff pedicels at an erect angle and the flowers dangling from them, again like *Digitalis*. It is important to understand that this arrangement is symmetrical and that a well-grown plant has a perfect steeple of color.

The flowers are tubular bell-shaped, vertically pendent, and with the lower lip curving slightly upward. They are about 2 inches long, red above and yellow beneath, with a flare of about ¾ inch, the lobes being only ¼ inch long and rounded. The throat is light, with red dots. The spike may be 6 to 9 inches long and thickly packed on all sides with these beautiful flowers. Note that the nodding position does not detract from *Smithiantha* as it does from the species *Sinningia speciosa*, because the flowers are carried high and the tube rather than the flare makes its beauty.

Smithiantha fulgida is similar to *S. cinnabarina* but with green leaves and scarlet flowers with a yellow throat containing red spots in horizontal rows. It has contributed patterning and color to some of the hybrids.

Smithiantha multiflora is similar. Leaves are dark green and the flowers are somewhat narrower than *S. cinnabarina*, the lobes more reflexed, and the lower one jutting forward. Their color is creamy white.

Smithiantha zebrina. In this species the stems reach to 2½ feet, and the leaves are slightly larger than those of *S. cinnabarina*, dark velvety green with a suffusion of purple or brown. The flowers are ¾ inch across the tube, and the mouth is wide open, the lobes ¼ inch long. The lobes are not flared or reflexed and the lower lobe is larger and juts forward. The tube is scarlet with yellow, the lobes yellow, and the inside of the throat yellow spotted with red.

The treatment of smithianthas is much the same as for the florist gloxinias with Rich Mix and lime, temperature over 65°, and humidity over 50 percent. But they are less light demanding. Time and again they have bloomed for us on the side of the light garden, set on the floor with the shelf above, because they were too tall to be accommodated. That would indicate that 250 footcandles at most are needed. In fact the development of the plant was much better at the low light level than at greater intensities. A maximum of 500 footcandles is advisable as an excess seems to stunt the plant—and not in a favorable manner. Largish pots are required even for the smaller plants—4 inches being a minimum. The roots are shallow and spread widely, and pot binding only induces a poor growth pattern. Leaves have a tendency to brown at the edges in excessive heat, coolness, or moisture, and a *Smithiantha* with ragged leaves is not an enjoyable sight. The plant is a big feeder requiring regular doses of balanced fertilizer.

Plants grown from seed sown in the spring will bloom the following midwinter. But the amateur is better advised to acquire rhizomes from friends or trade. A feature of *Smithiantha* is the size of the rhizomes which may be 2 inches long and ½ inch thick. A healthy plant produces a considerable number of these monsters. After flowering is completed, it is not advisable to attempt to keep the plant going. Let the stem die down and shake the rhizomes out of the soil. They are easy to store in a plastic bag with slightly moist peat moss or vermiculite. Revival is in the early fall, and then starts the long haul, for the plant develops slowly till the following blooming season.

SMITHIANTHA HYBRIDS

Plants close to the species *cinnabrina* and *zebrina* are still grown, but most of the plants of this type in cultivation are old and often complex hybrids in many interesting color combinations—in the yellow red complex—and spottings, plus pure rich yellow and reds. In fact the opulent coloring is a consistent feature of these lovely plants.

At Cornell, Dr. Robert E. Lee made crosses between *S. fulgida* and *S. zebrina* producing a series of ten hybrids on which much of the European production has been based. Green-leaved varieties were named *S.* 'Abbey,' 'Cathedral Cloisters,' 'Matin,' and 'Vespers.' Red-leaved ones were labeled *S.* 'Capistrano,' 'Carmel,' 'San Gabriel,' 'Santa Barbara,' and 'Santa Clara.' The choice of names was suggested by an oft-used common name for *Smithiantha*, namely Temple Bells.

In backing the compact hybrids, Park has partially met the needs of the indoor grower. *S.* 'Little One' is described as having been "Created by Mr. Wiegelt, a devoted plantsman who lives by the Rhine River in Germany." Devoted or not and without disclosure of the secret of where he "lives on the Rhine River," Mr. Wiegelt's dwarfs are handsome, compact plants, 8 inches high with zebrina-type leaves and flowers in many combinations of yellow and red. In addition Park has offered mixed seed of compact hybrids. Another dwarf has been *S.* 'Little Tudor,' which is quite similar. Such plants have attracted great attention at flower shows and houseplant society conventions and have enjoyed short bursts of popularity. But the average grower soon deserts plants that maintain so long a dormancy.

xAchimenantha. This is the name of intergeneric crosses between *Smithiantha* and *Achimenes.* A large number of cultivars have been developed and described, but none has come into general acceptance by amateur growers, as the habit is generally less attractive than *Smithiantha* and the flowers are no improvement on either genus. The best-known of these hybrids is Mrs. Frances Batcheller's 'Kuan Yin' which is compact with *Achimenes* foliage and flowers, "yellow ochre shaded with purple.' Mrs. Batcheller writes that it does well in a greenhouse but poorly under fluorescent lights.

xGloxinantha. This is a hybrid of *Smithiantha* with the genus *Gloxinia.* The most famous of these is 'Evlo,' developed by Lois and Everett Hammond. It has leaves like *Smithiantha* and pink lavender flowers.

The difficulty with these plants is not so much cultural as aesthetic. The elements which are combined lead to no special improvement and to rather odd shades and foliage textures. They have, it seems to us, been a disappointment, as something better might have been expected from the combinations of such beautiful genera.

Incidentally, one of the reasons for the recent shuffling of species from one genus to another having been the ability to create intergeneric hybrids, one wonders why the triad *Smithiantha, Gloxinia,* and *Achimenes* has been spared. It has always been taught that the existence of a genus is established to a large extent by its inability to hybridize with other genera. But where this has been possible and even rampant—as in the *Epidendrae* of the orchid family—the pundits of that hobby have preferred to leave well enough alone, as many of the names had been established for a long time and a whole industry and its records built up on them.

Solenophora

Central American large shrubs with large leaves. Funnel-shaped flowers in red, yellow, or white.

Streptocarpus

We consider *Streptocarpus* the gesneriad of the future. It is already widely grown by houseplant amateurs, but we can envisage a much greater popularity when investigation and hybridization of this wonderful genus have gone further. Hitherto, our cultivars have come from Europe, where lower home temperatures are the rule. American hybridizers should therefore deal with the problem of developing plants with a higher temperature range, more suited to our needs. When this happens, *Streptocarpus* will really take off, for there are few flowers which match it for beauty and variety.

The following can only be a very superficial look at *Streptocarpus.* Readers will find the full story altogether fascinating as told by O. M. Hilliard and B. L. Burtt in *Streptocarpus, An African Plant Study,* 1971, University of Natal Press, Durban, South Africa. This is a beautifully organized and written book, jam-packed with information both esoteric and of general interest to the horticulturist, as well as containing precise and readable descriptions of all the species presently known. Books of this quality are rare in botanical literature. *Streptocarpus* might well serve as a model for others, which have been written as if scientific description required translation from the Latin via Bulgarian into English. Our technical people need a course in writing simple sentences in their native tongue.

This beautiful flowering, and botanically remarkable, genus is mostly concentrated in Africa and Madagascar. There are two distinct kinds of plant which have been designated as subgenera. Subgenus *Streptocarpus,* with thirty-two chromosomes, is unifoliate and is represented here by the large and colorful Wiesmoor Hybrids and 'Constant Nymph' strain. It has a range from southern Ethiopia nearly to the Cape and across the continent to Angola. Subgenus *Streptocarpella,* plants with normal growth patterns, has a chromosome number of thirty and ranges from Angola to Madagascar and then to a small number of species in Southeast Asia. The familiar *S. saxorum* and *S. holstii* belong to this very different group.

The following description of subgenus *Streptocarpus* is an attempt to put into simple language the careful analysis of Hilliard and Burtt. Most of the gesneriads of the Old World have cotyledons (the first two "leaves" which are really the splitting of the two halves of the seed—as in beans) which are unequal, but usually the adult plant shows no sign of this early abnormality. In the subgenus *Streptocarpus,* something else and most remarkable takes place.

The seed is extremely small for the very large species. When it germinates, there are two minicotyledons which are equal in size as in most dicotyledenous (two-parted seed) plants. Shortly thereafter one of the cotyledons, or seed leaves, starts to grow, while the other one withers away. Growth continues from the base of the cotyledon. In other words, whereas in the normal way the cotyledons both serve merely to provide nourishment for the starting roots and subsequent true leaves, eventually shriveling and disappearing, in *Streptocarpus* subgenus *Streptocarpus* one cotyledon becomes a true leaf and can grow to monstrous size. Furthermore, in many species this leaf is the only leaf each plant ever produces.

The very short stalk connecting the cotyledons with the anchoring root is called a hypocotyl. It thickens as the single leaf enlarges. From the lower part of the hypocotyl roots start forth from a section called the petiolode. They form the main root system of the plant. The anchoring root never becomes a fully developed taproot. But the roots from the petiolode are numerous and fibrous, though they never penetrate the soil very deeply.

The single leaf in some species eventually reaches a length of 3 feet and a breadth of a foot or more. But this is not typical, for there are leaves of all sizes. The flower stalks, or peduncles, arise from the point where the leaf joins the thickened hypocotyl, and successive growths occur in the direction of the leaf blade. This results in the first stalks being pushed backward and the last ones ending up at the base of the midrib of the leaf. The production of flowering stalks may be quite fantastic as in *S. dunnii.*

Plants of this type are annuals and, once they have flowered and fruited, they die.

Another group of plants with a single cotyledon-leaf develops one to three other leaves on the petiolode some distance below the inflorescence of the first one. The new leaves produce their own roots in turn. These are perennials.

The third form, called rosulate, is the one to which *S. rexii* and our modern hybrids belong. These plants produce a rootstock from elongation of the erect or prostrate petiolode from which the individual leaves arise, each capable of producing a series of flower stalks. They are, therefore, capable of spreading slowly along the ground in a manner similar to rhizomatous begonias. The orchid plant offers an even closer analogy. Those with pseudobulbs develop new horizontal growths, each of which is capable of blooming only once. There are a number of variations of this arrangement in *Streptocarpus.*

In the fourth form of this strange growth pattern, there are several leaves growing from the petiolode and, in addition, the lengthened petiolode of one or more of the leaves may produce a secondary leaf, also able to produce flowers, thus giving some of the aspect of a branching plant.

Subgenus *Streptocarpella* also starts out with one cotyledon leaf developing and the other withering and with a thickening of the petiolode. But the plant then develops from a vegetative bud on the petiolode in a normal way. In other words we have short-stemmed rosette plants and regular branching herbs with normal leaves.

In some species there is another oddity. Hilliard and Burtt give the examples of *S. grandis,* which rarely blooms the first season. In autumn an "abscission zone" develops across the leaf as a distinct line. The leaf from there to the tip proceeds to wither and dry up. Plants are rarely found with complete leaves. Further wilt takes place during the winter drought, but the leaf recovers with the spring rains and begins to grow again.

Note also that a typical feature of *Streptocarpus* is that the terminal inflorescences of the peduncles are always in pairs—a feature of many other gesneriads.

The characteristic on which the genus *Streptocarpus* has been based is the twisted seedpod. At first thought, this might seem insignificant, since many plants have long straight pods which, when ripe and dry, twist and release their seeds. *Streptocarpus,* however, is different because the twisting takes place at the very start of the growth of the pod. It is very easy to observe this phenomenon in pods developing on home-grown plants. The pod may be long or short. As usual this feature is not entirely restricted to *Streptocarpus* and has some suspicious representatives in other Old World genera so botanists have been obliged to use, in addition, some other criteria for inclusion in the genus.

Hilliard and Burtt also give us some indications of the habitat of subgenus *Streptocarpus.* The plants require summer rainfall, good drainage, and partial shade. Most are forest dwellers "along banks, stream sides and rock outcrops." On the rock outcrops they prefer "coarse granites and conglomerates" and are often found where humus or soil "has collected in the rock crevices, sometimes in cushions of moss." One other reporter states that they prefer alkaline soils.

The dry season lasts through the winter. If we reverse the South African seasons, this would be from October to April. Many of the plants are accustomed to an elevation of 3,000 to 5,000 feet, although some are in lower areas and even very dry ones. Nothing is mentioned of temperature, but we can assume that the ones from higher places require rather cool conditions, and this is confirmed by the sensitivity of our cultivated plants to very high summer temperatures.

Plants of subgenus *Streptocarpus* are always easy to recognize because of their leaves. It is easier to remember them than to describe them, for they look quite different from other gesneriad foliage. The narrower ones are often very long in proportion to their width—strap-shaped—and rather blunt-tipped. The surface is usually dull with the midvein sunken and the veining at wide-spaced intervals curving down to it from the edge. The edge is evenly scalloped. The texture is thin, and the edges of the leaves are turned down. Underneath the leaf is very pale and has prominent veins and a network that creates an allover appearance of cells. When the leaf is broad—sometimes almost as broad as long—it retains the same characteristics. Also the leaves often are shirred, as if one had taken a thread and pulled sections somewhat together, creating humps and forcing the whole leaf into a curve.

The flowers are extremely varied but the dominant shape is similar to *Achimenes* or, for instance, *Sinningia pusilla,* but of heavier texture. It is a long or shortish tube with an open-faced flaring of the lobes. Sometimes the lobes are distinct and deeply cut; at others they are short and rounded creating almost a bell shape. But normally the lower lip juts out below the upper. Where the lobes are deeply cut, this is most noticeable, for then the upper lobes are shorter than the lower. On the whole the shapes are very graceful.

The majority of *Streptocarpus* in cultivation are of the rosulate type, for these are perennial and have large flowers and great variety of coloring.

The truly popular ones are hybrids, principally the Wiesmoor Hybrids and the 'Constant Nymph' strains. The following list of species is, therefore, very short and includes only those plants with which amateurs here have had some experience. The longest description is of *S. rexii,* which has been involved in most of the major crosses. So look under that heading for more detail.

SPECIES, SUBGENUS STREPTOCARPUS.

S. candidus. Hilliard. Rosulate plant with an erect rhizome, grows above 3,000 feet in Africa. Leaves are 18 inches by 5 inches, numerous. Inflorescence, up to twenty-five flowers, many opening together. Flower over an inch long, white with yellow stripes and purplish spots in the throat. Lower lip has two purple wavy lines at the base.

S. confusus. Hilliard. Single leaf species which, along with its close relative *S. haygarthii,* is widely diffused in Natal. Leaf green above, purple below, 10 inches by 5 inches. Peduncles 8½ inches long with up to thirty-six flowers ¾ inch to 1½ inches long. Pale violet.

S. cooperi. C. B. Clarke. Related to *S. grandis.* Leaf up to 20 inches long and wide! Peduncles to 1½ feet. Flowers 1½ inches long, violet colored with lower lip marked with white wedges.

S. cyanandrus. B. L. Burtt. From 7,000 feet in Rhodesia. Hairy herb with leaves clumping together, up to 1 inch long and narrow, green above, purple reverse. Flower to 1 inch, the lobes oblong and the lower ones jutting forward. Pink with darker stripes on the lobes ranging to blue. All the plant surfaces are suffused with magenta pink. Often recommended for terrariums but obviously Alpine and a cool grower. The candy stripe effect is startling and has attracted the attention of commercial breeders. The problem is to adapt the plant to warmer temperatures and make it more tolerant in other respects.

S. cyaneus. S. Moore. This is a rosulate plant with 1-foot leaves, 3 inches wide. Inflorescences usually two-flowered. Hairy. Peduncle to 6 inches high. Tube an inch long, color white through deep purple with yellow streak on throat. In some variations the tube is broad and the corolla a beautiful bell shape. Widespread at rather high elevations.

S. dunnii. Hooker. Unifoliate, with leaf up to 3 feet long. But in some areas it grows as a perennial, so it depends upon the particular clone. Flowers range in color from rose to brick red. They are 1½ inches long, tubular with short lobes. This plant has aroused great interest and has been much used in hybridization for its color range which is rare in *Streptocarpus.*

Streptocarpus dunnii.
Photo L. H. Bailey
Hortorium of Cornell
University

The aspect of this plant in its large pot is quite extraordinary, for the huge single leaf curls and crimps over the side in quite a monstrous way. When in bloom, it presents an amazing appearance: the peduncles and flowers are all bunched at the base of the leaf; are very numerous; and form an incredible bouquet consisting sometimes of hundreds of flowers. In spite of its strangeness, greenhouse growers manage very well with it.

S. johannis. L. L. Britten. Similar to *S. parvifolius* and *S. polyanthus.* Rosette plant. Numerous leaves to 14 inches long and 4 inches wide. Scapes to 6 inches. Inflorescence is one to twelve flowered. Flower 1 inch long, white with variations to violet and yellow. Deep violet line in all lobes. Found at 3,000 to 5,000 feet. Important as a parent of 'Constant Nymph.'

S. polyanthus. Hooker. Both annual and perennial forms. Leaves to 7 inches by 3 inches. Flowering stalk 7 inches with as many as thirty-six flowers. Tube ⅓ of an inch long. Flower an inch long. Lobes flattened. Long flowering period. This plant has also been much used in hybridization.

S. primulifolius. Gandoger. Similar to *S. rexii.* Mauve flowers with purple lines in throat.

S. rexii. Lindley. This was the first *Streptocarpus* to be discovered, in 1828, probably for the reason that its home is the farthest south in Africa and the nearest to Capetown. It became the type species of the genus and has confirmed its chance distinction by proving most useful in hybridization. In fact it appears in so many crosses and has been cultivated for so long that chances are that plants labeled as *S. rexii* in the trade may well be actual cultivars. It is worth noting here that one of the problems of separating species in *Streptocarpus* is their gregariousness. Not only do plants of the same species vary to a

Streptocarpus johannis.

considerable degree in habit, size of flower, shape, and coloring, but they also interbreed in a most indiscriminate way. A great number of natural hybrids have been identified or suspected, and the process goes on constantly.

This is far from being a fault in the genus, however much we may deplore it on moral grounds. It is precisely those genera and species of any family which show the greatest amount of variability and the greatest ability to hybridize naturally that are the most convenient and rewarding tools of the artificial hybridizer. Anyone familiar with plants can think of species and genera, even families, which are relatively inflexible. Species do not interbreed, and they rarely change in appearance or behavior. Long isolation fixes the attributes of the plant in a rigid mold. If such plants are from the first adaptable to our needs, there is no problem but, if not, there is little we can do to change their natures to conform.

In those plants which are good natural hybridizers, Anderson noted a process which he called introgression. Continuous hybridization between two species produces in time a third stable species intermediate between the parents. And, in the process itself, the parents are genetically affected by the gene flow so that the dividing lines become obscured. In short that is how many species are born.

S. rexii is a rosulate plant with leaves up to a foot long and 2 inches wide, wavy: margined and blunt-tipped, narrowing into the petiole which is less than an inch in length. The flowering stalk or peduncle rises from the petiolode at the base of the leaf. It is up to 8 inches high and bears two to six flowers. Remember that in *Streptocarpus* there are always a few too many of these peduncles, each producing its quota of flowers, which accounts for the great floriferousness of the whole genus. All parts of *S. rexii* are covered with short hairs.

The calyx is divided into narrow segments 1/7 inch long . In the previous descriptions we have not mentioned the size of the calyx as we are not writing a botanical work, and the information we have given is for visual identification and an idea of the section of this genus as a whole. Also the calyx in these plants is quite insignificant in size and is a feature of the African *Streptocarpus.* It usually clasps the end of the tube closely but is so small or so narrow lobed that almost the whole of the tube is visible, and we have the impression of the flower's being suspended in air.

The pedicels are less than ⅓ inch long. The tube is narrowly funnel-shaped and 1 to 1¼ inches long. The corolla lobes spread 1½ inches, the upper lobes rounded and the lower three oblong and strongly spread out as they jut forward. The face of the flower is white or suffused with mauve or blue with seven violet stripes extending from the throat onto the lower lip.

This very beautiful flower marking, shared by *S. primulifolius* and *cyaneus* is responsible for the rich patternings of some of the Wiesmoor hybrids and most of the other *rexii* hybrids which have appeared in nurseries. We have seen large funnel-shaped flowers with a perfect inverted fleur de lys painted on the lower lip in a more intense or contrasting color. 'Constant Nymph' and its variations have retained the basic form of this flower with a strengthening of the blue coloration.

S. rimicola. Story. A plant very similar to *S. pusillus.* The leaf is up to 2 inches long by 1 inch wide. Unifoliate, but sometimes produces a second leaf and inflorescence. The peduncle is 2 inches long with from two to twenty flowers. The flower is white and ¼ to ⅓ inch long. Coming from an elevation of about 1,800 feet and a harsh environment, *S. rimicola* is rather easier in cultivation than *S. cyanandrus.*

S. wendlandii. Sprenger. The single leaf has a stout petiole and is 12 to 14 inches long by 8 to 10 inches wide. Peduncles to 18 inches high, pedicels ⅜ inch. Corolla is 1 to 1¼ inches long. The tube is curved downward and then outward. The lobes are reflexed, and the lower ones jut sharply forward. The color is violet with two darker blotches in the tube flanking a white stripe.

Streptocarpus sylvaticus. One of many attractive species which may eventually attract wider interest. *Courtesy Lauray of Salisbury*

If we consider the species descriptions in Hilliard and Burtt, we can very well understand the reasons why these plants and others have been used in hybridization with the object of developing more attractive and viable houseplants. For, though they would certainly be beautiful in the wild, they need considerable adjustment to suit our needs. The modern hybrids are a vast improvement—in terms of houseplant aesthetics—over these species.

What is more difficult to fathom is why some of the species have entered cultivation here at all except as a stunt, considering the difficulties in growing them. The habitats in many instances do not at all match the kind of conditions we can easily give these plants. On the other hand, it would seem that a more judicious choice, based on habitat relationship with normal house conditions, would turn up variations more attractive and more adaptable than those which have reached us thus far. It is the difference between botanists choosing the plants to distribute and horticulturists, specifically horticulturists who know our conditions, doing the job. That is a little too much to expect, but it would certainly save a lot of waste experimentation and lead to much more satisfactory results. The genus *Streptocarpus* subgenus *Streptocarpus* is loaded with material—as have been *Columnea, Episcia,* and others—that is susceptible of selection and hybridization to produce further magnificent additions to the houseplant repertory.

We have not described cultural requirements of these species. For one thing they are not being actively grown and the details are not available. For another, it is far more important to know how to grow the hybrids. On the other hand, as there are no hybrids of the subgenus *Streptocarpella*, we will deal with the culture of the two most popular species.

SPECIES OF SUBGENUS STREPTOCARPELLA

This section of *Streptocarpus* is relatively little known. Nevertheless, we are growing a few species and one of these, *S. saxorum,* is the most popular species of the whole genus.

S. caulescens. The plant is similar to *S. holstii,* because of its fleshy stem, but the leaves are less shiny and the whole plant is more hairy. The peduncles grow from the axils and bear up to twelve ½ inch, typically *Streptocarpus* flowers in deep purple, with variations into white with purple streaks on the upper lobes. The upper lobes are short and round, the lower ones jut forward and are nearly square. *S. caulescens* also likes it warm and wet as does *S. holstii.*

S. holstii. At first sight it is obvious that *S. holstii* is a plant of streamsides and generally wet places. Its shiny, juicy purple stems are complete giveaways. It is a much-branched plant up to 2 feet in height and, when well grown, forming handsome mounds of foliage. The leaves, varying in size up to 1½ inches are long and heart-shaped, with short stiff hairs but a brilliant shining green nonetheless. There are usually two bracts in the axils of the leaves.

The flowers are on a scape up to 3 inches long from the axils. There are anywhere from two to eight on thin 1-inch pedicels. Superficially they are very different from other *Streptocarpus* species. The hairy tube hangs vertically, and the lobes of the corolla are at right angles. Imagine a very large, flowered Kenilworth Ivy, and you are pretty close to the form of the limb. The two very short upper lobes turn upward and the three much larger lower lobes swell up to meet them, closing the mouth of the throat except for a narrow cleft. They then spread out in a downward curve until the edge of the middle lobe is at right angles to the tube. The deep pure blue flower with a white mark on the hump near the throat is about ¾ inch long.

Whereas plants of subgenus *Streptocarpus* present some ticklish problems indoors, those of *Streptocarpella* are quite easy. *S. holstii's* chief requirement is constant moisture, and it does not mind being decidedly wet. Give it Rich Mix with lime and high nitrate fertilizer. It is sensitive to temperatures below 60° and thrives best between 65° and 80°. Above that, trouble may be encountered in the form of stem rot. With good treatment the central stem may grow to be ¾ inch thick and the nodes become bloated.

Bloom is seasonal for a month or two in spring. It is far easier to come by in the country than the city. Presumably this is a matter of pollution. Cuttings root very quickly in moist vermiculite.

Since this is a very handsome foliage plant, it should become increasingly popular even without flowers. There are many green plants on the market which are more temperamental than this one and not nearly as handsome.

S. stomandrus, a very similar plant but less bushy and more suited to basket culture, with pale lavender flowers, has attracted attention lately and we may see more of it in the near future.

S. kirkii. This woody, hairy plant comes from Tanzania in the hilly country opposite Zanzibar. It grows to 12 inches and has little branches, sometimes straggling. The leaves reach a length of nearly an inch, are velvety and almost round. Flowers appear among the leaves on up to ten flowered peduncles each 2 inches long. The corolla is ½ inch long, pale lilac with purple spots in the throat. The tube is ¼ inch long, the upper lobes round and less than 1/10 of an inch in diameter, and the lower ones ¼ of an inch. This is a rather pretty little plant which, if nipped, can be grown in a terrarium. It is in cultivation mostly with hobbyists.

Streptocarpus stomandrus. Courtesy Lyndon Lyon

Streptocarpus saxorum. Of all the *Streptocarpus* in cultivation this is the most versatile plant and the one gaining national popularity most rapidly. The florists have recognized its great potential by the dubious process of renaming it the Dauphin violet although it has not the slightest resemblance to that flower. There is some excuse for the name African violet but none for this one. However, it is a princely plant.

Here we have a plant with an excellent growth habit suitable equally for pot or basket, providing a beautiful overall pattern of leaves and blooming, when it does bloom which is none too regularly, with beautifully held and delicately formed flowers of good size. Culture is easy and propagation is painless. The *Streptocarpus* hybrids are far more gorgeous in flower but we cannot add up as many virtues for them as yet. From the commercial point of view this has to be the more successful plant.

S. saxorum is an overall velvety gray green, much-branched plant, with thick but not very sturdy stems. The leaves are up to an inch long, oval, and turned down at the edges, which gives them an appearance of greater thickness. They are clustered at the end of branches. Growth is only a few inches high and spreading. A stranger to the plant would probably take it for one of the furry species of *Kalanchoe* or some other succulent genus of that type.

The flowers arise singly from the axils on 3-inch pedicels so threadlike that they look insufficiently strong to hold the flower—which they do, well over the foliage. The ⅝-inch-long narrow tube is white and opens out into a limb 1½ inches in diameter, with short upper lobes and larger rounded lower ones, the latter jutting sharply forward. The face is violet except at the throat. Despite the delicate coloring, the tint is attractive, and the form of the flower and its attitude are extremely graceful. Bloom is normally during the spring and early summer.

In spite of its half-succulent appearance, *S. saxorum* doesn't mind plenty of water during periods of growth. It is also tolerant of both cooler temperatures than some other gesneriads—down to 50°—and very high ones. When some of our other gesneriads are

Streptocarpus saxorum.

collapsing from the heat, *S. saxorum* carries on with no sign of discomfort.

Almost any mix will do, but we use Rich Mix with lime and fertilize rather sparingly because we don't want to encourage too rapid growth and consequent long internodes. A bit of starvation is good and keeps the plant compact. Trimming for branching is advisable. The light requirements are very low for maintenance—about 150 to 200 footcandles or reflected window light. For bloom, about 500 footcandles are required and an eastern window exposure.

During wintertime *S. saxorum* can be kept dry for a while between waterings. In fact, at any time, it has a very fair tolerance of dryish soil. About the only thing which will kill the plant in normal home conditions is excess water during a period when it is inactive. But it is certainly not fussy and will put up with considerable neglect. On the other hand, give it good care and you can develop a specimen foliage plant within a half year from a single rooted cutting. Cuttings do root with great speed in moist vermiculite, even without covering.

In short this is a good all around plant which can take its place with much coarser types in respect to adaptability to home conditions.

STREPTOCARPUS HYBRIDS

Streptocarpus xhybridus. For over a hundred years *Streptocarpus* have been bred by European nurserymen but, until quite recently, with little success in stablizing the plants. In addition to hybridization producing changes in leaf and flower, there were variations arising from leaf propagation due to the fact that *Streptocarpus,* like African violet, is capable of producing plants from single cells of the leaves. No doubt many of the resultant plants were improvements over the species, but it proved impossible to establish any line of continuity in the strains.

Cultivated plants were so unpredictable and their lineage was so scrambled that they were lumped together under the heading of *Streptocarpus xhybridus,* just as we speak of *Begonia rex cultorum* or *Pelargonium xhortorum.* Involved in this diffuse hybridizing where *S. cyaneus, S. wendlandii, S. dunnii, S. rexii, S. saundersii, S. polyanthus, S. parviflorus,* etc.

Streptocarpus rexii hybrid.

S. *dunnii* supplied red coloration which is much rarer than blue in *Streptocarpus*. S. *cyaneus* and others had strongly striped throats which appear in some of the prettiest variations. Flowers with more rounded lobes and with broader tubes led directly into the funnel shapes of the Wiesmoor Hybrids, while S. *johannis, parviflorus* and others with more oblong lobes and long upper ones are responsible for the 'Constant Nymph' type.

THE WIESMOOR HYBRIDS.   These famous plants appeared in 1952 in the catalog of Ernst Benary and were the result of work, over a period of two decades, by Carl Fleischmann of Wiesmoor, West Germany. They are a seed mixture which consistently produces a variety of colors and color designs with a flower of stabilized form. Recently the firm of R. Blossfeld, of Lübeck, has carried the matter a step further with their offerings of separate color strains derived from the Wiesmoors.

American nurserymen have named varieties of their own. The Wiesmoor Hybrids have also been confused with *Rexii* Hybrids. S. *rexii* was one of the major influences in the complicated parentage of *xhybridus,* but the form of the flower ends up as distinctly different from the Wiesmoors. Plants have also been offered under the 'Constant Nymph' label by color, but they have invariably been Wiesmoor types.

Wiesmoor *Streptocarpus* are rosulate plants with leaves up to a foot in length and occasionally as much as 3 inches across. They produce many 6- to 15-inch peduncles with several flowers. These are larger than the species *Streptocarpus,* being up to 3 inches across the face. The tube which is 2 inches long expands into a funnel shape with broad rounded lobes. These are quite shallow and often fringed or wavy edged. Colors range from white through deepest blue to deepest red, often with striking markings on the lower lobes. When well-grown these plants are as spectacular as the florist gloxinias and as varied in coloration. We have seen a row of basket plants at Lyndon Lyon's greenhouse which was unbelievably beautiful—great arching sprays of the large flowers in a multitude of brilliant colors. Improvement of these plants continues and they are by far the most spectacular *Streptocarpus* in cultivation.

We will discuss culture below, but we would like to remark here that young plants are of comfortable size in pots and produce flowers on shorter peduncles than later on when they have reached their full maturity.

'Constant Nymph.' The story of 'Constant Nymph,' as recounted by A. G. Brown of

Streptocarpus Wiesmoor hybrid.

John Innes Institute in the *Journal of the Royal Horticultural Society,* May 1973, is a most interesting one and indicates some of the problems which may arise on the long road leading from hybridization to commercialization.

In the 1930s, W. J. C. Lawrence at the Innes Institute made many interspecific *Streptocarpus* crosses as part of a study of inheritance of flower and plant characteristics. These resulted in a few selections of merit, including 'Merton Giant,' a hybrid of *S. grandis* and *S. hybridus,* and 'Merton Blue,' a selection of *S. hybridus.* But, in 1946, a far more successful cross was made betwen 'Merton Blue' and *S. johannis,* which was named *S.* 'Constant Nymph.'

'Constant Nymph' has clustered, green-wrinkled, strap-shaped leaves up to a foot long, each of which is capable of bearing as many as seven peduncles about 6 inches long with two to six flowers. These are a deep violet blue, almost 2 inches across, with distinct, longish oblong lobes. The throat is yellowish to white and the lower lobes marked with darker veining. It blooms from spring to fall and, under lights with good cultural conditions, can be nearly everblooming.

Increased attention to this plant was attracted in the mid 1960s through the work of Dr. M. E. Marston, of the University of Nottingham School of Agriculture, who experimented with vegetative propagation of the plants and publicized its virtues.

Although it seems that John Innes Institute kept the plants pretty much to themselves in the early stages, some of them appear to have "escaped" to Holland, were grown in the area of Wageningen by amateurs, and became popular there. Soon commercial nurserymen took up the plant and grew it in quantity so that the English, being slow to recognize its potential, found themselves buying plants from Dutch growers.

'Constant Nymph,' and other *Streptocarpus,* can be reproduced by cutting the two sides of the leaf apart from the midrib and planting each section with the cut edge down in propagating medium. As many as 50 plants per leaf will develop in this way. These plants are products of single cells—an observation which led to the next stage, for it indicated that changes in the cell genes could also produce mutations in the plants.

In 1966, Mr. C. Broertjes of the Institute of Atomic Sciences in Agriculture at Wageningen irradiated the leaves of 'Constant Nymph' with X rays and fast neutrons. "At the

Streptocarpus 'Constant Nymph.'

optimum dose of 3 krads of X rays, 60 percent or more of the plants had mutated for one or more characters"—an unbelievably high rate. Leaves were also treated with colchicine. The results were plants not very different from 'Constant Nymph' but with a sufficient number of distinct color changes to be selected and tried. They were introduced commercially in 1969. The following are the plants issued at the time:

S. 'Cobalt Nymph.' Dark blue with still darker veins on lower lobes. Greenish blotch in throat.

S. 'Mini-Nymph.' A more compact plant than *S.* 'Cobalt Nymph' and lighter blue with yellow blotch in throat. A tetraploid which is very free flowering.

S. 'Netta Nymph.' Dark blue with deeper blue veining. The throat is pale yellow with a violet blotch. This is at present the favorite of growers and the most floriferous of the group.

S. 'Purple Nymph.' Large purple flowers with yellow in the throat. Also at about the time these plants were issued a white-flowered form occurred spontaneously in the nursery of Mr. Maassen at Elst. It is pure white with a yellow eye. The plant is now increasingly seen in the trade under the name Maassen's White.

So we see that a cross first made in the 1930s began to be recognized around 1962 and was not widely grown here until 1968–70. Since then the increase in popularity has been rapid.

However, this is still not the whole story which is, in fact, an ongoing one.

S. 'Constant Nymph' proved an ideal plant under English and Continental conditions which are somewhat cooler and more humid than ours. In 1969, or perhaps somewhat earlier, Mr. A. G. Brown of John Innes Institute, realizing that a wider color range than that of blue 'Constant Nymph' was desirable, started a series of hybridizing experiments using *S. johannis* and crossing it not with a blue but various other colored forms of *S. hybridus.* The crosses were fertile and F1 hybrids flowered in 1970. Most of these seedlings were in the blue violet range. Some were attractive, free flowering, and fertile when self-pollinated. Of these "thirty F2 progenies were grown and flowered in 1971. The F2 generation, being the one where the greatest amount of variation takes place, 3,000 plants were grown." In addition to blues there "was a whole range of flower colour from white through pink to red, purples and new shades of blue as well as many new flower patterns and markings." One hundred and fifty were selected for trial, and these were eventually reduced to seven. These plants are being registered under the group name of Cape Primroses. The following is a description of the seven plants.

S. 'Diana.' Up to six flowers per peduncle which is 5 to 6 inches high. The flowers 1½ inches in diameter, deep cerise with white throat.

S. 'Fiona.' Peduncles 3 inches high bear up to ten flowers. almost 2 inches across. Color pink with no intensification on lower lobes, which are wavy edged

S. 'Karen.' Six-inch high peduncles bear six flowers. 2 inches in diameter. Magenta pink with more intense color and dark veins on three lower lobes extending into the throat.

S. 'Marie.' Up to ten flowered inflorescences 4–5 inches high. Flowers are 1½ inches in diameter and dusky purple. No intensification of color on lower petals but distinctly veined into white throat.

S. 'Louise.' Peduncle 5 inches, bearing up to six flowers. Flowers 1½ inches in diameter, deep blue violet with more intense color and darker veins on lower lobes. Color extends into the throat except for two bold lines.

S. 'Paula.' Six-flowered inflorescence on peduncles 6 inches high. Flowers 1¾ inches. Reddish purple. Lower petals darker with distinct lines extending into yellow throat.

S. 'Tina.' Peduncles 3 inches high bearing up to ten flowers. Flowers 1¼ inches wide.

Streptocarpus 'Fiona.' Photo John Innes Institute

Streptocarpus 'Marie.' Photo John Innes Institute

Streptocarpus 'Paula.' Photo John Innes Institute

Upper petals pale pink, lower bright magenta with distinct veins. A very compact plant.

In 1973 the following additional plants were registered.

S. 'Helen.' Peduncles 5 inches high with ten flowers. Flowers 1½ inches diameter, medium blue violet with white throat. Very compact and free flowering.

S. 'Olga.' Peduncles 4 inches, ten-flowered. Flowers 1¾ inches wide. Bold magenta color; three lower lobes more intense, with dark veins extending into the yellow throat.

S. 'Margaret.' Peduncle 4½ inches high, one- to six-flowered. Flowers 1¼ inches. Bluish violet with dark veins on three lower lobes extending into yellow throat. ". . . this new mutant flowers throughout the year."

In a comparison of 'Constant Nymph' with 'Margaret,' it was found that, in December in cool greenhouse conditions, 'Margaret' had seven flowering stalks average per plant and 'Constant Nymph' 1.16. The average number of flowering stalks throughout the flowering period was smaller for 'Margaret' than for 'Constant Nymph.' 'Margaret' produced its best flowering stem numbers on sixteen-hour photoperiods with an intensity of 13,000 lux (about 1,000 fc) with some bleaching of leaves. But the surprising figure was the performance on eight-hour photoperiods. 'Margaret' produced at the same light intensities very many more flower stalks than 'Constant Nymph.' In other words, 'Margaret' not only blooms throughout the year, but can do so at low light intensities or duration. Although no temperature levels are given, the presumption is that the English greenhouse means winter level will run between 55° and 60°.

We have given all these details because they concern a plant of the greatest interest for the future. They also reveal that, in line with previous experience, European nurserymen and hybridizers have sought plants which thrive on lower temperatures than are normal in American homes. This is exactly the problem with *Streptocarpus.* We believe that if the same kind of experiments were carried on here—but with the objective of

Streptocarpus candidus. Improved strain. Irradiation also produced this extraordinarily floriferous clone of one of the species used in the hybridization program by the John Innes Institute. *Photo John Innes Institute*

plants with less need for cool temperatures—plants would be produced compatible with our needs. When that happens, *Streptocarpus* will become one of the most popular plants in cultivation.

CULTURE OF SUBGENUS STREPTOCARPUS

From any practical standpoint the only plants we have to consider are the modern hybrids we have described in the previous pages. They are much alike in cultural requirements but do break up into two sections, one consisting of *S.* xhybridus, the *S. rexii* hybrids and the Wiesmoor Hybrids and the other of the 'Constant Nymphs.' The essential difference is simply that the 'Constant Nymphs' have been found to be somewhat easier and more trouble free than the others.

There has been some controversy about the right soil for *Streptocarpus.* Some claim that peat moss is an unsatisfactory component, while others seem to do quite well with it. We have noticed that most nurserymen use peat moss mixes with success. The real cause of the controversy is the fact that American amateur growers of the plants indoors, after initial success, often find that the plants die off sometime during the year. In other words it seems to be difficult to keep them happy throughout the four seasons.

In our opinion the real villain is temperature and we have convinced ourselves at least, without any scientific proof, that these plants are all cool growers and that the real difference between 'Constant Nymph' and the others is simply that it does not die off as quickly in the heat of summer.

Soil does come into the matter, because it is logical and also agrees with our experience that its lightness or porosity has a good deal to do with whether the plants can withstand a heat spell or not. And we believe that this is not just a matter of drainage. Drainage conditions decide whether a soil will hold still water or not. It is a matter of moisture content. But there is another aspect. We have often referred to this as aeration. Granular soils which do not compact have tiny air spaces all through the medium. In addition to the function of ensuring perfect draining away of excess moisture, they can be cooling.

Although rarely mentioned in indoor plant literature, cool soil is an important factor in all horticulture. We read of certain outdoor plants that they appreciate direct sunlight and plenty of it as long as their roots are cool. Heat up the roots and they collapse. The same applies to certain houseplants. Outdoors we provide for cooling of roots primarily by means of some sort of mulch. A fibrous, very loose material is spread to some depth over the roots. Air enters and cools whereas a hard soil would bake in the sun. We can also wet the mulch, and evaporation during midday heat will maintain relative coolness in the area even without shading.

We have pointed out that many indoor growers, lacking air conditioning, lose plants in July and August. We are no exceptions, and we confess that we have usually not taken measures to counteract the damage before it happens. *Streptocarpus* are not the only plants, then, which can't take these hot spells. They will all usually survive in a greenhouse, but we think this is because of the better ventilation. We are no great ventilation advocates, as we have already indicated, but there is no denying that, during those summer dog days, good moving air may mean the difference between life and death for many plants.

For two summers running we experimented with planting *Streptocarpus* in loosely packed long-fiber sphagnum moss which we kept just moist. And, for the first time, they all came through in good shape. Since peat moss is not very different from sphagnum moss, except in mechanical characteristics, we must assume that the superiority of the latter was due to its providing better aeration. This is the solution of the summer problem—long-fiber sphagnum moss or a soil mix so large grained that it permits an equivalent amount of aeration and evaporation.

At best *Streptocarpus* seem to require cooler conditions than our normal home temperatures. In the country, where home temperatures are not kept as high in winter, they do much better. We calculate that the proper range for all of them is 55° to 75°, with 'Constant Nymph' showing better tolerance up to a little over 80°.

Whatever soil mix we use, we can cool the roots of our *Streptocarpus* indoors by packing a layer of long-fiber sphagnum moss on top of the soil inside the pots. On summer days of extreme heat we can moisten this layer without adding so much water that it soaks the soil below. Evaporation will reduce the temperature considerably at that level. Good ventilation or moving air provided by a fan will greatly assist the process.

We believe that Lean Mix with eggshell or lime chips added is perfectly adequate for these plants. We can also recommend the following mix which is more gritty.

1½ parts peat moss
1 part perlite—medium to large grain
1 part vermiculite
2 parts granitic or conglomerate gravel, the particles not larger than ¼ inch
2 tablespoons lime chips to the quart

The light requirements of the plants is lower than that indicated by Mr. Brown as far as intensity is concerned. Seven hundred and fifty footcandles is ample. We keep the plants 6 inches under a two-tube fixture with a twelve- to fourteen-hour day length.

'Constant Nymph,' and perhaps 'Netta Nymph,' is everblooming under controlled conditions. That means that you must not have excessive temperatures. We do not mean killing temperatures but those which will prevent blooming. Altogether cool temperatures in the sixties will guarantee continued production.

The floriferousness is indeed remarkable. The peduncles come up in clusters and produce a great show of bloom even on a relatively small plant.

On the other hand the Wiesmoor Hybrids and others bloom rather later in their development and must grow into substantial large plants—usually in 6-inch azalea pots at least—before they can send out numerous long peduncles with flowers. In the early stages, the plants are quite short leaved and produce a single peduncle at a time with at the most four very large flowers in succession. These flowers in the Wiesmoor Hybrids are much larger and showier individually than the 'Constant Nymph' types. Thus a few flowers produce the same showy effect in one instance as the many do in the other.

As for fertilizer, we know that the *Streptocarpus*, besides living at medium high altitudes—accounting for their need for coolness indoors, usually grow in harsh environments. Therefore they should not be overfed. In our opinion they should receive a normal dose of high phosphate fertilizer once a month at most. Certainly they appreciate a richer diet than that to which they are accustomed, but don't carry it too far. Roots are delicate and burn easily.

The easiest way to propagate *Streptocarpus* is by division. Since the speed of growth is amazing at times, great clusters of leaves develop, exhausting the room in the pot. Repotting time offers a good opportunity for division.

The principal difficulty is due to the habit of the plant. There is no obvious center or divisions. The thickened petiolode spreads in all directions and the leaves grow out of it in a totally unsymmetrical fashion.

Take a long-bladed and very sharp, thin knife and cut apart the sections which by guess and by golly look the most concentrated. If the plant is studied carefully after removal from the pot and most of the soil being shaken off, you will see that there usually are some obvious separate centers of activity.

Cut straight through, then repot each section separately. The main thing to guard against is fungal rot attacking the wounded section. This can be overcome by the following device. See that the roots are well covered in the new pot but, in bringing the soil up around the base of the petiolode leave the area of the wound unfilled so that it is exposed to the air. The rest of the soil will be adequate support for the plant. After the wound has air dried for a few days you can fill in that section. In this way you will have no problems.

For seeding, follow our instructions in the section on general propagation of gesneriads. The seed, as so often with gesneriads, is exceedingly small.

The favored method of leaf propagation is the one described in the first part of this section. The two sides of the leaf are cut away from the midrib, then planted with the cut edge down in moist vermiculite. Do not cover the prop box. Alternatively, cut the whole leaf into a series of wedges with the point facing the bottom of the leaf and treat just like an African violet leaf.

Some of the *Streptocarpus* hybrids have very long leaves which are an embarrassment to the indoor grower. These can be cut across to make them almost any desired length without serious damage to the plant or, for that matter, to its appearance. Often the leaves are so brittle that you can break them off one-quarter or halfway down their length.

Titanotrichum

Titanotrichum is an individualist to such an extent that botanists have not known where to place it in their classifications, although it doesn't look so very different from

Titanotrichum oldhamii. Photo L. H. Bailey Hortorium Cornell University

some large *Smithiantha.* There is only one species, *Titanotrichum oldhamii,* which comes from Taiwan, that has been cultivated in England since 1941 and is occasionally offered by American plantsmen. The country of origin is not unexpected. What is peculiar is the fact that it is scaly rhizomatous, like several American genera but unlike those of the Old World. In addition the plant produces no viable seed. There has been some speculation that it might be a really weird hybrid.

In addition to the rhizomes it has very unusual aboveground vegetative propagules, suggesting that the species is real enough but has not been studied sufficiently. At the end of flowering, *Achimenes* produces propagules in place of blooms. But these look very much like the underground rhizomes. *Titanotrichum* bears clusters of small odd-shaped buds which, when planted, develop roots and grow into normal plants. It is also different from the American genera in having a superior ovary surrounded by a shallow ring at the base, and stamens joined in pairs.

In appearance *Titanotrichum* also reminds us somewhat of digitalis, reaching with a single stem a height of up to 5 feet. The numerous leaves are 7 inches long and 4 inches wide at the bottom, decreasing in size toward the top.

Deep yellow tubed flowers 1¾ inches long are borne on 1½-inch pedicels the length of a terminal raceme. The five-lobed limb is dark crimson with an edging of yellow and the yellow throat is speckled with crimson. The lobes of the limb are flattish, rounded, and broad—the flare not broad but like a cap.

We have never seen this plant except in photographs and know nothing of its cultivation. But its appearance and origin suggest warm treatment with moderately bright light—in other words *Smithiantha* might well serve as the cultural model.

As far as indoor growing is concerned, it is too tall and the dormancy period associated with its rhizomatous nature does not encourage greenhouse cultivation. Nevertheless it is a beautiful plant, and growers do report that pot binding results in a manageable plant which still flowers handsomely.

SOME ALPINE GESNERIADS

The *Gesneriaceae* include a number of Alpine species from Europe, Asia, and Japan. Mostly semihardy they are grown in England and this country by rock garden enthusiasts. The climate of the northwestern states, which is much like that of England, appears to suit them. However, this book is intended as a guide to members of the family which are adaptable as houseplants—the exotics and tropicals—which is an altogether different horticultural interest and use. For this reason we will, in this separate section, give only short descriptions of some of the better-known species with some hints regarding culture. A number of them are very attractive garden or cool greenhouse plants.

Asteranthera

This is one of the two well known Chilean genera, in this instance identical with the species, for there is only one. It is a long-stemmed vine, attaching itself to trees or rooting at the nodes. *Asteranthera ovata* has woody stems, opposite leaves 1½ inches in length, oval, on short petioles, toothed, and more or less hairy. The flowers are deep purple red, almost 2¼ inches long, with a small, narrow-lobed calyx and a narrow funnel expanding gradually to the limb. The two upper lobes are narrow and tend to overreach the lower which are rounded, striped with yellow, and with a veined design near the narrow throat. The spreading side lobes of the flower and the overhanging upper lip give it an appearance very reminiscent of *Columnea*. The fruit is a purple and green berry ¾ inch long.

Because of its woodiness *Asteranthera* can be trained as a shrub or grown in a basket. It will tolerate temperatures down to 40°, prefers high humidity and even moisture. The light requirements are 250–500 footcandles or moderate greenhouse light but it will bloom better with 500–750 fc. It flowers for a considerable period in the winter and early spring.

Briggsia

The genus consists of about twenty, mostly stemless, plants from the mountains of India and China, with thick rhizomes. The flowers are usually campanulate, the leaves generally large. *B kurzii* and *muscicola* have been listed as in culitvation at one time. These are hardy and semihardy Alpine plants.

Conandron

C. ramondoides is a deciduous Japanese plant with rosette leaves. It is rather exceptional in having a regular five-lobed flower and five anthers which are united in a tube surrounding the style. The leaves are 4 to 7 inches long and about 2½ inches wide, thin in texture, crinkled, and nearly hairless. Mrs. Frances Batcheller, who has grown these plants, has described the unusual method of overwintering in the following terms *(The Gloxinian* Mar/April 1970).

"This gesneriad forms tightly compressed resting buds, or rather entire miniature leaves, nestled at ground level and protected by the long brown hairs on the base of the plant. . . . The compressed leaves of *Conandron* expand rapidly in warm spring weather and soon flower buds appear on the leaf bases. Grown outdoors, *Conandron* flowers in June or July."

The flowers bloom on scapes 4 to 8 inches high which bear six to twenty-five flowers in a cluster. The triangular lobes of the corolla, an inch across, are creamy, pink, or lilac with orange lines or spots in the throat. A Japanese hobbyist reports collecting various colors of this plant, which has great beauty during its few weeks of bloom.

Conandron likes cool moist conditions and gritty soil. It will do well in a cool greenhouse, or outdoors if given winter protection.

Corallodiscus

This genus consists of about twenty species of rosette-leaved plants from high altitudes, which grow in limestone, in the Himalayas and China. They are considered very choice Alpines and have been frequently grown in England. Notable for the deep indentation of the veins of the leaves. Campanulate flowers in blue, white, or purple. Hardy to semihardy and among the difficult plants to grow.

Haberlea

This Alpine genus has at least two species, which grow in the mountains of Bulgaria. However, they are so much alike that they are often treated as one. Choice Alpine plants, they will do well in areas that are not subject to deep frost in winter or hot summers. Again, the Pacific northwest climate may be used as a model, and it is there that they are occasionally grown in this country.

The rosette consists of leaves 2 to 3 inches long, the upper surface hairy and coarsely toothed. The scapes are 6 inches high and the flowers pale lilac, about ¾ inch long on short pedicels. The calyx is hairy. The tube is broad and the five corolla lobes rounded and notched, the bottom lobe projecting. The tube is speckled with yellow and violet inside the throat. The two species are *H. rhodopensis* and *H. ferdinandi-coburgii. Rhodopensis* has a variety 'Virginalis' which is white flowered. *Ferdinandi-coburgi* is a slightly smaller plant with smoother leaves.

Jankaea

Only species of its genus, *J. heldreichii* is at home on Mount Olympus in Greece, on limestone at various levels from 300 to 6,500 feet. It is one of those rock garden plants which are equally famous for their small size, beauty, and difficulty of cultivation. They are reputed to be very intolerant of transplanting.

This little plant has a cluster of leaves only 1½ inches long and ¾ inch wide, white hairy above and reddish wooly below. The scapes are 2 to 3 inches long with one to four flowers, arising from leaf axils. The corolla is lavender with a wide tube ⅜ of an inch long and five nearly oblong lobes ⅓ of an inch long.

This is a spring blooming plant requiring a gritty, limy soil with perfect drainage. It is semihardy, which means it cannot withstand a long hard freeze but does well in a very cool greenhouse or in mild winter outdoor conditions.

Loxostigma

Three species from India and China with hairy seeds and a habit somewhat like *Chirita.* Semihardy Alpines.

Mitraria

M. coccinea is another single-species Chilean genus which is semi-hardy. In both the examples the existence of the genera seems to have been dictated by geography rather than botany, for both are sufficiently similar to other genera to warrant their inclusion. The differences which exist are no greater than those between species in these other

Mitraria coccinea. Photo Howard Conrad

genera. Taxonomy often has taken the nearest shortcut when the botanist had little knowledge of the plant family as a whole or simply wanted to garner notoriety by naming a genus rather than an unimportant species. In the confining studies to which many botanists are condemned, being on record as listing a new plant is a high distinction which impresses their fellow savants.

In any case, *Mitraria* is a plant with leaves very similar to those of *Asteranthera* both in size and appearance, except that it is less hairy. It is a branching, woody plant which seeks support, and, where it lacks it, it hugs the ground. That means that it may climb several feet up or crawl that distance horizontally. The flowers hang singly on long petioles from the axils of the leaves and are 1-inch tomato red tubes tipped with short rounded ¼-inch lobes. The throat is yellow.

This is as good a place as any to mention the variance that often occurs between the descriptions of plants and actual appearance. If the description is on the basis of the dried herbarium specimen it can, except for strictly botanical details, be very wide of the mark. If a botanist's type plant record is followed, it must be remembered that it is just one specimen and that plants in their habitat, growing in sun or shade, in one kind of soil or another, or in different localities, usually display differences which may change the visual appearance to a marked extent. For instance, a leaf described as hairy may, in one place, be quite shiny and the hairiness hardly noticeable. Elsewhere the hairiness may be much thicker and the surface appearance very different. In the same way flowers may be bigger or smaller, more or less intensely colored. Unless a color chart is used, the author's color adjective may be very different from the one you would use if you saw the plant. And so on. Classification of species sometimes arises because two botanists discover the same kind of plant in two widely spaced localities.

Mitraria is available from rock garden nurseries and has been grown in the Pacific northwest. The dangling flowers, somewhat like the original *Nematanthus* species, suggest the same uses at lower temperatures.

Opithandra

O. primuloides is a hardy Alpine, often found growing in association with *Conandron,* which requires cool summers and dry cold winters.

The leaves are oval, coarsely toothed, and 2½ inches by 1¼ inches. The whole plant is hairy. Scapes are 3 to 4 inches high with tight clusters of two to twelve lilac flowers with a white tube. The tube is down-curved and the flower distinctly two-lipped and trumpet-shaped, the lower lobes being longer. There are two stamens. The capsule is long and narrow with tiny seeds.

Oreocharis

Several species from China and the Philippines. Alpine rosette plants with straight tubes and symmetrical lobes in purple or yellow.

Platystemma

Himalayan genus with one pair of leaves. Flower like *Saintpaulia*. One species, *P. violoides*.

Ramonda

The ramondas are also rosette-type plants with charming flowers. These, and a number of the other Alpines, remind us somewhat of small primroses with their low leaves and delicate clear colorings. The stamens are five in number and very short, the broad anthers facing toward the stigma. The ovary is superior.

Ramonda myconii, from the Pyrenees, is the oldest cultivated species, sometimes listed as *R. pyrenaica.* The oval leaves are coarsely toothed and wrinkled, dark green and hairy, 2½ inches long by 2 inches wide. The reverse is reddish-hairy. The open-faced flower has five oval lobes, light to deep lilac, ½ inch long with a delicate fringe. The short tube is yellow in the throat.

R. serbica, a tetraploid, grows in the Balkans in limestone. The leaves are spoon-shaped, 2½ inches long by 1¼ wide. Scapes bear one to three lilac flowers with a yellow hairy throat. The corolla lobes are four to six in number and curved forward in a bell shape, ¾ to 1 inch across. The anthers are sometimes tipped with blue.

R. nathaliae, very similar to *R. serbica* but diploid, is also from the Balkans and is reported to be the most adaptable of these plants. It is a small one with up to twenty-six leaves in the rosette, orbicular, and 2 inches in diameter. Both sides are hairy. The stalks, 4½ inches high, carry one to three violet flowers with a deep yellow eye. The open-faced flower has four, five, or six lobes ½ inch long and a very short tube. Stamens, the same number as the lobes, are yellow or bluish.

Ramonda nathaliae. Photo Frances Batcheller

Gesneriad Update

In the last few years, the family of the African violet has made spectacular progress as America's most popular houseplant. *Saintpaulia* no longer attracts only the enthusiasm of hobbyists; it has become a major commercial crop and no florist, garden center, or variety store throughout the country fails to display them. The number and size of the nurseries producing them has greatly increased and the leading labels have become recognized trademarks. The African Violet Society, Inc., is the largest flower society in the country. Other gesneriads are appearing in the shops with ever-increasing frequency.

The superiority of the African violet is due not only to its spectacular clusters of flowers, the variety of colors, and the ease with which it can be grown, but the unique characteristic of bloom throughout the year. Whereas all other colorful houseplants are seasonal and identified with particular holidays, the African violet is always in bloom. It is, in short, a true miracle houseplant.

Recognition of these facts and our belief that other members of the gesneriad family would some day prove comparably popular, caused us to choose the title for this book. Our optimism has been confirmed by events. A popular interest in the other gesneriads is evidenced by their appearance in the shops.

The sensational performance of the African violets has encouraged major houseplant nurseries to investigate other possibilities in the family. The *Gesneriaceae* root from seeds, stems, leaves, and divisions of rhizomes and tubers, a combination found to such degree in no other family. Tissue culture has proved successful. Everbloom is shared by several genera. Those with tubers or scaly rhizomes all contain species with a potential of skipping dormancy that can be reinforced through intensive breeding. A small group of inspired hybridizers has already solved many problems. We are entering a new stage in the history of the family.

Already, row on row of Bill Saylor's *Nematanthus* hybrids are displayed by major distributors. *Aeschynanthus* is a common feature of florist shops and *A. hildebrandii* has turned up in the grocery chains. *Nautilocalyx* and *Episcia* are no longer unfamiliar to florists and dwarf gloxinias are replacing the older, larger varieties in popularity.

Most extraordinary has been the progress of *Streptocarpus,* the Cape Primrose. A gorgeous blooming plant, it has had the disadvantage of excessively long, brittle leaves and an intolerance of high temperatures that restricted its popularity to hobbyists. Now we see compact plants with the most beautiful flowers in the family and much improved ease of culture. It is rapidly becoming a large-scale commercial plant with the assurance of great popularity in the future.

When columneas are tamed to a more compact, upright growth, there will be no limit to their potential for popularity. Breeding will eliminate the partial dormancy of the rhizomatous plants and result in gorgeous everblooming kohlerias, smithianthas, and even *Achimenes*.

In due time, no doubt, the public will take to the everblooming miniature sinningias, for fashions change and smallness may not handicap the plant in the long run. Besides, many of the latest hybrids, especially those of Ted Bona, are sufficiently large to attract the same public that dotes on African violets. Gesnerias are also everblooming and amazingly prolific. At present they are terrarium plants but, again, breeding will improve their ability to grow in the open. If that happens, they will be hard to beat.

We expect much of intergeneric crosses. Improved techniques have made them possible and rapid progress can be expected in the future. We foresee the creation of whole new races of gesneriads, combining the best characteristics of different genera. As new plants arrive from the wild they will contribute to our stock of available genetic material.

Indeed, so great are the advantages offered by the *Gesneriaceae* that their popularity can only increase in the future. We foresee the day when flowering houseplants will be universally accepted and when the great majority of these will belong to The Miracle Houseplant Family.

IN MEMORIAM

Maude Cogswell is no more. She was one of the very first importers of botanical gesneriads in this country. Everybody knew of her place, Whistling Hill in Hamburg, New York, and sooner or later corresponded with her, receiving in return gossip about new plants along with reports on her visits to the local racetrack. She received regular shipments from Panama, propagated them, and supplied us all with unusual and often unnamed species. For Maude was impatient with names and took them very much on faith. It will do no harm to her memory to report a hilarious incident. In one of her letters she told me about a new blue *Columnea* that she was having the devil of a time trying to flower. Finally, I suggested that she send me a piece of the plant and she agreed. One day a big, long package appeared and I opened it with considerable anticipation. My mouth dropped when I saw what it contained—a very large hunk of a heart-leaved *Philodendron*. When I reported back to Maude, she was furious. Never had her shipper done such a thing before. All who knew her now miss her peppery personality and we are grateful to her for getting us started growing columneas, episcias, and many other plants of the family.

Mr. Easterbrook (I never knew his first name) and his splendid greenhouse are also gone. He was a more disciplined grower and was a prime source of both information and plants in the early days. His list was the best in the business and he was responsible for many cultivars—a number of which are still being grown by hobbyists. The most famous of these was and is *Episcia* 'Cleopatra,' a sport that appeared spontaneously in his greenhouse. It took no little skill to save and propagate this difficult plant. In the whole range of tropical houseplants, there is nothing to compare with the colorful foliage of that plant. At a time when the number of commercial growers is greatly reduced, the loss of this dedicated man is a calamity.

CULTURE

Temperature

The most popular gesneriads continue to be grown successfully in a temperature range between 65° and 85°. Only gradually have we discovered that failure to bloom a number of species is due to their requirement of a range that is 10° to 15° lower. These were originally few in number because the majority of really cool growers were simply stored for the record between herbarium sheets. But now more and more plants have been introduced from the wild and distributed to amateurs; they are difficult or impossible for most of us to grow because of their low temperature requirements.

Everyone who has searched for plants in the tropics is aware of the many gesneriads growing at altitudes above 1,500 feet. Hardly more than the height of our tallest buildings, it is surprising what a difference this small elevation makes. In St. Lucia, we saw magnificent plants of what we think was *Gesneria ventricosa*. The flowers were as large and beautiful as any *Aeschynanthus*. But, since we were obliged to wear sweaters, we did not consider so cool a plant to be of interest to our gardening friends at home. If the

African violet required 50°–55° night temperatures in order to bloom, it would not be the popular plant it is.

Another feature of the higher altitude plants is that they are often woody shrubs. The St. Lucia plant was five feet tall. For a long time at least, the larger shrubs brought back from expeditions were not distributed. Lately they have been lumped with all the others. We are quite certain that the ultimate failure of a number of small shrubs we have grown, such as bellonias and shrubby gesnerias was due to the temperature factor. In the early days of *Columnea,* it earned the common name of the 'Norse Fire Plant' because a few of the handsomest species were very cool growing. Today all the most successful columneas are adaptable to normal indoor temperatures.

In the future it will be very helpful if the description of a new species is accompanied by specific information regarding the temperature range in its habitat. Botanists usually don't bother to mention that but it is all-important for us growers.

When you have a new species that has reached maturity and failed to bloom, consider the possibility that it is one of these cool growers. Air conditioning or fans may solve the problem.

Light Sources

Our assessment of fluorescent light sources has not changed an iota since our first edition. There has been no improvement over the combination of Cool White and Warm White tubes as superior for growth and bloom of gesneriads, nor over Verilux tubes' ability to match them, with the added attraction of a far more natural-looking illumination.

However, there has been a breakthrough in bulbs. The Wonderlite, distributed by the Public Service Lamp Corporation in New York City, is, in our opinion, the only one that can be applied to the growing and blooming of gesneriads. All the other bulbs are either underpowered or possess an inadequate growth spectrum.

The Wonderlite is a 160-watt, mercury-vapor reflector lamp with a normal life of 10,000 hours. The reason it works so well is that a chemical has been added that provides the red part of the spectrum lacking in other lamps. Being self-ballasted, it screws into any ceramic incandescent lamp-light fixture. As its reflector is built in, it needs no reflector shade, though a more aesthetic appearance is achieved with one. All mercury vapor lamps take a few minutes to warm up before reaching full spectrum. If the lamp is turned off, it requires anywhere from ten to fifteen minutes to light up again. It is also typical of this type of lamp (with very complex innards) that an occasional one will be a blinker. The company replaces it promptly on request.

The Wonderlite is expensive when considered as a unit. But it does the work of four 40-watt fluorescent tubes, covering an equal circular rather than rectangular area. It has application for the illumination of circular tables with plants, of taller plants, such as drymonias, and of large terrariums. The lamp should be at all times no closer than 1½ feet above the plants, though it is much cooler than incandescent bulbs of the same wattage. Another use for this lamp is for corner and wall gardens at any level. Keep the lamp on the same length of time as you would a fluorescent lamp for best results.

Watering

Our ideas on watering have been somewhat modified since the first edition. We have learned that the epiphytes, identifiable as those most suited to baskets, are small drinkers and bloom best when watered sparingly. Many of them have quite succulent leaves and juicy stems, which is a sign that they bloom from the beginning of the dry season to which they are accustomed. Even the fibrous rooted and rhizomatous plants, heavier drinkers, should be treated similarly. The tuberous plants require the even moisture we have suggested, but that is difficult to maintain outside a terrarium. Daily heavy spraying, with the water running down the stems, is a good way of keeping the soil from drying out without subjecting the plants to the risk of over watering.

Wick culture, so popular at one time, has disappeared. Instead most growers are using mats. Mats are hard to keep clean and are an excellent means of insect communication from plant to plant. But they cut down on watering time and provide a good deal of ambient humidity. We prefer white horticultural matting to the gray-colored mixtures that are unsightly. Absorbent nondecaying fabrics of any kind will do as well.

Claims made about water or hydroponic culture are greatly exaggerated. The trick can be accomplished even with gesneriads but requires very precise care in following instructions. Nobody has won blue ribbons with plants grown in this way.

Soils

Since our first edition, a slight shift in our recommendations for soil mixes has occurred. This comes about because of two factors. One is a deterioration in the quality of vermiculite. Large-size clean cubes are very difficult to come by these days and much of the vermiculite being sold, besides being extremely fine in grain, contains a considerable amount of impurity that is damaging to plants in the long run. Perlite has been under suspicion for some time but originally for the wrong reasons. The real trouble seems to be that it accumulates salts in excessive quantities. An excellent medium at the start, it can cause damage later on, especially if the soil is not regularly leached with clear water.

At present we are using Ball Growing Mixes. No. 1, which is the more fine grained, consists of bark, vermiculite, and perlite. No. 2, which is coarser, consists of bark, vermiculite, peat, and perlite. In both mixes the proportion of vermiculite and perlite does not appear to be large. But the grind of the mix is the right size and results have been excellent. For soft-stemmed gesneriads we suggest the same proportions of lime as formerly. For the more woody plants we recommend cutting the amount in half.

Pests

It is well known that we were among the first to recommend Safer Agro-Chem's Insecticidal Soap for our houseplant insects. As we have a constant traffic in plants, insects are being introduced regularly with them. With Safer we have been successful in eradicating bad cases of mealybug, mite, and scale infestations. The pesticide is particularly effective with mites and increasingly less so with larger insects. Thus, mealybugs require a number of applications before they disappear completely. Another reason for their partial and temporary immunity to complete eradication is the ability of the young mealybug to crawl into the tiniest crevices in leaf buds and axils where water tension will protect them from the action of the pesticide. But, with patience, they can be driven out.

Our method is to follow instructions for mixing with water and apply a drenching spray every couple of days for up to two weeks. It's work, but it does the job.

The special merit of Safer is its relative safety in handling. The insecticidal soap is really a fatty acid that is far less dangerous than the usual chemical pesticides. However, it is a caustic material and should not be handled carelessly. Use gloves and protect your eyes. You may be allergic to its action on your skin; therefore wash hands after each application. And, of course, it is not something to drink. The odor is much less unpleasant than Kelthane.

In other words, Safer is a development of the frequently recommended use of detergents to combat insects. It is just more concentrated and more lethal to them.

THE HYBRIDIZERS

Our leading hybridizers have spent years adapting wild plants to the needs and tastes of indoor growers, and their work precedes and underlies mass marketing that leads to general popularity. It is they, too, who are mainly responsible for maintaining indispensable stocks of those rare botanicals that usually disappear from amateur collections.

Frances Batcheller of Durham, New Hampshire, is certainly the dean of gesneriad hybridizers. Her plants have gained worldwide fame and she continues to enchant us with her new creations. Some of her latest beauties are *Achicodonia* 'Isis' and kohlerias 'Lono,' 'Modron,' and 'Pamola,' successors to 'Rongo,' a permanent favorite. It is due to her that *Codonanthe* cultivars have improved and become so popular.

Ted Bona of Reading, Pennsylvania, is perhaps the most prolific of hybridizers. We are happy to see that there is renewed appreciation of his outstanding *Sinningia* hybrids.

Active in selecting and hybridizing exotic plants, Ken Freiling and Tom Winn maintain at Glasshouse Works, Stewart, Ohio, one of the most extraordinary collections in the world. They are a major source for botanical gesneriads and their cultivars, which are sold through the catalog of Country Hills Greenhouses in Corning, Ohio.

Gary Hunter of Drumore, Pennsylvania, has produced very fine *Streptocarpus,* notably 'Essue.' Many others are on the way.

Michael Kartuz and his partner, Patrick Worley, now moved to Vista, California, from Massachusetts, where they made their reputations, have not lost their touch. Worley has been especially active in *Kohleria* crosses and both have created many new *Sinningia* cultivars. Theirs is still a prime source of mail-order gesneriads.

Lyndon Lyon, the great African violet hybridizer, just rolls on and on, producing top plants. In recent years much of his effort has also been devoted to dwarf *Streptocarpus* and compact sinningias. The Lyon touch is justly famous.

Martin Mines of New York is a leader in the hybridization of mini-sinningias and in the propagation of his plants by tissue culture.

William Saylor of Brewster, Massachusetts, is Mr. *Aeschynanthus, Nematanthus,* and *Codonantanthus* all rolled into one. His achievement is a whole lexicon of new plants, superior to the natural species, many of which have substantial commercial potential.

Bartley Schwarz of El Monte and Roger Strickland of Valley Center, California, have been major creators of fine *Streptocarpus* and *Sinningia* hybrids.

Of the foreign hybridizers who possess a long tradition of gesneriad development, recent leaders have been the John Innes Institute in the U.K. and The Institute of Atomic Sciences in Agriculture (ITAL) in the Netherlands.

NEW DEVELOPMENTS IN GESNERIADS

Achimenes

Three outstanding new *Achimenes* from Patrick Worley of Kartuz Greenhouses are:
A. 'Desiree.' Fully double large flower, salmon-red, long lasting, semitrailing. Compact.
A. 'Rio Rita.' Large rose-pink flowers, ruffled and scalloped. Semitrailer.
A. 'Teresa.' Double and semidouble. Large flowered deep fuchsia. Dark foliage. Trailing.
For *xAchimenantha,* see Intergeneric Crosses, page 233.

Aeschynanthus

A. hildebrandii. The ever-alert Mrs. Batcheller reported on *A. hildebrandii* in *The Gloxinian,* May/June 1979. "This species is a most unusual *Aeschynanthus,*" she wrote. "It is not trailing, but erect and woody in habit. Being a dwarf species it has the potential for a superior bonsai subject. Despite the small size of the plant, it blooms prolifically, setting new buds wherever it is pruned. The orange and red flowers have the typical *Aeschynanthus* shape with a curved tube 2.5 cm. long. The calyx is very small. There can be twelve or more flowers in a cluster. The leaves are a dull green tapered to both ends, 5 cm. long and 1.5 cm. wide. The leaf texture is rather thin, without the usual succulent character of most *Aeschynanthus.*" Undoubtedly this is one of the great introductions of the last ten years.

Hildebrandii comes from Burma and grows at 4,000–5,000 feet. Hence ideal growing conditions are rather cool, in the 65°–70° range, with high humidity. As it is an epiphyte, it requires good drainage in a light peat mix. High temperatures and soggy soil will kill it.

Bartley Schwartz has made a cleverly calculated cross between *A. micranthus* and *A. hildebrandii* called 'Big Apple'—clever because it takes advantage of *micranthus*'s ability to bloom at every leaf node plus its larger size. The result is a bigger plant without the loss of *A. hildebrandii*'s general appearance. It reaches at least a foot in height and width. The plant has not yet become generally available.

With time our admiration for *A. longicaulis (A. marmoratus)* has increased. The flower is lost in the foliage but the pattern of the leaves is a delight in a sunny window or under room illumination at night. The handsome design of the leaves does not display well in the ambient light of flower shows and fails to attract the attention it deserves. The hybrid, 'Black Pagoda,' lacks the rich leaf patterning. *A. longicaulis* blooms freely from the nodes, like *A. micranthus* and *A. hildebrandii*. This makes the three far superior as hybridizing material to the other species being used. With further work it may be possible to combine the fine foliage with more colorful flowers while retaining the floriferousness.

We note that *A. evrardi,* the most shrubby of the other cultivated *Aeschynanthus,* continues to be listed, as are *A. speciosus, x-splendidus,* and *tricolor.* The attempt to produce shorter branches continues.

Bill Saylor never stops creating fine hybrids including the following:
'Firecracker.' *Micranthus*-type flowers on a compact plant with small leaves.
'Fireworks.' Dwarf, very compact. Many red flowers.

'Greensleeves.' A trailer with large red flowers striped with purple and yellow.

'Little Tiger.' Large red flowers striped with black. A compact trailer.

'Mandalay.' Large burnt-orange flowers. Purple marbled leaves. Upright habit. Nearly everblooming.

'Red Cascade.' Large red tubular flowers. Purplish-green leaves. Trailing.

'Tiger Stripe.' Red flowers striped with purple and yellow. Purple calyces.

'Bali.' Trailer with bright red, tubular flowers.

Lauray has produced 'Laura,' a cross between *A. micranthus* and *A. evrardii*. It mates *micranthus*'s flowering at the nodes to *evrardii*'s more shrubby habit, with the larger flowers of the latter. Long summer bloom.

Arndt's 'Kalimantan' is a 'Black Pagoda'-type plant with more vivid flowers.

'Coral Flame' is a small-leaved plant with dark red flowers.

Selby Garden's 'Red Elf' is described as a basket plant with small leaves and short upright red flowers with a cream throat.

'Holiday Bells' by Kartuz has short red flowers in a broad coral calyx.

Kartuz has also introduced a new species, *A. tricolor*. The flowers are striped red, yellow, and purple. A repeat bloomer.

'Hot Flash,' a Kartuz listing, has upright clusters of orange flowers with red stripes. Compact, upright, and everblooming.

Bucinellina

This is a new genus, mistakenly named at first as *Bucinella*.

B. nariniana. Colombia. Stems and leaves are described as similar to *Neomortonia rosea*. Pink calyx, trumpet-shaped corolla, yellow and maroon. "Everblooming."

Chirita

Chirita sinensis has maintained its popularity with hobby growers very well, especially the silvery leaved form. The annual species of the genus turn up occasionally. Considering their relative ease of culture and the pretty flowers, it is surprising that at least hobbyists do not take to them more. Our hopes for *C. asperifolia (blumei)* have not been confirmed. This outstanding plant hasn't been around for years though it is one that has few equals.

A number of new species have been introduced from Ceylon and China in recent years. For descriptions of these we are indebted to Mrs. Batcheller. In the Sept./Oct. 1982 issue of *The Gloxinian,* where she updates the genus, she also provides the information that *Chirita* "is a Hindustani word meaning gentian," adopted no doubt in reference to the bluish color of some of the flowers.

C. anachoreta. An annual to 14 inches with white flowers, having a wide range in southeast Asia. The photograph shows a weed plant with the flowers on short pedicels partly hidden by the numerous leaves.

C. involucrata is also an annual with a similar range. It reaches 18 inches in height and the corolla lobes are blue with blue-purple around the throat. Prefers limey soils.

C. pumila, from the same area. An inappropriate name for an 18-inch plant. This annual bears leaves with purple-brown patches. Corolla violet with a paler tube and an orange patch near the throat.

C. walkeri. A perennial, 24 inches high, the corolla deep purple, the tube narrow with a yellow streak. It comes from Sri Lanka. Lauray has offered it.

C. zeylanica is also from Sri Lanka, and the potential winner in the group. The flowers were shown on the cover of *The Gloxinian,* March /April, 1979. It is a perennial species to 24 inches high with leaves resembling those of *C. lavandulacea.* The trumpet flower has blue-purple lobes and a broad pale-lilac tube. The yellow stamens are prominent. Although the growth habit is not indicated, it seems to be shrubby as it does become woody with age.

Chrysothemis

We had the good fortune to see *C. pulchella,* both green- and bronze-leaved forms, growing in the little gardens of Tobago. There they were exposed to full sun, which kept them very compact, reduced the size of the leaves, and increased the number of flowers in a cluster. This is a very popular plant, and for good reason, for its calyces are brilliant orange and very long lasting. Most of the plants were grown in pots. In the forest, at 1,500 feet, barely emerging from a thin layer of moist, fallen leaves, we also encountered *C. villosa,* with its attractive, very hairy white calyx. It is significant that the local people prefer to grow *C. pulchella.* It was a lesson in the difference between wild and cultivated plants—namely, the superior growth that can be expected if they are protected and cared for. It made us wonder why so few are grown by our hobbyists.

In *The Gloxinian,* Nov./Dec., 1979, Laura Progebin reported obtaining *C. pulchella* 'Amazon' from the USDA. The flowers are much larger with a length of ⅝ inch and a diameter of ⅜ inch. In reality this does not seem to be any bigger than the flowers of well-grown plants in Tobago. It was found near Belem, Para, Brazil, which is very hot country indeed, a key to its cultivation and temperature tolerance. Incidentally, since *Chrysothemis* is a tuberous rooted plant, it produces offsets. It is when there is a colony of these growing in an azalea-type pot that the plants become more compact and make a greater show of flowers.

Cobananthus

This genus was established to accommodate *Alloplectus calochlamys,* which is now *Cobananthus calochlamys.* See page 62.

Codonanthe

A number of recently introduced plants have been given specific names, while older species made their reappearance and others have been transferred from one specific name to another. A detailed description of these species serves little purpose except for botanical researchers. The amateur will have to see these plants in juxtaposition with others in order to recognize the visual differences and make their choices. Among the survivors of interest are the following:

C. caribaea (triplinervia). Glossy, dark green leaves and small white flowers. Cv. 'Paria' has larger leaves and flowers.

C. chiricana is described as an upright species with long-tubed white flowers.

C. devosiana is an older species with small, hairy leaves and small white flowers.

C. digna is a small vine with white flowers in the leaf axils and orange berries from

Brazil. The plants were formerly listed under *C. carnosa.* Cv. 'Frances Batcheller,' with leaves that are green on both sides, has been very popular. Cv. 'Moonlight.' The reverse of the leaves is red.

C. luteola, a new species from Panama, has long yellow flowers.

C. picta (gracilis). Waxy, oval leaves and white flowers. Long pendent stems and orange fruits.

C. uleana is an older species with rounded leaves on a more upright plant. Pink berries.

Kartuz lists a new species, *C. elegans,* with large, waxy white flowers.

Codonanthopsis

Includes *C. ulei,* a warm-growing basket plant with large fleshy leaves and white flowers with lavender spots. Everblooming (?) Brazil.

Columnea (Bucinellina, Dalbergaria, Pentadenia, Tricantha)

Beginning in 1973, Wiehler assigned a number of *Columnea* species to the genera *Bucinellina, Dalbergaria, Pentadenia,* and *Tricantha.* The AGGS Nomenclature Committee chose to remain neutral and some other botanists did not agree to the changes. This created considerable confusion among amateurs, especially as some commercial nurseries adopted the new names in their catalogs while others did not. Even those who printed the new names, however, listed them under *Columnea.* Our first impulse was to change our original text and the captions of illustrations to conform to the new system. On second thought, we abandoned the idea. Because it is not the normal custom among hybridizers of gesneriads and nurserymen to list the seed and pollen parents of their plants, all of them had to appear under the general heading of *Columnea.* As regards the species, we decided to use Dr. Margaret H. Stone's invaluable listing of synonyms from *The Gloxinian,* Vol. 31, No. 4 of 1981, but without including the sequence of authors that is of minor or no interest to amateurs. We have also reprinted her introduction to the list because it clearly states the problem and the method she has used in making up her list.

Here is a reference list of related gesneriads which have caused some confusion in the gesneriad world because many of them have two validly published names in common use (Stone, 1981). Theoretically, either name may be used at flower shows, in the trade, or in publications. Whether you use one name or the other usually depends on the name given to the plant by the person who gave or sold it to you. Perhaps you don't care what it is called, as long as it is easy to grow and blooms continually. However, it is quite possible to purchase a new plant and find out it is actually an old friend with a different name, so it is wise to know both names.

The species in this list may be considered as belonging to one large genus *Columnea* (Morley, 1973, 1974, 1976; Skog, 1979), or to a complex of related genera: *Bucinella, Columnea, Dalbergaria, Pentadenia,* and *Trichantha* (Wiehler, 1973, 1975, 1977, 1978). Since this represents a difference of opinion based on different taxonomic concepts, *The Gloxinian* remains neutral. Species with two names may thus be cited either according to the traditional classification (left column) or according to the new classification (right column). The list contains only species in cultivation.

THE TRADITIONAL CLASSIFICATION		A NEW CLASSIFICATION
		The Genera of the *Dalbergaria* Alliance, with *Columnea* in the Narrow Sense
The Genus *Columnea* in the Broad Sense		
1. *Columnea affinis*	=	*Dalbergaria aureonitens*
2. *Columnea allenii*	=	*Columnea allenii*
3. *Columnea ambigua*	=	*Tricantha ambigua*
4. *Columnea ampliata*	=	*Dalbergaria ampliata*
5. *Columnea angustata*	=	*Pentadenia angustata*
6.	=	*Tricantha angustifolia*
7. *Columnea anisophylla*	=	*Tricantha anisophylla*
8. *Columnea argentea*	=	*Columnea argentea*
9. *Columnea arguta*	=	*Columnea arguta*
10.	=	*Dalbergaria asteroloma*
11. *Columnea aureonitens*	=	*Dalbergaria aureonitens*
12. *Columnea bilabiata*	=	*Columnea bilabiata*
13. *Columnea billbergiana*	=	*Columnea billbergiana*
14. *Columnea brenneri*	=	*Tricantha brenneri*
15. *Columnea brevipila*	=	*Columnea brevipila*
16.	=	*Pentadenia byrsina*
17. *Columnea calochlamys*	=	*Cobananthus calochlamys*
18. *Columnea calotricha*	=	*Tricantha calotricha*
19. *Columnea canarina*	=	*Columnea canarina*
20. *Columnea cerropirana*	=	*Tricantha cerropirrana*
21. *Columnea chiricana*	=	*Columnea chiricana*
22.	=	*Tricantha ciliata*
23.	=	*Tricantha citrina*
24.	=	*Pentadenia colombiana*
25. *Columnea consanguinea*	=	*Dalbergaria consanguinea*
26. *Columnea crassa*	=	*Dalbergaria crassa*
27.	=	*Pentadenia crassicaulis*
28. *Columnea crassifolia*	=	*Columnea crassifolia*
29. *Columnea cruenta*	=	*Dalbergaria cruenta*
30. *Columnea dissimilia*	=	*Tricantha dissimilis*
31. *Columnea dodsonii*	=	*Columnea dodsonii*
32.	=	*Tricantha dodsonii*
33. *Columnea domingensis*	=	*Tricantha domingensis*
34. *Columnea dressleri*	=	*Columnea dressleri*
35.	=	*Pentadenia ecuadorana*
36. *Columnea ericae*	=	*Dalbergaria ericae*

NOTE: Some of the species listed do not have alternate names, hence the blanks that occur in both columns.

THE TRADITIONAL CLASSIFICATION		A NEW CLASSIFICATION
37. *Columnea erythrophaea*	=	*Columnea erythrophaea*
38. *Columnea erythrophylla*	=	*Tricantha erythrophylla*
39. *Columnea fawcetii*	=	*Columnea fawcetii*
40. *Columnea fendleri*	=	*Columnea fendleri*
41.	=	*Tricantha filifera*
42. *Columnea flaccida*	=	*Columnea flaccida*
43. *Columnea florida*	=	*Dalbergaria florida*
44. *Columnea gallicauda*	=	*Columnea gallicauda*
45. *Columnea glabra*	=	*Columnea glabra*
46. *Columnea gloriosa*	=	*Columnea gloriosa*
47. *Columnea grisebachiana*	=	*Tricantha cristata*
48. *Columnea guianensis*	=	*Dalbergaria guianensis*
49. *Columnea guttata*	=	*Dalbergaria guttata*
50. *Columnea harrisii*	=	*Columnea harrisii*
51. *Columnea herthae*	=	*Tricantha herthae*
52. *Columnea hiantiflora*	=	*Columnea hiantiflora*
53. *Columnea hirsuta*	=	*Columnea hirsuta*
54. *Columnea hirsutissima*	=	*Columnea hirsutissima*
55. *Columnea hirta*	=	*Columnea hirta*
56. *Columnea illepida*	=	*Tricantha illepida*
57. *Columnea inaequilatera*	=	*Dalbergaria inaequilatera*
58. *Columnea incarnata*	=	*Columnea incarnata*
59. *Columnea kalbreyeriana*	=	*Columnea kalbreyeriana*
60. *Columnea kienastiana*	=	*Columnea kienastiana*
61. *Columnea kucyniakii*	=	taxonomic position unclear
62. *Columnea lepidocaula*	=	*Columnea lepidocaula*
63. *Columnea linearis*	=	*Columnea linearis*
64. *Columnea maculata*	=	*Columnea maculata*
65.	=	*Dalbergaria madisonii*
66. *Columnea magnifica*	=	*Columnea magnifica*
67.	=	*Pentadenia matudae*
68. *Columnea microcalyx*	=	*Columnea microcalyx*
69. *Columnea microphylla*	=	*Columnea microphylla*
70. *Columnea minor*	=	*Tricantha minor*
71. *Columnea mira*	=	*Tricantha mira*
72. *Columnea moorei*	=	*Tricantha moorei*
73.	=	*Bucinellina nariniana*
74. *Columnea nervosa*	=	*Pentadenia nervosa*
75. *Columnea nicaraguensis*	=	*Columnea nicaraguensis*
76. *Columnea oerstediana*	=	*Columnea oerstediana*
77.	=	*Pentadenia orientadina*

THE TRADITIONAL CLASSIFICATION		A NEW CLASSIFICATION
78. *Columnea oxyphylla*	=	*Columnea oxyphylla*
79. *Columnea panamensis*	=	*Columnea panamensis*
80.	=	*Bucinellina paranicola*
81. *Columnea parviflora*	=	*Tricantha parviflora*
82. *Columnea pectinata*	=	*Dalbergaria pectinata*
83. *Columnea pendula*	=	*Tricantha pendula*
84. *Columnea perpulchra*	=	*Dalbergaria perpulchra*
85. *Columnea picta*	=	*Dalbergaria picta*
86. *Columnea pilosissima*	=	*Columnea pilosissima*
87. *Columnea polyantha*	=	*Dalbergaria polyantha*
88. *Columnea proctori*	=	*Columnea proctori*
89. *Columnea pulchra*	=	*Tricantha pulchra*
90. *Columnea purpurata*	=	*Dalbergaria sanguinea*
91. *Columnea purpureovittata*	=	*Tricantha purpureovittata*
92.	=	*Dalbergaria puyana*
93. *Columnea querceti*	=	*Columnea quercetti*
94. *Columnea raymondii*	=	*Columnea raymondii*
95. *Columnea repens*	=	*Columnea repens*
96. *Columnea rubida*	=	*Pentadenia rubida*
97. *Columnea rubra*	=	*Columnea rubra*
98.	=	*Dalbergaria rubriacuta*
99. *Columnea rutilans*	=	*Columnea rutilans*
100. *Columnea salmonea*	=	*Columnea salmonea*
101. *Columnea sanguinea*	=	*Dalbergaria sanguinea*
102. *Columnea sanguinolenta*	=	*Tricantha sanguinolenta*
103. *Columnea scandens*	=	*Columnea scandens*
104. *Columnea schiedeana*	=	*Columnea schiedeana*
105. *Columnea schimpffii*	=	*Dalbergaria schimpffii*
106. *Columnea segregata*	=	*Tricantha segregata*
107. *Columnea septentionalis*	=	*Alsobia punctata*
108. *Columnea silvarum*	=	*Dalbergaria silvarum*
109. *Columnea spathulata*	=	*Pentadenia spathulata*
110. *Columnea strigosa*	=	*Pentadenia strigosa*
111. *Columnea subcordata*	=	*Columnea subcordata*
112. *Columnea sulfurea*	=	*Columnea sulfurea*
113. *Columnea tenensis*	=	*Tricantha tenensis*
114. *Columnea tenuis*	=	*Columnea oerstediana*
115. *Columnea tessmannii*	=	*Dalbergaria tessmannii*
116. *Columnea teuscheri*	=	*Tricantha minor*
117. *Columnea tomentulosa*	=	*Columnea tomentulosa*
118. *Columnea trollii*	=	*Pentadenia trollii*

THE TRADITIONAL CLASSIFICATION		A NEW CLASSIFICATION
119. *Columnea tulae*	=	*Columnea scandens*
120. *Columnea tulae* Urban var.	=	*Columnea tomentulosa*
121. *Columnea urbanii*	=	*Columnea urbanii*
122. *Columnea verecunda*	=	*Columnea verecunda*
123. *Columnea vinacea*	=	*Pentadenia vinacea*
124. *Columnea vittata*	=	*Dalbergaria vittata*
125. *Columnea weberbaueri*	=	*Pentadenia weberbaueri*
126.	=	*Pentadenia zapotalana*
127. *Columnea zebranella*	=	*Columnea zebranella*
128. *Columnea zebrina*	=	*Columnea zebrina*

COLUMNEA SPECIES

As the result of explorations by Hans Wiehler, a number of new *Columnea* species have been listed. None of these has proved significant as yet to hobbyists. We note them simply for future reference.

C. canarina. Calyx and corolla canary yellow.

C. cobana. Guatemala. Branches spreading. Flowers orange-red.

C. dodsonii. Ecuador. Branches pendent. Flowers small, red. Changed to *Alloplectus.*

C. dressleri. Panama. Calyx fringed, green, with maroon center. Corolla red.

C. gallicauda. Panama. Leaves "like a cock's tail." Calyx maroon. Corolla striped yellow and black.

C. hiantiflora. Panama. Leaves long and narrow. Calyx fringed. Corolla red.

C. kienastiana. Colombia. "Similar to *C. dodsonii*" but serrated calyx.

C. rubra. Leaves 5 inches long, red below. Calyx lobes almost an inch long, wine red. Corolla 3 inches long, lemon yellow.

Additional hybrids are:

C. 'Eureka' (Schwarz). Large yellow and orange flowers. Small leaved, trailing.

C. 'Mirage' (Schwarz). Small, variegated leaves, trailing.

C. 'Madame Butterfly' (Schwarz). Very large orange and yellow flowers on trailing stems. Everblooming.

C. 'Starburst' (Schwarz). Bright yellow, peloric (equal-lobed) flowers. The peloric blooms usually develop only on mature plants. Semitrailing.

COLUMNEA "INTERGENERICS"

As many botanists disagree with the splitting up of *Columnea* we have no compunction about including *xColbergaria* and *xColtricantha* hybrids here.

xColbergaria 'Miami Noon.' Upright plant with olive-green leaves and red hairs. Orange flower.

xColbergaria. 'Orange Fire.' Dark green foliage, reddish beneath. Orange flower.

xColbergaria 'Sarasota Sunset.' Large plant. Dark green leaves, red beneath. Dark yellow flower.

xColtricantha 'Golden Nugget' (Schwarz). Dangling yellow flower, red calyces. Bronze-green leaves red beneath. Upright. Everblooming.

xColtricantha 'Miami Sunrise.' Semitrailer. Yellow flowers with orange hairs.

xColtricantha 'Mountain Elf.' Trailing, light green foliage with red hair. Dark red bloom.

Corytoplectus

A genus redefined by Wiehler and now including a number of species taken from *Alloplectus*, namely: *A. capitatus, A. cristatus, A. schlimii, A. speciosus (vittatus)*, and *A. teuscheri*. See pages 61 and 62.

Cyrtandra

A big genus, some species of which are indigenous to Hawaii, but having a range from China to Australia and many other Pacific islands. The habit is varied for there are herbs, shrubs, and even small trees. The flowers are usually white, sometimes yellow or red, and clustered in the leaf axils. Mrs. Batcheller reports that *C. oblongifolia* makes a good pot plant, having white flowers in the lower axils. *C. splendens* bears large, *Episcia*-like leaves and red flowers.

Didissandra

This genus is included because of the description by Dr. Anton Weber in *The Gloxinian*, 1978, No. 2. It is a southeast Asian genus. The plant shown by Dr. Weber, *D. morganii*, has a habit similar to *Gesneria cuneifolia* and the leaves are also reminiscent except that they are more crenulated and sharp toothed. The large trumpet flower is violet, purple, or mauve. Not very floriferous on the moist rain forest floor that is its habitat, it may well be rewarding in a terrarium or greenhouse environment. We anticipate that there will be many more Asiatic gesneriads available to collectors in the next few years.

Didymocarpus

A large genus ranging from the Himalayas to Borneo, many of which are alpine. They are herbs bearing some resemblance to *Chirita*.

Dr. Anton Weber in *The Gloxinian*, 1981, No. 6, described *D. bakoensis*, from Borneo. The plant is 6 inches in diameter with leaves very much like *Gesneria cuneifolia*. The inch-long flower is mauve, the tube long, the lobes reflexed. The upper two are distinct, the lower three form a large lip with reduced lobes. The plant grows not on the forest floor but on boulders with a thin covering of soil. Other species mentioned from the same area are *D. angustifolius* and *scabrinervus*.

Drymonia

Among the new species of *Drymonia* are the following:

D. conchocalyx. Large plant with spreading branches and leaves up to 8 inches long. Calyx green, flushed red. Flower large, magenta-rose with white edges. Throat with yellow streaks and rose dots. Panama.

D. ecuadorensis. Flowers similar to *D. stenophylla.* Leaves to 8 inches, red beneath.

D. killipii. Colombia. Tall plant with thick stems and large, white-veined leaves. Calyx yellow-green, tube creamy white, lobes deep purple. Yellow streaks in throat.

D. macrantha. Central America. Single stemmed to 3 feet with an ''umbrella'' of nine to seventeen (!) leaves. Flowers are waxy-white with yellow lines in the throat. Up to 2½ inches in length. Hardly a houseplant but fine for the greenhouse.

D. multiflora. Panama. Thin stemmed basket plant with small leaves. Flower with maroon calyx and yellow corolla.

D. pulchra. Ecuador. Similar to *D. turrialvae.* Upright plant with thick green leaves, maroon calyx and bright yellow corolla, the lobes fringed.

D. rhodoloma. Ecuador. Spreading basket plant with leathery leaves. Calyx green, maroon veined. Lobes of corolla cream, tube pinkish.

D. serrulata. Central America, Caribbean and northern South America. A rampant, branching vine. The 6-inch leaves are bright green above and wine red below. The flowers are up to 2½ inches long, white or creamy yellow or pink flushed, the throat sometimes lined with red.

D. strigosa. Shrub to 3 feet in height. Leaves unequal, as in *D. stenophylla,* up to 6 inches long. Large, pinkish red sepals and long yellow flower.

We doubt that drymonias will ever become great favorites with the public. But for many greenhouse and indoor growers, they possess the attraction of handsome foliage and eventual flowers that are produced off and on throughout the year. Selections of smaller plants would be helpful.

Episcia Cultivars

Some of these are older plants whose virtues, having been passed around by word of mouth, settled in for a longer career than expected.

'Abalone Shell.' Pink and green veins on brown. Red flowers.

'Bronze Queen.' Raised leaves, red flowers.

'Butter Oak' (Freiling). Succulent brown leaves with silver veining. Red-orange flowers. Selected for cold tolerance.

'Canal Zone Hybrid.' An old timer with dark foliage and orange-red flowers. Fast grower.

'Chocolate n' Cherries.' Blooms in low light. Cherry red flowers.

'Chocolate Kiss.' Umber-green leaves. Orange flowers.

'Chocolate Velour.' Leaves with a deep pile.

'Cleo's Sport.' Yellow-orange flowers.

'Cora Weigel.' Old hybrid. Dark leaves, red flowers. An easy grower and bloomer.

'Cotton Candy.' Flowers fringed pink, throat cream. Leaves green with silver.

'Faded Jade.' Quilted leaves, deep green and silver. Flowers crimson.

'Gladiator' (Freiling). Chestnut leaves with lime veining. Bright red flowers.

'Gray Lady.' Slate gray leaves. Yellow veins. Orange-red flowers.

'Harford Renick' (Baker). Semierect. Silver-pebbled leaves. Red flowers with yellow eye.

'Helen O.' Metallic rose leaves. Orange-red flowers. Popular favorite.

'Lady Killer.' Tolerates low humidity. Large mahogany leaves, silver veined. Deep orange flowers.

'Mint Julep.' Moss green leaves with silver. Coral-red flowers. Compact.

'Nancy Lou.' Basket plant. Silvered leaves and large orange flowers.

'Noel.' Emerald leaves with chartreuse overlay. Holly red flowers.

'Pinkiscia.' Still a favorite. Coppery leaves, pink flowers.

'Pink Panther.' Bronze and silver leaves. Deep pink flowers freely produced.

'Quilted Beauty.' An old clone with heavily quilted leaves and blue flowers. Magnificent but not easy.

'Ruby Red Dress' (Lyon). Red and silver leaves. Large crimson flowers.

'Silver Gladiator.' Small, oval, silvery leaves. Large red flowers.

'Simon's Seedling.' Semierect bronze leaves. Red flowers often rimmed with yellow.

'Strawberry Fields' (Worley). Flowers profusely pink spotted on white. Leaves silver and black. Compact.

'Strawberryfields Forever' (Freiling). Leaves with cream centers. Large red flowers.

'Sun Dog' (Lyon). Quilted chocolate leaves. Red flowers.

'Temptation' (Kartuz). Metallic rose leaf with thin darker edge.

'White Lightning.' Leaves with olive edge, the center green, white, and silver.

The most recent arrivals have been:

'Benden Wine' (Jeans). Silver leaves bordered rose-purple. Red flowers.

'Country Carnival' (Blansit). Silver veined overlaid with salmon-pink. Orange-red flowers.

'Country Cowgirl' (Blansit). Coppery green leaves with broad pink midrib. Light red flowers.

'Pink Brocade.' Similar to 'Cleopatra.' Terrarium culture.

'Queen Dragon' (Jeans). Coppery brown leaves with broad silvery midrib. Red flowers.

Most of the new episcias seem hardly new in any real sense, with the exception of the dwarfs.

Eucodonia

As noted on page 50, *Achimenes andreuxii* and *A. ehrenburgii* have become, respectively, *Eucodonia andreuxii* and *E. verticillata*.

Cultivars of *E. andreuxii* are:

Cv. 'Naomi' with red-haired pendant stems, brown beneath. Small, orchid-colored flowers.

Cv. 'Tinctacoma' covered with red fuzz. Flower small, orchid in color.

Cultivars of *E. verticillata* are:

C. 'Ehrenburgii.' Large orchid and white flowers. Oval leaves are hairy beneath.

Cv. 'Frances.' Large violet lobed, white-throated, bell-shaped flowers. Flat rosette growth. Also called 'Naomi II.'

E. 'Adele' (Worley) is new. Large orchid, nodding flowers. Silvery haired leaves, red beneath. Compact.

Culture is the same as for *Achimenes*.

Gasteranthus

A South American genus from Ecuador and Peru.

G. atratus is a plant attracting considerable attention because of its unusual leaves and flowers. It is erect to 15 or more inches, with serrated, puckered, shiny oval-pointed, nearly black leaves 3 inches long. The flowers are bright yellow, slipper shaped, 2 inches long or more. An unforgettable plant but requiring very high humidity and moderately cool conditions. Only a few have managed to bring it to flower, notably Phyllis Rosenbluth of New York. Perhaps a more tolerant clone will be found through selection.

G. corallina grows to 8 inches with dark green, elliptic leaves crowded on the stem. Thick peduncles bear tightly packed little scarlet pouch flowers reminiscent of *Pearcea*. Terrarium culture.

G. acropodus may be in cultivation. It is a terrestrial from Panama a foot high with 1 ¼-inch, bell-shaped yellow flowers dotted with red. Requires high humidity.

G. dressleri. is described as having flowers similar to *Sinningia richii*. Quilted leaves, calyx gray-green, corolla white with magenta veins in throat. Panama.

Gesneria

There is not too much to report on these charming plants. A couple of name changes are worth mentioning along with some description of other species.

G. albiflora has become *G. pedunculosa*.

G. cuneifolia 'El Yunque' has become a new species, *G. reticulata*.

G. saxatilis, the small shrub, is now to be called *G. pulverulenta*.

The inferiority of *G. acaulis, christii,* and *pedicellaris* to *G. cuneifolia*, which they resemble, has been confirmed. Of the three, *G. christi* seems to be the best and is still widely grown.

G. humilis is a small plant with a yellowish flower, requiring high humidity.

G. pauciflora is a little shrub with 4-inch long leaves and bright orange, 1-inch flowers. It has proved quite floriferous.

G. pumila is a miniature with white flowers.

It has always seemed to us that *G. cuneifolia* could gain wider favor if it were sold in bloom planted in covered glass bowls. Few plants can perform as well under these conditions.

G. 'Sun Drop' (Worley) is an improvement over 'Lemon Drop.' Yellow, tubular flowers on a *G. cuneifolia* habit plant. *G.* 'Lemon Drop' is more decorative but presents great difficulty in propagating.

Gloxinia

Sightings of *Gloxinia perennis* in both Jamaica and Tobago have convinced us that our illustration of the plant does not do it justice. Those we found were far more compact—not over 15 inches in height—and had much larger, bell-shaped flowers. In Jamaica, we thought it might be altitude and coolness that made the difference, for we saw them at 2,500 feet in the Blue Mountains. But, in Tobago, they were growing at 400 feet above sea level. The secret must be either other elements in their culture or a difference in clones. Our interest was aroused because, as a more compact plant, it is much more beautiful and could be very much more popular. Selection of the more intensely perfumed flowering plants for propagation would add still another attraction.

The transference of *Seemannia sylvatica* to the genus has brought a special luster to it. As more clones have been tested, it has been discovered that by keeping them warm and moist, dormancy can be prevented. This results in stronger, larger, second-year plants. Selection and hybridization have led to other improvements.

G. sylvatica 'Yellow Bird' is a yellow flowering clone.

Mrs. Batcheller's hybrids, 'Medusa' and 'Turan,' have led to others, namely, 'Island Sunset,' 'Cardinal Glow,' 'Cherry Belle,' Michael Worley's 'Scarlet,' and Lyndon Lyon's 'Chic.' The last has maintained its popularity with hobbyists.

G. 'Yellow Bird.' The tube flowers are yellow tipped with orange.

xG. 'Scarlet Letter' (Worley) is an *xGlokohleria* with red flowers and dark, coppery leaves. It is virtually everblooming.

Thus we end with a *G. sylvatica* hybrid having its season greatly extended. Further work along these lines should lead to more reliable everblooming plants with commercial possibilities.

The latest important cultivar comes from Mrs. Batcheller with *Gloxinia* 'Arion.' This great improvement over *Gloxinia perennis* has richly scented, rosy-purple, companulate flowers on upright stems. Scalloped, oval leaves. Much easier to grow and flower than *G. perennis*.

Intergeneric Crosses

xACHIMENANTHA

An intergeneric hybrid name that is only one of several that have replaced others. This one was formerly *xEucodonopsis*.

'Cerulean Mink.' A compact plant with woolly leaves and lavender-pink open-pouched flowers.

'Ginger Peachy' (Worley). Large peach-colored flowers and small dark leaves. Long blooming period.

xCODONANTANTHUS

This is Bill Saylor's bailiwick. He started them and has persisted in producing these pretty, shrubby, little plants with colorful small flowers in abundance. Seasonal bloomers in part and a few everbloomers under the right conditions.

'Antique Gold.' Yellow flowers and glossy leaves. Trailer.

'Aurora.' Pink tube and yellow lobes. Tiny, dark leaves.

'Fiesta.' Ruby-red tube and pink lobes. Leaves dark red beneath. Long bloom.

'Rosy Dawn.' Pink tube, yellow lobes. Glossy leaves. Trailing.

'Springtime.' Pink flowers. Dwarf everbloomer.

'Tambourine.' Rosy tube and yellow lobes. Tiny leaves. Trailing everbloomer.

xGLOKOHLERIA

'Scarlet Letter' (Worley). Deep red tubular flowers. Dark plush leaves. Everblooming.

xMOUSSONIANTHA

'Cornellian.' Small clusters of white flowers on long stems. Dark green, oval foliage.

xNIPHIMENES

'Lemonade.' Clusters of yellow flowers. Trailing, quilted foliage.

xSMITHICODONIA

'Denise' (Worley). Rose-pink, slipper flowers with spotted throat. Hairy, textured foliage.
'Elizabeth' (Worley). Violet-purple flowers with spotted throat. Bronzy foliage.

xKoellikohleria is listed under *Koellikeria.*

KOELLIKERIA

These attractive little plants are still being listed. Kartuz has two cultivars.
'Judy' has charcoal leaves with silver spots. Red and white flowers.
'Red Satin' has coppery-brown leaves speckled with silver and red beneath. Ruby and white flowers.
For most growers, these will remain, of necessity, terrarium plants. Hence *Koellikohleria rosea,* which is taller and has a longer blooming period, is suitable only for those who live in a climate where it can be grown in the open.

Kohleria Species

A number of kohlerias have become better known since our first edition, though the appeal of the genus is principally maintained by the hybrids. There have been name changes but none, thankfully, affecting the more frequently grown species. Because the poor things lacked rhizomes, *K. elegans, deppeana, hirsutissima,* and *strigosa* have set up business under a new genus, *Moussonia.* You will find them there.

Of the remainder, those listed continue to be of interest mainly for their use in hybridization. It has been suggested for more than one that the species may well be a natural hybrid. Some gesneriad genera have species that are distinct and stable. But a great many more show a tendency to variability in nature that is difficult for the northern grower to imagine. Gesneriads are not as variable as orchids but it is a common experience in the field to find colonies of a species among which there are plants varying as to leaves, flowers, or growth habit. Botanists attempt to collect these plants when they are especially attractive, along with the typical ones. This tendency to vary is very useful in hybridization and has the potential of resulting in plants that have a greater chance to gain popularity. *Kohleria* is rich in material of this kind.

K. allenii is a tall shrub with dark green leaves. Flowers are borne near the ends of the stems. The fat corolla tube is yellow, blanketed with red hairs. The interior of the tube and the lobes are dotted with red spots and lines. Incidentally, much of the beauty of kohlerias is the result of hairs that contrast in color with the background of the corolla. From Costa Rica.

K. bella. Usually single stemmed covered with reddish hairs and reaching 16 inches. The leaves are green with whitish or reddish hairs. The flowers appear successively from clusters. They are pale, greenish-yellow with flushes of scarlet on top and the rest of the tube orange. Purple dots are strewn on the greenish-yellow lobes of the limb.

K. hirsuta. The tubes are yellow covered with red hairs and the corolla lobes dotted with crescent shapes in red. Northern South America.

K. lanata. Mexico. The corolla is orange-pink, flowers dotted in red.

K. magnifica. Colombia. The flowers are red-orange with dark stripes on the tube.

K. peruviana. A 4-, or more, foot plant, white, hairy. Red-haired flowers with dotted orange-red lobes.

K. spicata (K. longifolia), (K. schiedeana). Single stemmed with bright red to red-orange flowers. The tube is narrow at the base, swollen in the middle, the lobes flared.

K. tubiflora. Mexico to northern South America. A variable species with slender tubed flowers in colors ranging from greenish-yellow to reddish-orange. Leaves are also variable.

K. villosa. Originally introduced as *K. platylomata.* A smaller plant than the others and, therefore, useful in hybridization. Leaves are velvety, reddish-brown with a greenish margin. Flower deep orange-red, the throat yellow spotted with red.

KOHLERIA HYBRIDS

We quote in full Margaret H. Stone's and Helen T. Beaufort-Murphy's extremely useful listing in *The Gloxinian,* 1982, No. 4.

MARGARET H. STONE, GAINESVILLE, FLORIDA

HELEN T. BEAUFORT-MURPHY, TRENTON, FLORIDA

There have been many lovely *Kohleria* hybrids in cultivation for which the full parentage is not known. But a knowledge of species characteristics may give us a clue. For example, marbled foliage, pink flowers, and compact size usually indicates *K. amabilis* as a parent. A robust habit, large flowers, and dark leaves with a red edge surely come from *K. eriantha.* A very dark red on the underside of the leaf indicates *K. hirsuta.* Bright yellow flowers and dark leaves with pale green veins indicates *K. bogotensis.* A yellow green limb is the trademark of *K. digitaliflora.* A large corolla with a swollen tube indicates *K. allenii.* All of the species, except *K. bella,* seem to form crosses. Since no particular color seems overly dominant, a considerable range of mixing is possible.*

K. 'Carnival' (*K.* 'Longwood' × *K. bogotensis*) (Kartuz)
　　Large flowers with red dots on creamy yellow background. Leaves bright green, darker along the edge.
K. 'Cecilia' (cultivar of *K. amabilis*)
　　Larger flowers than species. Leaves dark yellowish green, flower tube deep pink

*The authors gratefully acknowledge the assistance of Frances Batcheller in the preparation of the list of *Kohleria* hybrids, and for additional information on their culture, based on her long experience with growing and hybridizing species of this genus.

outside, mostly white inside with red dots. The limb has very strong red lines and dotted lines radiating from the throat, almost obliterating the pink background.

K. 'Clown Prince' (Worley)

Dwarf plant, vigorous grower. Flowers clear rose heavily spotted with large deep rose dots on lower lobes.

K. 'Clytie' [*K*. 'Longwood' × (*K*. 'Rongo' × *K*. *amabilis*)] (Batcheller)

Compact plant with gray-green leaves with dark green veins. Pale pink corolla, upper lobes darker, small darker pink spotting; large flower.

K. 'Connecticut Belle' (*K*. *amabilis* × *K*. *eriantha*) (Clayberg)

Compact plant. Spotted pink flowers with red tube. Mottled leaves.

K. 'Dark Princess' (Kartuz)

Velvety light green leaves, marbled with brown. Corolla with creamy background, spotted dark pink and red tube.

K. 'Dragon's Blood' (Kartuz)

Dark coppery leaves edged in dark red; very deep red flowers spotted yellow. Good under lights.

K. 'Duchess' (Worley)

Beautiful shades of lavender flowers with deep rose-red tube. Dark leaves with lighter mid-vein. Very compact, free-flowering.

K. 'Firelight' (Spaugh)

Dark bronzy foliage marbled with chartreuse-green. Flowers bright yellow, spotted red.

K. 'Flirt' (*K*. *amabilis* × *K*. *villosa*) (Worley) New 1981.

Very compact. Blue-green leaves with dark veining. Solid red flowers, throat speckled deep cerise.

K. 'Gator Blood' (Spaugh)

Mutation of *K*. 'Rongo' with much darker corolla. Deep maroon red with velvety texture. Dark green and black leaves.

K. 'Jester' (Worley)

Same growth habit as *K*. 'Clown Prince,' except that the flowers are a lovely shade of amethyst violet. Good for growing under lights. Excellent hanging basket.

K. 'Kapo' (*K*. 'Longwood' × *K*. *sciadotydaea* hybrid) (Batcheller)

Compact plant with dark green leaves. Large deep burgundy-red flowers. Very compact, free-flowering; grows well under lights.

K. 'Laura' (*K*. *amabilis* × *K*. 'Connecticut Belle') (Lyon)

Compact plant. Beautiful marbled foliage, red spotted flowers with rose background.

K. 'Longwood' (Imported from Portugal by Longwood Gardens)

Very tall plant with large strawberry-red flowers. Bronzy-green leaves.

K. 'Lono' (*K*. 'Kapo' × *K*. *digitaliflora*) (Batcheller)

Flowers with distinctive light green face, boldly spotted with purple, light purple tube. Velvety dark green leaves.

K. 'Modron' (*K*. *eriantha* × *K*. *amabilis*) × *K*. *amabilis* (Batcheller)

Robust plant, leaves gray-green with red reverse. Large flowers, six to an axil, magenta pink.

K. 'Monarch' (Kartuz)

Large clusters of flowers spotted rose on a red cream background. Light velvety green leaves with red edges.

K. 'Pamola' (*K*. *amabilis* × *K*. *longifolia*) (Batcheller)

Dwarf compact plant with small green leaves and dark veins. Intensely red spotted flowers with white background. Shy bloomer.

K. 'Princess' (*K*. *amabilis* × *K*. *eriantha*) (Kartuz)

Compact, free-flowering plant, usually under 10 inches. Velvety green leaves with brownish markings. Large warm pink flowers spotted with rose. Excellent under lights.

K. 'Raspberry Ripple' (*K.* 'Connecticut Belle' × *K. eriantha*) (Spaugh)

The bottom petals are light pink with bright red spots; the two top petals are dark pink with small burgundy spots. The tube is orange-pink. Two white petaloids in throat. Small–medium green leaves.

K. 'Red Ryder' (Worley)

Very large fiery-red flowers with deeper red spots. Marbled foliage. Grows well under lights.

K. 'Regent' (Worley 1982)

Unusual flower colors of spotted purple on a yellow background. Free-flowering, compact.

K. 'Rongo' (*K. amabilis* × *K. sciadotydaea* hybrid) (Batcheller)

Foliage mottled light and dark green. Magenta-pink flowers with darker spots. Compact, free-flowering, excellent as a hanging basket. Colorful under lights.

K. 'Roundelay' (*K.* 'Strawberry Fields' × unnamed hybrid) (Worley)

Very large flowers spotted rose-pink on a white background; compact plant.

K. 'Strawberry Fields' (Worley)

Heavily spotted red flowers with white background. Marbled foliage; compact plant.

K. 'Sunny' (Kartuz)

Yellow flowers spotted pink, small leaves.

K. 'Tane' (*K. eriantha* × *K. hirsuta*) × *K. amabilis* (Batcheller)

Leaves dark green with maroon reverse, red-orange hairs on margin. Large orange-pink flowers with white patches and red spotting.

K. 'Trinidad' (Selection of *K. hirsuta*) (Selby Botanical Gardens)

Whorled bronze-green leaves with burgundy reverse. Corolla with orange-red tube, small yellow lobes.

K. 'Warrior' (Kartuz)

New. Large flowers with cream background, boldly spotted with red. Foliage velvety-green with darker green veins and wide red edges.

Monopyle

Mrs. Batcheller reports several species in cultivation. *M. grandiflora* bears the largest flower. *M. paniculata* is many-flowered, the color lavender with dark purple spots. *M. sodiroana* (or *sodieroiana*) is listed by Tiki Nursery as being semiupright, the leaves sticky, dark olive with red beneath. Small lavender flowers with a yellow throat.

Moussonia

Moussonia was redefined by Wiehler in 1975 and a number of species, previously listed under *Kohleria,* were transferred to it, principally because they lacked scaly rhizomes and possessed a chromosome count of $n = 11$ instead of $n = 13$. All, so far, are Central American plants.

Like more and more gesneriads that have been introduced to cultivation recently, these are plants from high altitude rain forests. They will grow very well in the 65-degree-minimum temperatures of most of our houseplants but can be induced to bloom only if lower temperatures (55°–75°) are maintained for six to eight weeks when they are approaching maturity. These are large plants that are unsuitable for indoor growing.

They can be trimmed but that inhibits bloom. See our remarks in the Temperature section, page 217.

M. deppeana (K. deppeana). A 3–6 foot, very hairy shrub with narrow leaves. Flowers, pendent from long peduncles, are in fours, orange-red, the tube much inflated.

M. elegans (K. elegans). Canes erect to 30 inches or more. Leaves in threes. Short, erect peduncles bear three or four 1-inch tube flowers, orange-red, the throat yellow with red dotted lines.

M. hirsutissima (K. hirsutissima). A 6-foot, very hairy shrub. Leaves to 6 inches. Peduncles carry six pale yellow flowers swollen on one side.

M. strigosa (K. strigosa). A somewhat smaller plant but with a similar habit to the others. Peduncles carry up to seven orange-red flowers, ¾ inch long.

Napeanthus

Napeanthus is found from Mexico to Brazil and Peru. Most of the plants are low rosettes with stalked white, short-tubed, open-faced, five-lobed flowers similar to *Bellonia* and *Niphaea*.

N. costaricensis is a compact, slow-growing plant with shiny leaves. The cup-shaped flowers are small and white. The flower opens at 4 P.M. and drops by morning.

Nautilocalyx

Since our first edition, *Nautilocalyx* has turned up from time to time as a foliage offering of major commercial nurseries. Without identifying labels, they have been sold, usually in 4-inch pots, through florists and garden centers. It would seem that growers have hoped for greater popular acceptance of a plant that has many of the necessary virtues; ease of culture and propagation, fast growth, sturdy, upright habit.

Alas, gesneriad leaves are never as solid and durable as those of aroids or any of the other cast-iron plants that have become standard houseplants. Leave *Nautilocalyx* on the shelf or expose it in the street and the leaves will curl, brown, and drop. For that reason alone it is and will remain the joy of indoor and greenhouse growers who buy direct from nurseries and give it the conditions that it requires. Among hobbyists its popularity has held up well. New, more compact species and cultivars should attract more amateurs to this handsome genus.

N. adenosiphon. Small, very hairy plant with white flowers.

N. aeneus 'Roezl's Bronze.' To 12 inches, the leaves bronze-purple, puckered, very hairy. Calyx maroon, tube inflated, white with a pink flush. This is one description. Another for the flowers is simply ''yellow.'' 'Strickland's Green' has emerald-green leaves.

N. 'Caribbean Pink' (*N. melittifolius* × *N. villosus*). The new arrival from *Episcia,* which has a bright pink flower, mated with a very hairy *Nautilocalyx*. The result is a nice-looking, free-flowering plant, erect to 15 inches with much the same pink blooms.

N. cataractarum. Rosette plant with puckered green leaves. Calyx green, corolla pink. An easy bloomer. Venezuela.

N. glandulifer. Compact plant with oval leaves covered with purple hairs.

N. porphyrotrichus. Venezuela. The best of several cultivars is 'El Blanco,' notable for its narrow leaves with a broad, feathered white band down the center and deep red, narrow tubed flowers.

Nematanthus

William R. Saylor of Brewster, Massachusetts, has made himself almost synonymous with the genus *Nematanthus* in the intervening years. His hybrids have really put it on the map and gesneriad enthusiasts everywhere are growing his plants. They have also been grown on a large scale commercially. This test, however, revealed problems. When grown along with other plants they are damaged by the heat of summer; leaves shatter and flowers blast. In fact the indoor grower has more success with these hybrids than this type of nursery. Bill's creations are lovely and floriferous plants whose leaves are often as attractive as the flowers but they must have good ventilation and be watered very sparingly during warm days. A good drying out between waterings is essential and for the same reason the soil must be very well aerated. Perlite should be avoided in the mix as it tends to absorb and retain salts. High humidity and misting are beneficial.

The following listing of cultivars also brings the name of Bartley Schwarz of California into the arena of *Nematanthus* hybridizers.

All the Saylor older hybrids have survived along with Wyrtzen's 'Marianne.'

'Bambino' (Saylor). A small plant with tiny dark leaves, reddish beneath. Flowers are orange and yellow pouches.

'Black Gold' (Schwarz). Compact trailer with very dark leaves. Deep yellow flowers.

'Cameo' (Saylor). Dangling orange flowers.

'Cheerio' (Saylor). Compact trailer. Small orange pouch flowers.

'Christmas Holly' (Schwarz). Shiny, green leaves and small red flowers. Compact trailer.

'Encore' (Saylor). Compact trailer. Orange flowers tipped with yellow.

'Freckles' (Schwarz). Yellow flowers speckled with red. Dark foliage. Compact.

'Golden West.' Foliage variegated, cream, yellow and light green with a pink tinge. Orange flowers.

'Jungle Lights' (Saylor). Dark purple leaves. Orange and pink pouched flowers.

'Lucky Strike' (Saylor). Yellow flowers.

'Moon Glow' (Saylor). Upright. Flowers yellow, spotted pink.

'Sambo' (Saylor). Purple leaves. Pendent orange and pink flowers.

It is unfortunate that when a series of hybrids, such as this one, may have long or short dangling pouches on thin pedicels, pouches in the axils, or some other shape, catalogs never specify. We have not seen all these plants and therefore are unable to provide this information. The claim of everbloom that turns up repeatedly may apply in a greenhouse but should certainly be used sparingly when addressed to indoor growers. Because of exaggerated descriptions and claims, a truly outstanding plant often is not featured as it should be.

Neomortonia

Neomortonia has gained whatever luster it possesses from the transference of *Alloplectus nummularia,* which was formerly a *Hypocyrta.* The wandering of some of these species reminds us of the successive hideouts of an embezzler on the run, with the detective (read "amateur gardener") in hot pursuit.

N. nummularia comes from Mexico and Central America. It is a creeping vine with thin, hairy red branches in nature though they are usually green in cultivation. The leaves have short petioles, are opposite and oval, usually 1 ½ inches by ¾ inch with toothed margins. The flowers are on short pedicels in the axils. The calyx is about ⅜-inch long, hairy and clasping, and the corolla is ¾-inch long.

The corolla is curious for, though a pouch like a number of *Nematanthus,* the shape is quite different. The top of the tube is nearly straight, but the bottom takes an acute turn downward and outward, then becomes almost reflexed upward to a tiny opening equipped with very small lobes. The color is a beautiful shade of vermillion that changes to a ring of deep purple just below the lobes, which are yellow. In other words, the pouch juts forward much more and is broader when seen from in front than *Nematanthus.*

Unfortunately, *N. nummularia* is a summer bloomer that goes into partial dormancy in the fall, when it should have very little watering or it will rot out. Carrying it over winter is not easy for this reason, and it needs constant attention. Cuttings root with comparative ease during the growing period. Be sure to give it a very lightly packed mix and a small pot. It does rather well in long fiber or live sphagnum moss. And don't let the temperature go over 80° for long, or it will start to drop its leaves. These problems are the reasons why the plant has not and probably will not become popular.

N. rosea. This small plant, somewhat similar in habit to *Alsobia dianthiflora,* has white fringed flowers with pink-flushed lobes.

Ornithoboea

We include this genus solely because of Dr. Anton Weber's fascinating report in *The Gloxinian,* 1979, No. 4, on *O. arachnoidea.* The extraordinary aspect is the obvious resemblance of the flowers to certain orchids. Other examples of imitation are found in nature between orchids and plants of different families that share the same pollinator.

The plant has a single stem, 15 inches tall with only a few pairs of oval, pointed leaves. The flowers, with short pedicels, are borne in clusters on stout peduncles from every node. The pedicels are covered with a mass of white wool. The white calyx is star-shaped and the flowers, pendent. The corolla consists of a white tube, an upper lip that presses against the tube and is, thereby, curled around forming a narrow throat. The much-enlarged lower lip has three lobes. The base where they join is covered with a thick pad of fine hairs. The color of the corolla is light blue to lilac. This curious plant is a honey of a challenge for a real gesneriad buff.

Paradrymonia

The genus *Paradrymonia* was just beginning to be represented in collections around 1976 when our first edition was published. It is, as its name implies, closely related to *Drymonia* and also to *Episcia* and *Nautilocalyx.* One difference noted between *Para-drymonia* and *Drymonia* is the unequal leaf pairs of the former and the equal leaf pairs of the latter. It is not important but it is amusing that *Drymonia stenophylla,* for which we have an affection, probably because of the foliage, and which we have grown for years, displays consistently irregular sized leaves. Of each leaf pair, one is no more than a quarter the size of the other. However, this occurs only on plants that have reached 15 or more inches in height. However, there are other differences that probably justify the separate genus.

Paradrymonia has the advantage over *Drymonia* that the flowers bloom in clusters rather than singly. Though they last only a day or two, like *Drymonia,* there are more of them, which makes a better show. Culture is as for *Drymonia.* There are now at least five species in cultivation. They are not easy plants but once they start blooming they are quite spectacular. They should be popular at least among enthusiasts for the family.

P. ciliosa. A big plant with a spreading, branching habit more suitable for a basket than a pot. The larger leaves are up to 16 inches long, green and shiny. The calyx lobes are narrow, rimmed with red and ragged. The 2-inch long white flowers have a fat, pouched middle that opens into fringed lobes, the lower one being much larger and the fringe very striking. They occur in clusters rising on short petioles from the axils of the leaves. In plants of this type, flowering does not occur continuously but in bursts. Brazil, Venezuela, and Peru.

P. decurrens. Costa Rica. The growth is similar to *P. ciliosa* but somewhat smaller, the leaves reaching a length of 12 inches. The narrow, red hairy calyx cups the spur and the narrow base that swells into the tube. The corolla is pale yellow and the lower lobe curves upward and is toothed, as in *Drymonia stenophylla.* The latter unusual detail makes one rather suspicious of the generic separation, at least in regard to this plant.

P. hypocyrta. Ecuador. A spectacular flowering plant with narrow, shiny leaves. Peduncles from the axils bear a number of red pedicels leading to a cupped red calyx with long reflexed lobes. The smaller white corollas are pouched.

P. lineata. Panama. Narrow olive-green leaves, 12 inches long. Petiole and calyx lobes are reddish. The corolla expands gradually and is whitish or yellow with rusty lines around the center of the tube. The plant offsets readily and the flower clusters occur at the base of the stem as well as higher up in the plant.

P. lurida. Erect, thick canes bear leaves up to 14 inches long and only a ½ inch wide. The distinctly five-lobed corolla is similar to *P. lineata* and is soft yellow with a wavy edge.

The following additional paradrymonias have been listed: *P. colombianensis, P. flava, P. lacera,* and *P. tylocalyx.*

Parakohleria

Parakohleria was proposed as a separate genus by Wiehler in 1978, as differing from *Kohleria.* Will it stick? We wouldn't bet on it. But, luckily, the species are new and therefore there is more complication without increased confusion. The following species are still in the try-out stage. Habit and culture are as for *Kohleria.*

P. abunda. Red hairy stems, bright green leaves veined with red. The inflated, small flowers are orange-red. Mrs. Batcheller reports the species as the easiest to bloom.

P. baezana. Bronzy green foliage, red beneath, the midrib silver bordered. Tubular red bloom with yellow throat, purple spotted.

P. rhodotricha. The foliage is covered with stiff, red hairs. The small flower is pouched, blue-black, with an orange calyx.

P. spruceii. Five-inch, light green leaves, the flowers tubular, orange, with a rose-spotted throat.

P. vinicolor is also known to be in cultivation.

Phinaea

Reports on other *Phinaea* species suggest that they differ principally with regard to foliage size, shape, and hairiness. The flowers are all white and cup-shaped, borne more or less erect on short pedicels. Strictly for a terrarium.

P. multiflora 'Tracery' is a popular cultivar with slightly larger flowers and leaves that are silver veined.

P. albolineata 'Wilbur' has larger flowers.

P. divaricata. Bronzy foliage.

P. lancerta.

P. viscida. Bright green leaves.

P. repens. A small trailer.

Rufodorsia

This is a new genus described by H. Wiehler. The plants grow in the cloud forests of southern Central America where they are epiphytic. Most are shrubby with rather inconspicuous flowers. The four species thus far are *R. congestiflora, R. intermedia, R. major,* and *R. minor.* Only the last has received some attention and all are difficult to grow because of the cool, very humid conditions they require.

Rufodorsia minor. An epiphyte with stems to 20 inches long. The leaves, clustered at the tips of branches, are about 2 inches long and half as wide, oval-pointed, light green, covered with silky white hairs. The small flowers have a reddish upper lip, and a white, three-lobed lower lip.

Saintpaulia

Since our first edition saintpaulias have retained unchallenged leadership among flowering houseplants. And for good reason. For they are the only ones that are available in the shops every working day of the year; the only ones that retain their bloom for weeks on end in that difficult environment and never flag when brought to a new home. They have every virtue, except fragrance, that one could expect in a flowering houseplant and no other, as yet, can begin to vie with them in popularity.

Although the true gesneriad enthusiast enjoys collecting and growing the many other attractive, nay unique, plants in the family, hardly anyone fails to include African violets for the consistent bloom they alone bring to any collection of plants. There has even been a revival of interest in the original species, some of which retain an unsophisticated charm that is very attractive. Unfortunately, the connecting links between the species and their innumerable progeny of cultivars have virtually disappeared. There may still be some back crossing but the many new cultivars that appear every year now exist on their own, bearing no other names than those provided by their hybridizers.

The African violet plant with a symmetrical leaf arrangement and clustered flowers in the center remains the norm and probably will not be superseded in the foreseeable future. The hybridizers of distinction remain mostly the same. Of those who cater to the hobbyists, Lyon, Tinari, and Granger still produce the plants in greatest demand. Fredette has gained the favor of those who enter competitions at flower shows. Thanks to

Mrs. Leon Fiedler and the African Violet Society of America, Inc., we are able to print the Honor Roll for the years 1976 through 1982, which bears witness to the consistent success of the old masters. There is no better guide for beginners to the best plants in this genus.

In commercial hybridizing, Reinhold Holtkamp's Optimaras lead the field by a wide margin. The label is so ubiquitous in florist shops that it has become a trademark of excellence. We should, however, not fail to mention the Ballet series of Geo. J. Ball, Inc., which deserves greater recognition.

In the intervening years we have seen many more plants with variegated leaves, the development of trailers, and, finally, the minis. None of these has great commercial significance but the last, the minis, have become exceedingly popular especially among those with limited growing space. Among them are plants of a somewhat different character, as regards flowers and leaves, than their larger relatives. In the future some of the forms may be carried over to the standard size plants and result in new series, providing greater variety still to the commercial repertory.

HONOR ROLL OF AFRICAN VIOLETS
1976–1982
by
Mrs. Leon Fiedler
Honor Roll Compiler

1976

Fashionaire No. 2223 (Granger)
Nancy Reagan No. 2167 (Reinhardt)
Happy Harold No. 2165 (Reinhardt)
Top Dollar No. 2168 (Reinhardt)
Poodle Top No. 2053 (Tinari)
Chanticleer No. 1386 (Granger)
Jennifer No. 2006 (Tinari)

Royalaire No. 2023 (Granger)
Floral Fantasy No. 1986 (Lyon)
Softique No. 1957 (Richter)
Granger Peach Frost No. 2216 (Granger)
Granger Peppermint No. 2227 (Granger)
Pink Panther No. 2108 (Lyon)

1977

Garnet Elf No. 2339 (Granger)
Like Wow No. 2329 (Lyon)

Mary D. No. 2675 (Maas)
Miriam Steel No. 2276 (Granger)

1978

Ballet Lisa No. 2898 (Geo. J. Ball, Inc.)
Cordelia No. 2466 (Lyon)
Granger's Pink Swan No. 2577 (Granger)
Pocono Mountain (De Sandis)

Richter's Step Up No. 2458 (Richter)
Starshine No. 2349 (Granger)
Whirlaway No. 2210 (Lyon)
Wisteria No. 2056 (Tinari)

1979

Ballet Marta No. 2899 (Geo. J. Ball Inc.)
Blue Storm No. 2464 (Lyon)

Christmas Holly (Reed)
Double Black Cherry No. 1178 (Anderson)

Dora Baker No. 2084 (Vern Lorensen)

Duet (Richter)

Granger's Musetta No. 2575 (Granger)

Granger's Serenity No. 2578

Granger's Swiss Ballet No. 2579 (Granger)

Like Wow Sport (Lyon)

Rhapsodie Mars (Holtkamp)

Spring Deb No. 2348 (Granger)

Vern's Delight No. 2271 (Vern Lorenzen)

1980

Becky No. 2669 (Maas)

Coral Caper No. 2727 (Lyon)

Corpus Christi No. 3075 (Utz)

Crimson Frost No. 2706 (Granger)

Edith Peterson No. 2561 (Constantinov)

Gotcha No. 2205 (Lyon)

Granger Eternal Snow No. 2573 (Granger)

Granger Regina No. 2716 (Granger)

Lavender Tempest No. 2709 (Granger)

Midget Bon Bon No. 2280 (Champion)

Mrs. Greg No. 2361 (Vern Lorenzen)

Pink Viceroy No. 2714 (Granger)

Pixie Blue No. 2598 (Lyon)

Sailor's Dream No. 3108 (Kolb Grhse.)

Tina No. 2680 (Maas)

The King No. 2698 (Maas)

The Parson's Wife No. 2317 (Rev. Blades)

1981

Faith No. 2707 (Granger)

Flamingo No. 2670 (Maas)

Helene No. 2885 (Lyon)

Jason No. 3004 (Maas)

Mark No. 3007 (Maas)

Orion No. 2069 (R. Anderson)

Ruffled Red No. 2679 (Maas)

Sweet Mary No. 2489 (Vern Lorenzen)

Tommie Lou No. 1744 (Ogden)

1982

Alouette No. 2787 (Fredette)

Amazing Grace No. 2688 (Saultz)

Ballet Anna No. 2890 (Geo. J. Ball, Inc.)

Firebird No. 2818 (Granger)

French Lilac No. 2844 (Swift)

Granger Starburst No. 2874 (Granger)

Granger Sylvan Blue No. 2875 (Granger)

Joyful No. 3168 (Lyon)

Little Delight No. 3169 (Lyon)

Little Jim No. 3005 (Maas)

Millie Blair No. 3020 (Granger)

Pink N' Ink No. 3173 (Lyon)

Sam N/R (Lyon)

Winter Grape No. 2789 (Fredette)

Sinningia

ADDITIONAL SPECIES

S. cooperi. Similar to *S. cardinalis.* The many 3-inch-long flowers bloom in a cluster, nod more, and are more orange in color than *cardinalis.*

S. magnifica. Also similar to *S. cardinalis* but are clustered on a peduncle well above the foliage. A very handsome species.

S. tuberosa. Additional note. The plant goes through alternate cycles of foliage and flower production. The flowers rise directly from the leafless tuber. Development from seed is slow, requiring as much as four years to produce flowers.

S. warszewiczii. A name change to *S. incarnata* has been proposed. The tuber remains dormant for six months or more.

MINIATURE SINNINGIAS

Plants now listed under this heading are a mix of all kinds of hybrids throughout the range of *Sinningia* species and running in size from a little bigger than *S. pusilla* through 'Cindy' and the old, formerly named *xGloxineras* of Ted Bona to large slipper-type nodding flowers that are crosses with *S. speciosa* or *regina* on much more compact plants. The old hybrids have stood up so well that we have not seen it necessary to change the original text. The new ones are often not so very different and more and more look-alikes are appearing.

Of the original hybridizers, Lyndon Lyon, Kartuz, and Ted Bona are the most active. Ted's scattered progeny are beginning to reappear, as they deserve, and he continues to pour out new ones. A careful study and selection of his output would, we believe, reveal many more real beauties of a kind that have not been duplicated by anyone. Country Hills (Glasshouse) is offering more and more of Bona's creations. We remember one he was kind enough to call 'Jinny Elbert,' which we, ourselves, were responsible for losing. It was an *xGloxinera* with a glowing tan tube and white flare and throat. Unique. But it has disappeared as far as we know.

New hybridizers entering the lists include Marty Mines, who has concentrated on the real minis, and Bartley Schwarz.

We have probably seen most of the plants listed below but, without labels attached, it is difficult to be sure of which ones. Where plants of this size are concerned, the measurements of the flowers should be printed along with the rest of the description. There is considerable variation in consistency of flowering and that should be mentioned, too. The fascination of the whole group is largely based on their ability, though tuberous plants, to flower off and on throughout the year. Those that do not are definitely less desirable. The real criterion is not whether the plants bloom continuously in a greenhouse and as juveniles, but whether they perform as well indoors with normal care. Only time and experience will separate the best performers from those that are less reliable.

'April Snow.' Well-flared white flowers with rose throat.

'April Starr.' Similar plant with pink flowers and rose throat.

'Aurora Borealis' (Bona). Leaves variegated pink, white, and green.

'Bob W.' Large slipper in purple. Small, dark leaves.

'China Seas' (Bona). Monstrose, variegated leaves.

'Claire Roberts' (Bona). Very dwarf *S. speciosa* type. Upright pink flowers, white throat with pink ring.

'Coral Baby.' Coral-salmon flowers in clusters.

'Diploid Dollbaby.' More floriferous than the original.

'Don D.' (Bona). Coppery, velvet leaves. Pink bell flowers.

'Eileen' (Schwarz). Nodding flowers, lavender-blue, darker veined. Free flowering. Handsome.

'Jimminy Cricket' (Bona). Dwarf *speciosa* type with bright red flowers. Dark foliage.

'Lavender Queen' (Selby). *Speciosa* type orchid-blue flowers. Very dwarf.

'Little Venus' (Worley). Large, pure white flowers with faint rose in throat. Free flowering on tiny plant.

'Maiden's Blush' (Saylor). Very light pink. Compact.

'Margaret Heald' x *lineata* (Bona). Apparently *S. aggregata* crosses. Not true miniatures. Two forms: A. to 10 inches with tubular red flowers, ivory throat with violet dotted lines; B. rich pink. Floriferous and easy.

'Marty Mines' (Bona). Mini florist gloxinia with red flowers and deeper throat.

'Minarette' (Kartuz). Salmon-pink, nodding flowers.

'Mod Imp' (Kartuz). Fine pink mini with tubular flowers.

'Mother of Pearl.' Pink flowers.

'Norma Jean.' Mini-slipper with pink flowers.

'Poupee' (Nixon). Lavender-blue flowers similar to Dollbaby. Has proved popular. Free flowering.

'Premier Pink, Premier White' (Schwarz). Large flowers with red in throat. Compact and free flowering.

'Scarlet Red.' Scarlet tubular flowers. Neat foliage.

'Silhouette' (Belanger). Large, dark violet-purple slippers with spotted throat.

'Snowflake' (Clayberg). 'White Sprite' with fringed lobes. Popular.

'Stuckup.' Dark purple flowers with white spotted throat. Popular, free flowering.

'Ted Bona' (Mines). Red miniature typical of the Mines group of floriferous narrow-tubed pink, orange-red, and red flowers.

Streptocarpus

SECTION STREPTOCARPELLA

To the species we listed in the first edition, several others have been added:

S. glandulosissimus. A lax, straggling, branching plant; the leaves 1 inch wide by 3 inches long. The inch-long flowers are deep violet. Widely distributed in East Africa.

S. muscosa. A small plant, the crawling stems no more than 3 or 4 inches in length. Leaves are 1 inch wide by 2 inches long. Flowers similar to *S. rimicola.* Madagascar.

S. stomandrus. This is certainly a very floriferous species, bearing up to twenty flowers to an inflorescence. It is now being used more frequently in hybridization. However, this is as good a place as any other to lodge a protest against those who, carried away by their enthusiasms, describe certain gesneriads as everblooming without qualifying the statement. Some plants deserve this description even when they receive minimum normal culture. Others have the potential of everbloom but require special conditions and special care. For the average grower, they are not constantly in bloom. Furthermore, by the very nature of their structure, most everblooming plants, after a burst of flowering, require time to put out new growths bearing inflorescences. *S. sto-mandrus* is *potentially* everblooming. The average grower, especially in regions of the United States where summer heat can climb over the 90-degree mark, is not able to maintain bloom and is lucky if the plant survives. Hybridization along lines that raise its temperature tolerance may succeed in producing an everblooming plant in the true sense. You can be sure that if any of these plants were really everblooming they would compete with African violets for public favor and we would see them everywhere. Everybody wants an everblooming plant. This is not to deny that *S. stomandrus* shares with the other species of the subgenus a greater ease of culture than the subgenus *Streptocarpus*.

S. *thysanotis*. A large plant, up to 30 inches in height. The stiff stem is marked with brown spots. Leaves are 3 inches long by 2 inches wide. Flowers are pale violet, about a half-inch long, the throat fringed with hairs. Described as particularly easy both under lights and on the windowsill.

S. *nobilis*. Reaches 3 feet in height with 6 inch leaves 3 inches wide. It is peculiar for producing normal and cleistogamous, or closed, flowers. Flowers are deep purple, 1 inch long. Less than 10 hours of light are necessary for flower production. We suspect that *S. saxorum,* also, is a short day plant, for it does much better as a basket plant outdoors or in the greenhouse than under long days of artificial light.

SECTION STREPTOCARPELLA HYBRIDS

These stemmed and branched Cape Primroses are essentially basket plants and require fairly strong light to bloom. We suspect that they will prove of interest principally to greenhouse growers except on the Pacific Coast where the climate is favorable to these plants.

S. 'Ballerina' (Strickland). Orchid-rose flowers "all year."

S. 'Boysenberry Delight' (Strickland). Violet-rose flowers "all year." Self-branching.

S. 'Concord Midnight' (Schwarz). Deep violet-purple flowers.

S. 'Good Hope' (Saylor). Medium-blue flowers. The plant has caught on and is, thus far, the most popular of the group.

S. 'Powder Blue' (Schwarz). Light-blue flowers.

S. 'Sassy' (Strickland). Deep-blue flowers "at all times."

S. 'Sparkle' (Strickland). Purple flowers "all year."

Note that, like the species, these are small flowered plants and the ultimate test will be whether they actually flower as early and often as is claimed.

SECTION STREPTOCARPUS

The frenzy of activity in the stemless Streps presages a major future for these plants. Their large flowers, produced in compact clusters, the great range of coloring and patterning, and the durability of blooms have encouraged commercial growers to take an interest in the genus. When firms like Geo. J. Ball, Inc., engage in distribution we know that another gesneriad has made a major step to general popularity, perhaps even on the level of the African violet.

The large, brittle leaves have been a handicap but there has been considerable success in shortening them so that they can be transported more easily and take up less room in the house. Overcoming high temperature intolerance is another matter and the returns on that are not yet in. But we are sure that even this major stumbling block will be dealt with successfully. The finest looking plants we have seen thus far are from Bodger Seeds, Ltd., of El Monte, California. They are of the Wiesmoor type in a number of colors with attractive dark lines in the throat. The leaves are wide and short, suiting them for a fine show in a 4-inch pot. As Bodger only sells seeds, we must wait until the plants appear in florist shops and garden centers to test the actual plants. But the trend is in the right direction.

Meanwhile, Rexii and Wiesmoor hybrids have retained their popularity with hobbyists as have the various Constant Nymph variations. The John Innes plants, beautiful though they are, seem suited mainly to such climates similar to that of England, as the northwest. None of these plants are good survivors in high temperatures.

The number of hybrids and hybridizers is now very considerable. Each new plant is greeted with ecstasy but we are still some time away from completion of test in growing. For that matter, there is also the hurdle of commercial display and sales to be overcome—how well the plants stand up in shops. It is essential that the flowers remain showy long enough to attract buyers. Even now we can say, however, with some assurance that *Streptocarpus* is ready for the gift market where the requirement is more for showy appearance than a long and repeated burst of flowering.

The new plants fit into two categories: those with large flowers, often hybrids of the Nymphs and Wiesmoors, and those that can be called dwarf or miniature, the result of crosses with smaller species. Lyndon Lyon has been working on these for years, using *cyanandrus* and related species.

As we predicted, *Streptocarpus* is on the threshold of becoming a major commercial houseplant. This is, however, entirely due to hybridization. The species play their necessary role but are mostly grown by amateurs because of the challenge. To our list of species we now add the following because they were listed by Frances Batcheller in "Gesneriads One by One" (*The Gloxinian*) as being in cultivation.

S. daviessi. A perennial producing one new leaf a year. The leaf is heart-shaped and 10 inches long. The 2-inch (max.) flower is greenish-white flushed with violet and a yellow blotch in the throat.

S. erubescens. Annual unifoliate with leaf 6 inches long and 4 ½ inches wide (max.). Corolla about 2 inches long, white flushed pink and with magenta stripes on the lobes.

S. fanniniae. Fragrant, like *S. candidus.* Leaf blade close to a yard long and flowers rising as high. Corollas white to violet.

S. gardenii. Rosulate perennial. Similar to *S. rexii* but with a greenish tube.

S. grandis. Similar to *S. cooperi* but leaf is only 14 inches long and flowers smaller. Color from white to medium violet.

S. schliebenii. Possesses an erect stem that may attain more than a yard in height. Small white flowers. A curious, transitional form.

S. silvaticus. Produces two to five leaves up to 6 inches in length. Flower similar to *S. daviessi.* Flower pale violet.

S. variabilis. A small rosette perennial 2 to 8 inches in diameter. Half-inch long tube, pale violet at base and deeper at top. Lobes white, sharply edged with violet.

S. wendlandii. Single leaf 18 inches in length, dark green above and beet-red below. The violet and white flowers are 2 inches long.

Some of the other single leaved *Streptocarpus* in cultivation are *S. cooksonii, eylesii, michelmorei, molweniensis, vandeleurii,* and *wilmsii.*

These short descriptions suggest the wide variation in form to be found in the genus. And, as they hybridize quite readily in the wild, they offer a field day to artificial hybridizing botanists and nurserymen. The rise of *Streptocarpus* is really their story.

The following is a list of some recent cultivars.

The leading hybridizers are Lyndon Lyon, Kartuz, Bartley Schwarz, and Gary Hunter of Drumore, Pennsylvania.

'Albatross.' The tetraploid of 'Maasens White.' This is an improvement over the original plant, still the best white.

'Ambrosia.' Big, deep pink ruffled flowers with striped throat.

'Blue Lace.' White veined and netted blue.

'Candy Pink' (Schwarz). Pink flowers, yellow throat, wine stripes. Easy bloomer.

'Cape Jewel' (Lyon). Compact plant with clusters of light pink flowers, the lobes striped deep pink.

'Cape Lynda' (Lyon). A similar plant with textured foliage.

'Captain Blood.' Ruffled deep red flowers with striped throat.

'Cloud Nine.' Ruffled pink, striped yellow throat.

'Essue' (Hunter). Deep blue with still darker lines. A very showy and popular plant.

'Frilled Red' (Lyon). Dark red with maroon stripes and yellow throat.

'Glacier' (Kartuz). Large white. Leaves variegated.

'Isabelle White.' Ruffled white flowers. Free flowering.

Little Gems 'Candy Pink' (Schwarz). Dwarf. Light pink with red and yellow lines in throat.

Little Gems 'Flashy' (Schwarz). Dwarf. Dark vermillion-magenta with yellow throat.

'Merry Sunshine.' Large, deep cerise-pink flowers, yellow throat.

'Mighty Mouse' (Lyon). Nymph-shaped flowers, lavender with purple lines.

Mini-streps. Line of commercial dwarf *Streptocarpus* in a wide range of colors by Schwarz.

'Network' (Kartuz). Heavily netted light blue flowers.

'Nosegay' (Schwarz). Miniature. Purple with black lines in throat.

'Peach Glow.' Large, salmon-pink ruffled flowers with yellow throat.

'Peppermint' (Hunter). Pink with darker lines.

'Pink Blush.' White with pink lines in throat.

'Pink Rosebud' (Schwarz). Double-flowered pink.

'Purple Rosebud' (Schwarz). Double-flowered purple.

'Royalty' (Kartuz). Very large royal purple, ruffled flowers with dark stripes in throat.

'Ruby' (Schwarz). Ruby-red flowers with yellow throat.

'Sizzler' (Lyon). Dark red with maroon stripes and yellow throat.

'Snow Sparkle' (Lyon). Compact, pure white flowers.

'Velveteen' (Worley). Deep violet flowers with white striped throat.

'Winter Dreams' (Kartuz). Ruffled pink. Leaves variegated.

'Wintermint' (Hunter). Near white with wine-colored lines.

The floriferousness of these unique plants depends on several factors. Because the peduncles grow from the bases of the leaves, the continuity of flowering is controlled by the rate of growth of new leaves. As each leaf may bear from one to several peduncles in succession, the concentration of flowers is partly in relation to the number of peduncles produced and the sequence of their development. Finally, a peduncle may bear from one to several flowers. Obviously, the more the merrier. A rating scale based on these factors would be very useful in judging progress. That, however, would not tell us the length of the blooming season. In fact, nobody is being very specific about that.

Glossary of Words
Used in This Book

We have tried to avoid the use of technical words in our text. However, such words as stem and stalk can lead to much ambiguity, and we are forced in the circumstances to differentiate by means of petiole, pedicel, and stem. Usually we have explained the meaning of a technical word we have used at some place in our text. We have been very colloquial in our description of leaves and other parts of plants, where possible, rather than use the complex terms which require a novice to refer constantly to a chart or list. In regard to colors we are very approximate. We could have referred to a particular color fan or chart recognized in botanical circles, but the average reader does not have access to them. Colors strike different viewers differently, and so we have left it at simple descriptive adjectives with plenty of room for imagination and variation. As a matter of fact, flower color does vary to a large degree both in nature and in cultivation.

Alternate.   Leaves or flowers which are on opposite sides of a stem but arranged at alternate intervals.

Annual.   A plant which dies after a season, perpetuating itself only by means of seed.

Anther.   The pollen-bearing (male) organ of the flower which is supported by a stalk or filament.

Axil.   The point at which the parts of a branch meet. A commoner word might be "joint." There is an axil where the branch meets the stem. But usually here we refer to the angle between the petiole of the leaf and the branch. Vegetative and flowering buds grow from the axils in the *Gesneriaceae*.

Biennial.   A plant which lives for two years, continuing its cycle by means of seed. Many biennials flower only in the second year after germination.

Bract.   A modified and subsidiary leaf usually growing in the regular leaf axil or in the inflorescence.

Bulb.   The thickened underground fleshy root of certain plants, mostly of the amaryllis and lily families.

Calyx.   Plural calyxes. The part of the flower which is at the top of the pedicel or stem and to which the corolla is attached. The calyx may be almost entirely tubular or be divided into leafy segments that are called sepals in some families of plants.

Campanulate.   A bell-shaped flower. The tube of the flower is broad and generally round, the lobes almost equal. Usually nodding or pendent.

Chlorophyll.   The green matter in plants which, under the influence of light, converts carbon dioxide, water, and various chemicals in the soil into sugar, glucose, and other plant foods.

Clone.   A group of plants produced by vegetative propagation from a single plant. It is not often pointed out that the parent plant is also part of the clone. We speak for instance of a "good clone," namely a single plant which is worth propagating vegetatively for its merit.

Corm.   A woody or solid water-storing organ, such as that of *Sinningia.* We have used "tuber" incorrectly throughout in place of this less familiar term.

Corolla.   The petalliferous parts of a flower. The tube and the limb together when the parts are fused. Usually the colorful part of a flower.

Cross.   The mating of two species, expressed by the letter x, as *Sinningia pusilla* x *Sinningia eumorpha.* The word is often applied to the resultant plant—in this case, *S.* "Dollbaby."

Cultivar.   Any plant which is altered from the species through cultivation. A variation of a species not occurring in nature is a cultivar and so is a hybrid.

Cutting.   Any section of a plant which is cut off and planted for propagation.

Deciduous.   A plant which loses its leaves seasonally.

Decussate.   A word not usually seen in texts and which we use reluctantly. But, without it, certain arrangements of leaves require a lengthy explanation that authors usually neglect. When the first pair of leaves on a stem are opposite, the next pair are at a 90° angle, the third pair is in the original position, and so forth, we say that the arrangement is decussate. It is a very common leaf system.

Dormancy.   A period during which a plant is inactive. It may, as in tuberous or scaly rhizomatous plants, die down to the ground. The tuber or rhizome is then totally inactive for a period, reviving spontaneously.

Epiphyte.   Epiphytic. Plants that grow on rocks or trees, not in the ground. Most epiphytes are not parasitic.

Family.   The largest classification of plants with which we deal in this book. The family of the gesneriads is the *Gesneriaceae*. Subsidiary classifications are the genus and species.

Flare.   We have used this word, which is not a botanical one, to express the spread of the lobes of a flower.

Footcandle.   An arbitrary measure of the amount of light falling on an object. There are footcandle meters, and an ordinary photographic light meter can be used when the readings are properly translated. However, light effectiveness for growth is another matter. So this is a rather useful but crude measure.

Genus.   The largest subdivision of a family. *Sinningia* is a genus of the family *Gesneriaceae*. Every family consists of one or more genera. Every genus consists of one or more species.

Habitat.   The normal environment of a plant in nature.

Hybrid.   The result of a cross, which see.

Inflorescence.   The flowering of a plant and the structures which bear the flowers.

Limb.   When the parts of a flower are separate we speak of these as petals. When they are fused at their base a tube is created, no matter how short, and the segments, or lobes, are called the limb. We speak of the petals of the rose but the lobes of a gesneriad flower. The limb is the sum total of the divisions of the tube.

Lip.   Tube flowers generally have an unequal division of the upper and lower lobes. In the *Gesneriaceae* there are two upper lobes which are usually smaller than the three lower lobes as in *Saintpaulia* species or *Sinningia regina*. But it may also be just a division as in some of the columneas in which the two upper lobes are fused into a hood and the lower lobes are separate. The lower lobes in all cases are the lower lip and the upper lobes the upper lip.

Lobe.   Any projecting segment of a corolla tube. See *Limb*.

Mutation.   An inheritable change in a plant due to a change in the genes or chromosomes. The change of *Sinningia speciosa* from a nodding slipper plant to a peloric or funnel-shaped flower was a mutation.

Node.   The point of attachment of a branch or leaf. The ring of scars left by leaves. The sections of stem between leaves or branches.

Opposite.   The position of leaves which are arranged in pairs opposite each other on a stem—for instance, most columneas.

Pedicel.   The stalk of a single flower.

Peduncle.   A stalk bearing several flowers each of which may be and usually is provided with a pedicel.

Peloria. Peloric.   Reversion of a flower with unequal lobes to the simpler form of equal lobes. The mutation from a slipper shape to a funnel or rotate shape as in *Sinningia cardinalis* 'George Kalmbacher.'

Petal.   Sections of the corolla of the flower. We have preferred to use "lobe" to describe these in the gesneriads. See *Lobe.*

Petiole.   The stalk or stem of a leaf. When leaves clasp the stalk or stem of the plant, they are without petioles.

Pistil.   The whole female organ of the flower, consisting of the ovary, style, and stigma.

Rhizome.   A specialized portion of the root of a plant, usually swollen, which has the same function as a tuber or bulb but is usually elongated rather than orbicular. The scaly rhizomes of the gesneriads look like miniature pine cones. The whole rhizome carries the plant through dormancy and produces new growth. Each scale of the rhizome is also capable of producing a new plant.

Rosette.   Usually applied to leaves which form a flat circular pattern close to the ground, sometimes stemless, sometimes developing a stem with age. *Saintpaulia* and *Boea hygroscopica* are rosette plants.

Segment.   We have used this on occasion to describe any separate part of a calyx or corolla. Each lobe of the corolla may be a segment.

Sepal.   The projecting parts of a calyx—its segments. Strictly speaking sepal should no more be used for gesneriads than the word petal for the corolla.

Shrub.   Any woody plant not a tree.

Species.   The smallest division of a family and a part of a genus.

Stamen.   The pollen-bearing anther and its supporting stalk or filament.

Stem.   The central structure of a plant aboveground. Some plants, for instance some *Streptocarpus,* are stemless.

Stigma.   The receptive portion of the style to which pollen adheres. It is usually seen as a swollen, sticky tissue at the tip of the style.

Stolon.   A stem that grows horizontally, usually without nodes, a leaf cluster, and eventually roots, developing at the tip. As in *Episcia.*

Style.   Connective between the ovary and the stigma. The support or stem of the stigma. The pollen grows down the style to the ovary.

Throat.   The inside of the tube of the corolla. Sometimes used for the mouth of the tube.

Tube.   The tubular, fused portion of the corolla.

Tuber.   A woody food and water-storage root as in the iris. We have used tuber instead of the more correct word *corm* to describe this organ in *Sinningia.*

Whorl.   Leaves or flowers arranged in a spiral around a stem.

Plant Sources

ALL OR PARTLY GESNERIADS OTHER THAN AFRICAN VIOLETS

Ron Brenton. 30840 Wentworth, Livonia, MI 48154. African violets and mini-sinningias.

Buell's Greenhouse. P.O. Box 218 MH, Eastford, CT 06262. African violets, gloxinias, gesneriads. Cat. $1.00.

Burpee, W. Atlee, Co. Warminster, PA 18974. Free catalog.

Country Hills Greenhouses. Rt. 2, Corning, OH 43730. African violets and numerous gesneriads. Cat. $2.00.

Country Violets. Rt. 2, Box 214, Great Bend, KS 67530. Episcias and African violets. 2 stamps for list.

Far North Gardens. 16785 Harrison, Livonia, MI 48152. Gesneriads, etc. Cat. $1.25.

Fischer Greenhouses. Oak Avenue, Linwood, NJ 08221. African violets and gesneriads. List 25¢.

Glasshouse Works. Stewart, OH 45778. See *Country Hills Greenhouses.*

Green's, Doris, House. 7260 Brickey Lane, Knoxville, TN 37919. African violets, gesneriads, supplies. List 50¢.

Hunter's Greenhouses. R.D. 1, Box 2A, Drumore, PA 17518. *Streptocarpus.*

Island Gesneriads. P.O. Box 853, Anna Maria, FL 33501. *Achimenes* and kohlerias. Not shipping at present. Cat. $1.25.

Kartuz Greenhouses, Inc. 1408 Sunset Drive, Vista, CA 92083. Numerous gesneriads. Cat. $1.00.

Lauray of Salisbury. Undermountain Rd., Salisbury, CT 06068. Numerous gesneriads. Cat. $1.25.

Logee's Greenhouses. 55 North Street, Danielson, CT 06239. Gesneriads, etc. Cat. $2.50.

Lyndon Lyon. 14 Mutchler Street, Dolgeville, NY 13329. African violets and other gesneriads. Stamp for list.

McFarland Greenhouses. 1609 South Lea Circle, Bryant, AR 72022. African violets, episcias, and other gesneriads. 2 stamps for list.

McKinney's Glassehouse. 89 Mission Rd., Eastborough, Wichita, KS 67207. African violets and gesneriads. Cat. 75¢.

Miree's Gesneriads. 70 Enfield Avenue, Toronto, Canada M8W 1T9. Gesneriads. 75¢ for list.

Park, Geo. W., Seed Co. Greenwood, SC 29646. African violets and other gesneriads. Free catalog.

Patty's Plant Place. P.O.B. 117, Cheney, KS 67025. African violets, episcias. List 40¢.

Peterson Son, J. A. 3132 McHenry Avenue, Cincinnati, OH 45211. Wholesale African violets and gesneriads.

Petrovffsky Greenhouses. 14867 Indian Springs Rd., Rough & Ready, CA 95975. African violets and gesneriads. Cat. 50¢.

Plants 'N' Things. Pollock Rd., RR#2, Keswick, Ontario, Canada L4P 3E9. African violets and gesneriads. Cat. $1.00.

Pleasant Hill African Violets. Rt. 1, Box 73, Brenham, TX 77833. African violets and gesneriads. SASE for list.

Quality Violet House. Box 947, Walkerton, IN 46574.

Small, Earl J., Growers, Inc. P.O.Box 425, Pinellas Park, FL 33565. Wholesale.
Tiki Nursery. 25555 SW 147 Ave., Naranja, FL 33032. Cat. $1.00.
Tinari Greenhouses. Box 190, 3525 Valley Rd., Huntingdon Valley, PA 19006. Cat. 35¢.
Tropical Treasures. Box 1693, New Port Richey, FL 33552. SASE for list.
Village Plants. P.O.Box 319, Westminster, MA 01473. Stamp for list.
Violets at the Ernst's. 221 S.E. 70 St., Gainesville, FL 32601.
Violets by Karen. 6072 No. Dower, Fresno, CA 93711. List 50¢
Zaca Vista. 1190 Alamo Pintado Rd., Solvang, CA 93463. Cat. $1.00.

MOSTLY AFRICAN VIOLETS

(Outstanding nurseries for gesneriads other than African violets are preceded by an asterisk.)

African Violetry, The. 926 E. 14 St., Houston, TX 77009. No shipping.
Alice's Violet Room. Rt. 6, Box 233, Waynesville, MO 65583. List 25¢.
Annalee Violetry. 29-50 214th Place, Bayside, NY 11360. List 50¢.
Annex Violets. P.O.B. 212, Pocono Lake, PA 18347.
Baker's African Violets. 1930 Red Road, Alpharetta, GA 30201.
Bay Valley Violets. P.O.B. 1052, Midland, MI 48640. List 50¢.
Bloom Room, The. 3459 East St., Birmingham, AL 35243. List $1.50.
Bluewater African Violets. P.O.B. 306, St. Clair, MI 48079.
Bohn, Jeanne P. P.O.B. 174, Hygiene, CO 80533. List 25¢.
Bri-Lea Greenhouses. Rt. 1, Box 235, Bilter Rd., Aurora, IL 60504.
*Buell's Greenhouses. Eastford, CT 06262. Cat. $1.00.
Bugtussle Violets. 5280 Haven Rd., Leonard, MI 48038. List $1.00.
Burpee, W. Atlee, Co. Warminster, PA 18974. Free cat.
Butler's. 10052-136 Ave. N.E., Kirkland, WA 98033.
Buttram's African Violets. P.O.B. 193, Independence, MO 64051.
California Violets. P.O.B. 3053, Ontario, CA 91761. List 50¢.
Cape Cod Violetry. 28 Minot Street, Falmouth, MA 02540. Cat. $1.00.
Cedar Hill's Violet House. Rt. 1, Box 285, Omaha, TX 75571. List $1.00.
Champion's African Violets. 8848 Van Hoesen Rd., Clay, NY 13041. Wholesaler.
Cheryl's Violet Patch. 1915 Flora Rd., Clearwater, FL 33515. List 35¢.
*Country Hills Greenhouses. Rt. 2, Corning, OH 43730. Cat. $2.00.
Country Violets. Rt. 2, Box 214, Great Bend, KS 67530. Two stamps for list.
Crestwood Violetry. 7314 Jervis St., Springfield, VA 22151.
Dar-Let Violets. 14 Lorio Dr., Yardville, NJ 08620.
Far North Gardens. 16785 Harrison, Livonia, MI 48152. Cat. $1.25. Seeds of gesneriads.
Fischer Greenhouses. Oak Ave, Linwood, NJ 08221. List 25¢.
*Glasshouse Works. Stewart, OH 45778. See *Country Hills Greenhouses.*
Goetz, Josephine. 461 Eisenhower Ave., Angola, NY 14008. List 25¢.
Good's Hybrids. 281 Sabrina Ct., Woodstock, GA 30186.

Granger Gardens. 1060 Wilbur Rd., Medina, OH 44256. Wholesaler of African violets.

Greenbrier Violet Nursery. P.O.B. 316, Greenbrier, AR 72058. List 35¢

Green's, Doris, House. 7260 Brickey Lane, Knoxville, TN 37918. List 50¢.

Hale's House of Violets. 76 London Rd., Hebron, CT 06248. List 50¢.

Hardens Gardens. 910 W. Hillsboro, Seffner, FL 33584. SASE for list.

Heavenly Violets. 9 Turney Pl., Trumbull, CT 06611. List 35¢.

Hortense's African Violets. 12406 Alexandria St., San Antonio, TX 78233. List 25¢.

House of Violets, The. 936 Garland St. SW, Camden, AR 71701.

Humphrey's African Violets. 46 Glen Ave., Harrington Park, NJ 07640.

Hunter's Greenhouses. R.D. 1, Box 2A, Drumore, PA 17518. Streptocarpus.

Innis Violets. 8a Maddison Lane, Lynnfield, MA 01940. Stamp for list.

Island Gesneriads. P.O.B. 853, Anna Maria, FL 33501. Cat. $1.25. Temporarily not shipping.

Janice's Violets. Box 62, Rt. 1, Gainesville, MO 65655. List 35¢.

J&J African Violets. P.O.B. 273, Pitman, NJ 08071. Large SASE.

Just Violets. Pembrook Drive, New Orleans, LA 70114. Free list.

Kartuz Greenhouses, Inc. 1408 Sunset Dr., Vista, CA 92083. Cat. $1.00.

Kent's Flowers. 320 West Eagle, Arlington, NE 68002.

Knee-Deep in Violets. 103 Shenandoah Dr., Winston-Salem, NC 27108. List 50¢.

Knull Enterprises. 26614 Timberlane Dr. S.E., Kent, WA 98031. List 50¢.

Kolb's Greenhouses. 725 Belvedere Rd., Phillipsburg, NJ 08865.

Lakeside Violets. 82 Brady Rd., Lake Hopatcong, NJ 07849. List 50¢.

Lauray of Salisbury. Undermountain Rd., Salisbury, CT 06068. Cat. $1.25.

Leix's Village Violetry. P.O.B. 238, Millington, MI 48746. List $1.00.

Lindstrom, Wayne. 3632 No. Woodland Pl., Mt. Vernon, WA 98273.

Little Plant Haven, The. 1331 La Porte, Waco, TX 76710. SASE for list.

Lloyds African Violets. 2569 East Main St., Cato, NY 13033. List 50¢.

Logee's Greenhouses. 55 North St., Danielson, CT 06239. Cat. $2.50.

Lynde Violets. 910 W. Hilsboro, Seffner, FL 33584. SASE for list.

Lyndon Lyon. 14 Mutchler St., Dolgeville, NY 13329. Stamp for list.

McFarland Greenhouses. 1609 South Lea Circle, Bryant, AR 72022. African violets and other gesneriads. 2 stamps for list.

McKinney's Glassehouse. 89 Mission Rd., Eastborough, Wichita, KS 67207. Cat. 75¢.

McLester African Violets. 308 Meadowood Circle, Kannapolis, NC 28081.

Madame Butterfly. 2166 Broadlawn, Dubuque, IA 52001. List 50¢.

Marilu's Violets. P.O.B. 1074, Azle, TX 76020. List 50¢.

Mary's African Violets. 19788 San Juan, Detroit, MI 48221.

Meek's African Violets. 214 Goodrich Ave., Syracuse, NY 13210. List $1.00.

Messin' Round Violetry. 4040 Squirrel Rd., Lake Orion, MI 48035.

Miderski, R. J. 20983 N. Exmoor Ave., Barrington, IL 60010.

Miree's Gesneriads. 70 Enfield Ave., Toronto, Canada N8W 1T9. $1.00 for list.

Nadeau Saintpaulia Seed Co. 48 Queenbrook Pl., St. Louis, MO 63132.

Napa Valley Violets. 636 Cunard Dr., Napa, CA 94558. List 50¢.

Park, Geo. W., Seed Co. Greenwood, SC 29647. Cat. free.

Patches and Pots. 583 El Cajon Blvd., El Cajon, CA 92020.

Pat's Flowerland. Box 237, Stroud, Ont., Canada LOL 2MO. List 50¢.

Patty's Plant Place. P.O.B. 117, Cheney, KA 67025. List 40¢.

Peterson Sons, J.A. 3132 McHenry Ave., Cincinnati, OH 45211. Wholesale.

Petrovffsky Greenhouses. 14867 Indian Springs Rd., Rough & Ready, CA 95975. Cat. 50¢.

Phillips, Candy. Rt. 5, Box 1518, College Station, TX 77840.

*Plants 'N' Things. Pollock Rd., R.R. #2, Keswick, Ontario, Canada L4P 3E9. Cat. $1.00.

*Pleasant Hill African Violets. Rt. 1., Box 73, Brenham, TX 77833. African violets and gesneriads. SASE for list.

*Quality Violet House (Susan Feece). Box 947, Walkerton, IN 46574.

Rainwater Violets. 609 N.E. 3rd St., Blue Springs, MO 640115. Stamp for list.

Ray's African Violets. Rt. 4, Box 212, College Station, TX 77840. List 50¢.

Reigning Violets. Star Rt. 940, Box 730, Pocono Lakes, PA 18347. List $1.00.

Roberta's Violetry. 1650 Cherry Hill Rd., State College, PA 16801. List 50¢.

*Roseann's Violets. 5247 Hauserman Rd., Parma, OH 44130.

Rosemeyer's African Violets. R.R. #3, Box 267, Sunman, IN 47041. List 75¢.

Scagliola's Greenhouse Violets. 750 Gull Ave., Foster City, CA 94404. List 50¢.

Shirley's Bloomin' Blossoms. P.O.B. 67, Somerset, MI 49281. List $1.00.

Sims'. 1308 South Sandusky, Tulsa, OK 74112. List 35¢.

Sitting Pretty Violetry. 2239 S. 61 St., Cicero, IL 60650. List 40¢.

*Small, Earl J., Growers, Inc. P.O.B. 425, Pinellas Park, FL 33565. Wholesale.

Susan's Sweetheart Violets. 4367 Franklin Ave., Loveland, CO 80537. List 50¢.

Susan's Violets. 2447 Gus Thomasson, Dallas, TX 75226.

Swift's. P.O.B. 28012, Dallas, TX 28012.

Thelma Jean's Violets. 16 Oxbow Rd., Fairport, NY 14450. SASE for list.

*Tiki Nursery. 25555 S.W. 147 Ave., Naranja, FL 33032. Cat. $1.00.

Tinari Greenhouses. Box 190, 2325 Valley Rd., Huntingdon Valley, PA 19006. Cat. 35¢.

Tomara African Violets. Rt. 3, Fayette, MO 65248.

Travis Violets. P.O.B. 42, Ochlocknee, GA 31773. List 40¢ in stamps.

*Tropical Treasures. Box 1693, New Port Richey, FL 33552. SASE for list.

*Village Plants. P.O.B. 319, Westminster, MA 01473. Stamp for list.

Violet Connection. Box 11, Glencoe, IL 60022.

Violet Haven. 3900 Carter Creek Pkwy., Bryan, TX 77801. 50¢ for list.

The Violet House. P.O.B. 1274, Gainesville, FL 32601.

Violet Park. 33 North Park Ave., Buffalo, NY 14216. List 50¢.

Violetria, The. 3394 N.E. Indian Dr., Jensen Beach, FL 33457.

Violet Showcase, The. 3147 S. Broadway, Englewood, CO 80110.

Violets Are Blue. P.O.B. Plymouth, PA 18651. List 35¢ plus SASE.

Violets Atlanta. P.O.B. 722, Conley, GA 30027.

*Violets at the Ernst's. 221 S.E. 70 St., Gainesville, FL 32601.

Violets by Bess. 808 N. Sonoita Ave., Tucson, AR 85711. List 35¢.

Violets by Betty Terry. 4100 38th Way, S. St. Petersburg, FL 33711. List $1.00.

Violets by Beverly. 1325 Paseo Sereno, San Dimas, CA 91773. List $1.00.

Violets by Cort. 87 Mahan St., West Babylon, NY 11704. SASE for list.

*Violets by Karen. 6072 N. Dower, Fresno, CA 93711. List 50¢.

Violets Collectible. 1571 Wise Rd., Lincoln, NE 68002. List 50¢.

Violets c/o Cookie. 2400 Knightway Dr., Gretna, LA 70053. SASE for list.

Violets from the Starrs. 2602 Graupera St., Pensacola, FL 32507.

Violets Galore—at the Gorals. 132 Joan Ave., Green Bay, WI 54302. 45¢ for list.

Violets Galore of Georgia. 3482 Misty Valley Rd., Decatur, GA 30032.

Volkmann Bros. Greenhouses. 2714 Minert St., Dallas, TX 75219. 37¢ SASE for list.

Wilkening, Karter G. 2705 S. 45th St., Milwaukee, WI 53219. List 35¢.

*Zaca Vista. 1190 Alamo Pintado Rd., Solvang, CA 93463. Cat. $1.00.

Houseplant
Supplies

African Violetry, The. 926 E. 14 St., Houston, TX 77009. Supplies, lighting equipment. No shipping.

Alpa Plants Inc. Box 528, Lincoln, MA 01773. Automatic planters.

Bab'lon Tower Gardens. 7691 Liberty Rd., Salem, OR 97306. Circline light garden.

Bateman, Charles, Limited. Box 480, 67 Rodinea Rd., Unit 7, Ontario LOJ 1EO, Canada. Fertilizer.

Bay Valley Violets. P.O.B. 1052, Midland, MI 48640. Supplies. List 50¢.

Burpee, W. Atlee, Co. Warminster, PA 18974. Supplies. Free cat.

Cape Cod Violetry. 28 Minot Street, Falmouth, MA 02540. Supplies. Cat. $1.00.

Cherry, Elaine. 1014 11th St., No. 103, Bellingham, WA 98225. Indoor gardening books.

Clarel Laboratories, Inc. Deerfield, IL 60015. Fertilizers.

Dode's Gardens, Inc. 1490 Saturn St., Merrit Island, FL 32952. Supplies, light stands, books. Cat. 2 stamps.

Dolan, R. A. 4 Joseph St., Meriden, CT 06450. Soil.

Environmental Concepts. 710 N.W. 57 St., Ft. Lauderdale, FL 33309. Light meter.

Floralite Company. 4124 East Oakwood Rd., Oak Creek, WI 53154. Fluorescent light units.

Green House, The. 9515 Flower St., Bellflower, CA 90706. Fluorescent lighting carts.

Green's House, Doris. 7260 Brickey Lane, Knoxville, TN 37918. Supplies. List 50¢.

Greeson, Bernard D. 3548 North Cramer, Milwaukee, WI 53211. Supplies. List 50¢.

Home Grow Products. 8000 Baker Ave., Cleveland, OH. Floracart. Free cat.

House of Violets, The. 936 Garland St. S.W., Camden, Ark. 71701. Supplies.

Hydrofarm. 1299 4th St. #308B, San Rafael, CA 94901. Power Twist Tubes.

IDAI, Ltd/Gesneria. 309 Montauk Hwy, East Moriches, NY 11940. New Hybrid Directory.

Indoor Gardening Supplies. P.O.B. 40567, Detroit, MI 48240. Fluorescent gardening supplies. Free cat.

J. F. Industries. P.O.B. 275 Locust Grove, OK 74352. Supplies. Legal size SASE for list.

Lynde Violets. 910 W. Hilsboro, Seffner, FL 33584. Supplies. SASE for list.

McKee's House Plant Corner. Box 96, Northfield, NJ 08225. Supplies. Cat. $1.00.

McKinney's Glassehouse. 89 Mission Rd., Eastborough, Wichita, KS 67207. Supplies. Cat. 75¢.

Mary's African Violets. 19788 San Juan, Detroit, MI 48221. Soils, fertilizers, books, etc.

Ofiduca. P.O.B. 161302, Miami, FL 33116. Soils.

Optiflora, Inc. P.O.B. 8158, Nashville, TN 37207. Optimara plant food.

Orchid Art Gallery. 1765 Victory Blvd., Staten Island, NY 10314. Floracart.

Park, Geo. W., Seed Co. Greenwood, SC 29647. Supplies, light units.

Plant Collectibles. 103C Kenview Ave., Buffalo, NY 14217. Indoor gardening supplies.

Plantsmith. 1924 Plymouth St., Mountain View, CA 94043. Spoonit fertilizer.

Public Service Lamp Corp. 410 W. 16 St., NY 10011. Wonderlite growth bulbs.

Schultz Co. St. Louis, MO 63043. Green Thumb fertilizer.

Texas Growing Media. 11100 Finchley Rd., Louisville, KY 40243. Soils.

Tinari Greenhouses. Box 190, 2325 Valley Rd., Huntingdon Valley, PA 19006. Supplies, plant stands, books. Cat. 35¢.

Tropical Plant Products. 1715 Silver Star Rd. P.O.B. 7754, Orlando, FL 32804. Osmunda, tree fern, bark, Peters fertilizer.

Tube Craft, Inc. 8000 Baker Ave., Cleveland, OH 44102. Floracart watering wand.

Verilux, Inc. 35 Mason St., Greenwich, CT 06830. Verilux growth fluorescent tubes.

Violet House, The. P.O.B. 1274, Gainesville, FL 32601. Supplies.

Violet Showcase, The. 3147 S. Broadway, Englewood, CO 80110. Plant stands, supplies, books.

Vitaloam. Box 310, New Knoxville, OH 45871. Vitaloam medium.

Volkmann Bros. Greenhouses. 2714 Minert St., Dallas, TX 75219. Fluorescent plant stand. 37¢ SASE for list.

Index

A

xAchimenantha, 233

Achimenes, 50–54
    cultivars, 52–53, 221
    culture, 48
    species, 50–52

Aeschynanthus, 55–60
    cultivars, 221–22
    species, 58, 221

African Violet Society of America,
    Inc., 46

Agalmyla, 60

Air conditioning, 4

Alloplectus, 61–62

Alpine gesneriads, 210–14

Alsobia, 62–64
    'Cygnet', 62–64

American Gloxinia & Gesneriad
    Society, 46

Arnold, Paul, 180

Asteranthera, 210

August, Iris, 122, 123

B

Baskets, 25

Batcheller, Mrs. Frances, 5, 68,
    84, 121, 220

Bellonia, 84

Besleria, 66

Blooming plants, growing, 3

Boea, 66

Bona, Ted, 220

Box, propagation, 28

Briggsia, 210

Brown, A. G., 201, 202, 203

Bucinellina, 222, 224

Bulb, Wonderlite, 218

Burtt, B. L., 11, 68, 191–92

C

Cable heating, 30

de Candolle, A., 11

Capanea, 68, 69

Chirita, 68–71, 222–23

Chrysothemis, 72, 223

Clayberg, Carl D., 11, 167

Cobananthus, 61, 223

Codonanthe, 74–76, 223–24

xCodonantanthus, 233

Codonanthopsis, 224

Cogswell, Maude, 217

xColbergaria, 228

xColtricantha, 229

Columnea, 77–90, 224–29
    Cornell hybrids, 85
    cultivars, 86–90
    culture, 78–79
    intergenerics, 228
    species, 79–84, 228

Conandron, 210

Corallodiscus, 211

Corytoplectus, 61, 229

Crandall, Jane, 102

Cuttings, propagating, 32–33

Cyrtandra, 229

D

Dalbergaria, 79, 224

Day length, 15

Diastema, 90–92

Didissandra, 229

Didymocarpus, 92, 229

Division, propagation by, 40

Drymonia, 93–96
    new species of, 230

E

Episcia, 96–107
    cultivars, 103–6, 230-31
    culture of, 98–99
    look-alikes of, 101

species, 99–101
survivors and new cultivars of,
  106–7
training of, 99
Eucodonia, 50, 231
Eyerdom, Hugh, 86

F
Fertilizer, 23–25
Fertilizing, rules for, 24
Fiedler, Mrs. Leon, 243
Fish emulsion, 23, 25
Florist gloxinias, 162–66
Fluorescent lighting, 14–15, 218
  ballast for, 14
  fans for, 14
  fixtures for, 14
  lamps for, 15
  reflectors for, 14
  timers for, 15
  valances for, 14
  Verilux TruBloom tubes for, 15
Foggers, 22
Foliar feeding, 25

G
Gasteranthus, 232
Gesner, Konrad, 11
Gesneria, 107–10, 232
Gesneriaceae, 6
  description of, 7
  genera of, 10
  organs of, 7
  terminology of, 47
Gesneriad Hybridizer's Association, 46
Gesneriads, 2, 218
  cool growing, 218
  mutation of, 2
  name changes, 44
  repertory of, 5
  suitability for indoors of, 2
  superiority of, 2
  taxonomic changes in the, 5
  what are the, 6–9

Gesneriad-Saintpaulia News, 5
Gesneriad Society International, 46
xGlokohleria, 233
Gloxinia, 111–16, 232–33
  sylvatica, 113
Gloxinian, The, 102, 107
Gonzalez, Mrs. M. G., 147, 149
GSN, 5

H
Haberlea, 211
Hormone powder, 35
Humidity, 21
Hunter, Gary, 221
Hybridizers, 220
Hypocyrta, 116

I
Indoor Light Gardening Society of
  America, Inc., The, 46
Intergeneric crosses, 233–34
Intergeneric hybrids, naming, 45

J
Jankaea, 211

K
Kalmbacher, Dr. George, 167
Kartuz, Michael, 86, 220
Koellikeria, 117–19, 234
Kohleria, 119–22, 234
  hybrids, 120, 235

L
Lamps, fluorescent, 15
  distance from, 15
  HID, 16
  high output, 16
  mercury vapor, 218
  Verilux TruBloom, 15
  Wonderlite, 218

Leaf propagation, 33–38
   of *Saintpaulia,* 34–37
   of tuberous gesneriads, 37
Lee, Dr. R. E., 50, 84
Lietzia, 122
Light, fluorescent, 14, 16
   incandescent, 16
   sources of, 218
   window, 4
Light gardens,
   cost of, 5
   fluorescent, 14
Lighting fixtures, 14
Lime, 17, 31
Loam, garden, 19
Loxostigma, 212
Lyon, Lyndon, 86, 220
Lysionotus, 122

M
Marston, M. E., 202
Martius, K. F. P. von, 11
Mats, watering, 219
Mercury vapor lamp, 218
Mines, Martin, 220
Mitraria, 212
Mixes, soil, 16–19
   Cornell, 18
   lean, 17
   packaged, 19
   rich, 17
Monophyllaea, 123
Monopyle, 123, 237
Moore, Dr. Harold E., 5, 11, 50, 68,
      77, 107, 112
Morley, Dr. Brian, 11
Moss, long fiber, 32
   milled sphagnum, 2
   peat, 17, 31
   propagation, 36
   sphagnum, 19, 31
Moussonia, 237–38
xMoussoniantha, 234
Multiplying plants, 28–40

N
Naming intergeneric hybrids, 45
Napeanthus, 239
Naultilocalyx, 123–25, 238–39
Nematanthus, 126–31, 239
Neomortonia, 239–40
Niphaea, 131
xNiphemenes, 234

O
Opithandra, 213
Oreocharis, 213
Ornithoboea, 240

P
Paliavana, 132
Paradrymonia, 132, 240–41
Parakohleria, 241
Pearcea, 133
Peat moss, 17, 31
Pentadenia, 224
Perlite, 17, 31
Pests, 25, 219
Petrocosmea, 134
Phinaea, 135, 242
Plant societies, 46
Platystemma, 214
Pots, 25
Potting, 25
Propagation, 28–41
   box, 28–30
   from leaves, 34
   from stems, 32, 38
   from stolons, 39

R
Ramonda, 214
Rechsteineria, 137–38
Reflectors, 14
Rhabdothamnus, 139
Rhynchoglossum, 139
Rhytidophylum, 139
Rufodorsia, 242

S

Safer Insecticidal Soap, 219
Saintpaulia, 139–53, 216, 242–44
    culture, 152
    Honor Roll 1965–75, 148–49
    Honor Roll 1976–82, 243–44
    hybrids, 147
    mini-history of, 141
    species, 142–46
Sand, 30
Sarmienta, 153
Saylor, William, 216, 220
Schwarz, Bartley, 220
Seed, propagation by, 40
Sinningia, 155–88, 244–46
    Buell hybrids, 159
    canescens, 173
    cardinalis, 166
    concinna, 168
    confusion with *Gloxinia*, 156
    cultivars of, 158–87
    culture of, 187–88
    florist *Gloxinia* cultivars of, 162
    Fyfiana group of, 157, 161
    new miniatures of, 245–46
    pusilla, 175
    regina, 177
    species, 157–58
    speciosa, 157
    speciosa cultivars, 158
Skog, Laurence, 11
Smithiantha, 188–90
    hybrids of, 189–90
xSmithicodonia, 234
Societies, plant, 46
Soils, 16–20, 219
Solenophora, 190
Streptocarpus, 190–208, 246–49
    culture of subgenus *Streptocarpus*,
        206–8
    hybrids, 200–206, 247–49

hybrids of subgenus *Streptocarpella*,
    247
hybrids of subgenus *Streptocarpus*,
    200–206
species of subgenus *Streptocarpella*,
    197–200, 246
species of subgenus *Streptocarpus*,
    193–97, 247–49
Stroxinia, 178

T

Talpey, Dr. Thomas, 107, 109
Temperature, 22, 217
Terminology, 47
Terrarium culture, 42
Teuscher, Dr. Henry, 11, 118, 153
Timer for fluorescent fixtures, 15
Titanotrichum, 208
Tricantha, 224

V

Ventilation, 23
Verilux TruBloom tube, 15
Vermiculite, 17, 31

W

Wand, watering, 21
Ward, Dr. Nathaniel, 2
Wardian case, 2
Watering, 20, 219
    automatic, 21
Water propagation, 38
Wicks, watering, 21
Wiehler, Dr. Hans, 63, 119
Wiesmoor hybrids, 201
Wonderlite bulb, 218
Worley, Patrick, 220